162-0

A CUBS PERFECT SEASON

DAN McGRATH

BOB VANDERBERG

TRIUMPH
B O O K S

Library of Congress Cataloging-in-Publication Data

McGrath, Dan, 1950-

  162-0 : a Cubs perfect season / Dan McGrath and Bob Vanderberg.

    p. cm.

  Includes bibliographical references.

  ISBN 978-1-60078-362-3

  1. Chicago Cubs (Baseball team)—History. I. Vanderberg, Bob, 1948- II. Title. III. Title: One hundred sixty two to zero. IV. Title: Cubs perfect season.

  GV875.C6M45 2011

  796.357'640977311—dc22

                            2010047577

This book is available in quantity at special discounts for your group or organization. For further information, contact:

Triumph Books
542 South Dearborn Street
Suite 750
Chicago, Illinois 60605
(312) 939–3330
Fax (312) 663–3557
www.triumphbooks.com

Printed in U.S.A.

ISBN: 978-1-60078-362-3

Editorial and page production by Red Line Editorial

Photos courtesy of AP Images and Getty Images unless indicated otherwise

DEDICATION

ABOUT THE AUTHORS

Dan McGrath grew up on Chicago baseball and was in the stands at Wrigley Field for Ferguson Jenkins' debut with the Cubs in 1966, as well as the Cubs' epic meltdown in Game 6 of the 2003 NLCS and too many games to count in between. A journalist for nearly 40 years, McGrath supervised coverage of Chicago baseball as sports editor of the *Chicago Tribune* for 12 years and lists the 2005 World Series as his favorite event. McGrath was a baseball beat writer in the 1980s, covering the San Francisco Giants for the *San Francisco Chronicle*. He has worked for newspapers in Freeport, Ill., Reno, Nev., and Sacramento, Calif., as well as New York and Philadelphia. He believes he will go to his grave without seeing the Cubs in the World Series.

Bob Vanderberg, who grew up in Chicago's western suburbs, spent nearly 40 years as an editor and reporter in the *Chicago Tribune*'s sports department. The graduate of Hope College (Holland, Michigan) has written three previous books, all on the Chicago White Sox. Even so, he has seen his share of Cub games, attending his first in July 1955, when the North Siders swept a weekday double-header from the defending world champion New York Giants. Among his talents is a splendid (but not often requested) impression of the late Wrigley Field P.A. announcer, Pat Pieper. Vanderberg lives with his wife and son in Lemont, Illinois.

CONTENTS

INTRODUCTION

The late-'90s TV series *Chicago Hope* was about a quirky, well-meaning, struggling Chicago hospital, not a Chicago National League ballclub, even though the team fits the same description.

The Chicago Cubs have been dealing in hope for more than a century—as the 2011 season dawned, it had been 102 years since their last World Series championship and 65 years since their last Series appearance. Teams that didn't even exist when the Cubs were losing to Detroit in the 1945 Fall Classic—Florida's Marlins, Toronto's Blue Jays, even New York's hated Mets, for gosh sakes—have won multiple Series titles since the Cubs last competed for one. Twelve U.S. Presidents have occupied the White House, and man has walked on the moon.

The late, great Chicago columnist Mike Royko, as the defiant embodiment of the term "long-suffering" Cub fan, once sought to rationalize his frustration with a rather charitable observation: Any team can have a bad century. Too true—and the Cubs are working on a second one.

Yet through decades of failure—frequently hopeless, abject failure, interspersed with the occasional 1969-style near-miss that was even more painful to endure—Cub fans have been among the most unswervingly loyal and irrepressibly optimistic people in sports. Next year is just around the corner. And it's bound to be better.

It rarely is, and yet a Cub fan keeps coming back for more. It's partly the nostalgic charm of Wrigley Field, it's partly the old-school allure of day baseball. But it's largely because the Cubs, for all their myriad flaws, often present a beguiling, endearing cast of characters—only a Cub (Jose Cardenal) could miss a game because his eyelid was stuck open.

And only the Cubs could trade a swift, dynamic, Hall of Fame-bound outfielder for a broken-down, used-up pitcher who would win a total of seven games for them. Lou Brock for Ernie Broglio. Forty-four years later, it's still enough to make a grown fan cry.

The eight-team National League in which the Cubs prevailed in 1945 has doubled in size, and a quarter of the teams are eligible for two rounds of playoffs that didn't exist when the Cubs last won the pennant. They have been playoff participants six times in those 65 years, but five times they failed to win a series and three times they failed to win a game.

In fact, the losses have far outnumbered the wins in most Cubs seasons. But because of their relative rarity, the victories tend to stand out more, and many of them are as cherished as family heirlooms. Wouldn't it be fun, then, to comb through Cubs history and pick a win that truly stood out on each date of a typical season? That's the premise of this book—162-0: A Perfect Cubs Season. Think about it—a perfect *Cubs* season? Totally fanciful, sure, but lots of fun.

Some of the choices were obvious: 72 years after it took place, Gabby Hartnett's "Homer in the Gloamin'" remains one of the most significant moments in baseball history. Based on "eyewitness" accounts, a lot more than 5,264 people were in the stands at Wrigley Field on that May day in 1970 when the great Ernie Banks took Pat Jarvis deep for his 500th career home run. Similarly, 15,758 was the paid crowd for Kerry Wood's magnificent 20-strikeout game against the Houston Astros in May of 1998, but Wood says he has met at least 25,000 people who claim to have been there.

Before Banks there was Hack Wilson, and after him came Sammy Sosa. Not a similarity among them, save for their crowd-pleasing ability to hit long home runs. Frank Ernaga did it a time or two, and so did Bob Speake and Art Schult and Julio Zuleta.

Ryne Sandberg launched an MVP season and a Hall of Fame career with two game-tying home runs off Hall of Famer Bruce Sutter in June of 1984; mention "the Sandberg Game" to any Cub fan and he or she knows exactly what you mean, down to the last detail.

Adolfo Phillips had a day like that once. So did Lee Walls, and Hank Sauer, "the Mayor of Wrigley Field."

A game-winning grand slam off Don Nottebart 23 years earlier might not have had the same pizzazz as Sandberg connecting off Sutter, but it gave Al Heist a place in Cubs lore. Dick Drott is in there, too, along with Art Ceccarelli, Leo Burke, Moose Moryn and Willie Smith.

The Cubs have been notorious for breaking hearts over the years—there's no getting around it. But they also have dispensed some thrills, no question. We hope you will enjoy reliving some of them in these pages.

APRIL

"Mr. Cub" Ernie Banks hit his 300th home run in April 1962. He completed his two-time MVP career with 512 homers.

The Willie Smith Game
Gave Cubs Hope

It's fitting that one of the most memorable seasons in Cubs history would begin with one of the most memorable games.

The Willie Smith Game. It's the only description needed. And in Philadelphia it might be remembered as the Don Money Game if fate hadn't intervened in the person of Smith, a cheerful, amiable pitcher-turned-outfielder who also sang professionally during a fairly obscure baseball career that featured one unforgettable moment.

The 1969 season was the Cubs' fourth under firebrand manager Leo Durocher. They had improved in each of the previous three campaigns after ruefully living up to Durocher's takeover pronouncement that "this is not an eighth-place team" by finishing 10th in 1966.

Even before it started, the 1969 season was historic. Expansion added two

Cubs manager Leo Durocher's hunch led to an
Opening Day walk-off home run. It was the first
taste of the wild summer ahead.

teams to each major league—Montreal and San Diego in the National, Kansas City and Seattle in the American—and four six-team divisions were created to facilitate scheduling and emphasize geographical rivalries. The schedule remained at 162 games, with the division champions then meeting in two best-of-five playoff series to determine each league's World Series representative.

The Cubs were assigned to the National League East, one of the toughest divisions with the two-time pennant-winning Cardinals, the hard-hitting Pirates and on-the-rise young clubs in New York and Philadelphia. But the Cubs were a confident team when they took the field for the April 8 season opener against the Phillies, and a standing-room crowd of 40,796 at Wrigley Field shared in that optimism.

Ernie Banks was still "Mr. Cub," still a productive, dangerous hitter at 38. All-Stars Billy Williams, 30, and Ron Santo, 29, added more thunder to the middle of an imposing batting order. Young veterans Glenn Beckert and Don Kessinger joined Santo and Banks in the league's best infield. Randy Hundley was a rock behind the plate and deft handler of a pitching staff that featured Ferguson Jenkins, Ken Holtzman and Bill Hands in a strong rotation.

The bench, the bullpen and rookie Don Young in center field were the team's only question marks, but nobody wanted to hear a discouraging word on Opening Day. The call to "Play Ball!" produced spine-tingling anticipation.

A single, a sacrifice, his own error and Deron Johnson's RBI single put Jenkins in a 1–0 hole in the first inning, but Banks got him out of it when he powered a three-run homer into the left-field bleachers off Chris Short in the bottom of the first.

At a Glance

WP: Regan (1–0)

HR: Banks 2 (1, 2), Smith 1

Key stat: Banks and the Phillies' Don Money combined for 10 RBIs.

It remained a 3–1 game when Banks faced Short with Williams on first and one out in the bottom of the third. Banks took the veteran lefty deep again for a 5–1 lead as Wrigley rocked.

Jenkins had a propensity for giving up solo homers throughout his career, so no one flinched when the rookie Money tagged him for one leading off the seventh inning, cutting the Cubs' lead to 5–2. Jenkins settled down and was three outs away from a complete-game victory when Johnny Callison and Cookie Rojas opened the ninth inning with singles. That brought Money to the plate, and the 22-year-old shortstop was money once again, slamming a three-run homer off Jenkins that tied the game 5–5 and turned the raucous crowd deathly quiet.

Barry Lersch, in his major league debut, had shut the Cubs down on two hits over four innings in relief, and Phillies manager Bob Skinner demonstrated his faith in the rookie right-hander by letting him bat in the 11th, after an RBI double by that man Money had given the Phils a 6–5 lead. Money was 3-for-5 with 10 total bases and five RBIs for the day.

Lersch stayed in the game and got Banks on a fly to right leading off the 11th, then gave up a single to Hundley. With Jim Hickman due up, Durocher played one of the hunches for which he was famous. Hickman was 0-for-4 with a strikeout, and Durocher didn't like his chances against the hard-throwing Lersch in the gathering dusk. So he went to his bench for the left-handed-hitting Smith, a former pitcher who'd been converted into an outfielder while playing for the Angels because of how well he swung the bat.

Smith, 30, had one thing in mind as he stepped to the plate with darkness falling. And when Lersch threw him a 1–1 fastball, he produced it, sending a high drive into the right-field bleachers. The two-run, game-winning, pinch-hit homer touched off pandemonium at Wrigley Field. Hundley fairly danced around the bases in front of Smith. Jack Brickhouse's call on television—"Willie Smith!!! Willie Smith!!!"—was simple but eloquent, one of the most memorable in Brickhouse's Hall of Fame career. Throughout Chicago there was a sense that this could be the start of something big.

The feeling lasted throughout the summer as the Cubs played championship-caliber baseball, drew record crowds to Wrigley Field and turned their "Bleacher Bum" followers into cult figures. The end of their World Series drought—then a modest 24 years—seemed to be in sight.

But it was not to be. Their lack of depth exposed the Cubs as a tired team over the season's final six weeks. Meanwhile, the Mets caught fire behind a dominant young pitching staff. They not only overhauled the Cubs to win the NL East, they swept the Atlanta Braves in the first National League Championship Series and stunned the heavily favored Baltimore Orioles in a five-game World Series, earning a place in baseball lore as the "Miracle Mets."

History is less kind to the Cubs. Their 92–70 record and second-place finish is viewed as an epic collapse, and there's no denying it was a dispiriting letdown, mostly because of the day-to-day thrills and high-wire excitement that preceded it. But no one who experienced that 1969 season will ever forget it, least of all Willie Smith.

He died of a heart attack in his hometown of Anniston, Ala., in 2006. He was 66. He had modest numbers: a .248 career batting average, 46 home runs, 211 RBIs ... and one moment that will live forever in Cubs history.

Willie Smith!!!

The New Tradition Arrives with Green

As a major league pitcher, Dallas Green had modest talent but a fierce competitive drive. As a novice major league manager he railed against the complacency and sense of entitlement he found in the Philadelphia clubhouse, then cracked the whip and drove the Philllies to the 1980 World Series championship.

Anybody who expected business as usual at Wrigley Field after Tribune Co. bought the Cubs and installed Green as general manager before the 1982 season was in for a surprise. Green gagged at the "lovable losers" image that permeated the place—"Even the vendors had a hang-dog, defeatist attitude," he observed—and vowed that the "new tradition" he was implementing would be all about winning.

Cubs fans had heard that before, of course, but Green took a jackhammer to the Cubs' roster to prove he was serious about changing the culture. First baseman Bill Buckner, left fielder Steve Henderson and center fielder Ty Waller were the only starters from the '81 season finale who were in the lineup for the '82 home opener, and Waller had moved from third base to accommodate rookie Ryne Sandberg.

At a Glance

WP: Jenkins (1–0)

S: Smith (1)

HR: Buckner (1)

Key stat: Jenkins won his 148th game as a Cub.

With a curious crowd of 26,712 looking on, manager Lee Elia's Cubs kicked off the home portion of the new tradition by invoking a big name from their past. Ferguson Jenkins, 39, who'd been brought back as a free agent the previous winter, pitched 6 $2/3$ innings of scoreless, five-hit ball, combining with Lee Smith to shut out the Mets. Buckner hit a two-run homer off Mike Scott in the fourth inning. The other big contributors were Philadelphia émigrés who accompanied Green to Chicago: shortstop Larry Bowa went 2-for-4 and scored three runs, and catcher Keith Moreland was 2-for-4 with a two-run single in the eighth inning.

The Cubs lost the next two games and six of their next seven, finishing April with a 7–14 record en route to a 73–89, fifth-place showing.

But change would be a constant during the Green regime, and it would frequently be change for the better. Sandberg (now at second base), Leon Durham (now at first) and Bowa would be the only holdovers from the '82 home-opener lineup who took the field in Pittsburgh on Sept. 24, 1984, when the Cubs beat the Pirates behind Rick Sutcliffe to clinch the NL East title and reach the postseason for the first time since 1945.

Game-Winner Is Callison Deal's First Dividend

The 31-year-old left-handed batter stepped into the box. There were two outs, he had made no hits this Friday afternoon in Montreal's Parc Jarry and his new team, the Cubs, appeared to be on the verge of beginning the season 0–3. He himself had not fared all that well thus far, having collected one hit in 10 at-bats.

This is not what general manager John Holland and manager Leo Durocher had anticipated the previous Nov. 17, when they traded pitcher Dick Selma, a 12-game winner in '69, and 19-year-old outfield prospect Oscar Gamble to the Phillies for the veteran outfielder—a mainstay in Philadelphia for a decade, a three-time National League All-Star and the Midsummer Classic's MVP in 1964, when his three-run walk-off homer had stunned the American League.

The batter was Johnny Callison, pride of the Chicago White Sox farm system in 1958, when he too was 19, the year he hit 29 homers and batted .283 at Triple-A Indianapolis and was so impressive in a September call-up that the Sox named him their Opening Day left fielder for 1959. An ill-advised trade had sent him to Philly for third baseman Gene Freese in December 1959, and Callison soon established himself as a Phillies hero.

On the day the Cubs landed him, Durocher had declared: "Callison has the best arm in the league outside of Roberto Clemente. He not only adds to a solid defense, he also gives us another big bat in the lineup."

The big bat had been silent, but that was about to change. The host Expos had led 1–0 since the fifth inning, when a two-out RBI single by Marv Staehle—like Callison a onetime White Sox rookie hopeful—had given Joe Sparma the lead over Bill Hands. Glenn Beckert opened the ninth with a walk, but when Billy Williams rapped into a double play, the Cubs were staring at 0–3.

> ### At a Glance
>
> **WP:** Aguirre (1–0)
>
> **SV:** Abernathy (1)
>
> **HR:** Callison (1)
>
> **Key stat:** Callison's home run was the 190th of his career. He finished with 226.

But then Ron Santo singled to left, and now Callison was the batter. Sparma, a former Ohio State quarterback, went into the stretch and delivered. Callison swung and the ball sailed over the right-field fence for a 2–1 lead. A few minutes later, after Ted Abernathy had retired Adolfo Phillips, Bob Bailey and Bobby Wine, the Cubs had their first triumph of 1970. Callison was hitting .313 by May 1, and the Cubs were 13–5 and in first place.

'Toothpick' Sam Jones' Debut One to Remember

As befitting his status as the ace of the Cubs' pitching staff, Bob Rush was given the Opening Day start for the 1955 season. The assignment took Rush and the Cubs to Cincinnati, where the Reds played the traditional season opener a day earlier than everybody else in recognition of their status as baseball's first professional team.

It was a rough outing for the veteran right-hander—the hard-hitting Reds touched up Rush for four runs and 10 hits in just 3 ⅔ innings. But one man's struggle is another man's opportunity. Sam Jones, acquired from Cleveland the previous winter, took over in the fourth inning and earned his first Cubs win in his debut with five innings of two-hit relief pitching as the Cubs beat the Reds 7–5 before 32,195 fans at Crosley Field.

Dee Fondy doubled home Ernie Banks and Ransom Jackson in the second inning, and after Harry Chiti's double scored Fondy, Rush had a 3–0 lead.

In the third, Joe Nuxhall took over for embattled Reds starter Art Fowler, and Gene Baker greeted the Old Left-Hander with a home run for a 4–0 Cubs lead.

The Reds got half of it back on Ted Kluszewski's two-run homer in the third, but not to worry: Fondy singled to right and Chiti homered to left to put the Cubs up 6–2 in the top of the fourth.

At a Glance
WP: Jones (1–0)
S: Jeffcoat (1)
HR: Baker (1), Chiti (1)
Key stat: Chiti's 3 RBIs were half of his April total.

Rush, though, couldn't finish the bottom of the fourth. Wally Post singled to center and pinch-hitter Hobie Landrith doubled to right. After Johnny Temple's RBI groundout and Gus Bell's RBI single scored two runs, Jones replaced Rush and retired the dangerous Kluszewski on a grounder to first.

The lanky right-hander known as "Toothpick" for the ever-present toothpick he kept in his mouth, even while pitching, would keep the Reds quiet until the ninth, when Bell's double and a pair of two-out walks loaded the bases. Hal Jeffcoat relieved Jones. Jeffcoat hit Ed Bailey with a pitch to force in a run but retired Post on a grounder to preserve the 7–5 victory and a 1–0 start to a 72–81, sixth-place season.

The 2-for-4, three-RBI day was an encouraging start for Chiti, a catcher who was never known as a robust hitter during 10 major league seasons. Jones, meanwhile, would make history of a more dramatic sort one month later when he became the first African-American pitcher to throw a major league no-hitter.

The Hall of Fame Battery

No one suspected it—no one could have, as the Baseball Hall of Fame wouldn't open for another 14 years—but the Cubs trotted out a Hall of Fame battery to face the Reds in the 1922 season opener on April 12 at Cincinnati's Redland Field.

And it's not likely anyone suspected Cubs catcher Charles Leo "Gabby" Hartnett was Cooperstown-bound after the 21-year-old went 0-for-2 in his major league debut, a 7–3 Cubs victory.

The pitcher, however, was another story. Sturdy right-hander Grover Cleveland "Pete" Alexander was an established star with a 190–88 career record and a 2.18 ERA when the Cubs obtained him from the Philadelphia Phillies for the unforgettable Pickles Dillhoefer, Mike Prendergast and $55,000 on Dec. 11, 1917.

Alexander was beginning his fifth season with the Cubs when he faced the Reds this day. If he didn't exhibit Hall of Fame stuff, he got the job done with a complete-game seven-hitter and helped himself with an RBI double.

The Cubs staked Alexander to a 2-0 lead in the second inning on Hack Miller's RBI single and Marty Krug's fielder's-choice grounder. The Reds got on the board in their half of the second when Babe Pinelli singled home Sam Bohne, but the Cubs got the run back in the sixth when John Kelleher singled, stole second and scored on Bernie Friberg's single.

> ## At a Glance
>
> **WP:** Alexander (1–0)
>
> **Key stat:** Hall of Famer Hartnett was the only Cub to go hitless.

Alexander's run-scoring double and RBI singles by Kelleher and Jigger Statz were the big hits as they broke open the game with a four-run seventh, chasing losing pitcher Eppa Rixey.

The Cubs would finish 80–74 and in fifth place. Alexander, 35, would go 16-13 with a 3.63 ERA and 20 complete games, a far heavier workload than Hartnett's. Backing up catcher Bob O'Farrell, the rookie hit just .194 with no homers and four RBIs in 31 games, a quiet beginning to a distinguished career. Over 20 big league seasons, Hartnett would hit .297 with 236 homers and 1,179 RBIs. Along the way, he earned a reputation for his stellar defense and excellent handling of pitchers. He was elected to the Hall of Fame in 1955, still the only Cubs catcher so honored.

Alexander, 373–208 lifetime and a three-time 30-game winner, entered the Hall in 1938.

Catcher Gabby Hartnett made his debut with the Cubs in 1922 and enjoyed a Hall of Fame career.

Cubs 5, Mets 4

Monday Delivery

Perhaps it was optimism born of a 2–1 start to the season in St. Louis.

Mets	AB	R	H	RBI
Garrett 3b	6	0	0	1
Milner lf	5	1	3	2
Kranepool 1b	3	0	1	0
Boisclair pr-cf	0	0	0	0
Kingman rf	4	0	1	0
Unser cf	4	0	0	0
Torre ph-1b	1	0	1	0
Millan 2b	4	1	1	0
Grote c	3	1	3	0
Harrelson ss	4	1	1	1
Swan p	3	0	0	0
Koosman p	0	0	0	0
Ayala ph	1	0	0	0
Lockwood p	1	0	0	0
Totals	39	4	11	4

Cubs	AB	R	H	RBI
Monday cf	5	0	2	1
Cardenal lf	3	0	0	0
Madlock 3b	3	2	1	0
Morales rf	3	2	2	4
Thornton 1b	4	0	0	0
Trillo 2b	4	1	2	0
Swisher c	3	0	0	0
Summers ph	0	0	0	0
Rosello ss	3	0	1	0
Wallis ph	0	0	0	0
R Reuschel p	1	0	0	0
P Reuschel p	1	0	0	0
LaCock ph	0	0	0	0
Mitterwald ph	1	0	0	0
Knowles p	0	0	0	0
Garman p	0	0	0	0
Hosley ph	1	0	0	0
Totals	32	5	8	5

											R	H	E
NYM	0	0	0	3	0	0	0	1	0	-	4	11	0
CHI	2	0	0	0	0	2	0	0	1	-	5	8	2

Mets	IP	H	R	ER	BB	SO
Swan	6.1	6	4	4	2	3
Koosman	0.2	0	0	0	0	0
Lockwood L (0-1)	1.2	2	1	1	2	1
Totals	8.2	8	5	5	4	4

Cubs	IP	H	R	ER	BB	SO
R. Reuschel	3.2	6	3	3	3	4
P. Reuschel	3.1	3	0	0	1	2
Knowles	0.2	1	1	1	1	1
Garman W (1-0)	1.1	1	0	0	1	1
Totals	9	11	4	4	6	8

E—Chicago Cardenal, Trillo. DP—Chicago. 2B—New York Millan, Milner; Chicago Trillo. 3B—Chicago Trillo. HR—New York Milner (1); Chicago Morales 2 (1,2). HBP—New York Grote; Chicago Madlock. LOB—New York 15; Chicago 6. SB—New York Harrelson. Attendance: 44,818.

Perhaps it was the belief that a young Cubs nucleus would continue to develop and lift the team into contention.

Or perhaps it was anti-Mets passion that had been virulent in Chicago since the sorry end to the '69 season.

Whatever the reason, 44,818 fans jammed Wrigley Field for the Cubs' 1976 home opener. They were treated to a 5–4 victory over the despised New Yorkers in which Jerry Morales, Manny Trillo and Rick Monday were the hitting stars and Paul Reuschel stole some of the pitching thunder from his more accomplished brother, Rick.

Craig Swan was the Mets' starter, and the Cubs got to him in the first inning when Bill Madlock singled with two outs and Morales followed with a long home run to left.

But the Mets countered with three runs in the fourth, chasing Rick Reuschel. Felix Millan doubled, Jerry Grote was hit by a pitch and Bud Harrelson singled for the first Mets run. Wayne Garrett's fielder's-choice grounder tied the game, and the Mets went ahead 3–2 on John Milner's RBI double, finishing Rick Reuschel, who surrendered six hits and three walks in 3 $^2/_3$ shaky innings. Paul Reuschel, the elder of the Reuschel brothers from Camp Point, Ill., took over and worked 3 $^1/_3$ scoreless innings.

The Cubs still trailed 3–2 in the sixth inning when Swan hit Madlock with a pitch and Morales cracked his second homer of the game into the bleachers in left-center. The 4–3 score stood until the eighth, when Milner defied a lefty-lefty pitching matchup and tied the game with a home run to right off reliever Darold Knowles. An error, a walk and an infield single then loaded the bases, but Mike Garman retired Millan on a liner to center, preserving the tie.

With one out in the Cubs' ninth, Trillo legged out a triple to right-center off reliever Skip Lockwood. The Mets walked pinch-hitters Champ Summers and "Tarzan Joe" Wallis to set up a force at any base. Pinch-hitter Tim Hosley was retired for the second out, but Monday came through with a game-winning single to center, sending the huge crowd home happy.

Only 9,307 were on hand the following day as the Cubs got to 4–1 by beating the Mets 6–5. Three games over .500 would prove to be the high-water mark of a season in which they'd finish 75-87 and in fourth place in the NL East. Their lack of firepower was the culprit—the Cubs hit just .251 as a team and averaged 3.8 runs a game, a recipe for disaster in Wrigley Field.

There were bright spots: Madlock won his second straight batting title with a .339 average and drove in a team-high 84 runs. Monday slugged a career-best 32 homers and scored 107 runs.

The season's most encouraging development would come a month after the home opener. In May, with their bullpen depleted, the Cubs summoned reliever Bruce Sutter from the minors. The 23-year-old master of the baffling split-finger pitch went 6–3 with a 2.70 ERA and 10 saves in 52 games, a sign of the great things to come.

Jerry Morales

Julio Ruben "Jerry" Morales was a solid player for the Cubs during some mid-1970s mediocrity. Acquired from San Diego for second-base fixture Glenn Beckert, the Puerto Rico-born Morales was a capable fielder at all three outfield positions from 1974 through 1977. A right-handed hitter, he held his bat distinctively high and had some pop for a slightly built 5-foot-10, 160-pounder, batting .276 with 54 home runs and 309 RBIs in his first four seasons with the Cubs.

Morales made the All-Star team in 1977 and was hit in the knee by a Sparky Lyle pitch in his only at-bat. Traded to St. Louis that winter, he bounced from the Cardinals to the Tigers to the Mets before returning to the Cubs as a free agent in 1981. Lifetime, he was a .259 hitter with 95 homers and 570 RBIs.

Larry Biittner's Moment

Woodie Fryman? Dave Rader? There were not a lot of buzz-creating new faces with the Cubs in 1978, but Chicago fans were nonetheless eager for a look at second-year manager Herman Franks' creation. A crowd of 45,777, then a record for a home opener, turned out to see the Cubs and the Pirates on Friday, April 14. They were treated to a bravura performance by some unlikely heroes.

Fryman, a well-traveled 38-year-old left-hander obtained in an off-season trade for pitcher Bill Bonham, got the start and took a no-hitter into the sixth inning before Dave Parker ended his dreams of Chicago glory with a two-out double.

Larry Biittner—that's two 'i's', two 't's' if you're spelling at home—broke a 4-4 tie with a ninth-inning home run off Jim Bibby, winning the game with a walk-off homer long before the term was fashionable.

The Cubs broke through in the first inning against Bucs starter Jerry Reuss when ex-Pirate Gene Clines reached on Rennie Stennett's fielding error and scored on Bill Buckner's double. Buckner took third on a wild pitch, but Reuss left him there, striking out Bobby Murcer and Dave Kingman to end the inning.

In the second, Reuss hit Manny Trillo with a pitch and Heity Cruz singled to center. Rader forced Cruz and Fryman struck out, but Ivan DeJesus and Clines delivered two-out RBI singles, putting the Cubs up 3–0.

Fryman, meanwhile, was keeping the hard-hitting Pirates off balance with slow breaking stuff, but they finally solved him in the sixth. Parker's two-out double ended the no-hit suspense, and Bill Robinson followed with a triple. After Jim Fregosi walked, Stennett singled home Robinson and Phil Garner singled home Fregosi, tying the game at 3–3.

There matters stood until the eighth, when star-crossed reliever Donnie Moore took over for Fryman and Willie Stargell pinch-hit for Frego-

Pirates	AB	R	H	RBI
Taveras ss	5	0	1	0
Brye cf	2	0	0	0
Moreno cf	1	0	0	0
Parker rf	4	1	1	0
Robinson lf	2	1	1	1
Fregosi 1b	2	1	0	0
Stargell ph-1b	1	1	1	1
Stennett 2b	4	0	1	1
Garner 3b	4	0	1	1
Sanguillen c	3	0	0	0
Reuss p	2	0	0	0
Gonzalez ph	1	0	0	0
Tekulve p	0	0	0	0
Jackson p	0	0	0	0
Bibby p	0	0	0	0
Totals	31	4	6	4

Cubs	AB	R	H	RBI
DeJesus ss	5	0	2	2
Clines cf	3	1	2	1
Gross ph-cf	2	0	1	0
Buckner 1b	1	0	1	0
Biittner 1b	3	1	2	1
Murcer rf	4	0	0	0
Kingman lf	4	0	0	0
Trillo 2b	3	2	1	0
Cruz 3b	2	0	1	0
Rader c	3	1	0	0
Fryman p	3	0	0	0
Moore p	0	0	0	0
Ontiveros ph	0	0	0	0
Hernandez p	0	0	0	0
Totals	33	5	10	4

```
PIT   0 0 0 0 0 3 0 1 0 - 4 6 3
CHI   1 2 0 0 0 0 0 1 1 - 5 10 0
```

Pirates	IP	H	R	ER	BB	SO
Reuss	5	6	3	2	1	4
Tekulve	1.1	1	0	0	2	0
Jackson	0.1	0	0	0	0	1
Bibby L (1-1)	1.1	3	2	2	1	0
Totals	8	10	5	4	4	5

Cubs	IP	H	R	ER	BB	SO
Fryman	7	4	3	3	6	4
Moore	1	1	1	1	0	0
Hernandez W (1-0)	1	1	0	0	1	0
Totals	9	6	4	4	7	4

E—Pittsburgh Stennett 2, Taveras. DP—Pittsburgh; Chicago 2. 2B—Pittsburgh Parker; Chicago Buckner, DeJesus. 3B—Pittsburgh Robinson; Chicago Biittner. HR—Pittsburgh Stargell (1); Chicago Biittner (1). SH—Chicago Cruz. HBP—Chicago Trillo. LOB—Pittsburgh 7; Chicago 10. Attendance: 45,777.

si. The Hall of Fame slugger lofted a home run into the right-field bleachers, giving the Pirates a 4–3 lead that lasted only until the bottom of the eighth, when Trillo singled and scored the tying run on DeJesus' two-out double.

That set the stage for Mr. Biittner, a former Texas Ranger who had taken over at first base after Buckner tweaked his ankle running out his first-inning double. Leading off the Cubs' ninth, Biittner drove a Bibby pitch into the bleachers in right-center field, touching off Willie Smith-like pandemonium in Wrigleyville.

The first of Biittner's four '78 homers was a definite highlight in a season that didn't offer many. The Cubs went 79–83 and finished third in the NL East, 11 games behind the three-time division champion Phillies and 9.5 behind the oncoming Pirates, who were a year away from their "We Are Family" world championship. An astonishing power shortage was the Cubs' biggest failing; they hit just 72 home runs as a team, with Kingman accounting for 28 and no one else hitting more than Murcer's nine. Kingman was also the team's RBI leader with a modest 79. Buckner batted .323 with 74 RBIs, and DeJesus hit .278 with 104 runs scored and 41 steals in a solid year.

On the pitching side, Rick Reuschel was the staff leader with 14 victories, but 26-year-old Mike Krukow was the only starter on the plus side of .500 with a 9–3 record. Willie Hernandez (8–2, 3.77 ERA) was strong in middle relief, and Bruce Sutter (8–10, 3.19 ERA) collected 27 saves.

A footnote on Donnie Moore, who gave up the game-tying home run to Stargell: Eight years later, pitching for the California Angels in Game 5 of the 1986 American League playoffs, Moore served up a game-tying, ninth-inning homer to Boston's Dave Henderson that probably cost the Angels their first American League pennant. Friends say Moore never got over the disappointment and wound up committing suicide three years later.

How easy it is to forget that baseball is only a game.

Willie Hernandez

Cubs fans bemoaned Guillermo "Willie" Hernandez as one who got away during his career year with the 1984 World Series champion Detroit Tigers.

Hernandez, a left-handed reliever, was 26–28 with a 3.81 ERA and 20 saves over seven seasons with the Cubs, who traded him to the Phillies for pitcher Dick Ruthven in May 1983. The Phillies moved him on to the Tigers in March 1984, and Hernandez proceeded to dominate the AL, going 9–3 with a 1.92 ERA and 32 saves. He won the AL Cy Young Award and was also the league MVP on a team that included Kirk Gibson, Alan Trammell, and Lou Whitaker.

Al Who?

A statue of Al Heist will never be erected outside Wrigley Field, and his number—he wore 18 in 1960 and 22 in '61—will not be retired to fly atop the ballpark's foul poles.

Born in Brooklyn in 1927, Heist didn't reach the major leagues until he was 32 years old, and his 177-game big league career is hardly the stuff of Cooperstown. But on April 15, 1961, Al Heist fulfilled a dream every aspiring ballplayer nurtures at some point in his life. With the Cubs and the Milwaukee Braves locked in a 5–5 tie in the ninth inning on a frigid Saturday at Wrigley Field, Heist faced Don Nottebart with the bases loaded and drove a pitch from the rookie right-hander out of the ballpark for a game-winning grand slam.

"He was probably the last guy in their lineup I expected to do that," Braves manager Charlie Dressen said.

Only 6,207 fans were on hand for Heist's moment, though in subsequent years, many more would no doubt claim to have been eyewitnesses. A snowstorm would postpone the next day's game.

Heist was in his 11th minor league season and his sixth as a center fielder for the Sacramento Solons of the Pacific Coast League when he got the call to Chicago in July of 1960.

"I had pretty much given up on a major league career," Heist said. "When the Cubs brought me up it was the biggest surprise of my life."

He was hitting .299 with 13 homers and 66 RBIs in the PCL, known as the "third major league" because of the high caliber of play it featured before MLB expansion diluted its talent.

"Don't sell him short," Cubs general manager John Holland advised reporters who wondered why the Cubs would turn to a relative old-timer. "He's an excellent outfielder, he can run and he has more power than people give him credit for."

The Braves had jumped out to a 5–2 lead against Cubs starter Glen Hobbie, but Ron Santo's two-run homer, Ernie Banks' triple and Ed Bouchee's RBI single got the Cubs even in the fifth inning.

Braves	AB	R	H	RBI
Maye lf	4	1	0	0
Crandall c	5	2	4	1
Mathews 3b	5	1	1	0
Aaron rf	4	0	0	0
Bolling 2b	4	0	1	1
Adcock 1b	4	0	1	2
Spangler cf	2	0	0	0
McMillan ss	4	1	1	0
Willey p	1	0	0	0
Nottebart p	2	0	0	0
Totals	35	5	8	4

Cubs	AB	R	H	RBI
Ashburn lf	4	0	1	0
Zimmer 2b	3	4	2	0
Williams rf	4	0	1	0
Santo 3b	5	2	3	4
Banks ss	3	2	1	0
Bouchee 1b	4	0	1	1
Heist cf	4	1	2	4
Bertell c	3	0	0	0
Taylor ph-c	1	0	0	0
Hobbie p	2	0	0	0
Will ph	1	0	0	0
Elston p	0	0	0	0
Totals	34	9	11	9

											R	H	E
MIL	3	1	0	0	1	0	0	0	0	-	5	8	1
CHI	1	0	1	0	3	0	0	0	4	-	9	11	2

Braves	IP	H	R	ER	BB	SO
Willey	4.1	5	5	5	5	2
Nottebart L (0-1)	4.1	6	4	4	2	1
Totals	8.2	11	9	9	7	3

Cubs	IP	H	R	ER	BB	SO
Hobbie	8	7	5	4	3	1
Elston W (2-0)	1	1	0	0	0	1
Totals	9	8	5	4	3	2

E—Milwaukee Mathews; Chicago Banks, Hobbie. DP—Milwaukee. 2B—Milwaukee Crandall; Chicago Heist. 3B—Chicago Banks, Zimmer. HR—Chicago Santo (1), Heist (1). SH—Milwaukee Willey; Chicago Williams. HBP—Chicago Zimmer. LOB—Milwaukee 7; Chicago 8. Attendance: 6,207.

The deadlock persisted into the ninth. Nottebart hit Don Zimmer with a pitch leading off, and Zimmer took second on a sacrifice by rookie left fielder Billy Williams, who would not often be asked to bunt during his Hall of Fame career. Santo reached on an infield single and Banks walked to load the bases, but Bouchee flied to short left.

That left it up to Heist, and he delivered, atoning for an earlier mistake when he was thrown out trying to go from second to third on pinch-hitter Bob Will's tapper to the mound after a leadoff double in the eighth inning.

"Hanging slider," Nottebart grumped.

Heist's heroics couldn't save the '61 Cubs, who went 64–90 and finished seventh in the National League, 29 games behind the pennant-winning Reds. Heist would hit .255 with seven homers and 37 RBIs in 109 games while playing an excellent center field. But with Williams and George Altman in place and Lou Brock on his way to Chicago, Heist was deemed expendable and was lost to the Houston Colt .45s in the 1962 expansion draft.

Houston released him after just 27 games. Heist played three more seasons in Triple-A before retiring with modest career numbers: a .255 batting average, eight homers and 46 RBIs.

And one indelible memory.

Al Heist

Al Heist isn't mentioned with Willie Mays, Mickey Mantle, Duke Snider, and the few others who made the 1950s a golden age of center fielders. But off baseball's main stage, Heist was regarded as "the best center fielder you never heard of" thanks to his defensive work for the Sacramento Solons of the Pacific Coast League, which was often described as a third major league because of its high-caliber play.

Heist combined great range with a strong throwing arm and once had 25 outfield assists in 1959, the same year he took part in eight double plays. He was Milwaukee property until July 15, 1960, when the Braves traded him to the Cubs for Earl Averill Jr.

Burt Hooton's Fluke Is Good Enough for Cubs

A baseball season is destined to be remembered as unusual when one of its most vivid highlights occurs on the second day.

That was the case in 1972, when the Cubs sent rookie right-hander Burt Hooton to the mound to face the Philadelphia Phillies at Wrigley Field on April 16. A dispute between management and the players union resulted in a work stoppage that delayed the start of the season by nearly two weeks, so Opening Day occurred on a mid-April Saturday. And it felt like mid-January for Hooton's Sunday start, with a brisk wind blowing in off Lake Michigan contributing to the arctic-like conditions.

But Hooton, a 22-year-old from Texas, was as cool as the elements.

In the fourth appearance of his major league career, Hooton tossed a no-hitter against the Phillies, beating them 4–0. It was far from effortless; he walked seven and had at least one baserunner in six of the game's nine innings. But he also struck out seven and got the big out each time he needed it as the Cubs backed him with flawless fielding despite the tricky conditions.

"A fluke," Hooton insisted afterward, but anyone who saw him carve up the Phillies' lineup with a slick combination of fastballs and knuckle-curves would beg to differ.

At a Glance

WP: Hooton (1–0)

Key stat: Milt Pappas would pitch a no-hitter less than five months later. The Cubs would go 36 years without another one (Carlos Zambrano, 2008).

There weren't that many eyewitnesses, as the frigid conditions limited the crowd to 9,583. Ron Santo doubled in the fourth inning and scored the only run Hooton would need on a throwing error. Catcher Randy Hundley gave him some breathing room with a two-run single in the seventh, and Jose Cardenal's triple and Glenn Beckert's single made it a 4–0 game in the eighth.

That left it all up to Hooton.

As a college pitcher, Hooton was the Mark Prior of his day, going 35-3 with two no-hitters at the University of Texas. The Cubs took him with the No. 2 pick in the 1971 amateur draft and brought him to Chicago for some major league exposure after he signed that summer. Hooton hardly looked overmatched, winning two of his three starts with a 2.11 ERA and allowing just eight hits while striking out 22 in 21.1 innings. The Cubs tentatively included Hooton in their pitching plans for the '72 season, and he secured a spot in the starting rotation with a strong spring.

"Ferguson Jenkins pitched the opener and I pitched the second game," Hooton said. "It was quite a thrill."

Willie Montanez was the Phillies' first baserunner, drawing a two-out walk in the first inning, but Hooton retired Deron Johnson on a fly ball. Greg Luzinski walked leading off the second, but Don Money forced him and was thrown out stealing.

Montanez walked again with one out in the fourth, but Luzinski forced him, and Denny Doyle bounced into a 6-4-3 double play after Money walked in the fifth.

Trailing 1–0, the Phils got the tying run to second on a walk and a sacrifice in the sixth, but Hooton got Tim McCarver to ground out, and he struck out Montanez.

The Phils put two runners aboard on two-out walks to Money and Mike Anderson in the seventh, but Hooton slipped a called third strike past Doyle. With history bearing down, he got the Phils in order in the eighth and ninth, striking out Johnson and Luzinski to end it as Jack Brickhouse shouted, "He did it!" to the WGN-TV audience. The man who would later be known as "Happy" for his all-business demeanor was all smiles as his teammates mobbed him at the mound.

"A fluke," Hooton repeatedly insisted. Hardly. He was 11–14 despite a splendid 2.80 ERA that year for a Cubs team that was 85–70 but finished 11 games behind the division champion Pirates.

A student of pitching for as long as he could remember, Hooton developed his knuckle-curve by accident. He tried to teach himself the knuckleball after watching Hoyt Wilhelm throw it in a game he had seen on television. "I got a lot of rotation on the ball, but I couldn't get it to butterfly, and I got angry," he later recalled. "The angrier I got, the harder I threw it, and the harder I threw it the better it worked."

The knuckle-curve became Hooton's signature pitch over a 15-year career that really blossomed after he left Chicago for Los Angeles. He was traded to the Dodgers for Geoff Zahn and Eddie Solomon in May of 1975 after going 34–44 for a Cubs team in decline. He won 12 straight decisions and finished 18–7 for the Dodgers in '75 and was runner-up to Gaylord Perry for the NL Cy Young Award after going 19–10 with a 2.71 ERA in 1978. He was MVP of the National League Championship Series in 1981 and helped pitch the Dodgers to their first World Series championship since 1965.

Overall, Hooton was 151–136 with a 3.38 ERA for his career. He had a 6–3 postseason record ... and one Wrigley Field moment that is literally frozen in time.

The Baron Announces His Presence

The Cubs hadn't had a Hall of Fame catcher—still haven't—since Gabby Hartnett retired in 1940. They couldn't be blamed for thinking they might have stumbled onto one after George Mitterwald's performance in his fifth game with the team.

The burly catcher, known as "Baron von Mitterwald" after being acquired from the Minnesota Twins for fellow catcher Randy Hundley in December 1973, slugged three home runs and drove in eight runs as the Cubs outslugged the Pirates 18–9 before 15,560 fans on an unseasonably warm, windy Wednesday at Wrigley Field.

Career day? Mitterwald, then 28, would hit seven homers that season and 26 in his four years with the Cubs.

Mitterwald was as surprised by his power surge as anyone; he wasn't supposed to play that day. Having caught nine innings of the previous day's 8–5 loss to the Pirates, Mitterwald was expecting a day off, and legend has it he decided to experience a night out in his new town. But with left-hander Jerry Reuss pitching for the Pirates, the right-handed-hitting Mitterwald found himself in manager Whitey Lockman's lineup batting seventh when he got to the ballpark. And he wasted no time making a contribution.

The Cubs had one run in and the bases loaded when Mitterwald faced Reuss in the first inning. He lofted a drive into the wind that carried into the bleachers for a grand slam and a 5–3 Cubs lead.

In the second, Jerry Morales and Rick Monday hit back-to-back homers off Reuss, and in the third, Mitterwald went deep again after doubles by Jose Cardenal and Bill Madlock. That finished Reuss, who left with a yield of 10 earned runs on eight hits in just two innings. His successor, Steve Blass, fared no better.

Pirates	AB	R	H	RBI
Stennett 2b	6	0	3	0
Hebner 3b	6	2	4	2
Oliver cf	5	1	0	0
Stargell lf	5	2	3	3
Parker rf	5	0	0	0
Robertson 1b	5	1	1	0
Sanguillen c	5	2	2	2
Maxvill ss	4	0	1	0
Zisk ph	1	1	1	2
Reuss p	0	0	0	0
Morlan p	0	0	0	0
Bevacqua ph	1	0	0	0
Blass p	2	0	0	0
Kirkpatrick ph	1	0	1	0
Totals	46	9	16	9

Cubs	AB	R	H	RBI
Harris 2b	5	1	1	1
Monday cf	4	3	2	1
Garrett c	0	0	0	0
Morales lf-rf	3	2	1	1
Williams 1b	4	2	2	3
Thornton 1b	1	0	0	0
Cardenal rf	4	2	1	0
Ward lf	1	0	0	0
Madlock 3b	3	5	2	2
Mitterwald c	4	3	4	8
Alexander pr-cf	0	0	0	0
Rosello ss	5	0	0	1
Hooton p	4	0	0	0
Totals	38	18	13	17

PIT	3 1 0 0 0 0 0 0 5 - 9 16 2
CHI	5 2 3 5 0 2 0 1 X - 18 13 4

Pirates	IP	H	R	ER	BB	SO
Reuss L (0-1)	2	8	10	10	2	0
Morlan	1	0	0	0	0	1
Blass	5	5	8	5	7	2
Totals	8	13	18	15	9	3

Cubs	IP	H	R	ER	BB	SO
Hooton W (1-0)	9	16	9	5	1	7
Totals	9	16	9	5	1	7

E—Pittsburgh Hebner, Maxvill; Chicago Thornton 2, Harris, Madlock. DP—Pittsburgh; Chicago. 2B—Chicago Cardenal, Mitterwald, Williams, Madlock. 3B—Pittsburgh Sanguillen. HR—Pittsburgh Zisk (2), Stargell (2), Hebner (4); Chicago Monday (1), Mitterwald 3 (1,2,3), Morales (2), Madlock (1). LOB—Pittsburgh 11; Chicago 5. Attendance: 15,560.

Mitterwald drew a bases-loaded walk in a five-run fourth inning that featured three walks, two errors and a wild pitch. In the sixth, Madlock and Mitterwald hit back-to-back homers off Blass to put the Cubs up 17-4. After Mitterwald doubled to left to complete a 4-for-4 day in the eighth, Matt Alexander pinch-ran for him, Lockman reasoning Mitterwald wouldn't get a chance at a fourth homer in such a one-sided game.

The Pirates made it slightly less one-sided with five runs in the ninth, all off starter Burt Hooton, who was left in to finish what he started. Hooton's line: nine innings, 16 hits, nine runs (five earned), one walk and seven strikeouts. It was clearly not a day for pitchers.

With the win, the Cubs improved to 4–3 in a season in which they'd finish 66–96 and last in the NL East, 22 games behind the division champion Pirates. Jim Marshall would succeed Lockman as manager after 93 games.

Randy Hundley

George Mitterwald's career day as a Cub was also a poignant reminder of the durable warrior for whom he'd been traded: Randy Hundley.

Averaging 151 games as the Cubs' catcher during 1966–69—including 160 games in 1968—took a toll on Hundley's knees. At 32, he was a shadow of himself in his lone season with Minnesota, appearing in just 32 games and batting .193. After the Twins released him, Hundley signed with San Diego and hit .206 in 74 games in 1975. He concluded his career with a 15-game cameo for the Cubs in 1976–77.

Mitterwald never appeared in more than 110 games during his four Cub seasons, in which he hit .231 with 26 homers.

The Cubs have never had a four-homer game, so Mitterwald shares the single-game club record with 37 others. He also tied the team record for total bases in a game (14), and his eight RBIs were within one of the club record set by Heinie Zimmerman in 1911 and Sammy Sosa in 2002.

A sad footnote to all that history: Steve Blass' appearance would be the last of his major league career. The classy right-hander won 103 games for the Pirates from 1964-73 and helped pitch them to the World Series title in 1971 with two complete-game victories over the Baltimore Orioles. But a mystifying inability to throw strikes—Steve Blass Disease—overtook him sometime after the 1972 season, when he won 19 games, sabotaging his career.

Blass was charged with eight runs on five hits and seven walks in his five-inning finale. It's not how he should be remembered.

Atta Boy, Ernie!

The Houston Colt .45s were one of two expansion teams added to the National League for the 1962 season, and their motley crew of misfits and discards looked like world-beaters in sweeping the Cubs in a three-game, season-opening series at Houston's Colt Stadium, their pre-Astrodome home.

The Friendly Confines weren't any friendlier to the Cubs. After departing Houston they dropped two games to the Cardinals and two games to the Pirates at Wrigley Field, leaving them a dispirited 0–7 as they faced the Colt .45s on April 18. And not to say Chicago had soured on the Cubs already, but only 3,318 fans were in the stands for the Wednesday matinee.

The Cubs were in their second year of employing a bizarre "college of coaches" rather than a traditional manager to run things from the dugout. And in some ways the '62 Cubs were a new-look team. Two-time MVP Ernie Banks had shifted from shortstop to first base to make room for Elder White, a slick-fielding 27-year-old rookie. Ken Hubbs, 20, had taken over at second base; he'd play 160 games, hit .260 and field superbly in a Rookie of the Year season. Lou Brock, 22, was on hand for his debut season as well, but he'd take a seat behind journeyman Jim McKnight on this day with left-hander Hal Woodeshick starting for the Colt .45s.

Fellow lefty Dick Ellsworth took the mound for the Cubs.

Woodeshick and Turk Farrell had combined for a 2–0 shutout of the Cubs in Houston the previous week, but the Cubs reached Woodeshick for a run in the first inning when White led off with a walk and came around on Banks' two-out triple to left-center field. The Colt .45s tied it in the fifth on Jim Pendleton's bases-loaded, fielder's-choice grounder, and they went ahead 2–1 in the fifth when Bob Aspromonte's sacrifice fly scored ex-Cub Al Heist.

After Moe Thacker singled to open the Cubs' seventh, Brock ran for him. He stole second and scored on White's one-out single for a 2–2 tie.

The Cubs reached Woodeshick for 11 hits in seven innings, and Farrell replaced him in the eighth. Houston manager Harry Craft let Farrell

Colt .45s	AB	R	H	RBI
Aspromonte 3b	3	1	1	1
Amalfitano 2b	4	0	1	0
Gernert 1b	4	0	1	0
Mejias rf	5	0	1	0
Pendleton lf	4	0	1	1
Smith c	3	0	0	0
Heist cf	4	1	2	0
Buddin ss	3	0	1	0
Woodeshick p	2	0	0	0
Farrell p	1	0	0	0
Totals	33	2	8	2

Cubs	AB	R	H	RBI
White ss	3	1	1	1
Hubbs 2b	5	0	1	0
Williams lf	5	0	1	0
Banks 1b	5	1	4	2
Santo 3b	4	0	1	0
McKnight rf	4	0	1	0
Altman cf	4	0	1	0
Thacker c	3	0	2	0
Brock pr	0	1	0	0
Barragan c	0	0	0	0
Will ph	1	0	0	0
Taylor c	0	0	0	0
Ellsworth p	4	0	0	0
Totals	38	3	12	3

HOU	0	0	0	1	1	0	0	0	0	-	2	8	0
CHI	1	0	0	0	0	1	0	0	1	-	3	12	0

Colt .45s	IP	H	R	ER	BB	SO
Woodeshick	7	11	2	2	1	4
Farrell L (0-2)	2.2	1	1	1	0	3
Totals	9	12	3	3	1	7

Cubs	IP	H	R	ER	BB	SO
Ellsworth W (1-0)	10	8	2	2	4	3
Totals	10	8	2	2	4	3

DP—Houston 2; Chicago 2. 2B—Chicago Altman. 3B—Chicago Banks. HR—Chicago Banks (2). HBP—Chicago White. LOB—Houston 8; Chicago 8. SB—Chicago Brock. Attendance: 3,318.

hit for himself with two outs in the ninth inning and he struck out, but the fireballing right-hander then struck out the side in the bottom of the ninth, sending the game to extra innings.

With two outs in the 10th, Banks guessed fastball and Farrell obliged him. Banks drove the pitch over the wall in left-center for a game-winning home run, No. 300 of his storied career.

Whether playing shortstop or first base, Ernie had downtown power.

Such highlights were a rarity in the '62 season. The Cubs would finish 59–103 and ninth in the National League, 42.5 games behind the pennant-winning San Francisco Giants. They were outscored 827–632 and allowed 102 unearned runs. Not a single starting pitcher had a winning record, and the 22-year-old Ellsworth was a hideous 9–20.

Elder White was hardly the answer at shortstop. He was hitting .151 in 23 games when he was sent back to the minor leagues in early June, never to return. His run-scoring single off Woodeshick in the seventh inning on April 18, 1962 represented the only RBI of his major league career.

Dick Ellsworth

Everyone Go Deep

Two weeks into his first year as Cubs manager, Jim Riggleman was happy to welcome Dr. Longball to Wrigley Field for a Friday matinee that attracted 17,662 fans.

With a brisk wind blowing out, the Cubs slammed six home runs in out-slugging manager Dusty Baker's San Francisco Giants, who were thought to have one of the National League's more power-packed lineups with Barry Bonds and Matt Williams in the middle of it.

Three of the Cubs' homers came in succession, and none of the six was particularly wind-aided. Ryne Sandberg, back with the Cubs after a 1 ½-year retirement, slugged two homers, one off the foul pole and one onto Waveland Avenue. Ozzie Timmons cleared Waveland with his second-inning blast, sending the ball bouncing up Kenmore Avenue. Sammy Sosa reached the center-field bleachers in the third, and Mark Grace also went convincingly deep in the sixth.

At a Glance

WP: Foster (3–0)

HR: Sandberg 2 (3,4), Timmons (1), Sosa (5), McRae (1), Grace (1)

Key stat: The first four hitters in the Cubs' lineup were 11-for-19 with 6 runs and 9 RBIs.

But the big shot came from Brian McRae: a sixth-inning grand slam off Allan Watson that erased a 5–4 deficit and broke the game open.

Timmons led off the Cubs' sixth by reaching on Williams' fielding error and took second on a wild pitch. Leo Gomez walked, and with two out, Todd Haney pinch-hit for pitcher Kevin Foster and kept the inning alive with an infield single. That loaded the bases for McRae, who promptly unloaded them and presented Foster with his third straight win.

Watson was so unnerved he gave up a second homer to Sandberg, then gave way to Steve Bourgeois. Grace greeted the righty reliever with the Cubs' third homer of the inning and sixth of the game.

The Cubs improved to 10–6 with the victory, only to lose their next seven in a row. One game over .500 would be their high-water mark for the rest of the season. They'd finish 76–86 and fourth in the National League Central.

Sandberg would play in 150 games in his comeback season, batting .244 with 25 homers and 92 RBIs. Grace would hit .331, a career-high.

Leo Gomez, the latest in a seemingly endless line of third basemen the Cubs employed between Bill Madlock and Aramis Ramirez, would hit .238 with 17 homers and 56 RBIs in 136 games, then disappear from the big leagues at age 30. The '96 season also was the end of the line for catcher Brian Dorsett (0-for-4).

Mark Grace joined the hit parade often for the Cubs.
His 1,754 hits topped all players in the 1990s.

A Historical Footnote, Sort of...

The Cubs were often last, or close to it, in the 1940s and '50s. But, quite surprisingly, they were a close second in one rather important area.

When the 1952 season opened, five years after the advent of Jackie Robinson, it was rather obvious that big-league clubs had not exactly sent tailors fanning out across the country to get black ballplayers fitted for uniforms. Indeed, only 17 (nine in the National League) were on Opening Day rosters in 1952 and just nine were in Opening Day lineups.

Five of them were in the lineup for that year's American League opener on Chicago's South Side: Larry Doby, Luke Easter and "Suitcase" Simpson for Cleveland and Minnie Minoso and Hector Rodriguez for the White Sox.

The Cubs? Like most ballclubs, the North Siders had been in no hurry to add black talent. By April '52, they had signed one African-American, infielder Gene Baker, who was still in the minors. The common perception, fair or unfair, was that the Cubs' front office and Cub fans preferred white players. Let the White Sox, whose fandom had been buoyed by the postwar migration of black families from the Deep South to the South Side, go after black players. And that they had: In addition to Minoso and Rodriguez, the Sox had signed Negro League stars Bob Boyd, Connie Johnson and Sam Hairston, all of whom were in the high minors and close to promotion.

Imagine the surprise, then, to discover that the Cubs—not the White Sox, not Cleveland, not the New York Giants—were the second major-league team to field a starting lineup consisting of five African-Americans. The first team to do so was Robinson's Brooklyn Dodgers. And the key number was five. Roger Kahn wrote about it in *The Boys of Summer*:

"There existed in 1953 what (noted sports columnist) John Lardner called the 50 percent color line; that is, it was permissible for a major-league team to play only four black men out of nine. The ratio, five whites to four blacks, substantiated white supremacy. But to have five blacks playing with four whites supposedly threatened the old order.... In (Dodgers) camp in 1953 was Sandy Amoros, a black outfielder from Cuba who, according to coach Billy Herman, had miracle wrists. Changeups fooled Miracle Wrists and he batted .250. But he might improve.... A 1953 lineup might include Robinson, Roy Campanella, Junior Gilliam, pitcher Joe Black and Amoros in left. Five out of nine would be black.

"(The Dodgers eventually) dispatched Amoros to the minors, and the 50 percent color line was not tested until a full year later, when it vanished without trace and without protest. But in that uncertain spring of 1953, the possibility of five black Dodgers playing at one time threatened uncertain men."

The Dodgers started five blacks for the first time on July 17, 1954, against the Braves in Milwaukee. The lineup included Robinson, Gilliam, Campanella, Amoros and pitcher Don Newcombe, who had been in the service the previous two seasons. Brooklyn had another first on Opening Day 1956, when it started five African-Americans: Newcombe, Robinson, Gilliam, Campanella and rookie second baseman Charley Neal.

Three days later at Wrigley Field, Cubs manager Stan Hack, whose team had lost its first two games of the season at Milwaukee, turned in his lineup card to the umpires at the pregame confab at home plate. Hack's lineup, as had Brooklyn manager Walter Alston's three days before, included five African-Americans: Baker, in his third year as the regular second baseman; shortstop Ernie Banks, starting his third season and coming off his first monster year; left-fielder Monte Irvin, the 37-year-old former Giants star; rookie center-fielder Solly Drake, whose main tool was his speed; and pitcher Sam "Toothpick" Jones, author of a no-hitter the previous May during his first year as a Cub.

At a Glance

WP: Jones (1–0)

HR: Banks (1), Irvin (1)

Key stat: Irvin 3-for-4, 3 runs scored, 3 RBIs

It didn't take long for the new-look lineup to make Hack look like a genius. With 13,973 chilled fans looking on, leadoff man Don Hoak surprised Cincinnati pitcher Art Fowler with a bunt single and moved to second on Drake's sacrifice bunt. Dee Fondy grounded to short for the second out, but Banks homered to left and the Cubs were up 2–0. Walt Moryn, like Hoak a winter acquisition from the Dodgers, followed with a single to left and took second when rookie left fielder Frank Robinson booted the ball. Irvin's single brought home Moryn, Baker's double plated Irvin and Baker came home on Hobie Landrith's double.

It was now 5–0, but the Cubs weren't through. Ex-Cub Hal Jeffcoat replaced Fowler; Jones greeted him with a single that scored Landrith, and it was 6–0. Drake doubled in a run in the third and scored on Moryn's sacrifice fly in the sixth. Irvin's double and Baker's single set up a run in the seventh, and Drake doubled and scored in a three-run eighth, capped by Irvin's two-run homer.

Jones, meanwhile, went the distance, allowed only four hits and struck out nine in the Cubs' 12–1 romp. All in all, a splendid debut for the new Cub lineup. But its success, like that of the Cubs, was short-lived. Banks, Baker, Jones and even the veteran Irvin had solid seasons, but no one could save this Cub team, which finished last at 60–94 and 33 games out of first place.

Cardinals	AB	R	H	RBI
Templeton ss	6	1	2	0
Oberkfell 2b	6	0	0	1
Littell p	0	0	0	0
Hernandez 1b	5	1	1	0
Simmons c	2	3	2	0
Bonds lf	5	2	3	4
Hendrick rf	5	1	3	1
Reitz 3b	4	1	2	3
Scott cf	5	1	1	0
Forsch p	2	2	2	1
Sykes p	0	0	0	0
Fulgham p	0	0	0	0
Hood p	0	0	0	0
Thomas p	0	0	0	0
Iorg ph	1	0	0	0
Herr 2b	0	0	0	0
Totals	41	12	16	10

Cubs	AB	R	H	RBI
DeJesus ss	6	2	5	2
Ontiveros 3b	4	1	1	0
Caudill p	0	0	0	0
Vail ph	1	0	0	0
Tidrow p	0	0	0	0
Sutter p	0	0	0	0
Kingman ph	1	0	1	0
Randle pr	0	1	0	0
Buckner 1b	5	1	2	2
Biittner lf	6	1	2	0
Martin rf	5	4	3	2
Foote c	6	2	4	8
Lezcano cf	4	1	2	0
Tyson 2b	3	1	1	1
Lamp p	1	0	0	0
Figueroa ph	1	0	0	0
McGlothen p	0	0	0	0
Capilla p	0	0	0	0
Thompson ph	1	1	1	1
Dillard 3b	2	1	1	0
Totals	46	16	23	16

STL	2	1	3	5	1	0	0	0	-	12 16 0
CHI	1	1	4	0	3	0	2	1	4	- 16 23 3

Cardinals	IP	H	R	ER	BB	SO
Forsch	4.2	14	9	9	2	2
Sykes	1.2	4	2	2	0	2
Fulgham	0.1	0	0	0	0	1
Hood	0.1	1	0	0	0	0
Thomas	1	2	1	1	0	0
Littell L (0-1)	0.2	2	4	4	2	1
Totals	8.2	23	16	16	4	6

Cubs	IP	H	R	ER	BB	SO
Lamp	3	7	6	5	2	0
McGlothen	0.2	4	5	5	1	0
Capilla	1.1	2	1	1	0	0
Caudill	2	1	0	0	1	2
Tidrow	0.2	1	0	0	2	1
Sutter W (1-1)	1.1	1	0	0	0	1
Totals	9	16	12	11	6	4

E—Chicago Biittner, Ontiveros 2. DP—St. Louis 2; Chicago. 2B—St. Louis Hendrick, Reitz, Forsch, Simmons; Chicago Martin, Foote, DeJesus Thompson, Lezcano. 3B—Chicago DeJesus. HR—St. Louis Bonds (1), Forsch (1), Reitz (2); Chicago Foote 2 (2,3), DeJesus (2). SF—Chicago Tyson. LOB—St. Louis 8; Chicago 9. SB—St. Louis Scott; Chicago Randle. Attendance: 18,889.

Barry Who?

Catcher has been one of those "black hole" positions for the Cubs for much of their history. Gabby Hartnett is the only Hall of Fame catcher ever to play regularly for them, and he retired in 1940. Capable catchers aren't a total anomaly at Wrigley Field, but for every serviceable Jody Davis or Geovany Soto there has been the nondescript likes of Elvin Tappe and Moe Thacker.

In February of 1979, general manager Bob Kennedy believed he had come up with a long-term answer to the Cubs' catching dilemma when he acquired Barry Foote from the Philadelphia Phillies along with outfielder Jerry Martin and infielder Ted Sizemore. The price was steep: popular second baseman Manny Trillo, plus outfielder Greg Gross and left-handed-hitting catcher Dave Rader. Foote seemed worth it. Just 28, he was viewed as a dependable two-way player who would hit .254 with 16 home runs and 56 RBIs in his debut season with the Cubs. And on Tuesday, April 22, 1980, he had a day that suggested he might be Cooperstown-bound.

In a 16–12 victory over the St. Louis Cardinals, Foote went 4-for-6 with two homers and eight RBIs. The Cubs rallied from 6–2 and 12–6 deficits and tied the game at 12–12 when Foote homered off Cards reliever Roy Thomas in the eighth inning. In the ninth, after Garry Templeton reached Bruce Sutter for a leadoff single, Foote threw Templeton out on an attempted steal of second. Then in the Cubs' ninth he settled things with a walk-off grand slam off Cards closer Mark Littell.

It's not often that a player hits for the cycle and it pretty much goes unnoticed, but that was the case for Ivan DeJesus; the Cubs' shortstop was 5-for-6 with two RBIs and completed his cycle with a fifth-inning triple. And the Cubs collected 23 hits. But it was Foote's big day that had 18,889 Wrigley Field fans buzzing as they left the ballpark on an unseasonably warm, windy day.

Martin doubled and Foote singled him home

to get the Cubs within 3–2 in the second inning. In the third he delivered a two-run double off Bob Forsch to complete a four-run inning as the Cubs rallied for a 6–6 tie. The Cubs chased reliever Lynn McGlothen and put up a five-spot in the fourth, and Forsch homered for 12–6 lead in the fifth. That's when the Cubs began chipping away.

Scot Thompson's pinch double and DeJesus' triple keyed a three-run fifth that made it a 12–9 game, and Bill Buckner's two-run single got the Cubs within 12–11 in the seventh. After Sutter pitched out of a bases-loaded predicament in the eighth, Foote tied it with his homer off Thomas. He was just getting started.

Dave Kingman batted for Sutter and singled with one out in the Cubs' ninth. Lenny Randle ran for him and stole second. Littell walked Buckner intentionally, and the runners moved up on a wild pitch. After a two-out walk to Martin loaded the bases, Foote took Littell out just over the wall in right-center field, capping a career day, one he never came close to duplicating.

Bothered by a sore back, Foote appeared in just 63 games in 1980, hitting six homers with 28 RBIs. He was dealt to the Yankees in 1981 and was finished as a player by 1982, though he later resurfaced as a coach with the White Sox and Mets.

Sutter earned the win with 1 ⅓ scoreless innings for the Cubs, while third baseman Ken Reitz was 2-for-4 with a homer and three RBIs for the Cardinals. They would exchange uniforms over the winter, Sutter moving to the Cardinals in a deal that brought Reitz and top prospect Leon Durham to the Cubs.

Buckner would win the batting title with a career-high .324 average and Sutter would lead the league with 28 saves.

Barry Foote

Barry Foote's eight-RBI day represented nearly 10 percent of his run production over the three seasons he spent with the Cubs—the burly catcher was a .240 hitter with 22 homers and 85 RBIs in 204 games.

The Cubs acquired Foote from Philadelphia in February 1979, but he was not part of the influx of Phillies who followed Dallas Green when he took over as Cubs general manager; Bob Kennedy was the GM when the Cubs sent second baseman Manny Trillo, catcher Dave Rader, and outfielder Greg Gross to the Phillies for Foote, second baseman Ted Sizemore, and outfielder Jerry Martin. Foote, a first-round draft choice of the Montreal Expos in 1970, had been dealt to the Phillies for catcher Tim Blackwell and pitcher Wayne Twitchell in June 1977.

The Cubs moved him on to the Yankees in April 1981 after Foote lost the catching job to Blackwell, whom they had signed as a free agent.

Say Hello to Mr. Jenkins

The Cubs were coming off a 72–90, eighth-place season in 1965, which was pretty much the norm for their performance in the early and mid-1960s. If there wasn't much optimism toward 1966, there was a great deal of curiosity— Leo Durocher had been named manager over the winter. The fiery, irascible skipper represented a startling change of direction for a sleepy organization, and Cubs fans sensed they were in for an intriguing ride.

"This is not an eighth-place ballclub," Durocher declared upon taking over. Eventually he'd be proved right, but not in the manner he intended.

Dodgers	AB	R	H	RBI
Parker 2b	4	0	1	0
Johnson lf	5	0	1	0
Lefebvre 3b	4	0	0	0
Griffith pr	0	0	0	0
Ferrara rf	4	0	1	0
Fairly cf	5	0	0	0
Torborg c	3	0	3	0
Oliver 2b	3	0	1	0
Kennedy ss	3	0	1	0
Davis ph	1	0	1	0
Shirley pr-ss	0	0	0	0
Sutton p	3	0	1	0
Roseboro ph	1	0	0	0
Perranoski p	0	0	0	0
Totals	36	0	10	0

Cubs	AB	R	H	RBI
Phillips cf	4	0	1	0
Beckert 2b	4	0	1	0
Williams rf	4	0	0	0
Santo 3b	2	0	0	0
Browne lf	4	0	2	0
Banks 1b	3	0	0	0
Hundley c	3	1	1	0
Kessinger ss	2	0	0	0
Hendley p	0	0	0	0
Jenkins p	3	1	2	2
Abernathy p	0	0	0	0
Totals	29	2	7	2

LAD 0 0 0 0 0 0 0 0 0 - 0 10 0
CHI   0 0 0 0 1 0 1 0 X - 2 7 1

Dodgers	IP	H	R	ER	BB	SO
Sutton L (1-2)	7	7	2	2	1	5
Perranoski	1	0	0	0	1	1
Totals	8	7	2	2	2	6

Cubs	IP	H	R	ER	BB	SO
Hendley	2.2	5	0	0	4	2
Jenkins W (1-0)	5.1	4	0	0	0	3
Abernathy S (2)	1	1	0	0	0	1
Totals	9	10	0	0	4	6

E—Chicago Hendley. DP—Chicago. 2B—Los Angeles Parker; Chicago Beckert. HR—Chicago Jenkins (1). HBP—Los Angeles Lefebvre. LOB—Los Angeles 14; Chicago 6. Attendance: 6,974.

Durocher's less publicized directive to "back up the truck" was meant to rid the roster of many of the players responsible for that eighth-place finish, and that was the impetus for an April 21 trade that sent veteran pitchers Larry Jackson and Bob Buhl to the Philadelphia Phillies for three players: pitcher Ferguson Jenkins, 23, outfielder Adolfo Phillips, 24, and outfielder/first baseman John Herrnstein, 28.

Jenkins, a Canadian who played more hockey than baseball growing up, had appeared in eight games over parts of two seasons with the Phils, compiling a 2–1 record. Cubs fans got their first look at the long-armed, 6-foot-5 right-hander two days after the trade, when he relieved struggling starter Bob Hendley in the third inning of a 0–0 game with the Dodgers at Wrigley Field. There were only 6,974 fans in the ballpark on an overcast Saturday afternoon, and if Jenkins reminded them of anybody, it might have been Babe Ruth.

He retired the first batter he faced, Chicagoan John Kennedy, on a fly to right field to retire the side with the bases loaded. He would blank the Dodgers on four singles over the next five innings, walking no one and striking out three.

Jenkins struck out in his first plate appearance in the third, but when Don Sutton tried to throw a fastball by him in the fifth, Jenkins jumped on it and pounded it out to left-center field for the first run of the ballgame. In the seventh, Durocher let him bat for himself after Randy Hundley reached on an infield single and Don Kessinger bunted him to second. Jenkins delivered a clean single to center, scoring Hundley with the Cubs' second run.

He then pitched out of a first-and-second mini-jam in the Dodgers' eighth and was rewarded with his first victory as a Cub after closer Ted Abernathy pitched a scoreless ninth.

The victory was the first of 167 for Jenkins as a Cub, fifth most in franchise history. And well earned: 5 1/3 scoreless innings, 2-for-3 at the plate with a homer and two RBIs. The Cubs had themselves a pitcher, and a hitter who was at least capable of helping himself—a .165 lifetime average with 13 homers, 85 RBIs and 73 sacrifices.

Jenkins would be the Cubs' Opening Day starter in 1967 and begin a run of six straight 20-win seasons, but Durocher used him mainly in relief in '66; he finished 6–8 with a 3.31 ERA in 60 games. Phillips batted .262 with 16 homers and 36 RBIs in 116 games. Herrnstein was 3-for-17 in nine games and was traded to the Atlanta Braves a month later.

True to Durocher's word, the Cubs were not an eighth-place team—they finished 10th at 59-103 with a roster in flux all season. But Fergie Jenkins' arrival was a clear sign that better days were ahead.

Don Sutton

Like Fergie himself, the losing pitcher in Jenkins' Cubs debut would go on to have a Hall of Fame career. But no thanks to the Cubs—Don Sutton dropped 13 straight decisions to the Cubs before beating them.

They were both right-handers and they're both in the Hall of Fame, but Jenkins' and Sutton's careers had little else in common. Whereas Jenkins would reel off six straight 20-win seasons upon becoming a rotation starter in 1967, Sutton would not have a winning record until his fifth season, and he wouldn't win 20—for the only time—until his 11th season. But he won 19 twice and at least 14 games every year from 1969 to 1978 while never missing a start.

As Sutton watched Jenkins circle the bases on his fifth-inning homer, he could not have known it was a feeing he would never experience. Sutton did not hit a single home run in 1,354 career at-bats.

'There's a High Popup...'

Critics who derided the Los Angeles Memorial Coliseum as a substandard playing facility for major league baseball had Lee Walls in mind—not that Walls was a substandard player.

Cubs	AB	R	H	RBI
Taylor 2b	4	2	1	1
Walls rf	6	3	3	8
Banks ss	3	2	0	0
Moryn lf	4	2	1	0
Thomson cf	3	1	1	1
Long 1b	3	1	0	1
Goryl 3b	3	2	1	1
Tappe c	5	1	2	2
Fodge p	3	1	0	0
Totals	**34**	**15**	**9**	**14**

Dodgers	AB	R	H	RBI
Reese ss	2	0	0	0
Zimmer ss	2	1	2	1
Cimoli cf	3	0	0	0
Gilliam lf	1	0	1	0
Snider lf	3	0	1	0
Demeter lf-cf	1	0	0	0
Hodges 1b	4	0	1	0
Neal 2b	4	1	2	1
Jackson 3b	4	0	1	0
Furillo rf	4	0	1	0
Roseboro c	4	0	1	0
Drysdale p	0	0	0	0
Craig p	1	0	0	0
Larker ph	1	0	0	0
Negray p	0	0	0	0
Valo ph	1	0	0	0
Koufax p	0	0	0	0
Walker ph	1	0	0	0
Totals	**36**	**2**	**10**	**2**

CHI	2 0 2 0 7 0 3 1 0 - 15 9 1
LAD	0 0 0 0 0 0 1 1 0 - 2 10 0

Cubs	IP	H	R	ER	BB	SO
Fodge W (1-0)	9	10	2	2	0	3
Totals	**9**	**10**	**2**	**2**	**0**	**3**

Dodgers	IP	H	R	ER	BB	SO
Drysdale L (0-3)	2.1	1	4	4	4	2
Craig	2.2	5	7	7	3	1
Negray	3	2	4	4	3	0
Koufax	1	1	0	0	0	0
Totals	**9**	**9**	**15**	**15**	**10**	**3**

E—Chicago Banks. DP—Chicago 2; Los Angeles. 2B—Chicago Moryn. HR—Chicago Walls 3 (2,3,4), Thomson (1); Los Angeles Neal (2), Zimmer (1). SH—Chicago Fodge. HBP—Chicago Goryl, Banks. LOB—Chicago 5; Los Angeles 7. SB—Chicago Taylor. Attendance: 10,194.

The Coliseum was built for football and track, but it served as the Dodgers' home for their first four years in Los Angeles after they arrived from Brooklyn in 1958, while elegant Dodger Stadium was under construction in Chavez Ravine.

The facility's oval shape made it problematic to accommodate a baseball diamond. The configuration chosen resulted in the left-field foul pole being situated just 251 feet from home plate—Little League distance. Even the installation of a 42-foot-high screen was unlikely to discourage right-handed power hitters. Babe Ruth's sacred home run records were as imperiled as a slow-moving junker car on an L.A. freeway.

That was the talk, and it reached a crescendo after Walls, the Cubs' 25-year-old right fielder, popped three balls over the screen on the afternoon of Thursday, April 24, leading the Cubs to a 15-2 rout of the Dodgers.

A three-homer, eight-RBI day was not out of the question for, say, Ernie Banks—the Cubs' shortstop would hit 47 homers that season and win the first of his two MVP awards.

But Lee Walls? The Cubs obtained him with Dale Long from the Pirates for Gene Baker and Dee Fondy in May of 1957. He hit six homers that entire season. Walls was a big, strong guy at 6-foot-3 and 205 pounds, but not exactly known as a slugger.

"I heard Ted Williams say that working with weights improved a hitter's strength, so I lifted all winter," Walls said. "That's why I have good power this year."

Tony Taylor was aboard with a walk when

Walls went over the screen off Don Drysdale in the first inning. In the fifth he connected off Roger Craig with Elvin Tappe and pitcher Gene Fodge on base, capping a seven-run inning. In the seventh, with Taylor and Johnny Goryl on via walks, Walls lofted his third homer of the game over the screen off Ron Negray.

He insisted it was not a fluke. "I'd like to point out that those three home runs were all well hit," Walls said. "They would have been home runs anywhere. Ask [Dodgers manager] Walter Alston. He said so."

Walls would set a club record with eight home runs in the month of April. He had 14 by early June, made the NL All-Star team and finished with 24 homers, 72 RBIs and a .304 average in the best season of his career by far.

The birth of a slugger? Not exactly. Walls would never hit more than eight homers in subsequent years and finished with 66 in his 10 major league seasons.

Other things took place on April 24, 1958. Gene Fodge, 26, went the distance to win it for the Cubs, scattering 10 hits. It was the only complete game and only victory of his major league career, which encompassed 16 appearances, a 1–1 record and a 4.76 ERA in the '58 season.

With the game out of hand, the Dodgers had a little-used 22-year-old lefty mop up with a scoreless ninth inning. Kid by the name of Koufax, Sandy Koufax. Down the road he'd do all right.

Gene Fodge

The Cubs signed pitcher Gene Fodge out of South Bend (Indiana) Central High School in 1950. Though his professional career was interrupted by two years of service in the Marine Corps, the slender right-hander was one of several pitching prospects for whom the Cubs had high hopes when he joined Dick Drott, Moe Drabowsky, Taylor Phillips, and Bob Anderson on a very young staff in 1958.

But his complete-game win over the Dodgers on April 24 would be Fodge's only major league victory. He was 1–1 with a 4.76 ERA in 16 games when the Cubs sent him back to Fort Worth of the Texas League in July. Fodge returned to South Bend after the 1958 season. He and his wife Eileen raised a son and three daughters, and Fodge was a constant presence at his grandkids' ballgames.

A longtime employee of the Morris Inn on the Notre Dame campus, Fodge was 79 when he died in October of 2010. In lieu of flowers, the family requested donations to South Bend's Eastside Little League.

The Amazing Mr. Prior

The scouting report describing Mark Prior as "maybe the best college pitcher ever" during his junior year at the University of Southern California was a bit hyperbolic, but the Cubs thought enough of the tall, powerfully built right-hander to take him with the No. 2 pick of the 2001 amateur draft, right behind Joe Mauer. They didn't know they were also getting a slugger.

On a Friday night before 32,162 fans at Denver's Coors Field, Prior demonstrated the full range of his abilities.

Facing Nelson Cruz leading off the third inning of a 0–0 game, Prior bombed a long home run to left-center field, giving the Cubs a 3–0 lead.

They were up 4–1 when he batted in the sixth. With runners on second and third and two out, the percentage move was to walk catcher Damian Miller, the eighth-place hitter, and pitch to the pitcher. Only Prior didn't fit the pitcher-as-hitter stereotype of a feeble-swinging "Judy." He promptly unloaded the bases with a loud double to center field, putting the Cubs up 7–1 and breaking open the game.

"Mark is not just a great pitcher, he's a great competitor," manager Dusty Baker said. "He takes his hitting seriously because he knows he can help himself and help the team."

Prior didn't pitch too badly, either, limiting the Rockies to two runs on five hits over seven innings with seven strikeouts. Just 22, he was 4–1 after five starts and on his way to a year that seemed to have him destined for greatness: an 18–6 record with a 2.43 ERA and 245 strikeouts in 211 1/3 innings. Prior finished third in the National League Cy Young Award voting behind Dodgers reliever Eric Gagne and Giants starter Jason Schmidt. He even batted .250 with 18 hits, four doubles and seven sacrifices.

But as all Cub fans know only too well, it was never the same for Prior after Game 6 of the 2003 National League Championship Series unraveled with him on the mound for Cubs. A succession of

Cubs	AB	R	H	RBI
Grudzielanek 2b	5	0	0	0
Gonzalez ss	4	2	1	0
Sosa rf	5	1	3	0
Choi 1b	4	1	1	1
O'Leary lf	4	2	2	2
Borowski p	0	0	0	0
Patterson cf	5	3	4	3
Bellhorn 3b	5	0	1	0
Miller c	3	1	1	0
Prior p	4	1	2	4
Remlinger p	0	0	0	0
Farnsworth p	0	0	0	0
Goodwin ph-lf	1	0	1	1
Totals	**40**	**11**	**16**	**11**

Rockies	AB	R	H	RBI
Belliard 2b	4	2	1	0
Payton lf	4	2	1	1
Helton 1b	5	1	3	4
Walker rf	5	1	1	1
Wilson cf	5	0	1	1
Hernandez ss	3	0	1	0
Fuentes p	0	0	0	0
Kapler ph	1	0	1	0
Jones p	0	0	0	0
Estalella c	4	0	1	0
Stynes 3b	3	0	0	0
Norton ph	1	0	0	0
Cruz p	2	0	0	0
Speier p	0	0	0	0
Butler ss	2	1	1	0
Totals	**39**	**7**	**11**	**7**

	1	2	3	4	5	6	7	8	9		R	H	E
CHI	0	2	2	0	0	3	1	0	3	-	11	16	1
COL	0	0	0	1	0	0	0	3	3	-	7	11	0

Cubs	IP	H	R	ER	BB	SO
Prior W (4-1)	7	5	2	2	1	7
Remlinger	0.2	3	2	2	0	2
Farnsworth	0.1	0	0	0	0	1
Borowski	1	3	3	2	0	3
Totals	**9**	**11**	**7**	**6**	**1**	**3**

Rockies	IP	H	R	ER	BB	SO
Cruz L (1-3)	5.2	9	7	7	2	3
Speier	1	2	1	1	1	0
Fuentes	1.1	0	0	0	1	4
Jones	1	5	3	3	0	1
Totals	**9**	**16**	**11**	**11**	**4**	**8**

E—Chicago Bellhorn. DP—Colorado 2. 2B—Chicago O'Leary, Sosa, Prior; Colorado Helton. HR—Chicago Patterson (4), Prior (1); Colorado Helton (6), Walker (3). SF—Chicago O'Leary. HBP—Chicago Miller; Colorado Payton. LOB—Chicago 8; Colorado 7. SB—Colorado Wilson. Attendance: 32,162.

shoulder injuries sabotaged his career. A master of the "towel drill," Prior spent more time on the disabled list than on the field over the next three years, going 18–17 as injuries aborted several comebacks.

We'll never know how good he could have been, but for much of 2003 Mark Prior was as good as anybody. His name was frequently invoked as Washington's Steven Strasburg made the transition from college phenom to big league ace. Strasburg should be flattered by the comparison.

The Cubs' hitting star on this Friday night in Colorado was Corey Patterson, who went 4-for-5 with a homer and three RBIs. Patterson, just 23, was the Cubs' best player for much of 2003—he was hitting .298 with 17 doubles, seven triples, 13 homers, 55 RBIs and 16 steals when a severe knee injury ended his season in late July. He returned, but was never the same player. The Cubs traded him to Baltimore before the 2006 season, beginning a five-team odyssey. Like Prior, Patterson is a symbol of promise unfulfilled.

Patterson and Prior

The hitting and pitching stars of this victory over Colorado are poster boys for the Cubs' star-crossed recent history.

Corey Patterson, the Cubs' first-round draft pick in 1998, looked like one of the best players in the NL as a 23-year-old in 2003, hitting .298 with 13 home runs, 55 RBIs, and 16 steals before a knee injury suffered on a tag play at first base ended his season in July. He has never been the same player. The Cubs traded Patterson to Baltimore in 2006. He has played for four other teams since, without recapturing the form that evoked comparisons with Hall of Famer Lou Brock.

Mark Prior, the No. 2 pick in the draft behind Joe Mauer in 2002, broke down after his breakout 18-win season in 2003. He matched that victory total combined over the next three injury-plagued years and hasn't pitched in the big leagues since 2006.

At age 30, Prior was planning to attempt yet another comeback with the New York Yankees in 2011.

Nice Knowing You, Joe

Pirates	AB	R	H	RBI
Womack 2b	4	2	2	0
Allensworth cf	5	1	2	0
Martin lf	5	1	2	1
Johnson 1b	3	1	1	1
Elster ss	5	0	2	2
Kendall c	5	1	2	1
Sveum 3b	4	0	0	0
Brown rf	3	0	1	1
Cooke p	2	0	0	0
Wilkins p	1	0	0	0
Ruebel p	0	0	0	0
Loiselle p	1	0	0	0
Rincon p	0	0	0	0
Totals	38	6	12	6

Cubs	AB	R	H	RBI
McRae cf	5	3	3	0
Glanville lf	2	0	1	3
Grace 1b	3	0	2	0
Sosa rf	4	0	1	2
Sandberg 2b	5	2	2	1
Dunston ss	1	0	1	0
Sanchez ss	2	0	1	0
Orie 3b	2	0	1	0
Servais c	4	1	2	0
Castillo p	0	0	0	0
Bottenfield p	1	0	0	0
Tatis p	0	0	0	0
Clark ph	0	1	0	0
Adams p	0	0	0	0
Kieschnick ph	1	0	0	0
Wendell p	0	0	0	0
Hansen ph	0	0	0	0
Hernandez ph	1	0	0	0
Patterson p	0	0	0	0
Rojas p	0	0	0	0
Totals	31	7	14	6

											R	H	E
PIT	3	0	1	1	0	0	1	0	0	-	6	12	1
CHI	0	1	0	3	0	1	1	1	X	-	7	14	0

Pirates	IP	H	R	ER	BB	SO
Cooke	3.2	8	4	4	2	4
Wilkins	1.1	1	0	0	2	1
Ruebel	0.2	2	1	1	0	0
Loiselle	1	1	1	1	1	1
Rincon L (2-2)	1.1	2	1	1	0	1
Totals	8	14	7	7	5	7

Cubs	IP	H	R	ER	BB	SO
Castillo	0	3	3	3	2	0
Bottenfield	3.1	5	2	2	1	2
Tatis	0.2	2	0	0	0	0
Adams	2	0	0	0	0	3
Wendell	1	1	1	1	2	2
Patterson W (1-1)	1	1	0	0	0	0
Rojas S (1)	1	0	0	0	0	0
Totals	9	12	6	6	5	7

E—Pittsburgh Johnson. DP—Pittsburgh 2. 2B—Pittsburgh Womack, Elster, Kendall, Brown. 3B—Chicago McRae. HR—Chicago Sandberg (2). SH—Chicago Sanchez. SF—Chicago Glanville. HBP—Chicago Glanville. LOB—Pittsburgh 10; Chicago 10. SB—Pittsburgh Womack 2; Chicago Dunston. Attendance: 29,323.

In the second inning of this Saturday matinee at Wrigley Field, Ryne Sandberg stepped to the plate and drove a pitch from Pittsburgh left-hander Steve Cooke over the wall in left-center field for a solo home run. Ryno would go 2-for-5 and score the tying run in the seventh inning of a game the Cubs would win on Sammy Sosa's tie-breaking single off reliever Ricardo Rincon in the bottom of the eighth.

Most of it seemed inconsequential. The Cubs opened the 1997 season with a 14-game losing streak, taking themselves out of the division race before it started. They "improved" to 4–17 with this win, and nine games under .500—23–32 on June 2—was the best record they would manage in a forgettable season.

Ryno had hoped for better in the final season of his noble 16-year career, and so had the many Cubs fans who revered him.

Ah, but that home run. It was Ryno's second of the year and his 267th as a second baseman, one more than Joe Morgan hit as a second baseman during his Hall of Fame career with the Cincinnati Reds and four other teams. Take that, Joe, Cubs fans chortled.

Ever since he entered the broadcast booth, there had been a suspicion in Chicago—perhaps unfounded, perhaps not—that Morgan was reluctant to give Sandberg his due as a player lest it jeopardize his own stature as baseball's best second baseman.

"I heard people say that, but I never sensed any of it," Sandberg said. "I always admired Joe as a ballplayer, and he's been nothing but respectful toward me."

Other second basemen deserve to be in on the discussion: Eddie Collins, Rogers Hornsby, Jackie Robinson, and Robby Alomar are Hall of Famers, and Jeff Kent will get some consideration—he couldn't field worth beans, but he was an RBI machine who wound up with more homers than

Sandberg or Morgan. Still, the argument most often comes down to Sandberg or Morgan, at least among contemporary players. Let's crunch the numbers, bearing in mind that Morgan played 22 years to Sandberg's 16 and that Sandberg sat out 1 ½ mid-career seasons to reconstruct his personal life.

Sandberg batted .285 to Morgan's .271 lifetime. He hit 277 home runs as a second baseman to Morgan's 266. Morgan had a big edge in runs scored (1,650 to 1,318), but he played on better teams. He had a comparably big edge in steals (689 to 344), but Sandberg was more often a middle-of-the-order hitter who didn't run as much. And there's more to base running than steals—Sandberg was almost automatic going first-to-third or second-to-home on a single. Morgan's slight edge in RBIs (1,133 to 1,061) is attributable to longevity.

Each was a 10-time All-Star, Sandberg starting nine All-Star Games to Morgan's seven. Sandberg won nine Gold Gloves to Morgan's five and set a record by playing in 123 consecutive games without an error. Morgan was a two-time MVP for the Big Red Machine of the mid-'70s and played in four World Series. Sandberg, the MVP in 1984, never reached the World Series and played in just two postseason series in 1984 and 1989, but he hit .385 in 10 postseason games to Morgan's .182 in 50. Morgan was elected to the Hall of Fame in 1990, Sandberg in 2005.

Who was better? Take your pick. Any team in baseball would have been delighted with either man.

Manager Sandberg

Regardless of what Joe Morgan might think of him, Ryne Sandberg is one of the most popular Cubs in team history. But his relationship with the organization came to at least a temporary end when he was passed over for the manager's job in October 2010.

Retired since 1997, Sandberg inquired about managing the Cubs when Lou Piniella was hired in 2007. He was told he needed to go to the minor leagues to gain experience. So he did, putting in four years at the Class-A, Double-A, and Triple-A levels. Most of the young prospects who made their Cubs debuts in 2010 played for Sandberg, including shortstop Starlin Castro and outfielder Tyler Colvin.

But when Piniella retired in August 2010, third base coach Mike Quade was named interim manager. The interim tag was removed after the Cubs went 24–13 under Quade, who signed a two-year contract. Sandberg returned to his baseball roots, agreeing to become the Philadelphia Phillies' Triple-A manager.

What Hangover?

The 1969 season featured some exhilarating highs for the Cubs, beginning with Willie Smith on Opening Day and extending through most of the summer. But because it ended on a devastating low note—the worn-out Cubs seemed stuck in mud while the "Miracle Mets" charged past them and went on to win the World Series—it was only natural to wonder about a carryover effect in 1970.

They filled a troublesome outfield hole by acquiring Johnny Callison from the Phillies for veteran pitcher Dick Selma and outfield prospect Oscar Gamble over the winter, and late in spring training they obtained backup catcher J.C. Martin from the Mets in hopes of giving ironman catcher Randy Hundley some rest behind the plate—Hundley caught a record 160 games in 1969. Joe Decker, a 22-year-old right-hander, was among the young pitchers on call when the schedule demanded a fifth starter behind Ferguson Jenkins, Ken Holtzman, Bill Hands and Milt Pappas, who was acquired from Atlanta in late June.

Otherwise, the Cubs were pretty much the same team that thrilled Chicago for much of the previous summer.

Early returns were not encouraging—the Cubs dropped three of their first four, in Philadelphia and Montreal. Coming home, they embarked on a streak that threatened to erase the memory of 1969's collapse. They swept a 10-game homestand, taking three from the Phillies, two from the Expos, two from the Cardinals and three from Houston. When they stretched the streak to 11 with a 1–0 win over the Pirates on a Monday night before 6,635 fans in Pittsburgh, they had every reason to believe things were breaking their way.

They scored the only run of the game in the third inning when Glenn Beckert hit a triple to right field, then came around to score when catcher Manny Sanguillen mishandled Roberto Clemente's throw home. Otherwise the Cubs managed just three singles off hard-luck loser Steve Blass and reliever Al McBean.

Decker combined with Hank Aguirre and Phil

Cubs	AB	R	H	RBI
Kessinger ss	4	0	0	0
Beckert 2b	3	1	2	0
Williams lf	4	0	0	0
Santo 3b	3	0	0	0
Callison rf	3	0	1	0
Banks 1b	3	0	0	0
Hickman cf	3	0	0	0
Martin c	3	0	0	0
Decker p	3	0	1	0
Aguirre p	0	0	0	0
Regan p	0	0	0	0
Totals	**29**	**1**	**4**	**0**

Pirates	AB	R	H	RBI
Alou cf	4	0	0	0
Hebner 3b	4	0	1	0
Clemente rf	4	0	2	0
Stargell lf	3	0	1	0
Robertson ph	0	0	0	0
Martinez pr	0	0	0	0
Oliver 1b	4	0	0	0
Sanguillen c	3	0	2	0
Jeter pr	0	0	0	0
May c	1	0	0	0
Alley ss	3	0	0	0
Mazeroski 2b	3	0	0	0
Blass p	2	0	0	0
Pagan ph	0	0	0	0
McBean p	0	0	0	0
Totals	**31**	**0**	**6**	**0**

CHI	0	0	1	0	0	0	0	0	0	-	1	4	1
PIT	0	0	0	0	0	0	0	0	0	-	0	6	1

Cubs	IP	H	R	ER	BB	SO
Decker W (1-0)	8.1	6	0	0	1	5
Aguirre	0.1	0	0	0	1	0
Regan, S (2)	0.1	0	0	0	0	0
Totals	**9**	**6**	**0**	**0**	**2**	**5**

Pirates	IP	H	R	ER	BB	SO
Blass L (2-2)	8	4	1	0	1	6
McBean	1	0	0	0	1	1
Totals	**9**	**6**	**0**	**0**	**2**	**5**

E—Chicago Beckert; Pittsburgh Sanguillen. DP—Chicago 2; Pittsburgh 2. 2B—Pittsburgh Stargell. 3B—Chicago Beckert; Pittsburgh Clemente. LOB—Chicago 3; Pittsburgh 6. SB—Pittsburgh Alley, Sanguillen. Attendance: 6,635.

Regan on a six-hit shutout, which survived largely because the great Clemente, a Hall of Famer, was thrown out at the plate twice. In the first inning, he was aboard with a single and was nailed at home trying to score from first on Willie Stargell's double. In the ninth, he tripled with one out. Aguirre, on in relief of Decker, speared Al Oliver's bouncer to the mound and trapped Clemente off third for the second out of the inning. Regan then took over for Aguirre and retired Jerry May for the final out of the game as the Cubs improved to 12–3 after 15 games.

They were an up-and-down team all season and would offset this hot streak by losing 12 in a row from June 21 to June 30, falling from 35–25 to 35–37. Nine games over .500 would be the best the Cubs would subsequently do in a season in which they'd finish 84–78 and second in the National League East behind the Pirates.

As impressive as he was in earning his second major league victory, the game did not portend great things for Decker. He was 2–7 with a 4.64 ERA in 17 starts for the Cubs in '70 and 7–9 with a 4.37 ERA in parts of four seasons with them. He was a career-best 16–14 with a 3.29 ERA for the Minnesota Twins in 1974 but was out of baseball after winning just three games over the last three seasons. Decker was only 55 when he died of head injuries sustained in a fall at his home in Fraser, Mich., in 2003.

Callison, 31, was a useful addition, hitting .264 with 19 homers and 68 RBIs in 147 games. But the aging process began catching up with the nucleus of the '69 team. Ernie Banks, 39, and bothered by a sore knee, played in just 72 games and hit .252 with 12 homers and 44 RBIs. Man-about-town Joe Pepitone, obtained from Houston in July, was the first baseman for much of the second half and produced 44 RBIs in 56 games.

A serious knee injury also derailed Hundley after 73 games. The Cubs acquired Jack Hiatt from Montreal (for outfielder Boots Day) to fill in for him after deciding the light-hitting Martin (.156 in 77 at-bats) wasn't the answer.

The Cubs got a career year from center fielder Jim Hickman (.315, 32 homers, 115 RBIs), though he was better known for delivering the base hit that instigated the ferocious head-on collision between Pete Rose and Ray Fosse in the All-Star Game. And Billy Williams (.322, 42 homers, 129 RBIs) would probably have been the NL MVP in 1970 if catcher Johnny Bench hadn't hit .293 with 45 homers and 148 RBIs for the pennant-winning Cincinnati Reds.

As memories of '69 faded, the World Series remained as elusive a goal as ever.

So You're Mr. Dawson

How Andre Dawson came to be a Cub is a well-told tale.

As he got older, Dawson was desperate to get off the cement-like artificial surface that had ravaged his knees in the mausoleum that was Montreal's Olympic Stadium. He was eager to play real baseball on real grass before real fans in a real ballpark, so he played out his contract with the Expos. At 32, Dawson was a free agent, available to the highest bidder, not that far removed from "best player in the game" stature his MLB contemporaries had accorded him in a *New York Times* poll taken in 1983.

Only there were no offers.

Unable to rein in their own spending, major league baseball team owners had concocted a gentleman's agreement not to sign each other's players when they hit the market, thereby curtailing movement and holding down salaries. It was blatant collusion, and it eventually cost the owners millions when an arbitrator found them in violation of their own collective bargaining agreement. But it was common practice in 1987, and Dawson found himself hat in hand before the Cubs, offering to sign at a figure of their choosing if only they would rescue him from Montreal.

General manager Dallas Green's investment, reportedly $500,000, was probably the smartest money he ever spent.

Dawson found everything about Chicago to be invigorating. He hit 49 homers, drove in 137 runs, batted .287 in 153 games and won the National League MVP award, a rare achievement for a player from a last-place team.

Dawson's abilities were never more obvious than they were on this on Wednesday afternoon that drew 11,120 fans to Wrigley Field for a game with the Giants.

In the first inning, Dawson slugged a long home run to left-center field off Roger Mason, tying the game at 1–1. In the third he reached Mason

Giants	AB	R	H	RBI
Kutcher 3b	3	0	0	0
Clark ph	0	0	0	0
LaCoss p	0	0	0	0
Youngblood ph	1	0	0	0
Gott p	0	0	0	0
Davis cf	4	2	2	0
Leonard lf	4	1	1	1
Maldonado rf	5	0	2	1
Spilman 1b-3b	4	0	2	1
Melvin c	5	0	0	0
Williams ss	3	1	1	1
Speier 2b	2	0	1	0
Mason p	1	0	0	0
Minton p	0	0	0	0
Aldrete ph-1b	2	0	0	0
Totals	34	4	9	4

Cubs	AB	R	H	RBI
Walker lf	5	1	2	2
Sandberg 2b	4	0	0	0
Dawson rf	5	1	5	2
Moreland 3b	4	0	0	0
Lynch p	0	0	0	0
Durham 1b	4	2	2	0
Davis c	5	0	1	0
Dunston ss	3	2	0	0
Martinez cf	3	2	3	3
Maddux p	2	0	0	0
Mumphrey ph	1	0	0	1
Noles p	0	0	0	0
Trillo 3b	1	0	0	0
Totals	37	8	13	8

SF	1	0	1	1	0	0	1	0	0	-	4	9	4
CHI	1	0	2	3	1	0	1	0	X	-	8	13	1

Giants	IP	H	R	ER	BB	SO
Mason L (1-1)	3.1	6	6	5	1	3
Minton	1.2	4	1	1	1	0
LaCoss	2	2	1	1	1	0
Gott	1	1	0	0	1	1
Totals	8	13	8	7	4	4

Cubs	IP	H	R	ER	BB	SO
Maddux W (1-2)	5	7	3	2	2	6
Noles	1	1	1	1	3	1
Lynch, S (1)	2.2	1	0	0	2	0
Totals	9	9	4	3	7	7

E—San Francisco Davis, Speier, Maldonado 2; Chicago Maddux. DP—San Francisco; Chicago. 2B—San Francisco Davis, Maldonado; Chicago Dawson, Davis. 3B—Chicago Dawson, Martinez. HR—San Francisco Williams (2); Chicago Dawson (6). SH—Chicago Lynch. SF—San Francisco Spilman. LOB—San Francisco 11; Chicago 10. SB—Chicago Dunston, Walker. Attendance: 11,120.

for an RBI double during a two-run inning. In the fourth he singled off Greg Minton in the midst of a three-run flurry. In the sixth he reached Mike LaCoss for a triple, completing the cycle, and in the eighth he wrapped up a 5-for-5 day with a single off Jim Gott.

Dawson also contributed a fielding play that stood out by virtue of the skill and awareness required to make it.

Mason, the Giants' pitcher, batted with two out and a runner on first base in the second inning of a 1–1 game. After hitting what appeared to be a single to right field, he began loping toward first base. But Dawson knew the gangly 6-foot-6 pitcher didn't run well, so he charged the ball, fielded it on one hop and fired a strike to Leon Durham for the putout, ending the inning.

A 5-for-5 day at the plate, including the cycle. Two RBIs, a rare 9-3 putout on what should have been a Giants base hit … "The Hawk" looked like he might earn his keep.

Meanwhile, it was a day of what Lou Piniella might call "Cubbie occurrences" for both teams. The Giants committed four errors, two on one play by right fielder Candy Maldonado. Bob Melvin caught, which meant a day off for Bob Brenly; the future Cubs broadcaster would enjoy one of his better seasons in '87 with a .267 average, 18 homers and 51 RBIs.

Maldonado, Chili Davis and Harry Spilman had two hits each for the Giants, and rookie Matt Williams hit a homer.

Despite a balk, 21-year-old Greg Maddux earned his first win of his first full season, which would be a struggle for him—a 6–14 record with a 5.61 ERA.

Future Cubs GM Ed Lynch got the save with 2 ²/₃ scoreless innings, though his memories of '87 wouldn't be much better—he went 2–9 with a 5.38 ERA and four saves. Chico Walker was 2-for-5 with two of the seven RBIs he would accumulate in '87.

The Cubs got to 10–9 with their fourth win in five games, but they were ticketed for a sixth-place finish and a 76–85 record. You would have expected better from them in the Year of the Hawk.

Kieschnick's Big Day

Expos	AB	R	H	RBI
Stankiewicz ss	5	0	3	0
Lansing 2b	4	2	2	1
White cf	5	1	1	0
Segui 1b	5	1	1	1
Fletcher c	3	1	1	3
Rodriguez lf	4	2	2	2
Santangelo rf	3	0	0	0
Andrews 3b	4	1	1	1
Bullinger p	2	0	0	0
Telford p	0	0	0	0
Orsulak ph	0	0	0	0
Daal p	0	0	0	0
Valdes p	0	0	0	0
Obando ph	1	0	0	0
Urbina p	0	0	0	0
Totals	36	8	11	8

Cubs	AB	R	H	RBI
McRae cf	4	2	1	0
Dunston ss	4	1	3	2
Adams p	0	0	0	0
Grace 1b	5	1	2	1
Sosa rf	4	2	1	1
Kieschnick lf	4	2	3	6
Glanville pr-lf	1	1	0	0
Sandberg 2b	2	0	0	0
Bottenfield p	0	0	0	0
Clark ph	1	1	1	2
Patterson p	0	0	0	0
Sanchez ss	1	0	0	0
Orie 3b	4	0	0	0
Servais c	4	2	2	0
Trachsel p	2	1	1	1
Hernandez 2b	1	1	0	0
Totals	37	14	14	13

MON	5 0 1 1 0 0 1 0 - 8	11	2
CHI	3 0 3 2 0 6 0 0 X - 14	14	0

Expos	IP	H	R	ER	BB	SO
Bullinger L (1-4)	3.2	9	8	8	2	2
Telford	1.1	0	0	0	0	0
Daal	0.2	3	5	5	2	0
Valdes	1.1	1	1	0	0	0
Urbina	1	1	0	0	0	0
Totals	8	14	14	13	4	2

Cubs	IP	H	R	ER	BB	SO
Trachsel W (1-3)	5	8	7	7	3	9
Bottenfield	1	0	0	0	1	1
Patterson	1.2	1	1	1	0	2
Adams	1.1	2	0	0	0	1
Totals	9	11	8	8	4	3

E—Montreal Segui, Andrews. DP—Montreal 2; Chicago. 2B—Montreal Stankiewicz, Lansing; Chicago Grace, Dunston, Trachsel, Clark. HR—Montreal Fletcher (3), Rodriguez 2 (5,6), Andrews (4), Lansing (2); Chicago Kieschnick 2 (2,3). SF—Chicago Dunston. HBP—Chicago Sandberg. LOB—Montreal 5; Chicago 5. SB—Chicago Glanville, Sosa. Attendance: 21,886.

Brooks Kieschnick is one of the more intriguing players in Cubs lore.

He'd been an outstanding pitcher/outfielder/first baseman at the University of Texas, and the Cubs decided his bat was his most impressive asset after they took him with their No. 1 pick in the 1993 amateur draft.

The left-handed-hitting Texan never quite cut it as a position player, but he gave the 21,886 fans who were on hand at Wrigley Field on this brisk Tuesday something to remember. Kieschnick slammed a two-run homer off ex-Cub Jim Bullinger in the first inning and added a three-run shot off Bullinger in the third, finishing 3-for-4 with six RBIs.

Steve Trachsel got the win despite yielding seven runs in five innings. The Cubs "improved" to 6–18, but quickly reverted to the form they displayed in opening the season with a 14-game losing streak, dropping three in a row.

The six RBIs represented half of Kieschnick's 1997 total. He bounced around to three other teams before reinventing himself as a pinch-hitter/relief pitcher for the Milwaukee Brewers, making 74 relief appearances in 2003-04. He batted .248 with 16 homers and 46 RBIs over parts of six seasons with four teams.

In short, he did not measure up to GM Larry Himes' other first-round draft picks. As White Sox GM earlier, he had drafted, in successive years, Jack McDowell, Robin Ventura, Frank Thomas, and Alex Fernandez. Maybe the law of averages finally caught up with Himes.

The Sensational Mr. Soto

Banishing catcher Michael Barrett after a hard-to-miss dugout/clubhouse altercation with teammate Carlos Zambrano in 2007 left the Cubs with a hole behind the plate after they righted themselves and made a run at the NL Central title in Lou Piniella's first year as manager.

The July acquisition of Jason Kendall from Oakland was intended to address that issue; Kendall was a durable veteran who called a good game and could still hit. His experience would be an asset to a team with postseason aspirations. And it was really no reflection on Kendall that he lost his job to a September call-up.

Geovany Soto, 24, was MVP of the Triple-A Pacific Coast League in 2007, and the Cubs rewarded him with a summons to Wrigley Field. He was up to the challenge of a pennant race and big league pitching, hitting .389 with three homers and eight RBIs in 54 at-bats and slugging a home run in Game 2 of the Cubs' three-game loss to Arizona in the Division Series.

Thus Soto was anointed the Cubs' catcher for the 2008 season, with Kendall departing for Milwaukee as a free agent. On April 30, Soto showed he was serious about keeping the job, hitting two three-run bombs as the Cubs used six-, five- and six-run innings to bury the Milwaukee Brewers 19–5. Ryan Dempster (4–0) was the no-sweat winner.

Before a Wednesday night crowd of 39,908 at Wrigley Field, Soto faced Jeff Suppan in the first inning and drove a ball deep into the bleachers in left-center field, scoring Aramis Ramirez and Mark DeRosa ahead of him to complete a six-run inning.

The Cubs chased Suppan during a five-run fourth. Soto was the first hitter reliever Brian Shouse faced, and he greeted the young lefty rudely, connecting for another three-run homer that scored DeRosa and Kosuke Fukudome.

Ramirez and Ronny Cedeno drove in three

Brewers	AB	R	H	RBI
Weeks 2b	4	3	2	0
Cameron cf	3	0	0	0
Braun lf	3	0	2	3
Rivera 1b	1	1	1	2
Fielder 1b	3	0	1	0
McClung p	1	0	0	0
Turnbow p	0	0	0	0
Stetter p	2	0	0	0
Hart rf	2	0	0	0
Kapler rf	1	0	0	0
Hall 3b	4	0	0	0
Hardy ss	3	0	0	0
Suppan p	1	0	0	0
Shouse p	0	0	0	0
Gwynn ph-lf	3	0	0	0
Kendall c	3	1	0	0
Totals	32	5	6	5

Cubs	AB	R	H	RBI
Johnson lf	5	2	1	0
Theriot ss	5	3	2	1
Lee 1b	3	2	2	1
Cedeno ph-2b	1	2	1	3
Ramirez 3b	3	1	1	3
Ward ph-1b	3	0	1	1
Fukudome rf	4	2	2	1
Blanco c	1	0	0	0
DeRosa 2b-3b	3	3	2	2
Soto c	4	2	2	6
Howry p	0	0	0	0
Marmol p	0	0	0	0
Fontenot ph	1	1	1	0
Wuertz p	0	0	0	0
Pie cf	4	0	0	0
Dempster p	3	0	1	0
Murton ph-rf	2	1	1	1
Totals	42	19	17	19

```
MIL  0 0 1 0 2 0 2 0 0 - 5 6 1
CHI  6 0 1 5 0 1 0 6 X - 19 17 0
```

Brewers	IP	H	R	ER	BB	SO
Suppan L (1-1)	3.2	11	11	8	1	1
Shouse	0.1	1	1	1	0	1
McClung	3	1	1	1	4	5
Turnbow	0.2	4	6	6	4	1
Stetter	0.1	0	0	0	0	1
Totals	8	17	19	16	9	9

Cubs	IP	H	R	ER	BB	SO
Dempster W (4-0)	6	4	3	3	1	0
Howry	1	2	2	2	2	1
Marmol	1	0	0	0	2	0
Wuertz	1	0	0	0	0	0
Totals	9	6	5	5	5	1

E—Milwaukee Hall. DP—Chicago. 2B—Milwaukee Weeks, Braun; Chicago Cedeno, Ramirez, Ward, Fukudome, Lee. HR—Milwaukee Rivera; Chicago Soto 2. LOB—Milwaukee 5; Chicago 8. SB—Chicago Theriot. Attendance: 39,908.

runs apiece and Fukudome, DeRosa, Ryan Theriot and Derrek Lee had two hits each as the Cubs collected 17 in improving to 17–10, on their way to a 97–64 record, a second straight division title ... and a second straight division-series sweep, this one at the hands of the Dodgers.

But the last night in April was the impetus to a big year for Soto. He hit .285 with 23 homers, 35 doubles and 86 RBIs. He was the National League Rookie of the Year, the Cubs' first since Kerry Wood in 1998, and he made the National League All-Star team, getting two at-bats before his parents and several other family members at Yankee Stadium.

The Cubs believed they had themselves a catcher.

Ryan Dempster

Jim Hendry knew Ryan Dempster from their days with the Florida Marlins. After moving on to the Cubs and eventually becoming general manager, Hendry renewed his relationship with Dempster when the Cincinnati Reds released the versatile right-hander following two years of elbow problems in 2004.

Smart move. Dempster accumulated 85 saves in three seasons as the Cubs' closer, then made a seamless transition to the starting rotation, going a career-best 17–6 and making the NL All-Star team for the Cubs during their 2008 division championship season.

One of the most civic-minded Cubs, Dempster also has raised thousands of dollars for research into DiGeorge Syndrome, a rare genetic disorder that affects his daughter Riley's ability to swallow on her own.

MAY

Recognized as the best second baseman of his era, Ryne Sandberg was an All-Star for 10 years in a row.

'Moose' Masters Milwaukee

Braves	AB	R	H	RBI
Schoendienst 2b	4	2	1	0
Logan ss	3	0	0	0
Mathews 3b	2	1	2	2
Aaron cf	4	1	2	1
Torre 1b	4	0	0	1
Covington lf	2	1	1	2
Roach ph-lf	2	1	1	0
Hanebrink rf	2	0	0	0
Pafko ph-rf	1	0	0	0
Sawatski c	3	0	1	0
Burdette pr	0	0	0	0
Rice c	0	0	0	0
Conley p	3	1	1	1
Johnson p	0	0	0	0
Willey p	0	0	0	0
Adcock ph	1	0	0	0
Littlefield p	0	0	0	0
Totals	**31**	**7**	**9**	**7**

Cubs	AB	R	H	RBI
Taylor 2b	5	1	1	0
Walls rf	5	1	1	0
Banks ss	5	1	2	1
Moryn lf	4	2	2	2
Long 1b	4	0	2	1
Goryl 3b	2	0	0	0
Thomson cf	4	1	1	0
Taylor c	3	1	2	0
Adams ph	0	0	0	0
Tappe c	0	0	0	0
Drott p	1	0	1	0
Tanner ph	1	0	0	0
Mayer p	0	0	0	0
Bolger ph	1	1	1	3
Lown p	0	0	0	0
Ernaga ph	1	0	0	0
Elston p	0	0	0	0
Totals	**36**	**8**	**13**	**7**

```
MIL  1 0 0 3 2 1 0 0 0 - 7 9 2
CHI  0 0 0 0 0 1 6 0 1 - 8 13 1
```

Braves	IP	H	R	ER	BB	SO
Conley	6.1	9	5	5	1	3
Johnson	0.1	3	2	2	1	0
Willey	0.1	0	0	0	0	0
Littlefield L (0-1)	1.1	1	1	1	1	3
Totals	**8.1**	**13**	**8**	**8**	**3**	**6**

Cubs	IP	H	R	ER	BB	SO
Drott	5	7	6	6	2	3
Mayer	2	2	1	1	3	1
Lown	1	0	0	0	1	1
Elston W (3-0)	1	0	0	0	2	0
Totals	**9**	**9**	**7**	**7**	**8**	**5**

E—Milwaukee Torre, Mathews; Chicago Walls. DP—Milwaukee; Chicago 2. 2B—Milwaukee Schoendienst, Aaron. HR—Milwaukee Covington (1); Chicago Bolger (1). SF—Milwaukee Mathews, Torre. HBP—Milwaukee Conley; Chicago Moryn. LOB—Milwaukee 7; Chicago 7. Attendance: 5,751.

The 1958 season was a fun one for the Cubs and their fans, for several reasons:

• The Cubs hit a club-record 182 home runs, a mark that stood until 1987;

• The team was in contention into July, staying up there with an offense so effective that the Cubs seemingly were never out of a game;

• The Cubs, for the first time in the decade, stole the city's baseball headlines from the White Sox, who started slowly and, though finishing second, drew fewer than 800,000 fans after topping the million mark seven straight years. The Cubs, meanwhile, drew 979,904, their best home attendance total since 1952.

The homers started flying in April, and the feeling that no deficit was too great took hold in May. On the month's second day, the world champion Milwaukee Braves, whom the Cubs had beaten the day before, stormed to a 7–0 lead at the expense of 1957 rookie sensation Dick Drott at rainy, windy Wrigley Field. A Red Schoendienst double and an Eddie Mathews single started the scoring in the opening inning, and Wes Covington's two-run homer highlighted a three-run fourth.

Then came a sacrifice fly by Mathews and an RBI single by Henry Aaron in the fifth and a run-scoring single by pitcher Gene Conley in the following inning. Now it was 7–0, and it was getting late.

Walt "Moose" Moryn, a left-handed-hitting outfielder, began the comeback with a two-out homer in the sixth. In the seventh, after one-out singles by Bobby Thomson and Sammy Taylor, Jim Bolger, the bespectacled spare outfielder, batted for reliever Eddie Mayer and launched one onto Waveland Avenue, and suddenly it was 7–4.

Tony Taylor singled to center, and when third baseman Mathews threw wide to first on Lee Walls' bunt, runners were at the corners with one out. Ernie Banks singled home Taylor, and one out later, with Ernie Johnson having relieved Conley, Dale Long singled to score Walls, and it was 7–6. Johnson then uncorked a wild pitch, and Banks came in with the tying run.

The score remained 7–7 until the ninth. Braves pitcher Dick Littlefield, not looking anything like the oft-clobbered, well-traveled lefty (10 clubs in nine years) who had crafted a 5.35 ERA for the Cubs in '57, had retired pinch-hitter Frank Ernaga, Tony Taylor and Walls in order in the eighth following a leadoff walk and now began the ninth by striking out Banks. But then Moryn stepped up and drove one through the wind and into the right-field bleachers for an 8–7 victory—not to mention first place in the National League.

"I was just up there swinging," Moryn said afterward, "trying to get out of my slump."

Teammate Chuck Tanner, a huge optimist even then, surveyed the scene in the dressing room and proclaimed: "Anything can happen. Just take a look around this clubhouse. They look like a pennant-winning team to me."

Pennant-winning, no. Exciting, yes.

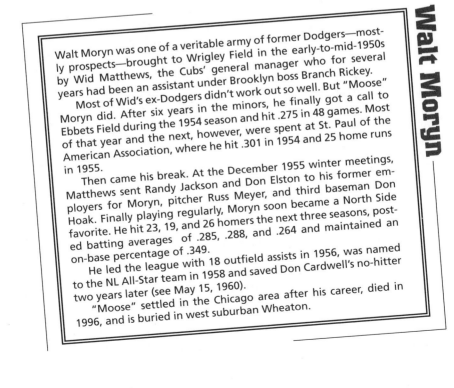

Walt Moryn

Walt Moryn was one of a veritable army of former Dodgers—mostly prospects—brought to Wrigley Field in the early-to-mid-1950s by Wid Matthews, the Cubs' general manager who for several years had been an assistant under Brooklyn boss Branch Rickey.

Most of Wid's ex-Dodgers didn't work out so well. But "Moose" Moryn did. After six years in the minors, he finally got a call to Ebbets Field during the 1954 season and hit .275 in 48 games. Most of that year and the next, however, were spent at St. Paul of the American Association, where he hit .301 in 1954 and 25 home runs in 1955.

Then came his break. At the December 1955 winter meetings, Matthews sent Randy Jackson and Don Elston to his former employers for Moryn, pitcher Russ Meyer, and third baseman Don Hoak. Finally playing regularly, Moryn soon became a North Side favorite. He hit 23, 19, and 26 homers the next three seasons, posted batting averages of .285, .288, and .264 and maintained an on-base percentage of .349.

He led the league with 18 outfield assists in 1956, was named to the NL All-Star team in 1958 and saved Don Cardwell's no-hitter two years later (see May 15, 1960).

"Moose" settled in the Chicago area after his career, died in 1996, and is buried in west suburban Wheaton.

'Handsome' Return on $6,000 Investment

It was a rather strange Friday afternoon at Wrigley Field.

The Cubs' Hank Edwards hit a home run in the first inning and a triple in the third. Then he departed in the sixth because of, according to one report, "an upset stomach." What the report didn't mention was that Edwards had swallowed his chewing tobacco while making a diving catch in right field.

Also, the wind was howling so hard from the west that the large pipe used to roll out the tarpaulin to cover the field after the game was blown almost to the outfield wall. Not only that, the Cubs committed five errors. And they still won the game, beating the powerful Brooklyn Dodgers 7–6, thanks to the first home run in the career of Randy "Handsome Ransom" Jackson.

Randy didn't win the third-base job until the following season, mostly because the Cubs still had hope for Bill Serena, a stocky fellow who had once hit 70 home runs (57 regular season, 13 more in the postseason playoffs) in the West Texas-New Mexico League. Eventually, Serena was found wanting and, after flunking a 1955 spring-training trial with the White Sox, spent his final ball-playing years in the Pacific Coast League.

Jackson, meanwhile, had signed in 1947 with the Cubs out of the University of Texas for $6,000 after leading the Southwest Conference in batting three straight years. He had also played football, operating in the same backfield as future All-Pro quarterback Bobby Layne. Now, as a Cubs rookie in May 1950, Randy knew he was going back to the minors later that month (when rosters were trimmed to 25) and that his time in Chicago was short. He had to make the most of his rare opportunities. This would be one of them.

> ## At a Glance
>
> **WP:** Vander Meer (1–0)
>
> **HR:** Sauer (1), H. Edwards (1), Jackson (1)
>
> **Key stat:** An Edwards on each club had a triple this day—the Cubs' Hank and the Dodgers' Bruce, who would become a Cub soon enough.

He entered the game in the top of the ninth, after Serena, having made two of the five Cub errors, was lifted for a pinch-hitter. The Cubs, trailing 6–3, sent the game into extra innings when, with two on and two out, Hank Sauer launched Carl Erskine's first pitch onto Waveland Avenue.

Johnny Vander Meer set down the Dodgers in their half of the 10th, and Jackson led off the bottom half against right-hander Bud Podbielan. He took the first pitch for a ball, then drove the second one into the bleachers in left-center for the game-winner.

The 'Kid K' Chronicles

Kerry Wood remembers feeling pretty good and plenty strong as he completed his bullpen warm-up session for the fifth start of his big league career, against a formidable Houston team that was destined to win the NL Central title.

In his first season as a Cub and less than three years removed from Grand Prairie High School in the Dallas suburbs, the strapping 6-foot-5 right-hander knew he had his work cut out for him. The Astros lineup he'd be facing featured two likely Hall of Famers, Craig Biggio and Jeff Bagwell, plus the dangerous likes of Moises Alou, Derek Bell and Jack Howell. Wood overpowered every one of them.

Brandishing what writer Bruce Jenkins described as "a fastball quick as a lightning bolt and a slider that broke from Waco to Galveston," Wood struck out the first five batters he faced. He struck out the side in the fifth inning and strung together seven 'Ks' in the seventh, eighth and ninth innings. When he blew away the hapless Derek Bell to end it, Wood had tied a major league record and "shot his age" with 20 strikeouts. He allowed only one hit, Ricky Gutierrez's infield single leading off the third inning. The oddly struck squibber glanced off third baseman Kevin Orie's glove and could just as easily have been ruled an error, which would have meant a no-hitter. Wood walked no one, which made it a totally satisfying afternoon for a young fireballer whose control had always been an issue.

"It was a completely dominating performance against a good club," Cubs manager Jim Riggleman said. "It was just electrifying, the way he was throwing the ball."

Mixing a crackling fastball with a knee-buckling breaking ball and an occasional change-up, Wood struck out Bagwell, Howell, and Alou three times each. He got Bell, Dave Clark, Gutierrez and Brad Ausmus twice and Biggio, losing pitcher Shane Reynolds and pinch-hitter Bill Spiers once each. Broadcaster Chip Caray's exuberant "Got him!" declaration became the soundtrack of a spring Wednesday as one Houston hitter after another trudged back to the dugout. The Astros were blown away by being blown away.

"He threw me one pitch that I thought was go-

Astros	AB	R	H	RBI
Biggio 2b	3	0	0	0
Bell rf	4	0	0	0
Bagwell 1b	3	0	0	0
Howell 3b	3	0	0	0
Alou cf	3	0	0	0
Clark lf	3	0	0	0
Gutierrez ss	3	0	1	0
Ausmus c	3	0	0	0
Reynolds p	1	0	0	0
Spiers ph	1	0	0	0
Totals	27	0	1	0

Cubs	AB	R	H	RBI
Brown cf	4	0	2	0
Morandini 2b	4	1	1	0
Sosa rf	4	0	1	0
Grace 1b	3	1	2	0
Rodriguez lf	2	0	0	1
Hernandez lf	1	0	0	1
Blauser ss	3	0	2	0
Martinez c	2	0	0	0
Orie 3b	3	0	0	0
Wood p	3	0	0	0
Totals	29	2	8	2

```
HOU  0 0 0 0 0 0 0 0 0 - 0 1 1
CHI  0 1 0 0 0 0 1 X - 2 8 0
```

Astros	IP	H	R	ER	BB	SO
Reynolds L (2-3)	8	8	2	1	2	10
Totals	8	8	2	1	2	10

Cubs	IP	H	R	ER	BB	SO
Wood W (3-2)	9	1	0	0	0	20
Totals	9	1	0	0	0	20

E—Houston Clark. DP—Houston. 2B—Chicago Grace, Blauser. SH—Houston Reynolds. SF—Chicago Rodriguez. HBP—Houston Biggio. LOB—Houston 2; Chicago 6. Attendance: 15,758.

ing to hit me in the face," Bagwell said. "Next thing I knew it was crossing the plate knee-high on the outside corner. How are you supposed to hit that?"

Wood was so totally in command that home-plate umpire Jerry Meals could have called the game from a rocking chair. Reynolds was pretty good himself, allowing two runs on eight hits with 10 strikeouts and two walks in eight innings. Mark Grace doubled and scored on Henry Rodriguez's sacrifice fly in the second inning, giving Wood the only run he needed. Mickey Morandini's single and Jose Hernandez's RBI groundout provided a bit of breathing room in the eighth.

"The most dominant pitching performance I've ever seen," said Grace, an 11-year veteran and one of the first Cubs to get to Wood as a mob of teammates engulfed him when strikeout No. 20 went into the books.

Fans in the left-field bleachers acknowledged each one by posting a 'K' placard on the back fence above Waveland Avenue, but Wood never stopped to count.

"I knew I had a lot, but I didn't know I had 20 until after the game," Wood said. "I knew they only had one hit. I knew I had a chance to throw my first complete game. I knew I had no walks."

Wood said catcher Sandy Martinez deserved just as much credit for the masterpiece. "We were on the same page," he said. "Every sign he put down, I already had the grip in my glove. We could have gone without signs."

Roger Clemens struck out 20 batters twice, and Randy Johnson did it once. Riggleman ranked Wood's performance among the all-time greats.

"I only had five years at Wrigley Field," he said, "but 20 strikeouts, one hit, no walks—I'm guessing it was the greatest game pitched in the history of the ballpark."

Wood would never come close to matching it, but his place in Cubs lore is nonetheless secure. Despite missing several weeks with a sore elbow, he would go 13–6 with 233 strikeouts in just 166 $^2/_3$ innings and be voted National League Rookie of the Year in 1998, the first Cub so honored since Jerome Walton in 1989. Wood would miss the 1999 season because of elbow surgery, and over the next several years his star-crossed career became an unrelenting series of trips to disabled list.

But the resolve he showed in battling back from each injury endeared him to Cubs fans just as much as this amazing day in May had. And when healthy he remained a prime-time contributor, helping the Cubs to a division title with a career-best 14 wins and a league-high 266 strikeouts in 2003, then reinventing himself as a closer and pitching them to the playoffs with 34 saves in 2008.

Rookie Kerry Wood struck out 20 batters in his fifth major league start, joining Roger Clemens and Randy Johnson as the only pitchers to accomplish the feat.

Wood was 77–61 with a 3.65 ERA and 1,407 strikeouts in 1,291 $^1/_3$ innings as a Cub, and he'll be back for more in 2011, having re-signed with the Cubs as a free agent.

He never bought into the theory that 20 strikeouts as a 20-year-old crushed him under the burden of unrealistic expectations. Wood never bemoaned his injuries, never second-guessed how the Cubs used him, never made excuses of any kind. He was a flinty-eyed gamer every day he wore the uniform, though he remains amused by the response the 20-strikeout game still elicits years after the fact.

The paid crowd on an occasionally drizzly afternoon with a Bulls playoff game scheduled for that night was 15,758.

"I think I've met everybody who was at the game," Wood said. "Fifteen thousand? I've met at least 26,000 people who say they were there."

Whether you were there, or you watched on television, or you listened to the radio, you'll never forget it.

Sammy's First Cubs Homer

The 23-year-old outfielder whom Cubs GM Larry Himes had to have was not exactly tearing up the National League. Nor were the Cubs.

The Cubs were 10–16 and at the bottom of the NL East on May 7, and Sammy Sosa—the flashy Dominican acquired by Himes from the White Sox six weeks earlier for veteran slugger George Bell—was hitting just .206 through 26 games with no home runs and three runs batted in.

But on this Thursday night, Sosa was to begin his climb toward the top of the North Siders' career home run list. He stepped into the box to lead off the home half of the first inning against Houston Astros right-hander Ryan Bowen, who had been staked to a 2–0 lead but like Sosa had been struggling so far this season (0–3, 10.20 ERA).

Sosa swung at Bowen's very first pitch and drove it deep to left and over the wall for the first of his 545 home runs in a Cubs uniform. Sammy's shot cut the lead in half and ignited a rally that resulted in a four-run first inning and an early shower for Bowen. Sosa added a double in the second and the Cubs went on to win 9–2, with Mike Morgan going the distance for the "W."

Injuries, however, wrecked Sosa's chances to make his first Cub season a success. A fastball from Montreal's Dennis Martinez broke his wrist on June 12, sidelining him for six weeks. Then came a fractured ankle, which put him out of action another four weeks. He finished at .260 with eight homers and 25 RBIs.

Astros	AB	R	H	RBI
Biggio 2b	4	0	1	0
Guerrero 2b	0	0	0	0
Finley cf	4	1	1	0
Jones p	0	0	0	0
Bagwell 1b	4	1	1	1
Incaviglia rf	4	0	2	1
Gonzalez lf	4	0	1	0
Ramirez ss	4	0	0	0
Taubensee c	4	0	0	0
Candaele 3b	3	0	1	0
Bowen p	0	0	0	0
Boever p	1	0	0	0
Distefano ph	1	0	0	0
Mallicoat p	0	0	0	0
Osuna p	0	0	0	0
Anthony ph-cf	1	0	0	0
Totals	**34**	**2**	**7**	**2**

Cubs	AB	R	H	RBI
Sosa cf	5	2	2	1
Grace 1b	4	1	1	1
Sandberg 2b	3	2	0	0
Vizcaino 2b	0	0	0	0
Dawson rf	4	2	3	0
Dascenzo pr-rf	1	0	0	0
May lf	4	2	2	2
Salazar ss	4	0	0	0
Girardi c	2	0	2	2
Strange 3b	4	0	1	2
Morgan p	4	0	0	0
Totals	**35**	**9**	**11**	**8**

HOU	2	0	0	0	0	0	0	0	0	- 2	7 1
CHI	4	1	0	3	0	1	0	0	X	- 9	11 1

Astros	IP	H	R	ER	BB	SO
Bowen L (0-4)	1	5	5	5	3	2
Boever	3	4	3	3	2	1
Mallicoat	2	2	1	1	2	2
Osuna	1	0	0	0	0	2
Jones	1	0	0	0	0	0
Totals	**8**	**11**	**9**	**9**	**7**	**7**

Cubs	IP	H	R	ER	BB	SO
Morgan W (3-2)	9	7	2	1	0	2
Totals	**9**	**7**	**2**	**1**	**0**	**2**

E—Houston Ramirez; Chicago Sosa. DP—Houston. 2B—Houston Finley; Chicago Dawson, May, Sosa. HR—Chicago Sosa (1). LOB—Houston 5; Chicago 9. Attendance: 21,614.

Cey Has His Say

Ron Cey was more than happy to see the San Francisco Giants come to town.
Back on Opening Day, April 3, he had homered in the City by the Bay, his
35th career home run against the Giants. He'd gone 2-for-5 the next day, and in
Chicago, in the opener of this two-game series, he had contributed a sacrifice fly
during a wild 10–7 Cubs victory. The Giants were the main rivals of Cey's former club, the Los Angeles Dodgers. Cey and minor-league teammates like Bill
Buckner, Davey Lopes, Bill Russell, Tom Paciorek and Joe Ferguson had been
taught by their managers—in particular Tommy Lasorda—to hate the Giants.
They had been told the tales of pennants snatched away by the Giants (1951,
1962), of beanball wars between the two clubs and of the Juan Marichal-Johnny
Roseboro fracas, to name a few.

So the Giants' presence was certain to serve as motivation for "the Penguin."

The Cubs trailed 3–1 when Bobby Dernier opened the home third inning
with a single and stole second. After Ryne Sandberg struck out, Giants rookie
right-hander Scott Garrelts walked both Gary Matthews and Leon Durham to
load the bases. Then Cey belted one over the wall in straight-away center for his
sixth career grand slam and a 5–3 Cubs lead.

The homer was his 36th against the Giants, easily the most of any opponent.
Explained Cey, smiling: "The club I played with last had, let's say, a deep tradition with the Giants."

Ignited by Cey, who would end up his second season in a Cub uniform with
25 homers and 97 RBIs, the Cubs went on to score three more runs in the inning for a seemingly safe 8-3 advantage. But this one was a long way from over.

Dickie Noles was touched for four runs in the Giants' seventh, enabling the
visitors to go up 9–8, but Jody Davis' RBI single tied it in the bottom half, and
Richie Hebner's pinch homer and Sandberg's run-scoring single in the eighth
put the Cubs up 11–9 entering the ninth.

The Giants were down to their final out when Jack Clark homered off
Lee Smith, after which Gene Richards singled, stole second and scored on Joel
Youngblood's triple. That made it 11–11,
but Keith Moreland's bases-loaded single in the home ninth gave the Cubs a
wacky 12–11 victory—and a half-game
lead in the NL East.

At a Glance

WP: L. Smith (3–2)

HR: Cey (5), Hebner (2)

Key stat: The teams combined for
33 hits, with both catchers—Jody
Davis and Bob Brenly—collecting
three apiece.

Cubs 3, Cardinals 2 (10 innings)

Shortstop, Long Ball

Five months later, he would be sharing the goat horns with Steve Bartman. But for an early-season stretch during the fateful campaign of 2003, Cubs shortstop Alex Gonzalez was anything but a goat.

The Cubs and Cardinals were tied 2–2 in the last of the 10th at Wrigley Field on this Saturday afternoon, the visitors having forced extra innings with J.D. Drew's run-scoring single in the ninth off closer Joe Borowski.

Now, in the Cubs' 10th, St. Louis right-hander Cal Eldred fanned Paul Bako for the first out. Next up was Gonzalez, who in his year and two-month stay with the North Siders had hit five game-winning home runs. Two had come already in 2003, one on May 1 in the 10th at San Francisco and the other May 4, when his 10th-inning shot had beaten the Rockies at Wrigley. Could Gonzalez do it again?

Said manager Dusty Baker a few minutes later, "I asked (pitching coach Larry Rothschild), 'Do you think he's going to do it? He said, 'I think he is.' Next thing I know, the ball is out of the park."

And the Cubs had a 1.5-game lead over the Cards in the NL Central, thanks to Gonzalez.

Observed Borowski, in a bit of understatement: "He seems to have a flair for the dramatic."

Gonzalez's third extra-inning, game-winning homer tied a club single-season record held by Ernie Banks, who did it in 1955, and Ron Santo (1966).

Cardinals	AB	R	H	RBI
Vina 2b	4	0	1	0
Palmeiro rf	4	0	0	0
Pujols lf	4	0	0	0
Edmonds cf	5	0	0	0
Rolen 3b	4	1	1	1
Martinez 1b	4	0	0	0
Renteria ss	3	1	1	0
Matheny c	3	0	1	0
Drew ph	1	0	1	1
Marrero c	0	0	0	0
Williams p	2	0	0	0
Cairo ph	1	0	0	0
Eldred p	0	0	0	0
Totals	35	2	5	2

Cubs	AB	R	H	RBI
Bellhorn 3b	4	0	0	0
Borowski p	0	0	0	0
Bako c	1	0	0	0
Gonzalez ss	5	1	2	1
O'Leary rf	4	0	1	0
Alou lf	4	1	1	1
Choi 1b	4	0	0	0
Patterson cf	3	1	2	0
Grudzielanek 2b	4	0	3	1
Miller c	1	0	1	0
Remlinger p	0	0	0	0
Wood p	0	0	0	0
Harris ph	1	0	0	0
Alfonseca p	0	0	0	0
Martinez 3b	1	0	0	0
Totals	32	3	10	3

STL	0 1 0 0 0 0 0 1 0 - 2										5 0
CHI	0 0 0 0 0 1 1 0 0 1 - 3										10 0

Cardinals	IP	H	R	ER	BB	SO
Williams	8	8	2	2	1	9
Eldred L (2-1)	1.1	2	1	1	2	1
Totals	9	10	3	3	3	10

Cubs	IP	H	R	ER	BB	SO
Wood	7	4	1	1	3	8
Alfonseca	1	0	0	0	0	0
Borowski	1	1	1	1	1	1
Remlinger W (1-0)	1	0	0	0	0	0
Totals	10	5	2	2	4	9

DP—St. Louis. 2B—St. Louis Vina. 3B—Chicago Patterson. HR—St. Louis Rolen (8); Chicago Gonzalez (4), Alou (4). SH—Chicago Wood, Miller. HBP—St. Louis Vina. LOB—St. Louis 8; Chicago 7. SB—St. Louis Renteria, Drew. Attendance: 38,106.

Maddux Magic

The 22-year-old right-hander pitching for the Cubs this Wednesday afternoon at Wrigley Field certainly had improved in this, his second full season in the big leagues.

Greg Maddux, working here against Robby Alomar, Garry Templeton, John Kruk and the rest of the San Diego Padres, had posted a wobbly 6–14 won-lost record and 5.61 ERA in 1987. But this clearly was a different year—and a different Maddux.

Through seven starts, he was 5–2 with a 2.48 ERA. He'd already pitched three complete games, including a three-hit shutout at Atlanta. Here, against the Padres, he was working on another shutout. But so was San Diego's Mark Grant.

Finally, in the eighth, the Cubs appeared set to break through. A one-out walk to Mark Grace brought reliever Lance McCullers onto the scene, and McCullers promptly gave up a double to Andre Dawson. Rafael Palmeiro was given an intentional walk to fill the bases, but Vance Law rapped into a 6-4-3 double play.

Maddux simply continued to mow down San Diego hitters, 20 of them in succession, waiting for his teammates to score the decisive run. It came in the 10th, after a leadoff triple by Ryne Sandberg and intentional walks to Grace and Dawson. Palmeiro bounced into a first-to-home forceout, and now it was up to Law again.

> ### At a Glance
>
> **WP:** Maddux (6–2)
>
> **Key stat:** Showing that Maddux had kept the ball down, first baseman Mark Grace posted 16 putouts.

With the count 2-2, Cubs manager Don Zimmer called for a suicide squeeze. Was Law surprised?

"Not particularly," he said later. "Zim told us in spring training not to be surprised at anything."

So down the line came Grace, here came Mark Davis' pitch, there went Law's bunt, perfectly placed, and across the plate slid Grace with the winning run. The Cubs were over the .500 mark at 16–15 and Maddux (6–2) had lowered his ERA to 2.10.

"I had a better changeup today than I've had," Maddux said, and then he took a shot at himself: "My fastball and changeup, you can't really tell the difference if you're sitting in the stands."

He was still able to say that in October, because Maddux finished 1988 with an 18–8 record and 3.18 ERA, his first big year. There would be many more.

Sam Jones' No-Hitter

On a chilly, overcast Thursday afternoon in Chicago, only 2,918 hardy souls paid their way into Wrigley Field, hoping to see the Cubs climb back to the .500 mark, heady territory for a franchise that only once in the preceding eight seasons had won as many as 69 games.

Also of interest was the African-American right-hander who was to start for the Cubs that day, the 6-foot-4 West Virginia native with the No. 27 on his back and the toothpick in his mouth. Sam Jones had come to the Cubs from the Cleveland organization with outfielder Gale Wade over the winter for the rapidly aging slugger Ralph Kiner. Jones, complementing his fastball with a big-breaking curveball, had taken special delight in facing Cincinnati hitters. Already he had beaten the Reds three times, once in relief, and in both starts he had struck out nine and walked seven.

But overall, entering this match with the Pirates, Jones was 3–3 with a 5.08 earned-run average. He was having trouble controlling his curve, but when he did control it, it was perhaps the best in the National League. "Tremendous curveball," Ernie Banks said, decades later. "I remember once Pee Wee Reese was facing Sam. Sam threw him that curveball, and Pee Wee, he saw it coming at his head, and he sat down—he sat down!—and it was a strike."

"You've never seen a curveball until you've seen Sam Jones' curveball," said former catcher Hobie Landrith, who caught Sam and batted against him. "If you were a right-handed batter, that ball was a good four feet behind you. It took a little courage to stay in there."

Stan Musial's swift summation: "Sam had the best curveball I ever saw."

The Pirates were getting their first look. They didn't like the view. Through eight innings, they had failed to get a hit off Jones, who had thrown 109 pitches. Sam only had three strikeouts, but the Bucs weren't making much solid contact. The only balls hit hard were by Frank Thomas, who lined out to third baseman Randy Jackson to end the fourth, and by Toby Atwell, who lined into a double play to end the eighth.

Pirates	AB	R	H	RBI
Saffell cf	3	0	0	0
Groat ss	4	0	0	0
Clemente rf	4	0	0	0
Thomas lf	4	0	0	0
Long 1b	0	0	0	0
Geo Freese 3b	3	0	0	0
Atwell c	2	0	0	0
Gen Freese 2b	2	0	0	0
King p	0	0	0	0
Montemayor ph	1	0	0	0
Law p	1	0	0	0
Ward ph	0	0	0	0
Mejias pr	0	0	0	0
Totals	24	0	0	0

Cubs	AB	R	H	RBI
Miksis cf	4	0	2	1
Baker 2b	3	1	1	0
Speake lf	5	0	1	0
King lf	0	0	0	0
Jackson 3b	4	0	2	0
Tappe rf	5	2	2	2
Banks ss	4	0	3	1
Fondy 1b	4	1	2	0
McCullough c	4	0	0	0
Jones p	4	0	2	0
Totals	37	4	15	4

```
PIT  0 0 0 0 0 0 0 0 0 - 0 0 0
CHI  1 1 0 0 1 0 1 0 X - 4 15 0
```

Pirates	IP	H	R	ER	BB	SO
King L (1-2)	2	5	2	2	1	2
Law	6	10	2	2	1	2
Totals	8	15	4	4	2	4

Cubs	IP	H	R	ER	BB	SO
Jones W (4-3)	9	0	0	0	7	6
Totals	9	0	0	0	7	6

DP—Chicago 2. 2B—Chicago Miksis, Tappe. 3B—Chicago Banks. HR—Chicago Tappe (2). SH—Chicago Baker, Miksis. LOB—Pittsburgh 4; Chicago 13. SB—Chicago Baker, Miksis, Fondy. Attendance: 2,918.

Meanwhile, the Cubs had built a 4–0 cushion, thanks in part to a run-scoring triple from Banks and a home run by outfielder Ted Tappe (no relation to Elvin). Now came the ninth. Future White Sox third baseman Gene Freese, then a 21-year-old Pirates rookie, led off with a walk, happy to have survived the at-bat.

"Sam's was the best curveball I ever saw, besides (Brooklyn star) Carl Erskine's," Freese remembered. "Well, I shouldn't say 'best I ever saw.' Because I never saw it. I was always running away."

Next came walks to pinch-hitter Preston Ward and leadoff man Tom Saffell to load the bases with nobody out. To the mound walked Cubs manager Stan Hack, carrying the proverbial hook. "I was out at the mound, too," Banks recalled. "I said to Stan, 'Don't do it! Don't do it!'"

"I was on third base," Freese said. "I was right there. Stan Hack comes out and says, 'Give me the ball, Sam.' Sam says, 'Are you nuts? You ain't getting the ball.' He started walking away."

Hack finally decided no change was necessary, even though the next three Pirate batters were youngsters who had given indications they would someday soon become excellent hitters: Dick Groat, Roberto Clemente and Thomas, later a Cub. Jones struck out all three on a total of 11 pitches to get his no-hitter, thus becoming the first African-American in big-league history to throw one. "Struck 'em all out on curveballs," Freese said. "All half-swings. Nobody had a full cut."

Sam Jones went on to pitch in the All-Star Game that July, posted a 14–20 won-lost record and led the NL in strikeouts (198) and walks (185)—and, of course, in chewed-up toothpicks.

Ernie Hits No. 500

Seventeen years before, on a sunny Sunday afternoon in St. Louis, a lanky 22-year-old shortstop named Ernie Banks had hit the first home run of his major-league career, a drive to left field off 18-game-winner Gerry Staley.

Here, the same player, now age 39, was in the batter's box at Wrigley Field, facing Atlanta right-hander Pat Jarvis in the second inning and well aware that the next home run he hit would be the 500th of his career.

Ernie had to be thinking of all the things that had happened to him and all he had accomplished since that day in St. Louis. He had:

- hit five grand slams, a single-season record, in 1955;
- hit 40-plus homers in 1955, '57, '58, '59 and '60;
- won back-to-back MVP awards in 1958 and '59;
- been named to the NL All-Star team 11 times;
- won the Gold Glove at shortstop in 1960;
- given Wrigley Field a second name, "The Friendly Confines";
- become universally known as Mr. Cub;
- become beloved by a city's baseball fans, even those of the White Sox;
- taken to giving out annual "predictions" for the Cubs, such as, "The Cubs will arrive in '55," or "The Cubs will roar in '64."

His sunny disposition was evident from the first words he would utter upon stepping onto the field each day for pregame warm-ups: "Let's play two!" One of his teammates, reliever Phil Regan, said this:

"He is an inspiration to the older guys as well as the rookies. Sometimes we complain about the travel or the conditions or something, and then we see Ernie lifting everybody up. All he wants to do is go out there and play ball. What a man."

Quite obviously, then, Banks had his own cheering section in that third-base dugout, especially this day. His teammates knew he was struggling. Indeed, ol' Ern was batting just .241 with two homers and 13 RBIs through 24 games.

Perhaps that's why Atlanta's Jarvis wasn't as careful with his 1-and-1 pitch to Banks as he would've been with it a year or two years earlier. He fired a fastball a bit up and in, but not up and in enough. Banks swung and lined the ball to left. Left fielder Rico Carty went back and watched the ball hit the wall above the "basket" and bounce back on the field. Umpires signaled home run, and the chilled audience of 5,264 began celebrating.

May 12, 1970
Cubs 4, Braves 3 (11 innings)

"I felt the ball had a real good chance," Banks said. "Then when I saw Carty turn and look up, I knew it was in."

Finishing his home run trot, he doffed his cap to the crowd and shook hands with every teammate he could find. When he took his position at first base at inning's end, he got another handshake, this from Carty, who was making his way to the first-base dugout.

There was a game still to be played, after all. Banks' 500th had cut the Braves' lead to 2–1. Atlanta led 3–1 in the seventh inning (thanks to Kenny Holtzman's third wild pitch of the afternoon), when the Cubs drew within a run, thanks to Banks' sacrifice fly. In the ninth, Billy Williams drove a Hoyt Wilhelm knuckler into the bleachers in right, and Ron Santo won the game in the 11th with a bases-loaded single off the glove of shortstop Sonny Jackson.

But Williams and Santo would be quick to remind one and all that this day belonged to Ernie Banks.

Sam Jones

Brock-for-Broglio isn't the only Cubs-Cardinals trade that did not work to the North Siders' favor. Go back to the winter meetings in 1956 and you'll see another clunker—and this time you can't blame Wid Matthews.

New general manager John Holland decided it was time to trade Sam Jones, even though Jones again had led the NL in strikeouts and had lowered his ERA from 4.10 in 1955 to 3.91 in 1956. Holland found a willing trade partner in "Frantic Frank" Lane, who was in his second season in St. Louis after spending seven years building the White Sox into contenders.

Lane, no doubt having trouble stifling a laugh, offered Holland pitchers Tom Poholsky and Jackie Collum and backup catcher Ray Katt for Jones, lefty Jim Davis, utility man Eddie Miksis, and catcher Hobie Landrith.

What happened? Poholsky had a horrid season, Collum got into just nine games as a Cub, and Katt was traded to the Giants on Opening Day. Jones, meanwhile, went 12–9 with a 3.60 ERA and cut his walks to 71. In 1958, he again led the NL in strikeouts (225) and was 14–13 with a 2.88 ERA. Traded to the Giants in 1959, "Toothpick" was 21–15 (those 21 wins were top in the NL) and led the league in ERA (2.83) and shutouts (4).

And then, in 1960, he had one final big year (18–14 and 3.19 ERA)—at age 34. Maybe trading Sam Jones was not such a good idea.

"Let's play two!" Ernie Banks provided the Cubs with some of their greatest moments, including hitting his 500th home run on May 12, 1970.

Banks Helps Bludgeon Padres

The Padres were the Cubs' favorite cousins in 1969. In fact, had it not been for expansion and the addition of new, hapless teams in San Diego and Montreal, plus the way the Cubs handled their other cousins, the 1969 club might not be revered as much as it still is to this day.

Against teams with winning records that year, the Cubs were an impressive 9–3 against the NL West champion Braves but just 8–10 against the East-winning Mets, 7–11 versus the Pirates, 9–9 vs. the Cardinals and 6–6 each with the Dodgers, Giants and Reds. Against the four with losing records, the Cubs were 8–4 vs. the Astros, 12–6 vs. the Phillies, 10–8 vs. the Expos and 11–1 against their beloved Padres.

They blanked the '69 Padres 1–0, 2–0, 4–0 and 6–0. And, on Tuesday afternoon, May 13, in front of a Wrigley Field gathering of 5,080—including Ernie Banks' daughter Jan and several schoolmates—the Cubs won by a National League-record-tying count of 19–0. And Ernie rewarded Jan and her friends by hitting two three-run homers and an RBI double in support of winnng pitcher Dick Selma, late of the Padres.

The seven RBIs equaled Banks' career high. On Aug. 4, 1955, he hit a pair of two-run homers and a three-run blast in an 11–10 decision over the Pirates at Wrigley; on May 1, 1963 at St. Louis, he had two three-run shots plus an RBI single in the Cubs' 13–8 triumph.

Ernie started his assault in the first inning this day, with two out and after two walks by lefty Dick Kelley. His drive over the wall in left-center put Selma up 3–0. In a four-run second, Banks doubled home Ron Santo. And in the fifth, with Don Kessinger and Santo aboard with walks, Ernie lined a pitch from a rookie right-hander named Leon Everitt into the bleachers in left. Now it was 12–0, and Everitt would not appear in another big-league game.

Padres	AB	R	H	RBI
DaVanon 2b	4	0	2	0
Pena ss	4	0	0	0
Gonzalez cf	3	0	0	0
Brown rf	3	0	0	0
Colbert 1b	1	0	1	0
Davis 1b	3	0	0	0
Ferrara lf	4	0	0	0
Spiezio 3b	2	0	0	0
Cannizzaro c	3	0	0	0
Reberger p	0	0	0	0
Niekro p	0	0	0	0
Kelley p	0	0	0	0
Baldschun p	0	0	0	0
Gaston ph	1	0	0	0
Everitt p	0	0	0	0
Krug c	1	0	0	0
Totals	29	0	3	0

Cubs	AB	R	H	RBI
Kessinger ss	3	3	2	0
Oliver 2b	5	3	3	4
Williams lf	5	2	2	2
Young lf	1	1	1	3
Santo 3b	2	3	0	1
Banks 1b	5	2	3	7
Smith 1b	1	0	0	0
Hundley c	2	1	1	0
Rudolph c	1	1	0	0
Hickman rf	5	0	0	0
Phillips cf	5	2	2	0
Selma p	4	1	1	0
Totals	39	10	15	17

SD	0	0	0	0	0	0	0	0	0	-	0	3	2
CHI	4	4	1	0	3	2	5	0	X	-	19	15	1

Padres	IP	H	R	ER	BB	SO
Kelley L (2-3)	1.1	4	7	6	3	2
Baldschun	0.2	1	1	0	1	1
Everitt	4	8	6	6	4	3
Reberger	1	2	5	5	3	1
Niekro	1	0	0	0	1	0
Totals	8	15	19	17	12	7

Cubs	IP	H	R	ER	BB	SO
Selma W (3-3)	9	3	0	0	4	10
Totals	9	3	0	0	4	10

E—San Diego Spiezio, DaVanon; Chicago Phillips. DP—San Diego. 2B—San Diego Colbert; Chicago Banks, Oliver, Kessinger. 3B—Chicago Williams. HR—Chicago Banks 2 (3,4), Oliver (1), Young (2). SH—Chicago Selma. HBP—Chicago Oliver. LOB—San Diego 6; Chicago 10. Attendance: 5,080.

Banks came up the next inning against Everitt with Billy Williams at third and Santo at first with two gone. The best he could muster, though, was a popup to third baseman Ed Spiezio.

His big day heartened Banks, who had come into it hitting .254 and having hit zero home runs and driven in 14 runs in the 32 games since his two-homer, five-RBI performance on Opening Day. He had gone just 6 for his last 39.

"I've been changing my stance in the last couple of weeks," he said after the game, "spreading out a little more and trying all kinds of things. But my big problem was that I was swinging too hard . . . and I'm not that type of hitter. I've got to swing easy and just try to meet the ball. Today I did that, and I went back to my old stance."

Ernie homered in the ninth the next day to tie the Padres 2–2, and the Cubs went on to win 3–2 on Willie Smith's pinch single later that inning. The Cubs were 23–11 and had a five-game lead in the new NL East, and the fun was just starting.

The Padres, however, were not enjoying it.

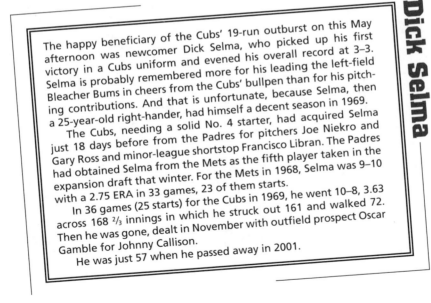

Dick Selma

The happy beneficiary of the Cubs' 19-run outburst on this May afternoon was newcomer Dick Selma, who picked up his first victory in a Cubs uniform and evened his overall record at 3–3. Selma is probably remembered more for his leading the left-field Bleacher Bums in cheers from the Cubs' bullpen than for his pitching contributions. And that is unfortunate, because Selma, then a 25-year-old right-hander, had himself a decent season in 1969.

The Cubs, needing a solid No. 4 starter, had acquired Selma just 18 days before from the Padres for pitchers Joe Niekro and Gary Ross and minor-league shortstop Francisco Libran. The Padres had obtained Selma from the Mets as the fifth player taken in the expansion draft that winter. For the Mets in 1968, Selma was 9–10 with a 2.75 ERA in 33 games, 23 of them starts.

In 36 games (25 starts) for the Cubs in 1969, he went 10–8, 3.63 across 168 2/3 innings in which he struck out 161 and walked 72. Then he was gone, dealt in November with outfield prospect Oscar Gamble for Johnny Callison.

He was just 57 when he passed away in 2001.

'What's Your Opinion of Kingman's Performance?'

It all began peacefully enough, with the Cubs' Ivan DeJesus flying out to the Dodgers' Reggie Smith in right field.

By the time it was over, some five hours later, this game would be remembered more for a manager's postgame tirade than the feat that caused it. It was one of Dave Kingman's most memorable days in baseball—and one of Los Angeles manager Tommy Lasorda's, too, but for different reasons.

While Lasorda had driven the Dodgers to the World Series the season before, Kingman had spent it bouncing around the major leagues on waivers, wearing the uniform of four different teams: the Mets, Padres, Angels and, for the final two weeks, the Yankees. Cubs GM Bob Kennedy realized his team needed power—only one Cub, Bobby Murcer, had hit more than 12 homers in '77, and Murcer had hit 27 in 154 games while Kingman had his 26 in 132 games. So Kennedy signed the 1967 Prospect High School (Mt. Prospect, Ill.) graduate as a free agent and hoped for big things.

The big things came in 1979, when Kingman blasted 48 homers, drove in 115 runs, hit .288 and had a .613 slugging percentage. Not that his '78 record was dreadful: He clouted 28 home runs and collected 79 RBIs in 395 at-bats spread across 119 games. But this particular Sunday afternoon in Los Angeles gave Cub fans an idea of what the 6–6 outfielder could accomplish with a bat in his hands.

At a Glance

WP: P. Reuschel (1–0)

HR: Kingman 3 (7), Murcer (2)

Key stats: Kingman had 8 RBIs; each club used 21 players.

Kingman, whose two-run homer in the ninth the evening before had ended winning pitcher Tommy John's shutout bid, had come into the weekend series hitting just .207 with three homers and eight RBIs in 23 games. The Cubs were 15–15, in third place in the NL East, two games back of Philadelphia after splitting the series' first two contests.

The Dodgers were up 3–0 until the sixth, when ex-Dodger Bill Buckner led off with a single and Kingman followed with his fifth homer, this one off lefty Doug Rau. The Dodgers snapped a 5–5 tie in the eighth on Smith's two-out, two-run single to center off Bruce Sutter, who had allowed just five earned runs and 14 hits in 23 innings thus far this season.

Dave Kingman (10) is congratulated by teammates Manny Trillo (19) and Bill Buckner (22) at home plate after Kingman hit his first of three home runs against the Los Angeles Dodgers on May 14, 1978.

Cubs 10, Dodgers 7 (15 innings)

So it was 7–5 L.A. going into the ninth, and although reliever Mike Garman walked DeJesus to open the inning, he quickly retired Steve Ontiveros and Buckner on fly balls. That brought up Kingman. Boom! This shot of some 430 feet, over the Dodger bullpen, sent the game into extra innings and Lasorda into a silent rage, his anger aimed at Garman, who lasted six more days with the Dodgers before he could be banished to Montreal for two minor-leaguers.

Lasorda's anger grew as his star-studded lineup—which included Steve Garvey, Ron Cey, Rick Monday, Davey Lopes, and Bill Russell in addition to Smith—was stopped cold through the 14th inning by Ray Burris and Rick Reuschel's chubby older brother, Paul. Meanwhile, the Cubs could do nothing with rookie Bobby Castillo and Rick Rhoden—until the 15th.

With one out, reserve infielder Mick Kelleher, a lifetime .213 hitter, singled to right off Rhoden, a starting pitcher pressed into relief duty. Lasorda surely was growing angrier. Ontiveros walked, but Buckner grounded into a force play, leaving Cubs at first and third with two outs. Up stepped Kingman, who crushed a Rhoden fastball deep into the bleachers in left. Kingman had his third home run of the afternoon and his sixth, seventh and eighth RBIs on the day, and the Cubs had a 10–7 lead.

It stayed that way, thanks to Paul Reuschel's third inning of shutout relief, and when Cey flied out to end the game, a mere spark was all that would be needed to get Lasorda going. It was provided by a poor soul named Paul Olden, a young radio reporter, who asked the manager: "What's your opinion of Kingman's performance?"

That was the cue to take cover. Lasorda was ready to erupt:

"What's my opinion of Kingman's performance!? What the bleep do you think is my opinion of it? I think it was bleeping horsebleep. Put that in—I don't bleeping care. Opinion of his performance!!? Bleep, he beat us with three bleeping home runs! What the bleep do you mean, 'What is my opinion of his performance?' How could you ask me a question like that—'What is my opinion of his performance?' Bleep, he hit three home runs! Bleep. I'm bleeping bleeped off to lose the bleeping game. And you ask me my opinion of his performance? Bleep."

Thirty years later, Lasorda told an Associated Press reporter, "I'm sorry that I did an interview like that, and I'm not proud of it. But when that guy talked to me, I was as low and depressed and dejected as you can get. I mean, we lose the game in 15 innings, I had to go into my starting pitchers and it knocked the daylights out of me. Then this guy comes in at the very moment I sat down and asked me, 'What is your opinion?' So I proceeded to tell him what my opinion was."

Cub fans would've had a much simpler, and less profane, response to the question. Like, "heroic."

Cardwell's No-Hitter Comes by a Shoestring

Three days earlier, the Cincinnati Reds had pounded the Cubs 14–1 at Wrigley Field. The team had fallen to 6–13 and was sharing the NL cellar with the 9–16 Phillies, both clubs already 8.5 games out of first place.

Something had to be done.

So the next day, the Cubs made a deal with, naturally, the Phillies. They traded away their rapidly improving 24-year-old second baseman, Tony Taylor, a flashy fielder, a base-stealer and a .280 hitter all in one snappy package. In return for Taylor and backup catcher Cal Neeman—actually, all Cub catchers were backups in those days—the Cubs received left-handed-hitting first baseman Ed Bouchee, a power hitter until the Cubs got him, and starting pitcher Don Cardwell, a big (6-foot-4, 210 pounds) fast-balling right-hander with three big-league seasons already under his belt despite being only 24.

Reaction to the deal was mixed—that is, until that Sunday, when Cardwell, before 33,543, pitched Game 2 of the afternoon's doubleheader and made Major League Baseball history by becoming the first man to throw a no-hitter in his first start for his new team after being traded.

Only one Cardinal reached base. That was Alex Grammas, later a teammate of Cardwell's in Pittsburgh. Grammas walked on a close 3-2 pitch in the first inning. Said Cardwell, 45 years later: "I asked him once, 'Grammie, how could you have taken that pitch? I thought it was right on the black.' And he says, 'Cardie, I didn't even see it.'"

The lack of lights at Wrigley Field certainly didn't hurt Cardwell. But the Cubs, despite the shadows, were able to score four times off St. Louis' Lindy McDaniel, so Cardwell obviously was bringing it that day. Even Stan Musial, who pinch-hit in the eighth, struck out on four pitches. Said Ernie Banks: "Stan told me later, 'I was swinging at sound.'"

The Cubs had broken a scoreless tie in the

Cardinals	AB	R	H	RBI
Cunningham rf	4	0	0	0
Grammas ss	1	0	0	0
Shannon ph-2b	1	0	0	0
White 1b-cf	3	0	0	0
Boyer 3b	3	0	0	0
Spencer 2b-ss	3	0	0	0
Wagner lf	3	0	0	0
Flood cf	2	0	0	0
Musial ph-1b	1	0	0	0
Smith c	2	0	0	0
Sawatski ph	1	0	0	0
McDaniel p	2	0	0	0
Crowe ph	1	0	0	0
Totals	**27**	**0**	**0**	**0**

Cubs	AB	R	H	RBI
Ashburn cf	3	1	2	1
Altman rf	4	0	1	0
Bouchee 1b	4	0	0	0
Banks ss	4	1	1	2
Moryn lf	3	0	0	0
Thomas 3b	3	1	1	0
Zimmer 3b	0	0	0	0
Rice c	3	0	1	0
Kindall 2b	3	1	1	1
Cardwell p	3	0	0	0
Totals	**30**	**4**	**7**	**4**

STL	0	0	0	0	0	0	0	0	0	-	0	0 0
CHI	0	0	0	0	1	2	1	0	X	-	4	7 0

Cardinals	IP	H	R	ER	BB	SO
McDaniel L (1-2)	8	7	4	4	2	5
Totals	**8**	**7**	**4**	**4**	**2**	**5**

Cubs	IP	H	R	ER	BB	SO
Cardwell W (2-2)	9	0	0	0	1	7
Totals	**9**	**0**	**0**	**0**	**1**	**7**

2B—Chicago Ashburn. HR—Chicago Banks (7). LOB—St. Louis 1; Chicago 4. SB—Chicago Kindall. Attendance: 33,543.

fifth when Frank Thomas came home on a fielder's-choice grounder by Jerry Kindall, and they extended the lead to 3–0 on Banks' sixth-inning homer with Richie Ashburn aboard. Ashburn doubled home Kindall, who had singled and stolen second, with the final run of the day in the seventh.

Now all the attention was on Cardwell. In the Cardinals' eighth, Daryl Spencer grounded out to Kindall, Taylor's replacement at second base, and Leon Wagner bounced to Bouchee at first. Then Musial fanned as a pinch-hitter for Curt Flood to become Cardwell's seventh strikeout victim.

Then it was the ninth. Carl Sawatski, a portly, lefty-swinging catcher whose career had begun as a Cub years before, hit for Hal Smith and crushed one, right at right-fielder George Altman, for the first out. Next was another left-handed pinch-batter, veteran slugger George Crowe, hitting for McDaniel. Crowe swung and drove a ball to deep right-center, where Ashburn pulled it in.

Now came another lefty, Joe Cunningham, who had batted .318, .312 and .345 the three previous seasons and was known for his terrific batting eye, a hitter who seldom swung at a bad pitch. In other words, here was one tough out.

The count was 3-1 when Cardwell threw a fastball on the outside corner. Umpire Tony Venzon called it a strike, and Cunningham made it clear to the man in blue that he disagreed. Regardless, both men prepared for the 3-2 pitch. Again, it was a fastball on the outer half. Cunningham stroked a liner toward left, a certain hit. Thirty-three thousand voices fell silent.

"I thought it was a base hit," Cunningham said, decades afterward. "I thought for sure I'd broken it up."

Left-fielder Walt Moryn, no defensive whiz, came running in. Thirty-three thousand hearts sank. Jack Brickhouse, in the WGN-TV booth, yelled, "C'mon, Moose!!" Unbelievably, Moryn reached down and caught the ball at his shoe-tops for the out that enabled Cardwell to make history.

Said Cardwell, an automobile dealer in Winston-Salem, N.C., until his death in 2008: "The thing I remember the most, like everyone else back there in Chicago, I suppose, is Walt Moryn making that running catch."

What many don't remember is that the game took just an hour and 46 minutes to play. To Don Cardwell, it must have seemed like an hour and 46 minutes from the time Joe Cunningham hit that line drive until the moment Walt Moryn caught it.

Cubs Finally Top Braves in 22 Innings

The Cubs have played four 20-inning games and a couple of 21-inning games—the most recent of which was on Aug. 18, 1982 at Wrigley Field, when the Los Angeles Dodgers won 2–1 when Steve Sax doubled and eventually scored on a sacrifice fly by Dusty Baker.

However, the longest game in club history, by innings, took place May 17, 1927 at Braves Field in Boston. The Cubs employed three pitchers, the last of whom—Bob Osborn—worked the final 14 innings, allowed only six hits and zero runs and lowered his ERA from 4.26 to 2.45. He was rewarded with a win, his first of the year to go with one defeat.

The host Braves, however, kept sending the same poor guy out there every inning. Meet Bob Smith, a 32-year-old right-hander and a former infielder. In fact, he had been the Braves' regular shortstop in 1923 and '24. Smith would wind up the 1927 season with a 10–18 won-loss record—and was to go 15–12 with a 3.22 ERA for the 1931 Cubs.

On this day, against his future team, he worked all 22 innings, was touched for 20 hits and even walked nine batters. And yet, after spotting the Cubs a 3-0 lead, he held them scoreless for 16 innings before the visitors broke through.

Hack Wilson, 4-for-8 on the day with two RBIs, led off the decisive frame with a walk and moved to second on Riggs Stephenson's sacrifice bunt. Charlie Grimm then lined a single, his third hit of the afternoon, past Smith's head and into center field. Wilson raced home and just beat the throw of Jack Smith, Boston's center fielder, and the Cubs led 4–3. And that's the way it stayed.

Cubs	AB	R	H	RBI
Adams 2b	6	0	3	0
Cooney ss	7	2	3	0
Webb rf	6	0	0	0
Wilson cf	8	1	4	2
Stephenson lf	8	0	2	0
Grimm 1b	9	0	3	1
Hartnett c	10	0	1	0
Beck 3b	9	0	1	0
Blake p	3	1	1	0
Brillheart p	0	0	0	0
Scott pr	0	0	0	0
Osborn p	5	0	2	0
Totals	71	4	20	3

Braves	AB	R	H	RBI
Richbourg rf	10	0	3	0
Bancroft ss	9	0	2	1
J Smith cf	7	0	0	0
High 3b	7	1	1	0
Burrus 1b	9	0	3	0
Brown lf	9	1	3	0
Moore 2b	8	0	0	0
Hogan c	9	0	2	2
B Smith p	8	1	1	0
Fournier ph	1	0	0	0
Totals	77	3	15	3

CHI	0	0	2	0	1	0	0	0	0	0	0	0	
BOS	0	0	0	0	0	1	2	0	0	0	0	0	

CHI	0	0	0	0	0	0	0	0	1 - 4R 20H 0E
BOS	0	0	0	0	0	0	0	0	0 - 3R 15H 0E

Cubs	IP	H	R	ER	BB	SO
Blake	7.1	9	3	3	2	1
Brillheart	0.2	0	0	0	0	0
Osborn W (1-1)	14	6	0	0	2	1
Totals	22	15	3	3	4	2

Braves	IP	H	R	ER	BB	SO
Smith L (1-3)	22	20	4	3	9	5
Totals	22	20	4	3	9	5

2B—Chicago Stephenson, Wilson; Boston Hogan. SH—Chicago Grimm, Adams 3, Stephenson, Wilson, Webb, Cooney; Boston Moore. LOB—Chicago 19; Boston 13.

This Family 'Feud' Alou-loo

Moises Alou's first two seasons as a Cub had fallen far short of expectations.

Slowed by injuries in 2002, the left fielder had limped home with 15 home runs, 61 runs batted in and a .275 batting average. The 2003 season had gone better for him (22 homers, 91 RBIs, .280 average), though the lasting impression Cub fans took with them from that year was Alou in a rage after Steve Bartman's ill-advised reach for a playable Florida foul ball in Game 6 of the NLCS.

But here in 2004, Alou was rolling, coming into this night's game against visiting San Francisco with a .315 average and nine homers and 25 RBIs. And the Cubs were 22–16 and a game behind Houston in the NL Central.

The Giants, meanwhile, were 16–23 after going 100–61 and winning the NL West title the season before under manager Felipe Alou, Moises' father. But for the younger Alou, there was no time for feeling sorry for his dad, especially with the Giants and lefty Kirk Reuter from downstate Illinois holding a 3-1 lead in the fifth.

Corey Patterson cut the lead by a run with a homer off Reuter in the Cub fifth, and spare outfielder Jason DuBois, in his big-league debut, delivered a game-tying sacrifice fly in the seventh to make it 3–3.

Soon it was the last of the 10th, the score still 3–3. Lefty-swinging Tom Goodwin flied out against lefty reliever Jason Christiansen to open the inning. Up stepped Alou, hitless on the night. From the visitors' dugout strode Felipe Alou, who waved in a right-hander, Jim Brower, to face his son.

At a Glance

WP: Borowski (2–1)

HR: Patterson (5), Alou (10)

Key stat: Baker's starting lineup included Jose Macias leading off and in right field, Damian Jackson batting second and playing second, and Ramon Martinez in the No. 8 spot at shortstop.

The count went to 3-2. Moises was certain a breaking ball was coming. "I've played against my dad for a long time and remember every at-bat," he said. "He doesn't give me a lot of fastballs."

Recounted Cubs manager Dusty Baker: "They threw him a changeup on 2-0 and a breaking ball on 3-1. Then Brower hung a breaking ball, and Mo didn't miss it."

Alou drove the pitch deep into the night, sending 39,047 fans home happy.

Rookies Hubbs and Brock Lead Sweep of Phillies

The summer before, at age 19, Kenny Hubbs was playing second base for Wenatchee in the Class B Northwest League, where he had hit .286.

The summer before, at age 22, Lou Brock was playing center field for St. Cloud in the Class C Northern League, where he had hit .361.

The Cubs had broken in Ron Santo as the regular third baseman in 1960. Left fielder Billy Williams had been named NL Rookie of the Year in '61. Now, here were two more outstanding prospects unearthed by Chicago scouts. What would the Cubs do with them?

The front office made a wise decision: The Cubs were not going anywhere in 1962, so Brock and Hubbs would start the season with the big club.

The kids batted 1-2 in the Opening Day lineup and stayed there most of the first month. Brock hit a home run his first time up in the home opener against St. Louis. Hubbs went 5-for-5 on April 17 against Pittsburgh.

At a Glance

Game 1

WP: Koonce (2–0)

S: Anderson (2)

HR: Brock (5)

Game 2

WP: Buhl (2–2)

HR: Williams (9), Banks (11), Altman (8)

Key stat: Hubbs 8-for-10

And then came a May 20 doubleheader at Philadelphia. When it was over and the Cubs had swept the Phillies 6–4 and 11–2, Hubbs was hitting .301 and Brock .279. Here's what the rookies did that day:

In the second inning of the opener, Brock launched a grand slam off Jim Owens to stake fellow rookie Cal Koonce to a big early lead. Then he walked and scored in the fourth, singled and scored in the sixth and was hit by a pitch in the eighth. Hubbs, meanwhile, singled in the first and second, grounded out to the right side to advance Brock in the fourth, then added a third single in the sixth.

In Game 2, while Brock singled once and scored a run, Hubbs added five more hits, all singles, and scored on home runs by Williams and Ernie Banks.

The two new Cub kids had served notice to the National League that they were up to stay. Hubbs would finish at a solid .260 and receive the Gold Glove for his standout defense. Brock ended up at a promising .263 with 16 steals. But neither player would achieve stardom in Chicago. Hubbs was killed when his small plane crashed near Provo, Utah, in February 1964. Four months later, Brock was traded to the Cardinals for sore-armed pitcher Ernie Broglio and developed into a Hall-of-Famer.

'Home Run' Hacker Just Misses No-Hitter

Warren Hacker was called "Home Run" Hacker for good reason. In successive seasons (1953 through '56), he surrendered 35, 28, 38 and 28 long ones. Had he only been as stingy as he was in 1952, when he gave up just 17 homers and went 15–9 with a 2.58 ERA, he might have had a far more successful career—and been spared that unfortunate nickname.

Thus far in 1955, however, he seemed to be getting things right. In six games, five of them starts—and four of those complete games—he had surrendered only two home runs over 41 ⅓ innings. Also, opponents had collected only 30 hits off Hacker.

In his last two outings, the right-hander from southern Illinois had lost to Brooklyn 3–0 when the Dodgers' Don Newcombe threw a one-hitter, and he'd beaten the defending world champion New York Giants 5–2, lowering his ERA to 1.74. Next he was to face the other member of the NL's Big Three, the Milwaukee Braves at County Stadium.

Hacker was at his best this Saturday afternoon. The Braves were missing one of their big guns—Eddie Mathews was beginning a stint on the disabled list—but the lineup still included people like Henry Aaron, Billy Bruton and big Joe Adcock. Hacker, though, brushed them all aside. He retired the first 11 batters before walking Chuck Tanner with two out in the fourth. Then he retired Aaron on a flyout. And then, as 26,279 looked on, he retired the Braves in order in the fifth, sixth, seventh and eighth. The Cubs had scored off lefty Chet Nichols in the sixth and in the seventh (on Dee Fondy's sixth homer of the year).

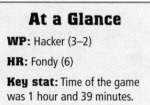

At a Glance

WP: Hacker (3–2)

HR: Fondy (6)

Key stat: Time of the game was 1 hour and 39 minutes.

It was still 2–0 when the Braves came up in the ninth, Hacker, still without a strikeout, needing only three more outs for his no-hitter. Milwaukee catcher Charlie White, a left-handed hitter, was up first. He sent a flyball to right, and Eddie Miksis caught it for the first out. Next was a pinch-hitter for Nichols, George Crowe, a veteran left-handed slugger from the Negro leagues who had hit .334 with 34 home runs in the American Association in 1954.

The count went to 1-2. Catcher Harry Chiti called for a fastball. Hacker shook him off. "I wanted to throw my knuckleball," Hacker said later that day. "Harry again insisted on a fastball. But I had my way and I threw the knuckler." The flutterball did not flutter. Crowe belted it into the right-field bleachers, the ball and the no-hitter dream both long gone. But two outs later, Hacker had a one-hitter and a 2–1 victory.

Deliverance?

In June 2001, the Cubs drafted a pitcher who looked as if he might be able to one-up Kerry Wood.

Not that Wood had fallen out of favor with the Cubs or their fans, but injuries had become a constant in his career. "Bad mechanics," pessimist critics chirped knowingly. And while he gamely battled back each time, each ailment heightened the concern that Wood would never fulfill the dazzling potential he had flashed in 1998, his rookie season.

Now this Mark Prior, he was the real deal. Bigger and stronger than Wood, if that were possible. Not quite as hard a thrower, but a more polished style of pitching after years of all-encompassing individual instruction from pitching guru Tom House. Near-perfect mechanics, according to the scouting reports, some of which described him as the best college pitcher ever after his two varsity seasons at Southern California.

At a Glance

WP: Prior (1–0)

S: Alfonseca (7)

HR: Sosa (17)

Key stat: Despite all those injuries, Prior was 42–29 with a 3.51 ERA and 757 strikeouts in 657 innings over his abbreviated career.

Prior had already said no to the New York Yankees, who drafted him out of San Diego's University High School, so the Minnesota Twins had no hope of landing him with the No. 1 pick of the 2001 amateur draft. They took a catcher named Joe Mauer instead, leaving Prior for the Cubs at No. 2. After signing for $10.5 million and dominating minor league hitters in nine starts early in the 2002 season, Prior was called to Chicago.

The largest crowd since the home opener—40,138 fans—jammed Wrigley Field for his debut, and he didn't disappoint. The Pirates used a walk, a hit batsman and Pokey Reese's RBI single to nick him for a run in the second inning, and Brian Giles reached him for a home run in the sixth.

Otherwise, Prior was in total control, as poised as advertised, with electric stuff to match. He gave up two runs on four hits with two walks in six innings and negated most of those six baserunners with 10 strikeouts. He fanned future teammate Aramis Ramirez three times.

Fred McGriff's two-run, first-inning double had given Prior some breathing room. Sammy Sosa's 17th homer made it 3–1 in the third, and the Cubs went up 5–1 in the fifth on Moises Alou's RBI single and Bill Mueller's sacrifice fly.

Prior would go 6–6 with a 3.32 ERA and 147 strikeouts in just 116 $2/3$ innings as a rookie. It was enough to get starry-eyed Cubs fans dreaming of a Prior and Wood-anchored rotation for years to come. And, as with most things that seem to good to be true, it was.

Nirvana for Ernaga

The town of Susanville is in the northeast portion of California, about 160 miles from the Oregon border to the north and about 80 miles from Reno, Nev., to the southeast.

"People don't know where Susanville is, but they know where Reno is," noted one of Susanville's better-known citizens, Frank Ernaga, whose exploits one Friday afternoon at Wrigley Field more than a half-century ago help him remain well known to Cub fans who were there.

On May 24, 1957, Ernaga (pronounced er-NOG-uh), a 26-year-old right-handed-hitting outfielder out of UCLA, made his big-league debut, playing right field and batting sixth against the World-Series-champs-to-be Milwaukee Braves and future Hall-of-Famer Warren Spahn.

"I can remember it well," Ernaga said. "That was at least 85 pounds ago."

The Cubs, who entered the action at 8–19, were trailing 1–0 in the second inning when Ernaga stepped up for the first time as a major leaguer and drove a Spahn pitch into the bleachers in left-center. Then, in the fourth, with the score 1–1 and teammate Jim Bolger on first base, Ernaga lined a hit to center. The ball took an odd hop and got past center fielder Billy Bruton and rolled to the wall for a triple. The Cubs led 2–1.

As for the rest of his day, Ernaga popped out in the sixth and walked in the eighth as the Cubs, with Moe Drabowsky going the distance, posted a 5–1 triumph.

"When I faced Spahn that day," Ernaga said, "I was in a daze. I just kinda floated around the bases on that home run. The triple, I remember where I hit that one. But the home run, I didn't even see it go into the seats."

He saw only a couple of pitches the next afternoon, when he grounded out as a pinch-hitter to end the eighth inning of a 7–6 Cub defeat. He sat out the first game of Sunday's double-header and watched from the dugout as fellow rookie Dick Drott struck out 15 and beat the Braves 7–5. In

Braves	AB	R	H	RBI
O'Connell 2b	3	0	0	0
Sawatski ph	1	0	0	0
Murff p	0	0	0	0
Thomson ph	1	0	0	0
Jolly p	0	0	0	0
Aaron rf	5	0	1	0
Mathews 3b	4	1	3	0
Adcock 1b	5	0	1	1
Tanner lf	3	0	0	0
Logan ss	3	0	0	0
Bruton cf	4	0	1	0
Crandall c	4	0	1	0
Spahn p	2	0	1	0
Torre ph	0	0	0	0
Cole pr-2b	1	0	1	0
Totals	36	1	9	1

Cubs	AB	R	H	RBI
Morgan 2b	3	0	2	0
Walls cf	3	0	0	0
Banks 3b	3	0	0	0
Long 1b	4	1	1	0
Bolger lf	4	2	2	1
Ernaga rf	3	2	2	2
Neeman c	3	0	1	2
Littrell ss	3	0	1	0
Drabowsky p	3	0	1	0
Totals	29	5	9	5

											R	H	E
MIL	1	0	0	0	0	0	0	0	-	1	9	0
CHI	0	1	0	2	0	2	0	0	X	-	5	9	0

Braves	IP	H	R	ER	BB	SO
Spahn L (4-2)	5	6	3	3	2	4
Murff	2	3	2	2	0	3
Jolly	1	0	0	0	1	0
Totals	8	9	5	5	3	7

Cubs	IP	H	R	ER	BB	SO
Drabowsky W (2-3)	9	9	1	1	4	5
Totals	9	9	1	1	4	5

DP—Milwaukee 2. 2B—Milwaukee Adcock; Chicago Littrell, Morgan, Long. 3B—Chicago Ernaga. HR—Chicago Ernaga (1). SH—Chicago Walls. SF—Chicago Neeman. HBP—Milwaukee Torre. LOB—Milwaukee 13; Chicago 5. Attendance: 6,487.

Game 2, however, Ernaga started against rookie lefty Juan Pizarro and this time doubled and homered as the Cubs rallied to win 5–4 for the sweep.

So these were Ernaga's numbers as a starter in his first weekend in the major leagues: 4-for-7 with a double, triple and two home runs. "The Cubs told me I was going to play right field against left-handed pitching," he said. "Well, I played right field against two left-handed pitchers, and then they sat me down."

Fifteen days and just 18 at-bats later, Ernaga took his .320 batting average to Fort Worth in the Texas League. He was, however, brought back as a September call-up and got a chance to face Spahn one more time, this on Sept. 20 in Chicago. He came through with a single and double in three at-bats, thus finishing the season having hit for the cycle (single, double, triple and homer) in six official at-bats against the masterful Milwaukee lefty.

And yet Ernaga would collect only one more major league hit, the following May, before he again was sent back to Fort Worth. The Cubs that spring had tried to make him into a catcher, without success. "I split a finger. Dick Littlefield, the lefty, a knuckleballer—I was catching him. My right hand caught it, but the glove was on my left hand. That was the end of that."

Eventually he returned to Susanville, where he became a building contractor.

"I always thought," he said, "that I should have gotten a better chance than I did."

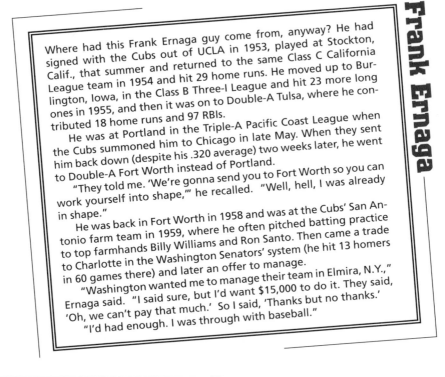

Where had this Frank Ernaga guy come from, anyway? He had signed with the Cubs out of UCLA in 1953, played at Stockton, Calif., that summer and returned to the same Class C California League team in 1954 and hit 29 home runs. He moved up to Burlington, Iowa, in the Class B Three-I League and hit 23 more long ones in 1955, and then it was on to Double-A Tulsa, where he contributed 18 home runs and 97 RBIs.

He was at Portland in the Triple-A Pacific Coast League when the Cubs summoned him to Chicago in late May. When they sent him back down (despite his .320 average) two weeks later, he went to Double-A Fort Worth instead of Portland.

"They told me. 'We're gonna send you to Fort Worth so you can work yourself into shape,'" he recalled. "Well, hell, I was already in shape."

He was back in Fort Worth in 1958 and was at the Cubs' San Antonio farm team in 1959, where he often pitched batting practice to top farmhands Billy Williams and Ron Santo. Then came a trade to Charlotte in the Washington Senators' system (he hit 13 homers in 60 games there) and later an offer to manage.

"Washington wanted me to manage their team in Elmira, N.Y.," Ernaga said. "I said sure, but I'd want $15,000 to do it. They said, 'Oh, we can't pay that much.' So I said, 'Thanks but no thanks.'

"I'd had enough. I was through with baseball."

Cubs Sweep Cardinals Behind Minner, Rush

During the 1950s, the phrase "great pitching" seldom came up in discussions about the Cubs. For a time in 1955, however, the Cubs' pitching staff—in particular starters Bob Rush, Warren Hacker, Sam Jones and, briefly, Paul Minner—was at the very least quite good.

In the magical month of May 1955, the North Siders registered five shutouts and, in eight other games, held the opposition to either one or two runs. The stinginess climaxed with a weekday doubleheader May 25 at Wrigley Field against the St. Louis Cardinals.

Facing a lineup that included veteran stars like Stan Musial, Red Schoendienst and Rip Repulski plus 1954 Rookie of the Year Wally Moon and 1955 rookie sensations Ken Boyer and Bill Virdon, Minner was at his very best in Game 1. The lefty, about to turn 32, allowed just four hits and set down Moon, Musial and Repulski in order in the ninth for a 1–0 triumph.

The only run support for Minner, who had been out since the opening week of May with shoulder pain, came on rookie outfielder Bob Speake's homer off Larry Jackson. But more on Speake later.

In Game 2, it was Rush's turn. The big right-hander, a Cub mainstay since 1948 and the staff ace most of his career, was as good as Minner had been. Thanks partially to Eddie Miksis' homer and Speake's RBI double—both coming in the first inning—Rush took a 3–0 lead *and* a one-hitter into the ninth. Musial flied out before Repulski wrecked the shutout bid with a home run. Undeterred, Rush retired Schoendienst and Moon to end it.

At a Glance

Game 1

WP: Minner (3–2)

HR: Speake (6)

Game 2

WP: Rush (3–2)

HR: Miksis (2)

Key stat: Barney Schultz pitched two hitless innings in Game 2 for St. Louis; the knuckleballer later had three decent years for the Cubs (1961–63) before posting a 1.64 ERA and 14 saves for the Cardinals' 1964 world championship team.

At day's end, Minner had a 3–2 record and had lowered his ERA to 3.82. Rush, also 3–2, had dropped to 2.23. And their team was 22–16, in second place, six games behind Brooklyn. (Incidentally, Howie Pollet made it a series sweep the next day with a 3–0 triumph over his former club.)

Now, about that Bob Speake fellow. Signed out of Springfield, Mo., in

1948, he had hit 20 homers but batted just .264 at Des Moines in the Class A Western League in '54. His power stroke, though, caught manager Stan Hack's attention during spring training, and Speake made the final camp cuts and came north with the Cubs.

He didn't get his first start until May 2 in Philadelphia, and the following day his bases-loaded triple in the first inning sparked the Cubs to a 6–0 victory in New York. He hit his first big-league homer two days later at the Polo Grounds, then homered in back-to-back games May 7-8 in Cincinnati.

Speake's bat continued to speak loudly, with a two-run homer May 18 against the Phillies, a triple off Lew Burdette and a game-winning homer in the 11th off Warren Spahn May 20 in Milwaukee. And so it went, the rookie capping the month with a pair of long ones in a Memorial Day doubleheader sweep in St. Louis (see sidebar).

A year later, he was back in the minors. Ah, but how bright that flash in the pan had been.

Rivalry Renews

The Cubs-Cardinals rivalry was pretty much dormant during the 1950s. Not until 1967 would Cub fans travel in great numbers to St. Louis—and Cardinal fans to Chicago—for meaningful series between the two clubs.

In any event, the Cubs surely gained much satisfaction when, on May 30, 1955, they completed a 20–9 month by sweeping the Cardinals in St. Louis, 9–5 in 10 innings and 4–3 in 11—just five days after they had swept a pair from the same team at Wrigley Field. That left the Cubs with a 27–17 record and in second place, six games behind the NL-leading Dodgers.

In the opener, before 28,258 at the original Busch Stadium, rookie Bob Speake's two-run homer in the ninth off Brooks Lawrence put the Cubs up 5–3, but fellow rookie Ken Boyer returned the favor in the bottom half to send the game into extra innings. Eddie Miksis' tie-breaking single, his third hit of the contest, keyed a four-run 10th that won it.

Then, in the second game, Larry Jackson and the Cards led 2–1 in the seventh until Ernie Banks' two-run shot put the Cubs ahead. Wally Moon singled home the tying run in the ninth, and the game remained tied until Speake stepped up to lead off the 11th—and slammed his 10th homer of the year—and 10th of the month—over the old pavilion in right off knuckleballer Bobby Tiefenauer. In the Cards' 11th, Howie Pollet got Red Schoendienst to roll into a Gene Baker-to-Banks force out to end the proceedings.

The '55 Cubs' success would last through June, and the North Siders stood at 44–36 and in second place, 12.5 games out, following completion of a doubleheader split with the Reds on July 4. Then the Cubs lost 17 of their next 19 and settled into their familiar second-division surroundings.

Rookie Drott Fans Record 15 Braves

Dick Drott, a rookie right-hander from Cincinnati, was still a few weeks shy of his 21st birthday, but he had given Cubs manager Bob Scheffing and pitching coach Fred Fitzsimmons every indication he was ready for his next assignment.

Thus far in 1957, in eight games (six starts), he had used his blazing fastball to post a 2–4 record and a 3.95 earned-run average. He had gone eight innings in his last outing, a game the Cubs won 4–3 over the New York Giants with two runs in the ninth.

Next for Drott was mighty Milwaukee—with Henry Aaron, Eddie Mathews and the rest—in Game 1 of a Sunday doubleheader at Wrigley Field, with 32,127 people on hand. The kid passed the test.

He struck out Billy Bruton to open the game and got Aaron to end the first inning. In the Cubs' half, Bob Speake's sacrifice fly, Dale Long's double and Walt Moryn's homer provided Drott with a quick 3-0 lead.

More strikeouts followed: Joe Adcock and Felix Mantilla in the second, opposing pitcher Gene Conley and Bruton again in the third. In the fourth, with Drott mixing in an effective curveball with his heater, Mathews and Aaron were victims, and in the fifth, Del Crandall and reliever Taylor Phillips went down swinging. Dick Cole fanned in the sixth, and in the seventh, Chuck Tanner—whose homer had given the Braves their lone run—struck out swinging and Crandall was called out on strikes to become victim No. 13.

After the Cubs gave Drott more breathing room with a four-run seventh, highlighted by Ernie Banks' homer with Jack Litrell aboard, Drott was touched for two runs in the eighth but escaped further difficulty by fanning Aaron for the third time to end the uprising. That broke the Cub record of 13 strikeouts, set by Lon Warneke in 1934 and matched in '56 by Sam Jones.

With two out in the ninth, Tanner blooped a

Braves	AB	R	H	RBI
Bruton cf	5	1	0	0
Cole 2b	3	0	0	0
Torre ph	1	0	0	0
Murff p	0	0	0	0
Mathews 3b	4	0	2	1
Aaron rf	4	0	0	0
Adcock 1b	4	0	0	0
Mantilla ss-2b	4	0	0	0
Tanner lf	3	2	2	1
Crandall c	4	1	1	2
Conley p	1	0	0	0
Phillips p	1	0	0	0
Logan ph-ss	2	1	2	0
Totals	**36**	**5**	**7**	**4**

Cubs	AB	R	H	RBI
Morgan 2b	3	1	0	0
Banks 3b	4	1	3	2
Speake lf	2	1	1	1
Long 1b	3	2	2	0
Moryn rf	3	1	2	3
Walls rf	0	0	0	0
Bolger cf	4	0	1	0
Neeman c	4	0	1	0
Littrell ss	4	1	1	0
Drott p	4	0	1	0
Totals	**31**	**7**	**12**	**6**

MIL	0	1	0	0	0	0	2	2	-	5	7	2
CHI	3	0	0	0	0	4	0	X	-	7	12	3

Braves	IP	H	R	ER	BB	SO
Conley L (0-2)	2	5	3	3	3	0
Phillips	5	6	4	4	1	3
Murff	1	1	0	0	0	1
Totals	**8**	**12**	**7**	**7**	**4**	**4**

Cubs	IP	H	R	ER	BB	SO
Drott W (3-4)	9	7	5	4	1	15
Totals	**9**	**7**	**5**	**4**	**1**	**15**

E—Milwaukee Aaron, Mantilla; Chicago Littrell, Moryn, Drott. DP—Milwaukee. 2B—Milwaukee Tanner; Chicago Banks, Long 2. 3B—Milwaukee Logan. HR—Milwaukee Crandall (4), Tanner (2); Chicago Banks (4), Moryn (3). SH—Chicago Moryn. SF—Chicago Speake. LOB—Milwaukee 5; Chicago 6.

double to left and Crandall homered into the first row of the bleachers in left. Now it was 7–5, but Drott was still throwing well. Johnny Logan dropped a pop fly into short center to bring the tying run to the plate and Scheffing to the mound for a conference.

Drott assured his manager all was well. It was. Within moments, Bruton had become Drott's 15th victim, and the Cubs had won 7–5.

"I've never had better control of my curve, that's for sure," Drott said in the clubhouse. "For that matter, I don't think I've had better control, period."

He said he had struck out Aaron each time with a curve, something his pitching coach never would have thought possible.

"Bob Scheffing told me this spring that Dick had a great curve," Fitzsimmons said. "Frankly, I didn't believe it. Certainly, he didn't show me one. But he made a believer out of me. He's got a curve, all right."

The Cubs made the day sweeter by rallying in the ninth for a 5–4 Game 2 win, and Drott went on after this day to finish his rookie year at 15–11 with a 3.58 ERA. He also had 170 strikeouts—and an NL-high 129 walks—in 229 innings. All those pitches took their toll: Dick developed arm problems, was 7–11 with a 5.43 ERA in 1958 and never had another winning season.

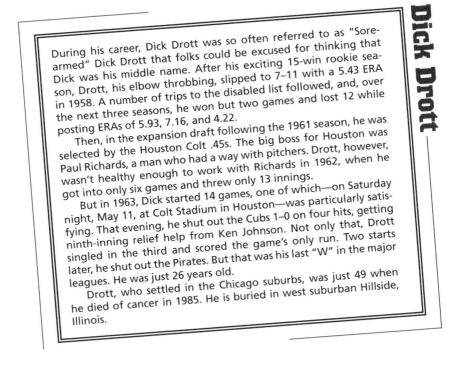

Dick Drott

During his career, Dick Drott was so often referred to as "Sore-armed" Dick Drott that folks could be excused for thinking that Dick was his middle name. After his exciting 15-win rookie season, Drott, his elbow throbbing, slipped to 7–11 with a 5.43 ERA in 1958. A number of trips to the disabled list followed, and, over the next three seasons, he won but two games and lost 12 while posting ERAs of 5.93, 7.16, and 4.22.

Then, in the expansion draft following the 1961 season, he was selected by the Houston Colt .45s. The big boss for Houston was Paul Richards, a man who had a way with pitchers. Drott, however, wasn't healthy enough to work with Richards in 1962, when he got into only six games and threw only 13 innings.

But in 1963, Dick started 14 games, one of which—on Saturday night, May 11, at Colt Stadium in Houston—was particularly satisfying. That evening, he shut out the Cubs 1–0 on four hits, getting ninth-inning relief help from Ken Johnson. Not only that, Drott singled in the third and scored the game's only run. Two starts later, he shut out the Pirates. But that was his last "W" in the major leagues. He was just 26 years old.

Drott, who settled in the Chicago suburbs, was just 49 when he died of cancer in 1985. He is buried in west suburban Hillside, Illinois.

Pirates Discover New-Look Cubs

Who'd have thunk it? Here were the Cubs, who had finished 75–87 and 26 games back in 1976, up there fighting for the NL East lead this Memorial Day weekend.

There was a new manager, Herman Franks; a new general manager, Bob Kennedy; and a whole bunch of new faces on this '77 club. The Cubs had traded their two top players—Bill Madlock and Rick Monday—and had received four solid performers in return: first baseman Bill Buckner and shortstop Ivan DeJesus from the Dodgers (for Monday) and right fielder Bobby Murcer and third baseman Steve Ontiveros from the Giants (for Madlock).

Also, new and valuable pieces for the bench, Gene Clines and Greg Gross, had arrived from Texas and Houston, respectively.

The changes had little effect on the field the first month: The Cubs were 7–9 through April 30. But then they slapped together a pair of six-game winning streaks and slowly climbed in the standings, despite the absence of their best player: Buckner's bad ankle was limiting him mostly to pinch-hitting duties.

Suddenly, the Cubs were 25–14 and trailed the first-place Pirates (26–12) by just 1.5 games as Chuck Tanner's band of sluggers and speedsters came to town on Friday, May 27. This would be a stiff test. The Bucs boasted scary thumpers like Dave Parker, Willie Stargell, Al Oliver and Bill Robinson, plus speedsters in Omar Moreno, Rennie Stennett and Frank Taveras. Were the new-look Cubs ready for prime time?

Part of the answer came Friday afternoon. Jerry Morales doubled and tripled, Manny Trillo and Murcer hit go-ahead homers and the Cubs and Bill Bonham (6–3) handed John Candelaria his first loss of the season. The next day, before 34,779, the Cubs trailed 2–0 before a five-run sixth—highlighted by

Pirates	AB	R	H	RBI
Moreno cf	4	0	0	0
Taveras ss	4	0	0	0
Parker rf	4	0	2	0
Oliver lf	4	1	2	1
Stargell 1b	4	0	1	0
Stennett 2b	4	0	0	0
Garner 3b	3	1	1	0
Dyer c	3	0	1	1
Reuss p	3	0	1	0
Gossage p	0	0	0	0
Totals	**33**	**2**	**8**	**2**

Cubs	AB	R	H	RBI
DeJesus ss	5	0	0	0
Clines lf	2	0	0	0
Buckner ph	1	0	1	1
Kelleher pr	0	0	0	0
Hernandez p	0	0	0	0
Sutter p	0	0	0	0
Biittner 1b	4	0	0	0
Murcer rf	4	1	1	0
Morales cf	4	1	2	0
Trillo 2b	4	0	2	1
Ontiveros 3b	3	0	1	0
Mitterwald c	2	1	2	0
Gross ph	1	0	0	0
Swisher c	0	0	0	0
Burris p	2	0	0	0
Cardenal ph-lf	1	0	1	1
Totals	**33**	**3**	**10**	**3**

PIT	0 0 0 1 0 0 1 0 0 - 2 8 1
CHI	0 0 0 0 0 0 1 2 X - 3 10 0

Pirates	IP	H	R	ER	BB	SO
Reuss	6.1	6	1	1	2	4
Gossage L (4-1)	1.2	4	2	2	1	3
Totals	**8**	**10**	**3**	**3**	**3**	**7**

Cubs	IP	H	R	ER	BB	SO
Burris	7	8	2	2	0	2
Hernandez W (1-1)	1.2	0	0	0	0	3
Sutter S (14)	0.1	0	0	0	0	0
Totals	**9**	**8**	**2**	**2**	**0**	**5**

E—Pittsburgh Taveras. 2B—Pittsburgh Reuss, Parker 2; Chicago Mitterwald, Murcer. 3B—Pittsburgh Garner. HR—Pittsburgh Oliver (6). SF—Chicago Cardenal. LOB—Pittsburgh 4; Chicago 10. SB—Chicago Ontiveros. Attendance: 39,517.

Morales' three-run double—sent them on to a 6–3 triumph and into first place by a half-game.

Now it was Sunday, and Wrigleyville was jumping. When the Cubs took the field, they were given a standing ovation by the throng of 40,146. But those folks didn't have much to yell about for the first six innings, as Jerry Reuss shut down the Cub offense and the Pirates led 2–0 on Oliver's homer and Duffy Dyer's RBI single, both off starter Ray Burris.

The Cubs cut the lead to 2–1 in the seventh when catcher George Mitterwald, who ended up throwing out five of seven would-be base-stealers in the series, doubled, went to third on Jose Cardenal's pinch single and scored on another pinch single, this by Buckner, off future Hall of Famer Rich "Goose" Gossage.

In the eighth, lefty reliever Willie Hernandez fanned Moreno, got Taveras on a roller to short and struck out the huge and dangerous Parker. Momentum swung to the Cubs, despite the presence of Gossage. "He has a changeup," said Murcer, "that's faster than most fastballs." Still, Murcer got to him for a leadoff double to center and went to third when Morales beat out a bunt. Trillo singled to left to tie the contest, and the old place was rocking.

Ontiveros drew a walk to load the bases, and, one out later, up stepped Cardenal, who had remained in the game. "I've been playing so little," he said later, "I almost don't feel like I belong to the ballclub." Jose, coming through again, lined a sacrifice fly to right for a 3–2 lead. It was up to the bullpen to hold it.

With ace closer Bruce Sutter throwing in the bullpen down the third-base line, Hernandez took the mound to open the ninth and retired Oliver and struck out Stargell. Next up was Stennett, a right-handed hitter. Franks called for Sutter, who retired the Pittsburgh second baseman on a grounder to Trillo, his Cub counterpart. Sutter had his 14th save, and the Cubs, winners of 21 of their last 26, had a 1.5-game lead.

And Wrigley Field was revitalized.

Said former Cubs catcher Randy Hundley, then a member of Franks' coaching staff: "It's just like 1969 all over again. Only this time, we're going to have a better ending."

Moryn's Memorable Memorial Day

Sure, the Cubs had been playing better ball in this new season, but who would have figured on a crowd like this one that stormed the gates of Wrigley Field for a doubleheader against the relocated Dodgers?

The Cubs were in fourth place but with a 20–23 record and trailing the first-place San Francisco Giants by eight games. The Dodgers, unable thus far to get acclimated to Los Angeles, were in last place at 15–24 and 11 behind.

The paid attendance was 37,799, including about 1,000 standees. The Cubs, particularly Walt Moryn, made sure that all of them got every penny's worth of the price of their ticket.

Moryn, a left-handed slugger, began his day's heroics in Game 1, but there were other heroes, to be sure. Like Moe Drabowsky, who pitched eight innings and departed with a 2–0 deficit, and right fielder Lee Walls, who collected three hits, the biggest of which came in the ninth.

Here's what happened:

Dodgers lefty Johnny Podres took a 2–0 lead into the last of the ninth before things came undone for him and the visitors. Bobby Adams lined to Carl Furillo in right for the first out before Walls belted his 13th home run of the season to make it a 2–1 game. Alvin Dark struck out looking, but Ernie Banks kept the Cubs alive by drawing a walk from Podres, who preferred facing Moryn, the left-handed hitter.

Moryn, though, lashed a liner to left-center for a double that scored Banks, and the score was 2–2. Now manager Walter Alston turned to reliever Ed Roebuck to face Bobby Thomson, but Bob Scheffing switched to Chuck Tanner, who was given an intentional pass. Another Scheffing switch from right-handed hitter to lefty swinger brought Sammy Taylor to the plate instead of Cal Neeman. Taylor singled up the middle, and Moryn raced home with the winning run.

The nightcap was more thrilling, though it did not start out that way. The Dodgers led 6–0 after 2 ½ innings, starter Taylor Phillips having been touched for seven hits, among them homers by Gil Hodges and Don Zimmer. It was 7–1 when the Cubs, in their half of the fourth, started on the road back against L.A. starter Don Newcombe. Banks opened with a liner into the bleachers in left, and Moryn launched one into the seats in right, and it was 7–3.

In the sixth, the Cubs scored three times against Don Drysdale to draw within a run. With two out, Sammy Taylor singled, Tony Taylor walked and pinch-hitter Thomson drove them both in with a double. Adams' single sent Thomson across, and it was 7–6.

Charlie Neal's triple set up a Dodger run in the top of the seventh, but that was merely Moryn's cue to step forward again. Facing Roebuck, the Game 1 reliever, "Moose" slammed his 10th homer of the season into the right-field bleachers. His round-tripper was followed by one from Tanner, and the game was tied 8–8.

Then it was the ninth. The much-maligned Cub bullpen stopped the Dodgers again, lefty Eddie Mayer doing the honors this time by retiring Pee Wee Reese and Randy Jackson to end the inning with Neal on second base with the potential winning run. So now it was the Cubs' turn, and a new pitcher, a young Sandy Koufax, was on the mound.

Banks led with a single, his fourth hit on the afternoon. Next was Moryn, who had finally won over his manager, who had harbored serious doubts as recently as spring training 1957—even after Moryn had hit .285 with 23 homers in his first season as a Cub.

"I'm just trying to find a place where he can catch a baseball," Scheffing told a reporter in March 1957. "He told me he could play first base and he couldn't. Then he told me he could play left field and he couldn't. Frankly, I'm not even impressed with his work in right field (his original spot). And he hasn't helped us much with his bat."

> ## At a Glance
>
> **Game 1**
>
> **WP:** Elston (6–2)
>
> **HR:** Walls (13)
>
> **Game 2**
>
> **WP:** Mayer (2–2)
>
> **HR:** Banks (12), Moryn 3 (11), Tanner (2)
>
> **Key stat:** Sammy Taylor, in addition to his game-winning pinch single in the opener, was 4-for-4 in Game 2.

But that was then; this was now. Koufax threw a 1-1 fastball and Moryn sent a drive to the opposite field, the ball landing in the first few rows of the left-field bleachers, and the Cubs were 10–8 winners.

Waiting for Moryn in the clubhouse were the writers and photographers, but they would have to wait a bit more. Because outside the clubhouse door was Walt's mom, Sophie, ready with a big hug after coming down from the family home in St. Paul, Minn., for a belated Mother's Day celebration. A special afternoon had become even more so.

His manager spoke for all: "He's proved to me that he's one of the most underrated players in baseball," Scheffing said. "I'll always want him playing for me."

Alexander Chalks Up 11th Straight Victory

By 1920, Grover Cleveland Alexander was halfway through his big-league career and already, for all intents and purposes, had presented a winning case for baseball immortality. He had won a record 28 games as a rookie with the 1911 Phillies and had won, in successive seasons, 31, 33 and 30 during the three-year period of 1915 to 1917.

At age 31, he had gone off to fight in France in spring 1918 and there he was gassed, suffered from shell shock and hearing loss and began experiencing the first signs of epilepsy. So all he did in 1919, his first full year as a Cub, was win 16 games and lead the National League with a 1.72 ERA.

Now, here he was at the end of May in a new season, riding a personal 10-game winning streak. Visiting newly named Cubs Park on the 31st for a morning-afternoon holiday twinbill were the defending world champion Cincinnati Reds, and Alexander was ready for them.

Alexander singled home Zeb Terry in the third inning to even the score at 1–1, and Charlie Deal's first homer of the year made it 2–1 Chicago in the seventh. Cincinnati tied things at 2–2 on Pat Duncan's RBI single in the eighth, and the game went into extra innings.

But with two out and the bases empty in the home 10th, Alexander decided this thing had lasted long enough. He swung at a Ray Fisher fastball and sent the pitch into the left-field bleachers for a 3–2 Cubs victory— the team's ninth straight win—and extended his own winning streak to 11.

> ### At a Glance
>
> **WP:** Alexander (11–2)
>
> **HR:** Deal (1), Alexander (1)
>
> **Key stat:** The 10-inning game took exactly 2 hours to play.

He finished that year 27–14, leading the NL in wins, ERA (1.91), innings (363 1/3), strikeouts (173), games started (40) and complete games (33). Alas, his team did not fare as well. At day's end, the Cubs were 24–16 and in first place, a half-game up on both Cincinnati and Brooklyn. They finished 75–79 and in fifth place.

JUNE

"It was easily my biggest day in all my years with the Cubs," Billy Williams said of the June 29, 1969, day named in his honor at Wrigley Field.

D-Lee De-livers

It's almost funny in hindsight, but there was some grumbling that the Cubs might have been taken after they traded cult-figure first baseman Hee Seop Choi to the Florida Marlins for Derrek Lee before the 2004 season. Choi flashed some early power for the Marlins, while Lee got off to a slow start, and Cubs fans conditioned to expect the worst were fretting, "Here we go again."

Lee had quieted much of the talk by the end of that season, hitting .278 with 31 home runs and 98 RBIs and playing first base like a magician. Over the course of 2005 he became a Wrigleyville favorite, and a 5-for-5, four-RBI night in this Wednesday victory at Dodger Stadium was the catalyst to a career year.

"D-Lee is one guy you pencil in and don't worry about because you know he's going to hit," manager Dusty Baker said.

Before a full house of 54,093 fans, Lee had singles in the first, third and fifth innings as the Cubs reached Dodgers starter Derek Lowe for six runs and 13 hits in 5 $^2/_3$ innings. Neifi Perez's three-run homer was the big hit in a four-run second inning.

Derrek Lee's 5-for-5 game with four RBIs on June 1, 2005, was only part of his impressive season. He was a contender for National League MVP.

Perez doubled and Lee singled to give the Cubs a 6–3 lead in the sixth, but the Dodgers got within 6–5 against Joe Borowski, Todd Wellemeyer and Michael Wuertz in the sixth and seventh. It was a 6–5 game in the eighth when Lee faced Dodgers reliever Duaner Sanchez with Perez and Enrique Wilson on base and two outs. He delivered a three-run bomb to break it open. Left-hander John Koronka, one of several pitchers to get starts in a patchwork rotation, picked up the only win he would earn in a Cubs uniform.

Beset by injuries to position players and the pitching staff, the Cubs never challenged in 2005, finishing in fourth place in the NL Central. Lee was the lone bright spot. He won the NL batting title with a .335 average, slugged a career-high 46 homers with 50 doubles, drove in 107 runs and scored 120. He had 99 extra-base hits, led the league in doubles and slugging percentage (.662) and made a strong run at becoming the Cubs' first MVP since Sammy Sosa in 1998, finishing third behind St. Louis' Albert Pujols and Atlanta's Andruw Jones.

At a Glance

WP: Koronka (1–0)

HR: Lee (17), Perez (6)

Key stat: Lee's 5 hits and 4 RBIs were season highs, as were Perez's 4 hits and 3 RBIs.

Perhaps a truer measure of Lee's worth came the following year, when a broken wrist limited him to 50 games and the Cubs plunged to a 66–96 record that cost Baker and team president Andy MacPhail their jobs.

Baker was heavily criticized for his reliance on veteran players such as Neifi Perez, but the Cubs would have been lost without the versatile switch-hitting infielder after Nomar Garciaparra went out with a torn groin muscle in late April. He didn't return until late August, so Perez took over at shortstop. Perez was 4-for-5 with a double, a homer and three RBIs in this game and wound up hitting .274 with 32 doubles, nine homers and 54 RBIs in 154 games, the most he'd played in since 2000.

As for D-Lee, he was still going deep long after Hee-Seop Choi had gone home to Korea.

A Smooth-Running Kaiser

Don Kaiser was a high school legend as a pitcher in Byng, Okla., winning 49 of 50 decisions, pitching a slew of no-hitters and tossing in an occasional perfect game. A 6-foot-5, 195-pound right-hander, Kaiser was an intriguing investment when the Cubs signed him to a bonus contract out of East Central Oklahoma State University as a 20-year-old in 1955.

According to roster rules then in effect to discourage outlandish spending, "bonus babies" such as Kaiser had to spend two years with the big league club that signed them before they could be sent to the minor leagues for seasoning. Kaiser joined the Cubs shortly after signing in 1955. Used primarily as a mop-up reliever, he compiled a 5.40 ERA with no decisions in 11 appearances.

He was still around in '56, and was pressed into service as a starter for Game 1 of a doubleheader against the Brooklyn Dodgers at Wrigley Field. Kaiser looked right at home—he threw a two-hitter against the defending world champions in his first major league start.

Just 21, Kaiser displayed a touch of first-inning jitters. He walked Pee Wee Reese, then gave up a single to Duke Snider and a sacrifice fly to ex-Cub Ransom Jackson, spotting Brooklyn a 1–0 lead. But after Gil Hodges grounded out to end the first, Kaiser retired the next 17 hitters. Hodges ended his spell with a two-out walk in the seventh, and Reese's ninth-inning single was the Dodgers' only other hit.

> ### At a Glance
>
> **WP:** Kaiser (1–0)
>
> **Key stat:** Though they completed a sweep in Game 2 of the doubleheader, the last-place Cubs were 6–16 against the pennant-winning Dodgers in 1956.

Meanwhile, the Cubs went to work against Brooklyn starter Carl Erskine, scoring twice in the third on a Hobie Landrith walk, singles by Eddie Miksis and Gene Baker and Dee Fondy's RBI groundout. Jim King's double, Moose Moryn's single and Pete Whisenant's sacrifice fly made it a 3–1 game in the fourth, and they broke it open by scoring four runs in the fifth, with King's two-run single the big hit.

Baker went 3-for-3 to lead the Cubs' 13-hit attack. Miksis, Moryn, King, Fondy and Ernie Banks had two hits apiece, and Fondy drove in three runs.

With 20,751 fans looking on, the Cubs completed a sweep with a 5–4 victory in the second game, Bob Rush outpitching Don Newcombe. It was a season highlight—the Cubs closed out April and began May with a seven-game losing streak from which they never seemed to recover.

Kaiser completed his three-season Cubs career with a 6–15 record and a 4.15 ERA in 58 games. He would never pitch in the big leagues again.

Corked Chaos Taints 'His Samminess'

Chicago's once-torrid love affair with Sammy Sosa had begun to cool when the Cubs faced Lou Piniella's Tampa Bay Devil Rays in an interleague game on a mild Tuesday evening at Wrigley Field.

For years, Sosa's slugging had captivated the city—he remains the only player in baseball history with three 60-homer seasons, the most notable a 66-homer barrage in 1998, when he won the National League MVP award for chasing St. Louis' Mark McGwire to the wire in a mesmerizing longball duel that energized baseball. But some diva-like behavior in subsequent years, over issues ranging from his salary demands to his control of clubhouse music, created a perception that "His Samminess" viewed himself as bigger than the team, bigger than baseball. That attitude never goes over well in Chicago, which prefers its heroes humble.

To compound matters, Sosa was off to a rough start in 2003. On April 20, an errant pitch from Pittsburgh's Salomon Torres shattered his batting helmet—he left the game and was lucky to escape serious injury. In mid-May he was put on the disabled list and missed 17 games when he had the toenail removed from his right big toe. Sosa refused a minor league rehabilitation assignment, but he clearly wasn't himself when he returned, going 2 for his first 15 with a five-strikeout game.

At a Glance

WP: Remlinger (4–0)

Key stat: Though he had just six home runs on the night of his corked-bat ejection, Sosa finished with 40 homers, the seventh time in his Cubs career he hit 40 or more.

He hadn't hit a homer since May 1 and had just six for the season when he stepped in against Tampa Bay's Geremi Gonzales, a former Cubs teammate, before 32,210 Wrigley patrons on a perfect night for baseball. Sosa clearly needed something to get him going, something to make him feel like the self-styled "Gladiator" once again. Even if it were inadvertent, as he would claim, the method he chose was as damaging to his reputation as subsequent steroid allegations would be.

With runners at second and third in the first inning, Sosa shattered his bat hitting a weak grounder to Rays second baseman Marlon Anderson. Those keeping score routinely marked "4-3, RBI" as Mark Grudzielanek crossed the plate with the game's first run. They probably didn't notice plate umpire Tim McClelland examining the barrel half of Sosa's splintered bat.

McClelland had spotted something: a half-dollar-sized, grayish-black substance he and his crew identified as cork after they huddled for a closer look.

Sosa was called out and ejected from the game for using an illegal bat, and Grudzielanek was sent back to third base. The Cubs would win, 3–2, when Rays reliever Al Levine wild-pitched the winning run home from third base in the ninth inning. But the story was just beginning.

Sosa could hardly deny that the bat had been doctored, so he didn't try. Instead, he said it was a bat he used to "put on a show" during batting practice, entertaining early-arriving fans by bombing long home runs. He claimed the tricked-out bat wound up among his game bats by accident and he didn't realize he had grabbed it and used it until it was too late.

"It's a mistake, I know that," Sosa said. "It's something I take the blame for. I feel sorry. I apologize to anyone who is embarrassed. I picked the wrong bat— I don't need [to use] that bat. I like to put on a show and make people happy. I do that in batting practice."

Baseball officials immediately confiscated more than two dozen Sosa bats. Because none of them was doctored, they had no choice but to accept his story. He still received an eight-game suspension, which was reduced to seven games on appeal.

Sosa regained his power stroke upon returning to the lineup, finishing with 40 homers, 103 RBIs and a .279 average in helping the Cubs to their first division title since 1989. He was 11-for-42 (.262) with two homers and seven RBIs in 12 postseason games, although a menacing fastball under the chin from Florida's Josh Beckett in Game 5 of the NLCS cooled him off as the Cubs blew a 3–1 lead and lost the series to the Marlins after an epic Game 6 meltdown.

It was never the same for Sammy Sosa in Chicago, and the love affair ended in acrimony a year later when he walked out on the team during the final game of a hugely disappointing season. Sosa was traded to the Baltimore Orioles that winter, and he was wearing a Texas Rangers uniform when he slugged his 600th career homer in 2007, amid allegations that the bulk of those homers had been chemically enhanced. Sosa denies those charges to this day.

Either way, it was a stunning fall from grace.

Kiki Cuyler Connects

If the adage is true, if everything really does "even out" in baseball, perhaps the Cubs' notoriously ill-fated Brock-for-Broglio trade in 1964 was payback for an earlier fleecing of the Pittsburgh Pirates.

In November of 1927, the Pirates concluded that a bitter salary dispute with Hazen Shirley "Kiki" Cuyler was irreconcilable, so they began shopping the standout center fielder. The Cubs were able to land him in exchange for 5-foot-5 infielder Sparky Adams and outfielder/first baseman Pete Scott.

Cuyler, from Harrisville, Mich., was recognized as one of the fastest players in baseball, a prototypical leadoff man. And though he stood just 5-feet-10 and weighed 180 pounds, he espoused the same from-the-heels hitting style as sluggers Rogers Hornsby and Hack Wilson, his Hall of Fame Cub teammates. The style served him well on this Thursday afternoon at Wrigley Field. Facing Brooklyn's Clyde "Pea Ridge" Day with teammate Charlie Grimm on first base and one out in the ninth inning of a 4–4 game, Cuyler, 32, slugged a two-run homer, lifting the Cubs to their 10th win in 12 games.

Les Sweetland went the distance and improved to 5–0 with the victory, but in the months to come he would embody the up-and-down nature of the Cubs' year, finishing 8–7 with a 5.04 ERA. The 1931 season was the 30-year-old left-hander's last one in the big leagues.

At a Glance

WP: Sweetland (5–0)

HR: Cuyler (3), Wilson (3)

Key stat: Sweetland was 5–0 with a 2.98 ERA after this win. He finished 8–7 with a 5.04 ERA in 1931 and was gone from the majors a year later.

The Cubs also got a homer from Wilson, who had begun paying the price for his infamous nocturnal lifestyle. A year after tearing up the National League with 56 homers, a still-standing-record 191 RBIs and a .356 batting average, the stocky slugger hit just .261 with 13 homers and 61 RBIs in 1931.

Wilson's decline was a factor in the Cubs finishing third in the National League with an 84–70 record in the Year of the Cardinal—St. Louis waltzed to the pennant with a 101–53 mark. Cuyler, 3-for-5 on this day, had a typical year with a .330 average, 202 hits and 110 runs scored. He hit nine homers and drove in 88 runs, an impressive total for a leadoff man who arrived via heist.

Julio Leaves the Ballyard

Cardinals	AB	R	H	RBI
Vina 2b	4	0	1	0
Edmonds cf	5	1	1	0
McGwire 1b	3	1	1	0
Marrero 1b	0	0	0	0
Polanco ph	1	0	0	0
Drew rf	3	1	0	0
Pujols 3b	3	1	2	1
Lankford lf	3	1	1	0
Renteria ss	4	1	2	3
Matheny c	4	0	1	1
Hermanson p	2	0	0	0
Christiansen p	0	0	0	0
James p	0	0	0	0
Bonilla ph	1	0	0	0
Benes p	0	0	0	0
Robinson ph	1	0	0	0
Totals	**34**	**6**	**9**	**5**

Cubs	AB	R	H	RBI
Young 2b	5	1	2	0
Gutierrez ss	4	0	1	1
Sosa rf	3	0	0	1
Stairs 1b	4	1	2	1
White lf	3	2	1	1
Coomer 3b	2	2	0	0
Ojeda 3b	1	0	1	0
Hundley c	4	2	2	0
Matthews cf	3	2	2	1
Lieber p	2	1	1	1
Cairo ph	0	0	0	0
Fassero p	0	0	0	0
Zuleta ph	1	1	1	4
Farnsworth p	0	0	0	0
Duncan p	0	0	0	0
Totals	**32**	**12**	**13**	**10**

STL	0	0	5	0	0	0	1	0	-	6	9	0
CHI	0	0	3	1	0	4	4	0	X	-	12	13	0

Cardinals	IP	H	R	ER	BB	SO
Hermanson L (5-4)	5	6	6	6	4	2
Christiansen	0	1	2	2	2	0
James	1	1	0	0	1	1
Benes	2	5	4	4	2	0
Totals	**8**	**13**	**12**	**12**	**9**	**3**

Cubs	IP	H	R	ER	BB	SO
Lieber W (6-3)	6	7	5	5	2	6
Fassero	1	0	0	0	0	1
Farnsworth	1	2	1	1	1	2
Duncan	1	0	0	0	1	1
Totals	**9**	**9**	**6**	**6**	**4**	**10**

DP—Chicago. 2B—St. Louis Vina, Matheny, Edmonds; Chicago Matthews, Ojeda. HR—Chicago Zuleta (6), White (9), Stairs (7). SH—Chicago Cairo. SF—St. Louis Pujols; Chicago Sosa. LOB—St. Louis 6; Chicago 7. Attendance: 37,912.

Don Baylor will remember 2001 as a good year—the Cubs' 88-74, third-place finish was his only winning record in two-plus seasons as their manager.

Jon Lieber will remember it as a great year—he won 20 games for the only time in his career. The sixth of those 20 Lieber victories was largely attributable to Julio Zuleta, a well-traveled journeyman whose Cubs career consisted of 79 games over parts of two seasons. The Panamanian-born first baseman had a night to remember on this balmy Tuesday before 37,912 at Wrigley Field.

Thanks to a four-run sixth inning, the Cubs took an 8–5 lead over St. Louis into the seventh. When they loaded the bases against Cards reliever Alan Benes, Baylor had Zuleta pinch-hit for pitcher Jeff Fassero. With the crowd imploring him to finish off the Cards, Zuleta, 26, pumped a grand slam into the bleachers in left-center field, breaking the game wide open. Walks to Rondell White and Gary Matthews Jr. and Todd Hundley's single loaded the bases for Zuleta, who promptly unloaded them.

Back-to-back homers by White and Matt Stairs had finished Cardinals starter Dustin Hermanson during the Cubs' four-run sixth. They piled up 13 hits off Hermanson and three relievers, with Matthews, Stairs, Hundley and Eric Young collecting two apiece. Lieber (6–3) won it despite giving up five runs and seven hits in six innings.

The Cubs' 12-game winning streak had ended two days earlier. This victory was the first of three in a row.

Zuleta, signed as a 17-year-old out of Panama in 1992, spent seven-plus years in the minors before getting the call to Chicago. He was a classic "4-A player"—too good for Triple-A, not quite good enough for the big leagues, cursed with one flaw that kept him from enjoying a productive career: an inability to hit a breaking ball. At 6-foot-6 and 230 pounds, Zuleta was capable of murdering a fastball, but any pitch with a little wrinkle in it gave him trouble.

Though his on-field contributions were ordinary—he hit .247 with nine home runs and 36 RBIs in 79 games in 2000-01—Zuleta was an extremely popular Cub, personable and cheerful, ever-smiling. Told earlier in the 2001 season that he bore a facial resemblance to Pedro Serrano, the brooding, voodoo-practicing first baseman from the *Major League* movies, Zuleta lined up the Cubs' bats in the dugout and performed a ritual over them to exorcise a team-wide hitting slump.

Unable to find a spot for him in the big leagues, the Cubs sold Zuleta's contract to the Fukuoka Daiei Hawks of the Japanese League later in 2001. Under the tutelage of Japanese hitting legend Sadharu Oh, Zuleta became an accomplished slugger overseas, hitting .319 with 43 homers and 99 RBIs in 2005 and wrapping up his career by playing two seasons for Bobby Valentine with the Chiba Lotte Marines.

Zuleta also played a year in the Mexican League and represented his native Panama in the 2009 World Baseball Classic. He's still involved with baseball, operating an indoor batting cage and offering hitting instruction in his adopted hometown of Fort Myers, Fla.

Cubs-Cardinals, of course, was the baseball story of the day in Chicago on June 5, but the Cubs made some news off the field as well. With the second overall pick in the amateur draft, they took Mark Prior, a heralded pitching prospect from Southern California. Prior was in the big leagues by 2002 and gone by 2007. His fortunes would mirror those of a star-crossed franchise.

Don Baylor

The 2001 season was by far the most successful of Don Baylor's 2 ½ years as Cubs manager; the team went 88–74 and finished third. After third baseman Bill Mueller's season-ending knee injury in June, Baylor platooned at five positions; only right fielder Sammy Sosa, shortstop Ricky Gutierrez, and second baseman Eric Young were assured of everyday duty.

Julio Zuleta shared time at first base with 5-foot-9 fireplug Matt Stairs and got into 49 games, hitting .217 with six homers and 24 RBIs in 106 at-bats. His days as a Cub were numbered when Fred McGriff arrived in a trade with Tampa Bay in July; McGriff took over as the regular first baseman. They also had Hee Seop Choi working his way through the system, which prompted the Cubs to part ways with McGriff after he hit 30 homers and drove in 103 runs in 2002.

Lucky Lindy Does It with His Arm and His Bat

Longevity and versatility were the hallmarks of Lindy McDaniel's distinguished pitching career.

An early proponent of the forkball that made Pittsburgh's Elroy Face famous, McDaniel combined unerring control with uncommon durability over 21 years with five teams. Long, lean and limber, he had 15 wins as a 21-year-old starter for the Cardinals in 1957 and 12 as a 37-year-old reliever for the Yankees in 1973. He collected 26 saves for the Cardinals in 1960 and 29 for the Yankees 10 years later.

A reliever for most of his career because of his ability to get ready quickly and pitch often, McDaniel spent three of those 21 years with the Cubs, arriving in 1963 to enjoy one of his best seasons. After coming over from the Cardinals with pitcher Larry Jackson and catcher Jimmy Schaffer in a trade for outfielder George Altman, pitcher Don Cardwell and catcher Moe Thacker, McDaniel compiled a 13–7 record with a 2.86 ERA and 22 saves in 57 games. He struck out 75 and walked just 27 (five of them intentionally) in 88 innings.

And with darkness falling on a cool Thursday afternoon at Wrigley Field, McDaniel turned in a performance that 11,240 eyewitnesses will never forget, even though he faced just one batter.

Having won the first three games of a four-game series with the San Francisco Giants, the Cubs were gunning for a sweep that would move them into a tie for first place in the National League—heady stuff for a team that had known more good times than bad since its last pennant in 1945. Pitcher Juan Marichal, one of four eventual Hall of Famers who took the field for the Giants, had outdueled Larry Jackson and took a four-hit shutout and a 2–0 lead into the eighth inning. But Ken Hubbs kept the inning alive with a two-out double and Billy Williams followed with a game-tying homer, forcing extra innings after neither team scored in the ninth.

Chuck Hiller opened the Giants' 10th with a

Giants	AB	R	H	RBI
Hiller 2b	5	1	2	0
Mays cf	5	1	3	1
McCovey lf	4	0	0	0
Alou lf	0	0	0	0
Cepeda 1b	3	0	0	0
Bailey c	5	0	2	1
Alou rf	4	0	0	0
Davenport 3b	4	0	1	0
Pagan ss	4	0	2	0
Marichal p	3	0	0	0
Pierce p	0	0	0	0
Totals	37	2	10	2

Cubs	AB	R	H	RBI
Brock rf	4	0	0	0
Hubbs 2b	4	1	1	0
Williams lf	3	1	2	2
Santo 3b	3	0	1	0
Banks 1b	4	0	0	0
Rodgers ss	4	0	0	0
Landrum cf	4	0	1	0
Bertell c	4	0	1	0
Jackson p	2	0	0	0
Will ph	1	0	0	0
Schultz p	0	0	0	0
McDaniel p	1	1	1	1
Totals	34	3	7	3

											R	H	E
SF	1	0	0	0	0	0	1	0	0	-	2	10	1
CHI	0	0	0	0	0	0	0	2	0	1	-	3	7	0

Giants	IP	H	R	ER	BB	SO
Marichal	9	6	2	2	2	7
Pierce L (1-4)	0	1	1	1	0	0
Totals	9	7	3	3	2	7

Cubs	IP	H	R	ER	BB	SO
Jackson	8	8	2	2	0	5
Schultz	1.1	2	0	0	1	2
McDaniel W (3-1)	0.2	0	0	0	0	1
Totals	10	10	2	2	1	8

E—San Francisco Bailey. 2B—San Francisco Hiller, Pagan; Chicago Hubbs. HR—Chicago McDaniel (1), Williams (7). SH—San Francisco Alou, Marichal. HBP—San Francisco Cepeda. LOB—San Francisco 9; Chicago 6. Attendance: 11,240.

single off Cubs reliever Barney Schultz. Willie Mays followed with another single, and Matty Alou sacrificed the runners to second and third. After an intentional walk to Orlando Cepeda loaded the bases, Cubs manager Bob Kennedy summoned McDaniel to replace Schultz. Talk about an escape act ...

Having noticed that Mays was wandering too far off second base, catcher Dick Bertell called a pickoff play. McDaniel whirled and fired a strike to short-stop Andre Rodgers, catching the great Mays as he scrambled back to second. He then struck out catcher Ed Bailey on three pitches to end the inning.

Kennedy figured McDaniel was on a roll, so he let him hit for himself leading off the Cubs' 10th. Longtime Chicago favorite Billy Pierce was on in relief for the Giants, and when his 2-2 pitch got too much of the plate, McDaniel pumped it over the left-field wall for a game-winning homer, the second of three he would hit in the big leagues and his first since 1957.

"I'll always remember it," McDaniel said. "I got a standing ovation as I walked to the dugout after picking off Willie Mays and striking out Ed Bailey. I was the first batter in the bottom of the 10th and I hit a home run to win the game. The entire team was waiting for me at home plate. The crowd was going crazy, and I received a prolonged standing ovation as I ran the bases. You know those Cub fans."

The Cubs improved to 31–23 with their fifth straight win and seventh in eight games. They seemed invigorated under Kennedy, who had put an end to the silly "college of coaches" rotation and declared himself the manager when he was hired to run the club before the '63 season. An 82–80 finish gave the Cubs their first winning season since 1946.

McDaniel had a 141–119 record with a 3.45 ERA and 172 saves in his career. He was a useful contributor over his three Chicago seasons, going 19–20 with a 3.06 ERA and 39 saves. He continued to help the Cubs after his departure; the December 1965 trade that sent McDaniel and outfielder Don Landrum to the Giants brought catcher Randy Hundley and pitcher Bill Hands to Chicago. Both enjoyed several productive years with the Cubs.

Finally, there's this: In the final transaction of his career, McDaniel was dealt from the Yankees to the Kansas City Royals on Dec. 7, 1973. The player he was traded for? Lou Piniella.

History ... and a Big Bang

This was the captivating tableau Baseball Commissioner Bud Selig had in mind when he began pushing for interleague play in the mid-1990s.

The New York Yankees and all the history that accompanies them appearing at Wrigley Field, one of the game's most storied venues. The visit would be their first since the 1938 World Series. Watching the Captain, Derek Jeter, and his fellow Pinstripers warming up on the field where Cubs legends Ernie Banks, Billy Williams, and Ryne Sandberg had created so many memories was one of those priceless baseball moments.

There was a definite buzz in the air for Friday's series opener, and the Yankees felt right at home, winning 5–3 behind David Wells before a full house. The crowd was into it, but if the game had the feeling of a prelim, it was understandable—Saturday's Game 2 was the highly anticipated main event, with Yankees ace Roger Clemens going for his 300th career victory. His opponent? Kerry Wood, who had grown up trying to emulate his fireballing fellow Texan. Wood-Clemens comparisons had been commonplace since 1998, when Wood, just 20 years old, matched Clemens' single-game record for strikeouts with 20 in his fifth major league start.

Every seat in the ballpark was occupied, and the surrounding rooftops were filled to overflowing for a pitching duel that lived up to the hype as the flinty-eyed Texans matched zeroes through three innings. In the Yankees' fourth, a frightening, freakish development almost overshadowed the entire weekend.

With Jason Giambi at the plate, the Cubs overloaded the right side of the field, as teams often did when facing the left-handed-hitting slugger. Third baseman Lenny Harris was playing near second base and had no chance at the towering infield popup Giambi hit when he batted with the bases empty and one out. Catcher Damian Miller never picked up the ball in the mid-day sun, but Wood and first baseman Hee Seop Choi did, and both gave chase.

At a Glance

WP: Wood (5–4)

HR: Karros (6)

Key stat: Choi, batting .244 with 7 homers and 22 RBIs when he was injured, finished with a .218 average to go along with 8 homers and 28 RBIs.

Neither heard the other call for it amid the din in the ballpark, and the two big men came together in a high-speed collision between the pitcher's mound and the third-base line. Choi fell to the ground and was knocked out when the back of his head slammed into the Wrigley Field turf. Somehow, he held onto the ball. He was momentarily unconscious, and still groggy but talking and moving his hands and feet when an ambulance pulled in through the gate in the right-field corner to take him to Illinois Masonic Hospital.

Wood, obviously shaken, observed the scene from one knee. "I've never seen anything like that on a ballfield. It was scary," he said. "But once he was able to talk and squeeze some fingers before he left the field, I felt better."

Dusty Baker retrieved the ball Choi had held onto so gamely and handed it to an ambulance attendant, with instructions to give it to "Big Choi" when he came to. With play about to resume, Baker visited the mound and urged Wood to "cowboy up"—to put the frightful incident behind him and go back to work. In the best Texas tradition, Wood did.

Hideki Matsui's solo home run in the fifth inning was the only run he allowed, but it gave the Yankees a 1–0 lead, which Clemens nursed into the seventh. Clemens was under duress because of a bronchial condition, though, and manager Joe Torre decided Clemens had gone far enough after Sammy Sosa reached him for a one-out single and Moises Alou walked. Juan Acevedo came on to face Eric Karros, who had taken over for Choi. Karros, a professional hitter, figured Acevedo would try to get ahead of him with a fastball, and he was ready for it. Bat meeting ball sounded like a rifle shot as Karros drove Acevedo's first pitch on a line into the bleachers in left-center field for a three-run homer.

"I cried," Wood's wife Sarah said later. "I know there's no crying in baseball, but I cried when Eric Karros hit that home run. I just knew what it meant to Kerry."

There was a lot of baseball to be played before anyone would celebrate. Singles by Matsui and Ruben Sierra and a walk to Jeter filled the bases with two outs in the Yankees' eighth. Wood departed to a standing ovation as left-hander Mike Remlinger came on to face Giambi. With the crowd on its feet, Remlinger struck him out on a gutsy 3-2 change-up.

The Cubs added two insurance runs in the eighth on singles by Ramon Martinez and Sosa and Alex Gonzalez's RBI double, but the Yankees didn't go quietly. Jorge Posada took Joe Borowski deep leading off the ninth, and the tying run came to the plate after Raul Mondesi and Matsui singled. But Borowski bore down and got pinch-hitter Todd Zeile on a groundout, preserving the Cubs' 5–2 victory.

Clemens' 300th win would have to wait one more start. Wood was the better man on this day, surrendering a run on just three hits while striking out 11 in 7 2/3 innings.

"Roger was one of my idols growing up," Wood said. "When he takes the mound, he gives off the attitude that 'You're not going to beat me—it's my mound, it's my plate, it's my game.' I just like the way he goes about it. I admire his whole pitching demeanor."

This was Kerry Wood's 50th victory in a Cubs uniform. None was more satisfying.

Mighty Moe Had the 'Mo' in One-Hitter

Moe Drabowsky, just 22, was one of four young, strong, talented right-handed pitchers whom the Cubs envisioned as their starting rotation for years to come as they all reached the big leagues in the late '50s.

Drabowsky, born in Poland and raised in Connecticut, signed for a $75,000 bonus and put together a 13–15 record with a 3.53 ERA in 1957, his first full season. The 239 $\frac{1}{3}$ innings he pitched as a 21-year-old hadn't yet caught up with him when he faced the hard-hitting Pirates on an overcast Sunday afternoon before 15,670 fans at Wrigley Field.

Drabowsky encountered a bit of trouble in the second inning when muscular slugger Ted Kluszewski led off with a broken-bat single that barely reached the outfield and Frank Thomas walked. But he coaxed a double-play grounder from Roberto Clemente and retired Bill Mazeroski on a fly to center, and that was it for the Pirates.

They had only two more baserunners all day: Clemente, who reached on an error in the fifth and was erased in a double play, and Bill Virdon, who reached on an error in the sixth. Drabowsky retired the last 10 hitters in order, completing his one-hitter with a lone walk and five strikeouts. It was the best game he pitched as a Cub.

Ernie Banks backed him with a solo home run off loser Ronnie Kline in the fourth inning, and after a 52-minute rain delay, Moose Moryn delivered a two-run shot in the eighth.

Drabowsky began experiencing arm problems during the '58 season, finishing 9–11 with a 4.51 ERA. They would recur throughout his time with the Cubs, and he was perceived as damaged goods when he was dealt to the Milwaukee Braves in 1961.

If Drabowsky was a victim of overwork, he wasn't alone. Dick Drott was the most intriguing of

Pirates	AB	R	H	RBI
Virdon cf	4	0	0	0
Skinner lf	4	0	0	0
Groat ss	3	0	0	0
Kluszewski 1b	3	0	1	0
Thomas 3b	2	0	0	0
Clemente rf	3	0	0	0
Mazeroski 2b	3	0	0	0
Foiles c	3	0	0	0
Kline p	2	0	0	0
Smith p	0	0	0	0
Powers ph	1	0	0	0
Totals	28	0	1	0

Cubs	AB	R	H	RBI
Adams 2b	4	0	1	0
Dark 3b	3	0	0	0
Walls rf	3	0	0	0
Banks ss	3	2	1	1
Moryn lf	4	1	3	2
Long 1b	4	1	1	0
Taylor c	4	0	0	0
Thomson cf	3	0	1	0
Drabowsky p	4	0	1	0
Totals	32	4	8	3

```
PIT  0 0 0 0 0 0 0 0 0 - 0 1 1
CHI  0 0 0 1 0 0 0 3 X - 4 8 2
```

Pirates	IP	H	R	ER	BB	SO
Kline L (6-6)	7.2	8	4	3	3	7
Smith	0.1	0	0	0	0	0
Totals	8	8	4	3	3	7

Cubs	IP	H	R	ER	BB	SO
Drabowsky W (4-5)	9	1	0	0	1	5
Totals	9	1	0	0	1	5

E—Pittsburgh Thomas; Chicago Banks, Adams. DP—Pittsburgh; Chicago 2. 2B—Chicago Thomson, Long. 3B—Chicago Adams. HR—Chicago Banks (17), Moryn (12). HBP—Chicago Thomson. LOB—Pittsburgh 2; Chicago 8. Attendance: 15,670.

Moe Drabowsky pitched a one-hitter on June 8, 1958. It ended up being a career highlight during his 17 seasons in the major leagues.

the Cubs' young starters, having compiled a 15–11 record with a 3.58 ERA and 170 strikeouts in 1957. But 229 innings may have been too much for his 21-year-old arm—Drott was an ineffective 12–35 over the remainder of his brief career.

Bob Anderson was 23 when he pitched 235 innings in 1959, and Glen Hobbie worked 234 innings as a 23-year-old and 258 $^2/_3$ innings at age 24. All three were out of baseball before they turned 30.

Drabowsky, though, reinvented himself as a reliever and pitched until he was 36, enjoying his greatest success with the Baltimore Orioles. He went 21–11 with a 2.33 ERA and 27 saves in four seasons. In the 1966 World Series, he replaced a struggling Dave McNally in the third inning of Game 1 and set a Series record for relievers by striking out 11 Dodgers. The Orioles won 5–2 and went on to a stunning four-game sweep.

Drabowsky was a direct participant in three other baseball milestones. Pitching for the Cubs, he gave up Stan Musial's 3,000[th] hit in May of 1958 at Wrigley Field. Pitching for the Kansas City Athletics, he was the losing pitcher when Cleveland's Early Wynn won his 300th game in July of 1963. Pitching for the Kansas City Royals, he earned the first victory in franchise history in April of 1969.

He also carried a well-earned reputation as a mischief-maker, particularly adept with bullpen phones. It was not uncommon for Drabowsky to get on the phone and order Chinese takeout for the opposing team in parks all over baseball. Once, while Jim Nash was pitching a two-hit shutout against the Orioles, Drabowsky called the Kansas City bullpen with a terse order to "get [Lew] Krausse up"—in the fifth inning.

Moe Drabowsky was 70 when he died of cancer in 2006. He had an 88–105 lifetime record with a 3.71 ERA and 55 saves in 17 seasons. He was a proud competitor who took his work seriously, but never himself.

Lighting the Lamp

Dennis Lamp managed a 7–15 record in his first year as a major league starter, although a 3.29 ERA would suggest he pitched better than 7–15 indicates.

Three of his seven wins were shutouts, too, including this game: a one-hitter, with Gene Richards' two-out single to left in the sixth inning the only thing keeping the performance from being one for the record book.

And yet, a one-hitter by a 7–15 pitcher who would fall to 2–10 by losing his next five starts was not the most unusual occurrence in a Friday matinee witnessed by 15,570 fans at Wrigley Field.

Slugger Dave Kingman, who went for the downs on every swing, reached base on a bunt single in the sixth inning. Kingman, notorious for wearing an iron glove in the outfield, made two nice running catches in left field.

Gold Glove infielders Ozzie Smith and Manny Trillo, meanwhile, each made an error.

Lamp, a .205 hitter with three RBIs all season, got two of them with run-scoring singles in the second and sixth innings.

The Cubs improved to 31–21 with their seventh win in eight games and would move a season-best 11 games over .500 three days later. But inconsistency would characterize their play thereafter and they'd finish 79–83.

Lamp, the Cubs' third-round pick in the 1971 amateur draft, was 25 when he took the mound to oppose Padres lefty Bob Owchinko. In the second inning he walked Gene Tenace. Lamp then retired the next 13 hitters before Richards ended the no-hit suspense by rifling a sharp single to left field with two out in the sixth.

Kingman had given him a 2–0 lead with a two-run, first-inning homer, his league-high 13th. Lamp singled home Steve Ontiveros during the Cubs' two-run second, and in the sixth, after Kingman stunned the Padres with his bunt single, Lamp brought him home with a bases-loaded infield hit.

A 5–0 lead put Lamp in a comfort zone. He struck out only two, but used a heavy sinker to record 13 ground-ball outs, while Kingman ran down most everything hit to the outfield—he really did.

Lamp improved to 2–5 with his second major league shutout, but six weeks would pass before he'd win again, getting to 3–10 with another victory over the Padres on July 23.

At a Glance

WP: Lamp (2–5)

HR: Kingman (13)

Key stat: Lamp and Juan Pizarro are the only pitchers to throw one-hitters for both the Cubs and White Sox.

Bombs Away for Phillips

Seventeen years before the fabled "Sandberg Game," there was "the Adolfo Phillips Game." Games, really, as the 25-year-old center fielder's power show encompassed both ends of a doubleheader sweep of the Mets on a warm, blustery Sunday at Wrigley Field.

At a Glance

Game 1

WP: Jenkins (8–3)

HR: Phillips (8)

Game 2

WP: Hartenstein (1–1)

S: Radatz (2)

HR: Phillips 3 (9, 10, 11), Hundley 2 (6, 7), Santo (8), Banks (9)

Key stat: The Cubs set a club record with seven home runs in Game 2. They have done it three times.

Spectacular as he was in slugging three homers and driving in seven runs in Game 2, after he'd hit a second-inning solo homer to help Fergie Jenkins to victory in Game 1, Phillips only heightened the mystery as to why he didn't achieve the stardom long predicted for him.

"He was the most disappointing player I ever managed," Leo Durocher once said, although Durocher's clumsy handling of the super-sensitive Panamanian was believed to have been a factor in Phillips' decline.

On this day, though, he validated the Willie Mays comparisons Durocher and others made after Phillips was acquired from Philadelphia with Jenkins and outfielder John Herrnstein for aging pitchers Bob Buhl and Larry Jackson in 1966. Jenkins had come up through the Phillies organization with Phillips and knew him well.

"He had great talent. He did things easily, without strain or strenuous effort," Jenkins said. "He had a strong arm, he could run, and he hit for power and average."

Phillips' three-run homer gave the Cubs a 9–4 lead in the third inning of Game 2. He hit a two-run homer in the fifth and a solo blast in the sixth, staking the Cubs to a 16–5 advantage. Randy Hundley homered twice and Ron Santo and Ernie Banks once each as the Cubs went deep seven times. The teams combined for a record-setting 11 homers in the Wrigley Field jet stream, with the Mets hitting three of their four in the ninth inning.

Phillips finished the day hitting .314, with a team-high 11 homers and 38 RBIs. He was the toast of Chicago. But his tenure would be short-lived. He batted just .223 with four homers and 22 RBIs after July 1. Phillips was in and out of the lineup in '68, hitting .241 with 13 homers and just 33 RBIs. He lost his job to rookie Don Young in the spring of '69 when Durocher decided Phillips was too slow recovering from a wrist injury he suffered when he was hit by a pitch in spring training.

The Cubs finally gave up on Phillips and traded him to Montreal for utility infielder Paul Popovich in June of 1969. They were left with a troublesome hole in center field when Young failed to hit, one reason for their infamous late-season collapse.

Phillips underwent surgery for a stomach disorder in 1970. "Adolfo was extremely sensitive," Jenkins said. "He had an ulcer caused by worry, pressure that had been put on him by Durocher and his teammates. He had to take tranquilizers to settle his nerves."

Phillips played in 12 games for the Cleveland Indians in 1972, then vanished from baseball, finished at age 30. No one among the 19,247 who were at Wrigley for "the Phillips game" five years earlier would have thought that was possible.

The Day the Story Was off the Field

Expos	AB	R	H	RBI
Raines cf	3	1	0	0
Rose 1b	3	1	3	1
Dawson rf	4	1	1	1
Carter c	4	0	1	1
Ramos c	0	0	0	0
Wallach 3b	4	1	1	1
Wohlford lf	2	0	0	0
Lucas p	0	0	0	0
McGaffigan p	0	0	0	0
Dilone ph	1	0	0	0
Reardon p	0	0	0	0
Flynn ss	2	0	0	0
James p	0	0	0	0
Francona ph-lf	2	0	0	0
Thomas 2b-ss	4	0	1	0
Rogers p	1	0	0	0
Little 2b	3	0	1	0
Totals	33	4	8	4

Cubs	AB	R	H	RBI
Dernier cf	2	1	0	0
Sandberg 2b	5	2	3	0
Matthews lf	4	2	2	1
Cotto lf	0	0	0	0
Durham 1b	5	1	3	2
Hall rf	3	1	1	0
Woods ph-rf	2	0	0	0
Davis c	3	0	1	2
Cey 3b	3	0	2	2
Bowa ss	4	0	2	0
Trout p	3	0	0	0
Stoddard p	0	0	0	0
Johnstone ph	1	0	0	0
Smith p	0	0	0	0
Totals	35	7	14	7

MON 0 0 0 0 1 3 0 0 0 - 4 8 1
CHI 0 1 2 0 1 3 0 0 X - 7 14 0

Expos	IP	H	R	ER	BB	SO
Rogers	4.1	9	4	3	4	1
James	0.2	1	0	0	0	0
Lucas L (0-1)	0.1	2	3	3	1	1
McGaffigan	1.2	1	0	0	0	1
Reardon	1	1	0	0	0	2
Totals	8	14	7	6	5	5

Cubs	IP	H	R	ER	BB	SO
Trout	5.1	3	2	2	2	3
Stoddard W (4-1)	1.2	4	2	2	2	1
Smith S (12)	2	1	0	0	0	3
Totals	9	8	4	4	4	7

E—Montreal Raines. DP—Montreal 2; Chicago 2. 2B—Montreal Dawson; Chicago Davis, Durham 2. 3B—Montreal Rose; Chicago Sandberg. HR—Montreal Wallach (10). SF—Chicago Cey. LOB—Montreal 6; Chicago 10. SB—Chicago Hall. Attendance: 22,388.

The alarm bells that sounded as the Cubs were taking their lumps in Arizona pretty much abated with the start of the regular season, quieted by a late March trade that brought Gary Matthews and Bob Dernier from the Phillies and gave the team a stronger looking outfield.

A crowd of 22,388 showed up at Wrigley Field on this Wednesday afternoon to see Steve Trout oppose Montreal's stingy Steve Rogers, who'd had the Cubs' number over the years. Not this time. The Cubs collected nine hits and four walks in 4 $\frac{1}{3}$ innings off Rogers, won for the fourth time in five games and moved a season-best nine games over .500 (34-25) despite squandering a 4–1 lead.

Bigger news was unfolding as the game was being played.

Ryne Sanberg was 3-for-5 with a triple, Leon Durham was 3-for-5 with two doubles and two RBIs and Ron Cey and Jody Davis also drove in two runs apiece. Durham and Davis had run-scoring doubles as the Cubs scored three times in the sixth inning to break a 4–4 tie the Expos created with three runs off Trout and reliever Tim Stoddard in the top of the sixth.

Immediately after Lee Smith pitched two scoreless innings for the save, the Cubs announced completion of a trade with Cleveland: outfielders Joe Carter and Mel Hall went to the Indians with two minor leaguers for pitchers Rick Sutcliffe and George Frazier and catcher Ron Hassey.

Sutcliffe, the 1979 NL Rookie of the Year with the Dodgers, had been banished to Cleveland after throwing a tantrum in manager Tom Lasorda's

Coming off consecutive All-Star seasons in 1982 and 1983, Leon Durham helped the Cubs advance to the 1984 National League Championship Series.

office when he learned he had been left off the 1981 postseason roster. He won 31 games in his first two seasons with the Indians and was off to a 4–5 start in '84, but a return to the National League was like a trip to Lourdes—Sutcliffe was a phenomenal 16–1 in pitching the Cubs into the postseason for the first time since 1945. He clinched the division title with a two-hitter at Pittsburgh on Sept. 24 and was a hands-down winner of the Cy Young Award as the NL's top pitcher.

The season was taking on storybook overtones when Sutcliffe blanked the Padres 13–0 in the NLCS opener and blasted a long home run. The Cubs won again the next day for a 2–0 lead in the best-of-five series, but they failed to get the job done in San Diego and extended two dubious streaks: 39 years without a World Series appearance, 76 years without winning one.

The trade was no steal—Joe Carter put together an exceptional career with five teams and won two World Series rings with the Toronto Blue Jays, one because of a Series-clinching homer he hit off the Phillies' Mitch Williams in 1993.

But Rick Sutcliffe was responsible for a lot of Wrigley Field magic. He earned his 'C.'

Rick Sutcliffe

Rick Sutcliffe, as competitive as he was professional as a big league pitcher, didn't react well when manager Tom Lasorda told him he was being left off the Dodgers' roster for the 1981 postseason. The big right-hander was 5–11 with a 5.10 ERA in the two seasons following his Rookie of the Year campaign in 1979.

Lasorda's Dodger Stadium office was a shrine to the Hollywood glitterati with whom he liked to hobnob, and Sutcliffe did a number on it, sweeping several artifacts off Lasorda's desk and onto the floor.

After the Dodgers won the 1981 World Series, Lasorda retaliated by exiling Sutcliffe to Cleveland, which must have seemed like Siberia after three years in Los Angeles. Two years later the Cubs rescued him in one of the best trades of the Dallas Green era. Sutcliffe showed his appreciation by pitching them to NL East title.

Making Spahn Work OT

Hall of Famer Warren Spahn was a 20-game winner 13 times in 17 years for the Boston/Milwaukee Braves between 1947 and 1963. His 363 career victories are the most ever by a left-handed pitcher. But it was games like this that helped saddle Spahn with a career-worst 19 losses in 1952, despite a 2.98 ERA in 290 innings.

Spahn went the distance in a 15-inning loss, one of 19 complete games he pitched as a 31-year-old that season. He matched Bob Feller's major league record with 18 strikeouts, although baseball didn't recognize it as a record because he required extra innings. He hit a home run for the Braves' only run of the day.

But the Braves' lineup was typically anemic, managing just four hits in those 15 innings off Cubs starter Willard Ramsdell and reliever Johnny Klippstein, who got the win after allowing two hits and no walks in eight innings of scoreless relief. The Braves were playing out the string in Boston, en route to a 64–89, seventh-place finish. The paltry crowd of 3,015 was typical, even for a summer Sunday.

Spahn, always capable of helping himself with the bat, led off the sixth inning with a home run off Ramsdell, one of two he would hit that year. Lifetime, Spahn was a .194 hitter with 35 homers and 189 RBIs.

He nursed his 1–0 lead through eight innings and was three outs away from a shutout victory when Bill Serena led off the ninth with a homer, the sixth of 15 the third baseman from California would hit in a career year.

The 1–1 deadlock stood until the Cubs' 15th, when Roy Smalley reached on a one-out walk and Klippstein bunted him to second. After an intentional walk to Eddie Miksis, Hal Jeffcoat delivered a two-run triple. Spahn took his fifth loss in 11 decisions when the Braves failed to score in their half of the 15th.

At a Glance

WP: Klippstein (4–4)

HR: Serena (6)

Key stat: The Cubs and the Braves played 15 innings in 3 hours, 14 minutes. There were 14 hits in the game, but only 5 walks.

Serena's homer was his only hit in seven at-bats; he struck out three times, as did Hank Sauer and Dee Fondy. Jeffcoat was an unlikely hitting star; he would bat .219 with four homers and 30 RBIs that season. In 1954 the strong-armed center fielder would make a full-time switch to pitching and compile a 39–37 record with a 4.22 ERA over the next six years.

The Cubs improved to a season-best 34–19 with their 10th win in 11 games. The next day they embarked on a nine-game losing streak on their way to a 77–77 finish.

Back...Back...Back... Sosa Chalks up Three of His 20 Homers in June

June was the month in which Sammy Sosa forcefully announced his presence in the Great Home Run Race of 1998. This Monday night meeting with Milwaukee before a full house at Wrigley Field was an exclamation point to his statement.

Sosa went deep against Milwaukee starter Cal Eldred with two outs in the first inning, a solo shot. He hit another bases-empty blast off Eldred with one out in the third. In the seventh, he reached the seats for the third time in the evening. Sosa began June with 13 home runs and finished it with 33, his 20 for the month setting a major league record that still stands. Eldred was one of his favorite foils— Sosa was 5-for-17 lifetime with four homers against the big Iowa-born right-hander.

In June alone, Sosa had this three-homer game, three two-homer games, a stretch of at least one homer in four straight games and a five-homer flurry in three games. He was in hot pursuit of St. Louis' Mark McGwire, who would finish the season with 70 homers to Sosa's 66. Their joint assault on Roger Maris' single-season record of 61, which had stood since 1961, was credited with revitalizing baseball.

Both men had transformed themselves into muscle-bound hulks as they approached baseball middle age, and the frequency of their home runs, combined with the distance they traveled, prompted speculation that there might be more to their regimen than weightlifting or an extra milk shake at the training table. But the baseball hierarchy and most fans seemed too caught up in long-ball excitement to concern themselves with the drug issue, even after a non-prescription performance-enhancer turned up in McGwire's locker.

Sosa, meanwhile, tried to allay any suspicion

Brewers	AB	R	H	RBI
Vina 2b	3	0	0	0
Cirillo 3b	3	1	1	0
Burnitz rf	3	0	0	1
Jaha 1b	3	0	0	1
Jackson pr	0	0	0	0
Jones p	0	0	0	0
Nilsson lf	2	1	0	1
Grissom cf	4	0	1	0
Valentin ss	4	1	1	2
Hughes c	3	1	0	0
Eldred p	2	0	0	0
Hamelin ph-1b	1	1	0	0
Totals	28	5	3	5

Cubs	AB	R	H	RBI
Brown cf-lf	4	0	0	0
Morandini 2b	4	0	0	0
Sosa rf	4	3	3	3
Grace 1b	4	0	2	0
Rodriguez lf	4	0	0	0
Beck p	0	0	0	0
Hernandez 3b	4	1	2	0
Martinez c	3	1	2	0
Servais c	1	0	1	0
Alexander ss	3	1	1	2
Wood p	3	0	1	1
Adams p	0	0	0	0
Lowery ph-cf	1	0	0	0
Totals	35	6	12	6

MIL	0 2 0 0 0 0 3 0 - 5 3 0
CHI	1 2 1 0 0 0 1 1 X - 6 12 0

Brewers	IP	H	R	ER	BB	SO
Eldred	7	10	5	5	0	6
Jones L (3-3)	1	2	1	1	0	1
Totals	8	12	6	6	0	7

Cubs	IP	H	R	ER	BB	SO
Wood	7.1	3	5	5	6	9
Adams W (6-3)	0.2	0	0	0	1	0
Beck S (17)	1	0	0	0	0	1
Totals	9	3	5	5	7	10

DP—Chicago. 2B—Chicago Martinez; Alexander. 3B—Chicago Hernandez. HR— Milwaukee Valentin (9); Chicago Sosa 3 (22,23,24). SF—Chicago Alexander. HBP— Milwaukee Vina. LOB—Milwaukee 4; Chicago 6. SB—Chicago Martinez. Attendance: 37,903.

with humor, ascribing his feats of strength to Flintstone vitamins. Subsequent events strongly suggest he was being disingenuous, and McGwire eventually came clean about his steroid use. But theirs was a feel-good story at the time it was unfolding.

Sosa was the undisputed star of the show at Wrigley for much of his Cubs career, and this game was an example of why—it didn't have much to offer outside of his three home runs.

Jose Valentin's two-run, second-inning homer was the only damaging hit among the three Kerry Wood allowed in 7 $\frac{1}{3}$ innings. The Cubs built a 5–2 lead on Sosa's homers, Wood's RBI single and Manny Alexander's run-scoring double. But Wood's control deserted him in the eighth. He walked three batters and reliever Terry Adams walked a fourth as the Brewers tied the game with just one hit—Jeff Cirillo's bunt single.

In the Cubs' eighth, singles by Jose Hernandez and Scott Servais put runners at first and third for Alexander, and he delivered the go-ahead run with a sacrifice fly. Rod Beck pitched a scoreless ninth for his 17th save.

Summer was starting to get very interesting on the North Side.

Did You Know?

It's difficult to compare players from different eras, and Babe Ruth was never dogged by steroid allegations. That being said, it can be argued that during his four peak years with the Cubs, Sammy Sosa was the most prolific slugger in baseball history.

Sosa is the only player with three 60-homer seasons, and the 50 he hit in 2000 gave him a four-season total of 243 from 1998 to 2001. He also drove in 597 runs and batted .310 during that period.

Barry Bonds became the single-season record-holder when he blasted 73 home runs in 2001, but that was the only year he exceeded 50 homers. From 2000 to 2003, Bonds hit 213 homers and drove in 443 runs while batting .334.

Babe Ruth's only 60-homer season came in 1927. From 1926–29 he hit 207 homers, but he drove in 606 runs and batted .348.

Long-Ball Lou

Brock-for-Broglio. The mere mention of the most disastrous trade in franchise history is enough give a Cubs fan indigestion.

Lou Brock was a raw 22-year-old when he came to the Cubs late in 1961, blessed with breathtaking speed and undeniable potential. But the Cubs had come to question whether he'd ever fulfill his potential in Chicago, and in June of 1964 they traded him to the Cardinals for a badly needed pitcher, Ernie Broglio.

Every Cubs fan knows the sad story. Brock became a Hall of Fame left fielder for the Cardinals, setting numerous stolen-base records and playing on three pennant winners. Broglio was a sore-armed shadow of his former self who would win just seven games in a Cubs uniform.

The specter of Brock-for-Broglio looms over every trade the Cubs have made in 46 subsequent years.

Brock was still a Cub when they faced the expansion New York Mets in a Sunday doubleheader at the Polo Grounds. In his first at-bat in the first inning of the first game, with Ron Santo on third after a two-run triple, Brock flashed some of that tantalizing potential. Turning on a fastball from left-hander Al Jackson, he drove the ball on a line over the wall in dead center field, about 480 feet from home plate. Only two other players reached that distant region of the venerable old ballpark. Those who were there still remember the rifle-shot crack of the bat.

"Lou wasn't known as a power hitter, but he had a lot of strength in his hands and wrists and he could get his bat through the zone really quick," teammate Billy Williams recalled. "He hit that ball about as far as I ever saw anybody hit one."

At a Glance

Game 1

WP: Gerard (1–0)

S: Elston (6)

HR: Brock (7), Banks (18)

Brock's massive homer, on the day before his 23rd birthday, capped a four-run inning. The Mets matched it in their first, with the type of play that made them famous, or infamous, in their first year as the Amazin' Mets.

With Gene Woodling and Frank Thomas on base, Marv Throneberry hit a deep drive to the gap in right-center field and steamed into third base with an apparent triple. But an umpire noticed he had failed to touch first base and called him out when the Cubs appealed. "Marvelous Marv" could hardly argue; he later admitted that he had missed second base as well.

When Charlie Neal followed with a homer, manager Casey Stengel came out of the Mets' dugout and into the infield to make sure Neal touched each base as he circled them.

Ernie Banks' homer gave the Cubs a 5–4 lead in the third inning, but the Mets pulled even in the fifth on a rare home run by Richie Ashburn. The former Cub hit only 29 homers in 2,189 career games and none in his two seasons as the Cubs' center fielder, but Ashburn managed a career-high seven as a 35-year-old in the final season of his Hall of Fame career.

Brock doubled home Banks with a tie-breaking run in the eighth, and Williams added a two-run triple in the ninth.

Santo's homer off Wilmer "Vinegar Bend" Mizell in the ninth inning of the second game completed the Cubs' sweep. They remained 18 games under .500 (24–42), on their way to a forgettable 59–103 record and a ninth-place finish, ahead of only the Mets, who bumbled their way to a 40–120 mark.

It was one of Lou Brock's better days in a Cub uniform. He'd make most of his magic for St. Louis and, much to Cubs fans' chagrin, he wore a Cardinals cap when he entered Cooperstown.

Did You Know?

Lou Brock was a casualty of the "College of Coaches" who provided dugout leadership for the Cubs in the early 1960s.

The system was the brainchild of owner P.K. Wrigley. Rather than a traditional manager, the Cubs employed eight coaches who provided instruction and were to rotate in and out of the head-coach position responsible for game management at various points of the season.

"Every one of those coaches had his own ideas about the type of player Lou should be," teammate Billy Williams recalled. "He was over-coached, listening to too many people. When he got to St. Louis, Johnny Keane put him out in left field and told him to just play his game. That's when Lou became a great player."

What Did Brown Do for You? Three Homers

A season that featured Kerry Wood's 20-strikeout game, Sammy Sosa rewriting baseball history and the Cubs' first postseason appearance since 1989 is also remembered for a radio call that did not involve any of that.

WGN analyst Ron Santo was three months from immortalizing Brant Brown when the Cubs faced the Phillies in the Thursday opener of a four-game series at Wrigley Field. Brown, an outfielder from Porterville, Calif., and Fresno State University who had been a third-round draft choice in 1992, was four days short of his 27th birthday when he enjoyed his best day as a Cub.

After the Phils jumped on Cubs starter Geremi Gonzalez for four first-inning runs, Brown led off the Cubs' first with a home run off Mark Portugal. Following a Jose Hernandez homer in the second, Brown made it a 4–3 game with an RBI single that scored Jeff Blauser. The Cubs took a 5–4 lead in the third on Henry Rodriguez's two-run homer, and Brown's second homer of the game made it 6–4 in the fourth.

Gonzalez's RBI double chased Portugal in the sixth. The Cubs added another run in the seventh on Mark Grace's double and Rodriguez's sacrifice fly, and they broke it open with a four-run eighth in which Brown's two-run homer off Darrin Winston was the big hit.

Brown's line for the day: 4-for-5 with three homers and five RBIs. Grace went 3-for-5, and winning pitcher Gonzalez had some fun at the plate, going 3-for-3 and knocking in a run before 21,267 spectators.

Brown's three-homer game was the sixth of the season in the majors and the Cubs' second in a week—Sosa had gone deep three times against Milwaukee just three days earlier.

Phillies	AB	R	H	RBI
Glanville cf	4	0	0	0
Jefferies lf	4	0	0	0
Rolen 3b	4	2	2	1
Brogna 1b	4	1	2	1
Lieberthal c	4	1	1	0
Abreu rf	3	1	1	2
Hudler ph	1	0	0	0
Jordan 2b	4	0	2	1
Relaford ss	3	0	1	0
Arias ph	1	0	0	0
Portugal p	2	0	0	0
Perez p	0	0	0	0
Amaro ph	1	0	0	0
Spradlin p	0	0	0	0
Winston p	0	0	0	0
Borland p	0	0	0	0
Totals	35	5	9	5

Cubs	AB	R	H	RBI
Brown cf-lf	5	3	4	5
Morandini 2b	5	1	1	0
Sosa rf	4	1	0	0
Grace 1b	5	2	3	1
Rodriguez lf	3	1	1	3
Lowery cf	1	0	1	1
Hernandez 3b	5	1	1	1
Blauser ss	3	2	1	0
Servais c	4	0	0	0
Gonzalez p	3	0	3	1
Pisciotta p	0	0	0	0
Mulholland p	1	1	1	0
Totals	39	12	16	12

```
PHI  4 0 0 0 0 1 0 0 0 -  5  9 1
CHI  1 2 2 1 0 1 1 4 X - 12 16 0
```

Phillies	IP	H	R	ER	BB	SO
Portugal L (2-2)	5.2	10	7	7	1	2
Perez	0.1	0	0	0	0	0
Spradlin	1.2	2	2	2	0	1
Winston	0	2	2	2	0	0
Borland	0.1	2	1	1	1	0
Totals	8	16	12	12	2	3

Cubs	IP	H	R	ER	BB	SO
Gonzalez W (6-5)	6	9	5	5	0	4
Pisciotta	0.2	0	0	0	0	0
Mulholland S (2)	2.1	0	0	0	0	0
Totals	9	9	5	5	0	4

E—Philadelphia Relaford. 2B—Philadelphia Abreu, Rolen; Chicago Grace, Lowery, Gonzalez. HR—Philadelphia Rolen (14); Chicago Brown 3 (8,9,10), Hernandez (11), Rodriguez (13). SF—Chicago Rodriguez. LOB—Philadelphia 3; Chicago 6. Attendance: 21,267.

The Cubs were 41–30 after this win. They would split the series with the Phillies, then drop six straight interleague games. Winning the division was pretty much out of the question as the Houston Astros rolled up 102 victories, and the wild card was anything but a given all season … in part because of Brown.

On Sept. 23, in the Cubs' 159th game, Brown was a late-innings defensive replacement against the Brewers at County Stadium. The Cubs took a 7–5 lead into the bottom of the ninth. Milwaukee loaded the bases with two outs, but closer Rod Beck appeared to be out of the inning when Geoff Jenkins hit a line fly to Brown in left field. He retreated a few steps to make what appeared to be a routine play, but the ball glanced off his glove and rolled away from him.

"Nooooo!" an anguished Santo cried as all three Brewers runners crossed the plate, pinning an 8–7 loss on the Cubs that manager Jim Riggleman described as "excruciating." To this day that "Nooooo!" remains Santo's signature call, and it was recalled often when the Cubs legend passed away in December 2010.

"I don't know how to explain it," Brown said. "The bottom line is I clanked it and we lost the game."

The play might have taken a more prominent place among all-time bad Cubs moments had they not finished tied with San Francisco in the wild-card race. Beating the Giants in a play-in game at Wrigley Field earned them a date with Atlanta in the division series; the Braves won in a sweep, and Brown got just one at-bat in the three games. He was traded to Pittsburgh for pitcher Jon Lieber in December, and he would play for Florida and the Cubs again before his major league career ended in 2000, when Brown was 29. He claims that awful day in Milwaukee was not a factor.

"Missing that ball made me a better person," Brown said. "If that's the worst thing that ever happens to me, I'll be fine. The whole thing has made me stronger."

Brown remains involved in baseball, having spent the 2010 season as hitting coach for the Frisco Rough Riders, Double-A affiliate of the Texas Rangers.

Don't I Know You?

Indians	AB	R	H	RBI
Carroll 2b	4	1	0	0
DeRosa lf	3	1	1	1
Crowe cf	0	0	0	0
Martinez 1b	5	1	1	3
Choo rf	5	0	2	0
Peralta 3b	5	1	1	0
Shoppach c	4	1	0	0
Valbuena ss	5	1	1	3
Francisco cf-lf	3	1	1	0
Lee p	1	0	0	0
Smith p	0	0	0	0
Perez p	0	0	0	0
Herges p	0	0	0	0
Hafner ph	0	0	0	0
Barfield pr	0	0	0	0
Wood p	0	0	0	0
Garko ph	1	0	0	0
Vizcaino p	0	0	0	0
Totals	36	7	7	7

Cubs	AB	R	H	RBI
Soriano lf	4	1	1	1
Theriot ss	6	0	1	1
Bradley rf	5	1	1	0
Lee 1b	5	2	3	2
Soto c	3	1	1	0
Fox 3b	4	0	0	0
Johnson cf	4	2	1	1
Gregg p	0	0	0	0
Blanco 2b	5	1	2	2
Harden p	1	0	1	0
Hoffpauir ph	1	0	0	0
Patton p	0	0	0	0
Miles ph	1	0	0	0
Heilman p	0	0	0	0
Fontenot ph	0	0	0	0
Hill ph	1	0	0	0
Marmol p	0	0	0	0
Fukudome cf	1	0	0	0
Totals	41	8	11	7

CLE	0	3	3	1	0	0	0	0	0	-	7	7 1
CHI	0	0	0	0	1	1	0	4	1	1	-	8 11 3

Indians	IP	H	R	ER	BB	SO
Lee	7	6	3	3	3	5
Smith	0.2	2	3	1	1	2
Perez	0	1	0	0	0	0
Herges	0.1	0	0	0	0	0
Wood	1	1	1	1	1	0
Vizcaino L (1-3)	0.2	1	1	1	1	0
Totals	9.2	11	8	6	6	7

Cubs	IP	H	R	ER	BB	SO
Harden	5	6	7	6	3	2
Patton	2	0	0	0	1	3
Heilman	1	0	0	0	0	0
Marmol	1	0	0	0	2	2
Gregg W (2-1)	1	1	0	0	0	1
Totals	10	7	7	6	6	8

E—Cleveland Peralta; Chicago Johnson, Soriano, Lee. DP—Chicago. 2B—Chicago Soto, Lee. HR—Cleveland Martinez (12), Valbuena (2); Chicago Johnson (4), Lee 2 (9,10). SH—Cleveland Lee 2. HBP—Cleveland Francisco. LOB—Cleveland 8; Chicago 10. SB—Chicago Soriano. Attendance: 40,155.

Kerry Wood's magical right arm has turned out to be as vulnerable as it is powerful, resulting in a series of injuries that left fans and Wood himself to wonder what he might have achieved had he been able to stay healthy.

The question became the Cleveland Indians' concern in the winter of 2008. Though Wood made a successful transition to relief pitching and collected 34 saves for the Cubs' 2008 division winners, the Cubs decided to "go in another direction" with the closer's position, obtaining Kevin Gregg from the Florida Marlins and allowing Wood to depart as a free agent. He signed a two-year, $20 million contract with the Indians and found himself back at Wrigley Field for an interleague series, along with teammate Mark DeRosa, another popular ex-Cub who had been dealt to the Indians over the winter to clear some payroll space for the Milton Bradley signing.

Hoo, boy.

Wood was his amiable self in a pre-game talk with reporters, expressing his appreciation for Chicago and Chicago fans and insisting he had no hard feelings toward manager Lou Piniella and general manager Jim Hendry for cutting him loose. DeRosa, meanwhile, acknowledged being slightly baffled, if not bothered, by his trade; he had been one of the Cubs' most productive hitters in his two years with the team and played well in the field at each of the five positions where he was used.

Torrential rains doused Chicago on Friday morning, but the storm blew out as quickly as it had blown in, and a capacity crowd of 40,155 filled Wrigley Field by the time the game got under way after an 86-minute delay. Cubs starter Rich Harden, however, left his game in the bullpen. Luis Valbuena and Victor Martinez reached him for three-run homers in the second and third innings and DeRosa chipped in an RBI single in the fourth as the Indians opened up a 7–0 lead.

It looked safe with Cliff Lee on the mound, but the Cubs began chipping away at the 2008 Cy Young Award winner with solo home runs by Reed Johnson and Derrek Lee in the fifth and sixth innings. Manager Eric Wedge pulled Cliff Lee after Bradley led off the Cubs' eighth with a single, and the Cubs went to work against the Cleveland bullpen, drawing within 7–6 in the eighth as Andres Blanco delivered a two-run single and Alfonso Soriano singled home another run.

Enter Kerry Wood, Cleveland closer. With one out and the bases empty, D-Lee got the better of his good friend and five-year teammate, guessing right on a Wood fastball and driving it out of the ballpark for a game-tying homer.

Gregg worked an uneventful 10th, completing five scoreless, one-hit innings by the Cubs' bullpen. They won it in the 10th as Soriano walked, stole second and scored when Ryan Theriot chopped a two-out single through the right side of the Cleveland infield.

Wood, greeted warmly by the Wrigley Field crowd, was philosophical about his blown save.

Mark DeRosa

Mark DeRosa's return to Wrigley Field was almost as eagerly anticipated as Kerry Wood's. DeRosa became a fan favorite for his multi-position fielding skills and his consistently productive bat during his two seasons with the Cubs. But his visit was cut short after he injured his thigh when he collided with the bullpen phone while chasing a foul ball during the series opener.

DeRosa batted .289 with 31 homers and 159 RBIs while playing a solid second base and filling in at five other positions on two division winners with the Cubs. Bobby Cox, his manager for seven seasons in Atlanta, was stunned when the Cubs traded De Rosa to Cleveland to clear payroll for the Milton Bradley deal after the 2008 season.

"Mark was one of the best kids I ever managed, in the clubhouse and on the field," Cox said.

"I made a bad pitch," he said, "and D-Lee did what a good hitter is supposed to do."

Said Lee: "Woody's a good guy and a good friend and we'll probably get together while he's here, but you can't think about that when you're competing on the field. He threw a fastball that got too much of the plate and I was fortunate enough to put a good swing on it. He's still a great pitcher."

Like Wood, D-Lee was one of the most popular Cubs during his six-plus seasons in Wrigleyville. Fourteen months after this game, he would follow his buddy out of town.

Murcer Has a Night

Bobby Murcer was a solid, capable, well-rounded ballplayer, universally respected as a pro's pro and a valued presence in every clubhouse he occupied during his 17-year big league career.

At times, he must have felt he'd been born under a bad sign.

Murcer grew up in Oklahoma, just as Mickey Mantle did. The scout who signed him for the Yankees, Tom Greenwade, also signed Mantle, so the comparisons were inevitable when Murcer got to New York, where he was expected to continue an iconic line of Hall of Fame outfielders that began with Babe Ruth and extended though Joe DiMaggio and Mantle.

Didn't happen. Murcer was good but not great in New York, and he didn't escape the burden of expectations when he was dealt to San Francisco. The Giants gave up Bobby Bonds to get him, much to the consternation of their fans, who embraced the fleet, powerful Bonds as the homegrown heir apparent to Willie Mays.

Murcer came close to matching his New York numbers over two seasons in San Francisco—he hit .279 with 34 homers and 181 RBIs—but he wasn't Bonds, so he was viewed as a disappointment, if not a failure. Frequent griping about sparse crowds and horrible playing conditions at Candlestick Park—Murcer once suggested the FBI look for kidnapped heiress Patricia Hearst in Candlestick's upper deck because nobody ever went up there—hardly endeared him to Giants fans, who barely blinked when he was moved along to the Cubs.

The reaction in Chicago was more heated—the Cubs gave up Bill Madlock, their 26-year-old, two-time batting champion and one of the most feared hitters in the National League. Madlock, who'd been obtained from Texas in a trade for Ferguson Jenkins, won over Cubs fans with his hard-nosed play, but he infuriated ownership with his hard-nosed salary demands as the age of free agency dawned. The order to trade him came from on high.

Cubs fans were not pleased. Welcome to Chicago, Bobby Murcer.

On this chilly Monday night, before a typical Candlestick "throng" of 4,344 fans, Murcer had the last laugh on his critics in all three cities. The game was scoreless in the fifth inning when Bill Buckner got the Cubs on the board with an RBI single, and Murcer followed with a three-run homer off veteran Jim Barr for a 4–0 lead.

With the Cubs trailing 5–4 in the eighth, Murcer lined a double to right-center field and scored on Jerry Morales' two-run homer, putting the Cubs up 6–5. It was an 8–6 game in the ninth when Murcer batted with one out and the bases loaded. He promptly unloaded them with a double to deep center field, giving the Cubs a 9–8 lead.

Jack Clark's RBI double tied it in the Giants' ninth, and they played on to the 12th, when Mick Kelleher's triple scored Joe Wallis with the winning run. The Cubs used 14 position players and six pitchers in the 3-hour, 57-minute marathon.

Murcer was 3-for-6 with six RBIs and enjoyed a typically solid year for the Cubs, hitting .265 with 27 homers, 89 RBIs and a .355 on-base percentage thanks to 80 walks. He hit .281 in 1978, but his power numbers dipped to 9 homers and 64 RBIs, and he was traded back to the Yankees midway through the 1979 season. He finished his career as a platoon player, sharing right field with future Cubs manager Lou Piniella.

Madlock and Murcer had one thing in common—they hated Candlestick Park. Madlock was always cold in the chilly dampness of the place. He batted .302 in his first year as a Giant, down from .339. His extra-base hits declined from 52 to 41, his RBIs from 84 to 46. He was dealt to Pittsburgh in mid-season 1979 and would win two more batting titles with the Pirates, plus a World Series ring.

Murcer joined the Yankees' broadcast team after retiring as a player. He never did become the next Mickey Mantle, but he was one of the most respected men in baseball when he died of brain cancer in 2008. He was 62.

Cubs	AB	R	H	RBI
DeJesus ss	3	1	1	0
Kelleher ss	3	1	2	1
Biittner lf	4	1	1	0
Darwin ph	1	1	1	0
Moore p	1	0	1	0
Rosello ph	1	0	0	0
R Reuschel p	0	0	0	0
Buckner 1b	6	2	1	1
Murcer rf	6	2	3	6
Morales cf-lf	3	1	1	2
Trillo 2b	5	0	0	0
Ontiveros 3b	6	0	0	0
Swisher c	6	0	0	0
Burris p	2	0	1	0
Hernandez p	0	0	0	0
Gross ph	1	0	0	0
P Reuschel p	0	0	0	0
Sutter p	0	0	0	0
Clines ph	1	0	0	0
Wallis cf	0	1	0	0
Totals	49	10	12	10

Giants	AB	R	H	RBI
Andrews 2b	5	3	2	0
Whitfield rf	2	0	0	0
Clark ph-rf	4	2	2	4
Evans lf-1b	7	1	2	1
Thomasson cf-lf-cf	6	0	1	1
McCovey 1b	4	0	2	1
Thomas pr-cf-ss	3	0	1	2
Madlock 3b	5	0	2	0
Foli ss	4	0	1	0
Elliott lf	1	0	0	0
Hill c	1	0	0	0
Sadek pr-c	1	1	0	0
Lavelle p	0	0	0	0
Harris ph	1	0	0	0
Moffitt p	0	0	0	0
Curtis ph	0	0	0	0
Cornutt p	0	0	0	0
Barr p	2	1	2	0
Alexander c	3	1	0	0
Totals	49	9	15	9

CHI 0 0 0 0 4 0 0 2 3 0 0 1 - 10 12 3
SF 0 0 0 0 2 3 0 3 1 0 0 0 - 9 15 2

Cubs	IP	H	R	ER	BB	SO
Burris	5.1	8	4	4	5	0
Hernandez	0.2	1	1	1	0	0
P Reuschel	1.1	3	1	0	0	0
Sutter	0.2	2	2	0	0	1
Moore W (3-0)	3	1	1	0	2	4
R Reuschel S (1)	1	0	0	0	1	0
Totals	12	15	9	5	8	5

Giants	IP	H	R	ER	BB	SO
Barr	7.1	7	6	6	2	5
Lavelle	1.2	3	3	2	1	2
Moffitt	2	1	0	0	2	1
Cornutt L (0-2)	1	1	1	1	1	1
Totals	12	12	10	9	6	9

E—San Francisco McCovey, Andrews; Chicago Ontiveros, Trillo 2. DP—Chicago; San Francisco. 2B—Chicago Murcer; San Francisco Clark. 3B—Chicago Kelleher. HR—Chicago Morales (4), Murcer (10); San Francisco Clark (7). SH—San Francisco Barr, Curtis. HBP—Chicago Trillo. LOB—Chicago 10; San Francisco 14. SB—Chicago Murcer. Attendance: 4,344.

Rookie Buzz-Heart One-Hits Phillies

John Buzhardt was John BUZZ-heart when he happened upon the North Side scene in September 1958 and promptly went 3–0 with a flashy 1.85 ERA in 24 innings.

He was John Buh-ZARD, though, by the time he reached the South Side White Sox in 1962.

Somewhere in between, the name had changed. Or maybe people simply had begun pronouncing it correctly. In any event, he was at his very best on Father's Day 1959, when the right-hander from Prosperity, S.C., reached new heights by throwing a one-hit shutout to beat Philadelphia 4–0 in front of 17,995 at Wrigley Field.

The only hit the 22-year-old allowed was a line single to right by former Cub/Sox catcher Carl Sawatski, this in the third inning. In the second, John had walked Wally Post, who was erased in a double play.

Thereafter, Buzhardt was terrific, retiring the final 20 batters to face him. Meanwhile, his batterymate and fellow South Carolinian, Sammy Taylor, provided all the necessary offense in the last of the third with a two-run home run off Ruben Gomez that hit the WGN camera halfway up the center-field bleachers.

Alvin Dark singled in a run in the fifth, giving the rookie a 3–0 lead, and in the eighth, Ernie Banks singled, took second on Walt Moryn's sacrifice bunt and scored on Dale Long's base hit to center.

Buzhardt closed it out with ease in the ninth. He got Sawatski on a fly to center and pinch-hitter Solly Drake, another former Cub, on a grounder to Tony Taylor at second. Finally, Joe Koppe popped to Banks at short, and Buzhardt, now 4–2 (with a 3.39 ERA), had helped the Cubs back to the .500 mark at 33–33 in a snappy 1 hour 48 minutes.

He didn't win another game that season—in fact made only three appearances in September—and in December was traded. To the Phillies.

At a Glance

WP: Buzhardt (4–2)

HR: S. Taylor (5)

Key stat: Buzhardt induced 19 groundball outs, a hint of what would come when he was going 7–0 vs. the Yankees as a member of the White Sox.

Heroics from Hickman

Perhaps it was the memory of that magical Opening Day, but the Cubs were imbued with the belief that anything was possible as the 1969 season rolled along.

There was no panic when the upstart Montreal Expos treated young lefty Rich Nye rudely in the first game of a Sunday doubleheader at Wrigley Field. Bob Bailey's RBI single gave Montreal a 1–0 first-inning lead, but the Cubs pulled even on Opening Day hero Willie Smith's fifth home run in the second.

Bailey's two-run homer capped a four-run fifth inning that chased Nye and gave the expansion Expos a 5–1 lead. After the Cubs cut it to 5–3 on RBI singles by Ernie Banks and Ron Santo in the bottom of the fifth, Bailey homered again in the eighth, and Montreal took a 6–3 lead into the ninth.

> ## At a Glance
>
> **WP:** Selma (7–3)
>
> **HR:** W. Smith (5), Hickman (2)
>
> **Key stat:** Hickman's 21 homers in 338 at-bats were a career-high to that point. He hit 32 the following season.

No sweat. Super-sub Paul Popovich singled to center field with one out, and Billy Williams followed with a single to right. After they moved up on a groundout, Banks delivered a two-run single to left, bringing the Cubs within 6–5.

As lumbering Jim Hickman came to the plate. Expos manager Gene Mauch decided to stick with Don Shaw, who was working his fifth inning in relief of starter Gary Waslewski. Hickman won the confrontation with his fellow former Met, slamming a two-run homer that gave the Cubs a 7–6 victory before 22,079 delighted Wrigley patrons.

Hickman had come from the Dodgers in April of 1968, one of general manager John Holland's better moves: Hickman and reliever Phil "the Vulture" Regan for journeyman outfielder Ted Savage and pitching prospect Jim Ellis. While Regan took over as the Cubs' closer and was 12–6 with 17 saves in '69, Hickman gave them some pop with 21 homers in 134 games, playing mostly right field.

He had a huge year in 1970, batting .315 with 32 homers and 115 RBIs. He made the National League All-Star team for the first time and contributed to a memorable All-Star moment: It was Hickman's hit that scored Pete Rose from second with the winning run—only after he barreled into A.L. catcher Ray Fosse with shoulder-shattering force.

The Expos kept it from being a perfect day for the Cubs with a 5–4 victory in the second game, which was called on account of darkness after six innings. The first-place Cubs' lead was five games over the Mets. No sweat?

The Sandberg Game

Can one game be credited with launching an MVP season? A Hall of Fame career? A franchise turnaround? In the case of Ryne Sandberg vs. the St. Louis Cardinals on a warm June Saturday in 1984, the answer to all three questions is yes. It was that kind of game.

Wrigley Field was packed with 38,079 spectators. Bob Costas and Tony Kubek were in the house for NBC's national *Game of the Week* telecast. The speedy Cardinals were not only the Cubs' arch-rivals, they were one of the dominant teams in baseball, in the midst of winning three pennants in six years.

St. Louis' Willie McGee hit for the cycle and drove in six runs. Ozzie Smith was 2-for-4 and scored four times; Tommy Herr was 3-for-6. When the Cards entrusted a 9–8 lead to Bruce Sutter—the Hall of Fame reliever who had won the Cy Young Award for the Cubs five years earlier and was on his way to a career-best 45 saves—it looked like Game Over.

Enter Sandberg. Leading off the bottom of the ninth, he caught a split-finger pitch from Sutter that didn't dive as sharply as Sutter's signature splitter typically did, and he drove it into the bleachers in left-center field for a game-tying home run.

The crowd erupted … and McGee countered. Facing Lee Smith, the Cubs' All-Star closer, with Ozzie Smith at second and nobody out in the 10th, McGee lined a double to right field, scoring Ozzie Smith with the go-ahead run. McGee came around on two groundouts, and the Cardinals led 11–9.

Sutter retired the first two Cubs in the 10th, then walked Bob Dernier, who got a favorable call when he checked his swing on Sutter's 3-2 pitch. That brought Sandberg to the plate, and he did it again, jumping on another hanging splitter and driving it out of the ballpark for another game-tying homer.

> ## At a Glance
>
> **WP:** Smith (4–4)
>
> **HR:** Sandberg 2 (8, 9)
>
> **Key stat:** NBC had already announced Willie McGee (4-for-6, 6 RBIs) as its player of the game before Sandberg went to work against Sutter.

"Do you believe it?" Costas asked the TV audience.

"He did it again!" Cubs broadcaster Harry Caray bellowed. "He did it again!"

The crowd summoned the reluctant Sandberg from the dugout for a curtain call, and they were still buzzing an inning later when Leon Durham led off the Cubs' 11th with a walk. He stole second and moved to third on catcher

June 23, 1984, will always be known as "The Sandberg Game" to Cubs fans. He went to become one of the greatest second basemen in major league history and was inducted into the Hall of Fame in 2005.

Darrell Porter's throwing error. After the Cardinals loaded the bases with two intentional walks, pinch-hitter Dave Owen delivered a game-winning single. Owen was the Cubs' last available position player.

"That game kind of put me on the map," Sandberg said with characteristic understatement. "It wasn't much to [Sutter's] career, but it was everything to mine."

Cardinals manager Whitey Herzog had a stronger reaction. "I always thought Babe Ruth was the greatest player in baseball," Herzog said. "Now I'm not so sure."

Sandberg and McGee combined to go 9-for-12 with five runs scored and 13 RBIs. McGee's bases-loaded triple was the big hit in a six-run second inning that chased Cubs starter Steve Trout and gave the Cardinals a 7–1 lead. He hit a two-run homer in the sixth, putting the Cards ahead 9–3, and finished his 4-for-6, six-RBI day with that run-scoring double in the 10th.

Sandberg singled in a run in the Cubs' first and had an RBI groundout in the fifth. His two-run single in the sixth capped a five-run uprising that brought the Cubs within 9–8, putting him in position to go to work against Sutter.

Sandberg finished 5-for-6 with seven RBIs. Dernier was 3-for-5 and scored four runs. The Cubs got seven innings of scoreless relief from Rich Bordi, Warren Brusstar, Tim Stoddard and George Frazier.

Sandberg didn't exactly "own" Sutter—he'd been 2-for-12 against him before this game. The genesis of his performance may have occurred in spring training. Jim Frey, the Cubs' first-year manager and an accomplished hitting coach, took note of Sandberg's size and strength and offered a suggestion.

"I told him, 'I know you're a team player, Ryno, and here's one thing you can do to help the team. You're a big, strong guy, and when you get a pitcher 2-0 or 3-1, you look for that fastball and pop it onto Waveland Avenue."

Sandberg totaled 15 homers in his first two big league seasons. Taking Frey's suggestion to heart, he hit 19 in '84, along with 36 doubles and 19 triples. He batted .314, drove in 84 runs, scored a league-best 114 runs, stole 32 bases and won a Gold Glove for fielding excellence. He was a runaway winner of the National League MVP award as the Cubs reached the postseason for the first time since 1945 ... and all agree it all began on a warm afternoon in June.

"After baseball got so home run-happy I heard some people say, 'What's the big deal about two home runs in a game?'" Sandberg said. "National TV, the Cardinals, the circumstances, Bruce Sutter, who threw nothing but ground balls and was a lights-out closer ... I guess it was a pretty big deal. I was amazed myself."

Brock Spends a Day on the Basepaths

Lou Brock, as Cubs fans know only too well, went on to a Hall of Fame career as a left fielder and leadoff man with the St. Louis Cardinals after the Cubs traded him in a fatally flawed exchange for sore-armed pitcher Ernie Broglio.

His ability to hit leadoff was one of the reservations Cubs brass had about Brock when the deal was made in 1964, but the author of that scouting report must have been absent for this Sunday doubleheader at Pittsburgh's Forbes Field. Leading off in both games, Brock made 11 plate appearances and reached base nine times as the Cubs pulled off a sweep of the Pirates.

At a Glance

Game 1

WP: Buhl (4–5)

S: Anderson (3)

Game 2

WP: Koonce (5–2)

S: Schultz (2)

HR: Banks (20)

Key stat: Lou Brock's on-base percentage was .306 with the Cubs, .347 with the Cardinals and .343 for his career.

Brock's five hits and four walks gave him an .818 on-base percentage for the day. He also stole a base. A leadoff hitter can't do much better.

"Lou was a college guy. He'd only played about a year in the low minors when he came to us, so he was pretty raw," teammate Billy Williams recalled. "But you could see his talent."

Brock doubled to left with two outs in the third inning of Game 1 and scored on Ken Hubbs' triple. Billy Williams doubled Hubbs home and Ernie Banks singled Williams home to complete a three-run inning that gave Cubs starter Bob Buhl the victory over Al McBean. Brock singled and was walked intentionally in two later plate appearances.

In the second game, Brock walked and scored as the Cubs reached Earl Francis for three first-inning runs, all of them unearned because of three Pirates errors. He singled and stole second but was stranded there in the fourth. He tripled home Moe Thacker and scored on Hubbs' single during the Cubs' three-run sixth, and he followed winning pitcher Cal Koonce's double with an RBI double for an 8–1 lead in the seventh. The Pirates walked him intentionally in the ninth.

To be fair, the performance was somewhat out of character for Brock, at least the 1962 Lou Brock. His on-base percentage for the season was .319—not good for a leadoff man. He was a hard guy to walk with just 35 in 477 plate appearances, as opposed to 96 strikeouts.

Cubs 10, Rockies 9

Howry's Helper

Anton Migursky's name isn't really prominent in Cubs lore, but if you were among the 40,269 fans at Wrigley Field on this balmy Monday evening, you witnessed his 15 seconds or so of productive, useful fame.

With Mike Fontenot enjoying a 5-for-5 night and Derrek Lee and Mark DeRosa each going 3-for-5, the Cubs took an 8–3 lead into the ninth inning of their game against Colorado. Manager Lou Piniella decided he'd seen enough of Scott Eyre after Kaz Matsui singled, Matt Holliday walked and Todd Helton doubled to open the inning, so he summoned Bob Howry.

Uh, bad idea. After Garrett Atkins and Brad Hawpe greeted Howry with RBI singles, rookie Troy Tulowitzki hit a bomb into the bleachers in left-center field, a three-run homer that gave the Rockies a 9–8 lead.

As a smoldering Howry stomped around the mound rubbing up a new baseball, an overserved fan named Brent Kowalkoski ran onto the field from his seat along the first-base line. He got close enough to Howry to ask, 'What are you doing?' but the confrontation went no further. Migursky, a Wrigley Field usher working security near the Cubs' dugout, had seen the trouble coming. He got to Kowalkoski and flattened him with a necktie tackle, probably sparing him a pummeling at the hands of the 6-foot-5, 220-pound Howry, who was in no mood for a personal encounter with a critic.

"I didn't even notice him," Howry said of the intruder. "I turned around and the security guard had already clotheslined him and taken him down."

"Best save I've ever seen in my life," catcher Koyie Hill said.

An even better one was immediately forthcoming. Blowing a five-run, ninth-inning lead could have been dispiriting for a team struggling to get back in playoff contention, but the Cubs got away with it. They loaded the bases in the bottom of the ninth, and Alfonso Soriano delivered a two-run single off reliever Brian Fuentes for a 10–9 victory.

Fontenot drove in two runs with his five hits, which included two doubles. Angel Pagan hit a three-run homer for the Cubs.

The win was the fourth for the Cubs in a streak that would reach seven. Reeling off 10 wins in 11 games, they climbed back into contention in the NL Central.

> ## At a Glance
>
> **WP:** Howry (4–4)
>
> **HR:** Pagan (3)
>
> **Key stat:** The Cubs' win was their 4th straight. They'd win 10 of 11 and get back into the NL Central race.

It was not such a productive night for Kowalkoski. The 24-year-old Elmwood Park, Ill., resident spent the night in police custody sobering up, and in January he pleaded guilty to felony trespassing.

Ron Santo Arrives

A 50-year love affair began on this day when the Cubs summoned Ron Santo from their Houston farm club and installed him at third base for a double-header against the Pirates at Pittsburgh's Forbes Field.

By any measure, his debut was a smash. Santo singled sharply to center field in his first major league at-bat and went 2-for-4 with three RBIs in the opener. He had a single, a sacrifice bunt and two more RBIs in the nightcap as the energized Cubs, bound for seventh place, took two from the Pirates, who were destined for the National League pennant and a seven-game World Series takedown of the mighty Yankees on Bill Mazeroski's Game 7 home run, one of the most dramatic blows in Series history.

Santo, who signed with the Cubs out of Franklin High School in Seattle, played well enough to make the team in spring training, but because he was only 20, the Cubs elected to have him open the season at Houston in the American Association and gain more experience. If he didn't wear out Triple-A pitching in his six weeks with the Buffs, he proved he could hit it.

At a Glance

Game 1

WP: Freeman (3–0)

S: Elston (5)

Game 2

WP: Morehead (1–6)

S: Elston (6)

Key stat: Ron Santo made his major league debut at 20; bonus-baby teammate Danny Murphy was nearly 3 years younger, two months shy of his 18th birthday.

Meanwhile, the Cubs were scuffling along with a losing streak that would reach nine games by the time Santo got the call to the big club. He didn't exactly enjoy a soft landing: the starters he would face in his debut games, Bob Friend (9–3) and Vern Law (11–2), would pitch the Pirates to the world championship, combining for 38 wins that season, 20 by Law in a Cy Young Award-winning performance.

But Santo was not intimidated—he would later joke that he was too nervous to be scared.

Santo had never been inside a major league ballpark, much less played in one, when he stepped in to face Friend in the second inning of Game 1 before 36,378 spectators. On the first pitch, Friend snapped off a breaking ball that buckled his knees.

"The catcher said, 'That's a big-league curve ball, kid,'" Santo recalled. "Then I hit a line drive up the middle and the weight of the world came off my shoulders."

In the fifth, after the Cubs rallied for a 3–2 lead on Richie Ashburn's single, Danny Murphy's double and Ed Bouchee's sacrifice fly, Friend walked left-handed-hitting George Altman to pitch to Santo with the bases loaded. "The

Kid" promptly unloaded them with a three-run double that gave the Cubs a 6–2 lead and sent Friend to the showers.

Facing Law in Game 2, Santo followed singles by Banks and Murphy, the 17-year-old bonus baby, with an RBI single in the fourth inning. In the sixth, third baseman Don Hoak misplayed his ground ball for an error, enabling Bouchee to score as the Cubs took a 5–2 lead with a four-run outburst. In the eighth, after Altman singled to right, Santo sacrificed him to second and Jerry Kindall singled him home with the go-ahead run.

Santo finished the day 3-for-7 with five RBIs against two of the National League's top pitchers. It wasn't always as easy as he made it look that day—he hit .251 with nine homers and 44 RBIs in 95 games as a rookie. But the Cubs were set at third base for the next 13 years as Santo became one of the great players in franchise history, finishing his Cubs career with a .279 average, 337 home runs and 1,290 RBIs. He made nine All-Star teams and won five Gold Gloves for fielding excellence. Why he isn't in the Hall of Fame is one of baseball's most perplexing questions.

And he did it all despite suffering from diabetes, diagnosed when he was 18. Santo required daily doses of insulin and constant monitoring of his blood sugar throughout his career. He lost both his legs to the disease in recent years, but the courage he showed in his determination to live a normal life, along with his tireless efforts on behalf of diabetes research, help explain why he was so popular among Cubs fans during his 21 years in the WGN Radio broadcast booth.

The Cubs retired his Number 10 during the 2003 season, an honor he said meant more to him than Hall of Fame enshrinement would have. If Ernie Banks is Mr. Cub, Ron Santo was Mr. Cub Fan before passing away after the 2010 season.

"This has been my life for 50 years," Santo said. "Every time I walk into Wrigley Field, I don't have a care in the world, other than moaning and groaning when the Cubs don't do well."

Martin and Much More

Jerry Martin was a versatile journeyman outfielder throughout his 11-season career, capable of an occasional long ball but better known for his fielding. His fourth home run in as many days might normally have occasioned headlines, but this was one of those games in which writers could choose from among several angles in crafting their stories.

The Cubs scored in each of the first six innings, roughing up loser Randy Lerch and three successors.

Mike Vail (4-for-5), Bill Buckner (3-for-4) and Ivan DeJesus (2-for-5) were a combined 9-for-14 as the Cubs collected 17 hits.

Catcher Bob Boone would drive in all four Phillies runs with a two-run double in the fifth inning and a two-run triple in the ninth.

Dave Kingman's homer, a two-run blast in the first inning, was no surprise—he led the National League with 48 dingers in '79. But pitcher Mike Krukow's solo shot in the fourth certainly was; Krukow hit one homer this season and five in his career. Krukow drove in another run with a sacrifice fly in the second.

At a Glance
WP: Krukow (5–5)
HR: Kingman (26), Martin (12), Krukow (1)
Key stat: Krukow, a .193 career hitter, batted .314 in 1979.

Krukow did some swinging of a different kind in the seventh, charging the mound to engage Phillies reliever Kevin Saucier, who had drilled him in the back with a fastball in apparent retaliation for Krukow hitting Garry Maddox a half-inning earlier, in apparent retaliation for Saucier hitting Steve Ontiveros in the fifth. Both benches emptied, and both pitchers were ejected.

Just another Wednesday at Wrigley before 29,858 spectators.

Martin went deep against reliever Rawly Eastwick in the third inning, a two-run shot that gave the Cubs a 5–0 lead. He homered in each game of the three-game series, enjoying a bit of revenge against his former team, after starting the streak with a three-run bomb off the Pirates' Enrique Romo in Pittsburgh on June 24.

The Cubs and the Phillies did a lot of business in those days; Martin was one of five former or future Phillies to suit up for the Cubs in this game, while the Phils employed the same number of former and future Cubs. Martin had been a fourth outfielder used most often for late-inning defense in Philly. The trade to the Cubs meant more regular work, and he responded with a .272 average, 34 doubles, 19 homers and 73 RBIs in a career-high 150 games.

Saucier, a hard-throwing 22-year-old lefty, would help the Phillies win the 1980 World Series.

Jurges' Busy Day

Billy Jurges was born and raised in the Bronx. He was a New York street kid with all that implies, a tough, no-nonsense competitor who played an artful shortstop and teamed with Hall of Famer Billy Herman to provide air-tight middle-infield defense for three Cubs pennant-winners in the 1930s.

He was also involved in several "escapades" during his career, at least two of them involving affairs of the heart.

This one ended favorably. On the morning of June 28, 1933, Jurges got married in Reading, Pa. He then hustled into Philadelphia and helped the Cubs to a doubleheader sweep of the Phillies with six hits, three RBIs and 18 innings of error-free fielding at short.

Busy day.

Billy Herman had three hits and Jurges, Babe Herman, Harvey Hendrick and Woody English added two apiece as the Cubs collected 14 hits and used a six-run eighth inning to prevail in the opener. Lynn Nelson got the win in relief of Pat Malone.

Infielders (from left) Rip Collins, first base; Billy Herman, second base; Bill Jurges, shortstop; and Stan Hack, third base, gave the Cubs a formidable defense in the 1930s.

In the nightcap, Jurges hit a solo home run in the fourth inning and went 4-for-4 with three RBIs. Billy Herman, Hendrick and winning pitcher Lon Warneke collected two hits apiece as the Cubs backed Warneke's route-going performance with a 12-hit attack.

Getting married may have represented a decision to settle down for the 25-year-old Jurges. A year earlier, on July 6, 1932, an encounter with a lady friend nearly cost him his life.

Violet Popovich Valli, an aspiring nightclub singer whom Jurges had been seeing, confronted him in his room at the Hotel Carlos, a facility three blocks from Wrigley Field where several Cubs players stayed during the season. According to reports, Valli grew distraught and brandished a gun when Jurges rebuffed her request for a commitment. The gun went off as Jurges tried to take it from her, and he was shot in the hand and the chest. Jurges declined to press charges, and Valli was never prosecuted.

The Cubs were en route to the National League pennant and a World Series date with the powerful Yankees, but Jurges was out of the lineup for more than two weeks recovering from his wounds. The Cubs signed former Yankees shortstop Mark Koenig to replace him, and the plot thickened.

Koenig played very well, hitting .353 in 33 games. But the Cubs awarded him only a half-share of their World Series purse, and his former Yankee teammates' contempt for the "cheapskate" Cubs formed the backdrop to the Series. Babe Ruth was particularly outraged by the Cubs' treatment of his buddy Koenig, and a lively exchange with the Cubs' bench is said to have precipitated his "called shot" home run off Charlie Root in the fifth inning of Game 3 of the Yankees' four-game sweep.

By comparison, June 28, 1933 was a quiet day for Jurges. All he did was play two games and get married.

Thanks, Billy

It's unusual for a team to salute a player with an official "day" unless that player is on a victory lap as he nears retirement or has already moved on.

Billy Williams was 31 when the Cubs honored him with Billy Williams Day between games of a Sunday doubleheader at Wrigley Field, and some of his best baseball years were still to come. But he was on the cusp of a significant milestone. In starting the first game, Williams tied Stan Musial's National League record for consecutive games played with 896. He broke Stan the Man's record in the second game.

Before the largest Wrigley crowd of the season, 41,060, the Cubs celebrated by beating Musial's former team twice. The Man of the Hour rose to the occasion with two doubles, two triples, five hits and three RBIs.

"It was easily my biggest day in all my years with the Cubs," Williams said.

On Sept. 21, 1963, manager Bob Kennedy decided to sit Williams against the Milwaukee Braves' Warren Spahn, a tough left-hander. Billy Cowan was the Cubs' left fielder, with Nelson Mathews in center and Ellis Burton in right. Williams was back in the lineup the next day, and he wouldn't miss another game until Sept. 3, 1970, when he told manager Leo Durocher it was time for a break.

Perfect attendance for 1,117 games over seven years, along with Hall of Fame-caliber hitting and outfield play.

"Billy Williams, day in and day out, is the best hitter I've ever seen," teammate Don Kessinger said. "He didn't hit for one or two days, or one or two weeks. He hit all the time."

True, but sometimes it took a while when Bob Gibson was pitching. Williams was 0-for-3 against the Cardinals' hard-eyed ace when he came to bat in the eighth inning of the opener and whaled a double off the wall in left-center field. One out later, Ernie Banks stroked a single to center, scoring Williams with the first run of the game. When Willie Smith followed with a two-run bomb onto Sheffield Avenue, Ferguson Jenkins had all the support he'd need to beat Gibson in one of their classic pitching duels, this one completed in a crisp 2 hours, 6 minutes.

At a Glance

Game 1

WP: Jenkins (10–5)

HR: W. Smith (7)

Game 2

WP: Selma (8–3)

HR: Banks (13) , Santo (15), Hundley (12)

Key stat: Fergie Jenkins was 5–2 head-to-head against Bob Gibson in his career.

Billy Williams raises his cap on Billy Williams Day in Chicago. The Hall of Famer smacked 426 home runs and drove in 1,475 runs in his 18-year career.

June 29, 1969
Cubs 3-12, Cardinals 1-1

The Cubs took all the suspense out of the second game with a four-run first inning. Williams was on third after a single when Banks slugged a three-run homer off Cards starter Jim "Mudcat" Grant. He doubled in the second, tripled home a run and scored on Ron Santo's homer in the fifth and tripled home two runs in the sixth as the Cubs made it easy for Dick Selma, who pitched a complete-game four-hitter.

Williams had a single, a double and two triples in his pocket when he came to bat in the eighth inning. He had hit for the cycle once in his career, and he was thinking about doing it again when he faced Cards reliever Dave Giusti.

"I went up there shooting for a home run," he said. "Naturally, I struck out. And I got a standing ovation. I don't know if anyone else ever got a sanding ovation for striking out. What a feeling that was."

The consecutive-games streak would stand as the NL record until 1983, when Steve Garvey of the Padres surpassed it. Williams was proud of the streak in that it symbolized the durability and dependability that defined his career. It also embodied his work ethic and his approach to the game.

"I was just doing something I liked to do, playing baseball," he said. "And I was getting paid for it, so I felt I should be out there trying to help my team as much as I could."

The Cubs improved to 50–26 with the sweep. Anything seemed possible as they put 14.5 games between themselves and the Cardinals in the NL East, while the upstart Mets were 8.5 games back. The memory of a blissful June Sunday became even more meaningful to Williams when the '69 season unfolded as it did.

"I guess you'd have to say it was my day," he said. "We won a doubleheader and I got five hits. I felt like I had to repay the people who had been so nice to me, and I had done it. I felt like the luckiest man in the world."

Good Day to Pitch

Larry Jackson enjoyed the game of his life in the year of his life.

Jackson, a lean right-hander from Nampa, Idaho, was one of the sturdiest, most durable pitchers in baseball when the Cubs acquired him from St. Louis with reliever Lindy McDaniel and catcher Jimmy Schaffer for outfielder George Altman, pitcher Don Cardwell and catcher Moe Thacker in October of 1962. But durability was not an issue on this day. Jackson, 33, needed just 85 pitches to subdue a hard-hitting Cincinnati lineup that featured Pete Rose, Vada Pinson, Frank Robinson and Deron Johnson.

Rose's seventh-inning single was all that stood between Jackson and a perfect game. He retired the first 18 Reds batters before Rose led off the seventh with a clean single to center, whereupon Jackson set down the final nine hitters in order, settling for a one-hitter.

He pretty much had to be that good in order to win, as Joey Jay pitched a two-hitter for the Reds. Rookie shortstop Jimmy Stewart was Jay's nemesis, doing away with any no-hit suspense with a first-inning double, then driving in the game's only run with a single in the sixth. That hit scored catcher Dick Bertell, who walked and moved up on Jackson's sacrifice.

So much for Wrigley Field being a hitter's park.

The Tuesday matinee, reeled off in a snappy 1 hour 40 minutes, was played in relative privacy—the paid crowd was 8,380.

Jackson would win at least 13 games for the final 12 years of his major league career, but in 1964 he was something special. In the age of Koufax, Marichal, Drysdale and Spahn, he led the National League with 24 victories and was second with 297 $^2/_3$ innings pitched, going 24–11 with a 3.14 ERA for an eighth-place Cubs team. He walked just 58 batters, eight of them intentionally, in those 297 $^2/_3$ innings. It was his only 20-win season, and he practically reversed it the next year, finishing 14–21 despite a 3.85 ERA.

> ## At a Glance
>
> **WP:** Jackson (10–5)
>
> **Key stat:** Jimmy Stewart batted .253 in 132 games as the Cubs' shortstop in 1964; he has scouted for several teams after a 10-season career as a utility man.

A four-time All-Star, Jackson was 194–183 lifetime and 52–52 in three-plus seasons as a Cub. He was a gift that kept on giving: The trade that sent Jackson to Philadelphia in April of 1966 brought six-time 20-game winner Ferguson Jenkins to the Cubs.

Grover Cleveland Alexander was not only known for his pitching ability, he was also among baseball's all-time great drinkers. And "Ol' Pete," as he was called, could handle his liquor. As Bill Veeck once wrote: "Deplore it if you will, but Grover Cleveland Alexander drunk was a better pitcher than Grover Cleveland Alexander sober."

Alexander's drinking is what finally caused the Cubs to get rid of him in June 1926. He argued almost constantly with new manager Joe McCarthy and, by mid-May, began arriving late for games, if indeed he showed up at all. One source reports that "Alex" came to the ballpark drunk six of his last 10 days as a Cub and twice didn't even bother to show. One time, completely drunk, he collapsed in the dugout.

So the Cubs sold him to the Cardinals, whom he helped win the pennant and World Series that year and for whom he won 21 games in 1927.

One other note: Alexander has the distinction of being named for one U.S. president and also of being portrayed in a motion picture by another. He was born during Grover Cleveland's presidency, and Ronald Reagan starred as Alexander in the 1952 film *The Winning Team*.

JULY

Ron Santo hit the first of his 342 home runs on July 3, 1960.

An 'Inside-the-Gutter' Home Run

Giants	AB	R	H	RBI
Alou rf	4	0	0	0
Spencer ss	5	1	2	1
Mays cf	3	1	1	1
Cepeda 1b	5	0	0	0
Jablonski 3b	4	1	1	1
Wagner lf	4	1	2	0
Schmidt c	4	1	2	1
Bressoud 2b	1	0	0	0
Speake ph	0	0	0	0
O'Connell 2b	0	0	0	0
Kirkland ph	0	0	0	0
Grissom p	0	0	0	0
Sauer ph	1	0	0	1
Miller pr	0	0	0	0
McCormick p	0	0	0	0
Gomez p	0	0	0	0
Antonelli p	0	0	0	0
Monzant p	1	0	0	0
Lockman ph	0	0	0	0
Crone p	0	0	0	0
Finigan ph-2b	2	0	0	0
Totals	**34**	**5**	**8**	**5**

Cubs	AB	R	H	RBI
T. Taylor 2b	5	3	3	2
Dark 3b	5	0	2	1
Walls rf	4	1	1	1
Banks ss	4	3	2	2
Thomson cf	4	0	2	2
Bolger lf	5	0	2	0
Long 1b	3	0	0	0
Neeman c	2	1	1	0
S. Taylor ph-c	2	0	0	0
Drabowsky p	3	1	1	1
Hobbie p	1	0	0	0
Totals	**38**	**9**	**14**	**9**

```
SF   2 0 0 0 0 1 1 1 0 - 5  8 1
CHI  2 2 0 1 0 0 1 3 X - 9 14 0
```

Giants	IP	H	R	ER	BB	SO
Antonelli L (8-6)	1	5	4	4	1	1
Monzant	3	3	1	1	1	3
Crone	2	1	0	0	1	0
Grissom	1	2	1	1	0	0
McCormick	0.2	3	3	3	1	1
Gomez	0.1	0	0	0	0	0
Totals	**8**	**14**	**9**	**9**	**4**	**5**

Cubs	IP	H	R	ER	BB	SO
Drabowsky W (7-7)	6	5	4	4	4	7
Hobbie (S)	3	3	1	1	2	4
Totals	**9**	**8**	**5**	**5**	**6**	**11**

E—San Francisco O'Connell. DP—Chicago 2. 2B—San Francisco Wagner; Chicago Taylor, Drabowsky, Thomson, Neeman. 3B—Chicago Walls. HR—San Francisco Spencer (11), Jablonski (6), Schmidt (11), Mays (15); Chicago Banks 2 (19,20), Taylor 2 (2,3). LOB—San Francisco 8; Chicago 9. Attendance: 16,549.

Inside-the-park home runs, more often than not, are rather exciting plays.

One Tuesday afternoon in 1958, Tony Taylor, then a rookie second baseman for the Cubs, hit the strangest and, yes, funniest inside-the-parker you ever saw.

Let's set the stage:

The wind was blowing out that day at Wrigley Field. The San Francisco Giants, starting the day in third place, three and a half games behind NL-leading Milwaukee, had gone ahead in the first inning with home runs by Daryl Spencer and Willie Mays off Moe Drabowsky. Now the fifth-place Cubs were coming up, and Taylor, the speedster from Cuba, was set to lead off.

He was about to hit a home run, but the wind was not going to be a factor.

"In Wrigley, if you hit a ground ball past third base fair, then it sometimes rolled to the rain gutter along the brick wall," Drabowsky told author Carrie Muskat. "One of the interesting things we did was right at the bullpen bench. We'd always drop our gloves in that gutter (when the opposition was at bat), so if a ball came in there, the ball would stop right where the gloves were so our outfielder could retrieve the ball. But, when we're hitting, we take the gloves out."

Taylor, facing lefty Johnny Antonelli, swung and sent a hard-hit grounder past third and into the gutter. Giants rookie left fielder Leon Wagner came running over, a bit confused. The Cubs' bullpen pitchers and catchers were peering under the bench, pretending to look for the ball—which was actually 40 to 50 feet farther down the gutter toward the left-field corner. It didn't occur to "Daddy Wags" that maybe the opposition was playing a trick on him, so he too joined the search under the bench. Third-base umpire Augie Donatelli could see where the ball was, but he wasn't about to tell Wagner. Taylor, meanwhile, sped around the bases, scoring easily as Wagner finally tracked down the elusive baseball.

Two batters later, Ernie Banks hit his 19th homer of the season, and the game was tied. More homers were to follow, including Taylor's second of the day, this one going out of the park. Chicagoan Ray Jablonski homered in the sixth and rookie catcher Bob Schmidt in the seventh for the Giants, and Banks belted his second of the day in the seventh off Marv Grissom to keep the Cubs ahead 6–4. A three-run, homerless eighth clinched a 9–5 triumph.

And the day wasn't a complete loss for Leon Wagner: The 24-year-old, playing in just his seventh major league game after his June 22 call-up, had a single and a double in four tries to raise his batting average to .400.

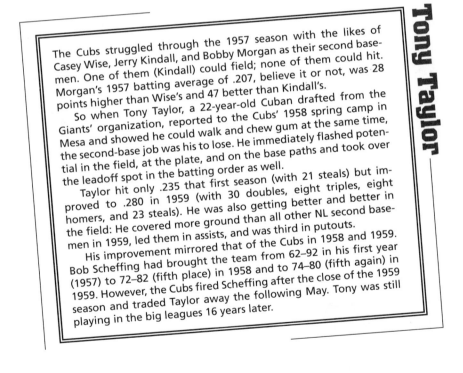

The Cubs struggled through the 1957 season with the likes of Casey Wise, Jerry Kindall, and Bobby Morgan as their second basemen. One of them (Kindall) could field; none of them could hit. Morgan's 1957 batting average of .207, believe it or not, was 28 points higher than Wise's and 47 better than Kindall's.

So when Tony Taylor, a 22-year-old Cuban drafted from the Giants' organization, reported to the Cubs' 1958 spring camp in Mesa and showed he could walk and chew gum at the same time, the second-base job was his to lose. He immediately flashed potential in the field, at the plate, and on the base paths and took over the leadoff spot in the batting order as well.

Taylor hit only .235 that first season (with 21 steals) but improved to .280 in 1959 (with 30 doubles, eight triples, eight homers, and 23 steals). He was also getting better and better in the field: He covered more ground than all other NL second basemen in 1959, led them in assists, and was third in putouts.

His improvement mirrored that of the Cubs in 1958 and 1959. Bob Scheffing had brought the team from 62–92 in his first year (1957) to 72–82 (fifth place) in 1958 and to 74–80 (fifth again) in 1959. However, the Cubs fired Scheffing after the close of the 1959 season and traded Taylor away the following May. Tony was still playing in the big leagues 16 years later.

Tony Taylor

A Belated Flag Day Celebration

In this summer of 1967, the summer Chicago rediscovered the Cubs, there were several indelible moments. One most certainly was this Sunday afternoon at Wrigley Field, when the Cubs met the Cincinnati Reds in the final game of a 12-game homestand—a wildly successful 12-game homestand.

The Cubs, 59–103 and 10th in the 10-club National League the year before, had ended a road trip by winning the final two games June 20-21 at Pittsburgh. Then they came home and swept four from Houston, split two with the Phillies, swept three from the Pirates and had won the opening two games of the Cincinnati series. That meant they had won 12 of 13 and had climbed to within a half-game of first-place St. Louis.

Now, to be in first place at day's end, all the Cubs and new pitching hero Ferguson Jenkins needed to do was to beat the Reds and hope the Mets at least split their twinbill with the Cardinals at Shea Stadium. A Cardinals sweep would keep St. Louis on top.

Wrigley Field shook with the fervor of 40,464 people, 36,062 of whom had paid their way in. These were exciting times. The ever-present trio of heroes in the lineup's middle—Ernie Banks, Billy Williams and Ron Santo—was finally playing in games that mattered.

The first crowd eruption came in the second inning, when Randy Hundley lined a pitch from Sammy Ellis to left-center for a double that scored Lee Thomas, who had started things with a single.

Vada Pinson tied it with a leadoff homer in the Reds' fourth, but the Cubs came back with three in their half: Al Spangler singled to score Santo, Thomas scored on Ellis' wild pitch and Jenkins tripled with two out to send Ted Savage home.

Fergie took care of the rest, retiring 17 of the last 18 Cincy batters and finishing with a three-hitter and striking out seven to improve his record to 11–5. When Art Shamsky flied to right-fielder Al Spangler for the final out, the crowd, instead of

Reds	AB	R	H	RBI
Pinson cf	4	1	1	1
Shamsky rf	4	0	1	0
Rose 2b	3	0	0	0
Perez 3b	3	0	0	0
Johnson 1b	3	0	0	0
Pavletich c	3	0	0	0
May lf	3	0	1	0
Helms ss	3	0	0	0
Ellis p	1	0	0	0
Lee p	0	0	0	0
Boehmer ph	1	0	0	0
Arrigo p	0	0	0	0
Robinson ph	1	0	0	0
Totals	29	1	3	1

Cubs	AB	R	H	RBI
Popovich ss	4	0	0	0
Beckert 2b	2	0	0	0
Williams lf	4	0	0	0
Santo 3b	4	1	1	0
L. Thomas 1b	4	2	2	0
Spangler rf	4	0	1	1
Hundley c	3	0	1	1
Savage cf	2	1	0	0
Jenkins p	3	0	2	1
Totals	30	4	7	3

CIN	0	0	0	1	0	0	0	0	0	-	1	3	0
CHI	0	1	0	3	0	0	0	0	X	-	4	7	0

Reds	IP	H	R	ER	BB	SO
Ellis L (5-5)	3.2	6	4	4	2	2
Lee	1.1	0	0	0	0	1
Arrigo	3	1	0	0	1	2
Totals	8	7	4	4	3	5

Cubs	IP	H	R	ER	BB	SO
Jenkins W (11-5)	9	3	1	1	0	7
Totals	9	3	1	1	0	7

DP—Chicago. 2B—Chicago Hundley, Jenkins. 3B—Chicago Jenkins. HR—Cincinnati Pinson (6). LOB—Cincinnati 1; Chicago 5. Attendance: 36,062.

heading for the exits, stood in place, cheering their favorites. Soon, it became obvious that most of the fans were sticking around for more than just the Game 2 result from Shea Stadium, where the Mets had won the opener but were trailing in the nightcap 3–1.

The workers in charge of arranging the scoreboard flags in correct standings order soon realized that, no matter what the result, the Cubs' flag, at the moment in the No. 2 spot, needed to be switched with the Cardinals' pennant. After all, a Cards victory would leave St. Louis at 45–29, same record as Chicago. Alphabetical order dictated that the Chicago flag be on top.

As some 30,000 or so roared their approval, the flags were reversed, with the Cubs' pennant moved to its rightful spot—on top of the National League.

It was a memorable moment in a memorable summer.

Did You Know?

When the Cubs moved into first place on Sunday, July 2 at Wrigley Field, it marked the first time since 1945 that they had been on top of the NL as late as July.

It also made Chicago the home of two first-place teams.

That same afternoon in Detroit, the White Sox had lost to the Tigers 3–0, despite Gary Peters' three-hit, 11-strikeout performance. Even with the loss, though, the Sox led the AL with their 43–29 record. They were 4.5 games ahead of each of the other three contenders: Detroit, Boston, and Minnesota.

But the excitement over the Sox was nowhere near that surrounding the Cubs. The Sox had been in first place in July or later a few times during the 1950s and 1960s, most recently in 1964, when they led the pack heading into Labor Day.

Oh, and the last time before 1967 that the Cubs and Sox both had been in first place in July? You have to go back a ways for the answer: July 13, 1915.

A Big First for Santo

Exactly one week before, 20-year-old third baseman Ron Santo had made his major league debut in Pittsburgh, going 3-for-7 with five runs batted in during a Sunday doubleheader. His first game, first hit, first RBI—all on the same afternoon.

A week later, Santo had cooled off somewhat, going 4-for-23 to drop his batting average to .233. But he was in manager Lou Boudreau's lineup to stay, batting fifth in the order this Sunday afternoon against visiting Cincinnati behind Frank Thomas and ahead of Dick Gernert.

Glenn Beckert (left) and Ron Santo relax in their hotel room at the Waldorf Astoria in New York after arriving for a series against the Mets in 1969. Santo, a hard-hitting third baseman who was a nine-time All-Star selection, had his Number 10 retired by the Cubs.

On the mound for the Reds was Chicago native Jim O'Toole, a left-hander destined to go 19–9 for the Reds' 1961 NL champs. He entered this game with a 6–7 record and a new bride: Jim had gotten married the day before.

The honeymoon, however, would have to wait.

The Reds, then in fifth place at 34–35, went up 2–0 in their half of the first on a two-run double by Harry Anderson off Glen Hobbie, but the last-place Cubs (27–41) came right back. With two out, Frank Thomas singled Ernie Banks to second, bringing Santo to the plate. He drove one deep to left and into the bleachers for his first big-league home run, and the Cubs, with 17,205 cheering them on, were on their way to a 7–5 victory.

Santo was to hit 336 more homers in a Cub uniform, which ranks him fourth in club history behind Sammy Sosa, Ernie Banks and Billy Williams.

Ron Santo

He had his detractors, as do most star-quality athletes. But there is no denying the fact that Ron Santo was one exceptional ballplayer.

Even as he battled diabetes, Santo won five Gold Gloves, was a nine-time All-Star, and drove in 1,290 runs across 14 seasons on the North Side. From 1963 to 1970, Santo averaged 105 RBIs per season, with a career-best 123 in 1969. He also posted five consecutive seasons of 300 or more total bases.

Santo led the league in walks four times, in on-base percentage twice and in triples once (13 in 1964). Four times he hit .300 or better, and four times he clubbed 30 or more home runs. He's the only third baseman in major league history with eight straight seasons of 90 or more RBIs. And in the field, he set or tied NL records by leading the league's third basemen in total chances eight times and in games, putouts, and assists seven times each.

After using his 10-and-5 rights to block a trade to the Angels in December 1973 (a player with 10 years in the majors, the last five with the same club, now had that power), Santo announced he would play only in Chicago or not at all. Off to the White Sox he went, for four players, including Steve Stone. He spent one uneventful year on the South Side and then called it a career.

It had been a grand one.

Now *That* Was a Fireworks Show

Hack Wilson was a fine outfielder and a dangerous hitter. He was also one of baseball's all-time drinkers and brawlers. His 56 home runs stood as the National League record for 68 years; his RBI record of 191 still stands.

What also remains is his reputation for drunken escapades and fights with fans, opposing players and hotel patrons.

"It wasn't fair, really, for Hack to have had to play in Chicago during the Roaring Twenties," wrote Bill Veeck, whose father was president of the Cubs in those days. "Nobody should have been forced to enjoy himself that much. Poor Hack, he never had time to go to bed."

One—actually two—of Wilson's better bouts took place on the 4th of July in 1929.

The Cubs were facing the Cincinnati Reds in Game 2 of the holiday doubleheader (the Reds had taken the opener 9–8). The Cubs had entered the day in first place, a half-game ahead of Pittsburgh; Hack, on his way to 39 homers, 159 RBIs and a .345 average that season, had entered with a .331 average and 19 home runs.

In the sixth inning, with the Cubs safely ahead 9–4, Wilson was standing on first base with a single. All afternoon, the Reds' champion bench jockey, pitcher Ray Kolp, had been heckling Wilson. He continued the verbal abuse as Hack stood on the bag. Suddenly, Wilson decided he'd had enough, and he dashed over and jumped into the visitors' dugout and began pounding lumps on Kolp. Players, umpires and police finally got him out of the battle zone, and Hack was escorted from the field.

The story did not end there. (Incidentally, the Cubs went on to win 10–5.)

That evening, both teams were at Union Sta-

Reds	AB	R	H	RBI
Swanson lf	5	1	0	0
Dressen 3b	5	2	3	0
Walker rf	5	2	2	1
Kelly 1b	2	0	2	3
Allen cf	5	0	2	1
Pittenger 2b	4	0	0	0
Lucas ph	0	0	0	0
Ford ss	4	0	1	0
Sukeforth c	1	0	0	0
Donohue p	1	0	0	0
Ehrhardt p	0	0	0	0
Purdy ph	1	0	0	0
May p	1	0	1	0
Totals	**34**	**5**	**11**	**5**

Cubs	AB	R	H	RBI
McMillan 3b	5	1	3	3
Beck 3b	0	1	0	0
English ss	5	1	2	2
Hornsby 2b	4	1	2	2
Wilson cf	3	1	1	0
Heathcote cf	1	0	0	0
Cuyler rf	5	1	1	2
Stephenson lf	3	0	1	0
Grimm 1b	3	2	1	0
Schulte c	4	2	2	0
Blake p	2	0	0	0
Totals	**35**	**10**	**13**	**9**

CIN	3 0 1 0 0 0 0 0 1 -	5	11	0
CHI	0 0 6 1 0 2 0 1 X -	10	13	0

Reds	IP	H	R	ER	BB	SO
Donohue L (3-9)	4	7	7	4	1	1
Ehrhardt	1	0	0	0	0	0
May	3	6	3	3	1	1
Totals	**8**	**13**	**10**	**7**	**2**	**2**

Cubs	IP	H	R	ER	BB	SO
Blake W (5-9)	9	11	5	4	6	3
Totals	**9**	**11**	**5**	**4**	**6**	**3**

2B—Cincinnati Allen, Kelly 2; Chicago McMillan. 3B—Cincinnati Walker; Chicago Hornsby. HR—Chicago Cuyler (8). SH—Cincinnati Sukeforth, Kelly 2; Chicago Blake 2. HBP—Chicago Heathcote, Stephenson. LOB—Cincinnati 11; Chicago 7.

Hack Wilson played for the Cubs from 1926 through 1931. His 191 RBIs in 1930 still stands as the single-season record in the major leagues.

tion, preparing to depart on eastern road trips. Wilson had not yet cooled down. He asked some of Kolp's teammates for his whereabouts, and a Reds pitcher named Pete Donohue told Hack, in so many words, to get lost. Donohue never saw the punch that knocked him to the Union Station floor.

As for Kolp, he had retired to his Pullman car, preferring perhaps to fight another day.

The net result was two bruised and battered pitchers for Cincinnati and a three-day suspension and $100 fine for Wilson, courtesy of NL president John Heydler.

Hack was still upset the next day. He told the *Chicago Tribune*'s Irving Vaughan: "I'm no Dempsey, but when anybody says I'm yellow (as Kolp had), I'm gonna try to show 'em they're wrong. The first man that opens his mouth and tries anything funny the next time we play the Reds will find out I haven't cooled off a bit. If any of their pitchers throws a beanball at me, I'll drop my bat and start out after him. I don't think Kolp or Donohue will try it. They don't want another lesson."

For the record, no one tried "anything funny" in the season's remaining 11 Cubs-Reds games, seven of which were won by the Cubs, the 1929 NL champions.

Call This Sweep Unrivaled

It took about 6 ½ hours and 23 innings to finish and required 13 pitchers, three of whom worked in both games. It featured 41 runs and 65 hits, among them six triples and three home runs. And it attracted a crowd of 39,240 to Wrigley Field.

When this Monday doubleheader was over, the first-place Cubs had won two important ballgames from their visiting rivals from St. Louis, 13–12 (in 14 innings) and 9–7, had picked up a game on second-place New York and improved their record to 44–25, good for a two-game lead on the Giants and a six-game bulge on the Cardinals.

Stan Hack spent his entire playing career with the Cubs (1932–47). Known as the top defensive third baseman of his time, Hack also compiled a lifetime batting average of .301.

July 5, 1937
Cubs 13-9, Cardinals 12-7

The heroes were many, ranging from 38-year-old pitcher Charlie Root, who entered the opener in the ninth inning and worked six scoreless innings to get credit for the win, to Phil Cavarretta, who though still a few days shy of his 21st birthday helped get the Cubs back into the first game with a two-run pinch triple and then belted a two-run homer in the second game.

Earlier in the afternoon, when the Cardinals were pounding starter Bill Lee to take a 7–1 lead in the third, the outlook was hardly bright. But then the Cubs put up six runs in the fourth, and the contest was tied. St. Louis seemed to take control with three runs in the seventh and two in the eighth (the latter rally keyed by Leo Durocher's two-run single) for a 12–7 lead.

Gabby Hartnett's two-run single, however, capped a four-run home eighth, and, in the ninth, Stan Hack tripled and scored the tying run on Rip Collins' sacrifice fly. Then came Root's brilliant relief job and, in the last of the 14th, the decisive rally.

Frank Demaree bounced a single to center, his sixth hit of the game. Billy Herman bunted Demaree over to second and Turk Stainback drew a walk. That's when Billy Jurges, with three hits already, singled to center to score Demaree for the 13–12 victory.

Manager Charlie Grimm figured Lee couldn't do any worse than he had in the opener, so he trotted out the right-hander to start Game 2 as well. Lee, much better this time, took an 8–2 lead into the seventh, when Pepper Martin's leadoff homer ignited a five-run burst that sliced the Chicago lead to a run. But reliever Clay Bryant, whose surprise single in the Cubs' seventh sent home Jurges with an insurance tally, shut the door in the eighth and ninth, and the Cubs had their sweep.

> ## At a Glance
>
> **Game 1**
>
> **WP:** Root (8–3)
>
> **Game 2**
>
> **WP:** Lee (9–6)
>
> **SV:** Bryant (2)
>
> **HR:** Cavarretta (1)
>
> **Key stats:** Demaree was 8-for-11 on the day to raise his batting average to .349. He finished at .324 with 36 doubles, 6 triples, 17 homers and 115 RBIs.

The Giants eventually caught the Cubs on Sept. 1, then handed them an 8–7 loss at Wrigley Field on Sept. 23 that left the Cubs 3.5 games back (instead of 1.5 had they won) with 10 games to go. The Cubs finished 93–61, three games off the pace.

Future Ump Provides the Thump

Frank Secory was an outstanding National League umpire, having worn the blue suit from 1952 through 1970, when he retired. He worked four World Series and six All-Star Games.

Interestingly, he also was the plate umpire for the game in which Ernie Banks hit his first big-league homer (Sept. 20, 1953) and was umpiring at first base the day Ernie hit No. 500 (May 12, 1970).

But what many people forget is that he was also a major league outfielder, albeit a part-time one, and that he had a few big moments, some as a Cub. He was 2-for-5 as a pinch-hitter in the 1945 World Series and, thus far in 1946, going into a July 6 twinbill with Cincinnati, he had gone 8-for-27 (.296) for the North Siders, almost exclusively in pinch roles.

At a Glance

WP: Schmitz (5–5)

HR: Secory (3)

Key stat: The sweep left the Cubs in third place, 7.5 games out of first.

Exactly one month earlier, his 12th-inning pinch grand slam off Giants lefty Dave Koslo had given the Cubs a dramatic 10–6 triumph at Wrigley Field. His next memorable performance came in Game 1 of this Saturday doubleheader against a Reds team so weak offensively that its No. 3 hitter was Grady Hatton (who was 0-for-8 that day and who 14 years later would resurface as a player-coach with the Cubs). Nonetheless, in spite of the lesser opposition, 38,217 fans had shown up at Clark and Addison.

Joe Beggs, who was to finish the '46 season with a 12–10 record and 2.32 ERA, matched the Cubs' Paul Erickson and reliever Johnny Schmitz (final 3 2/3 innings) zero for zero through 11 innings. Now there were two out in the home 12th and the bases were empty, thanks to Clyde McCullough's having just grounded into a double play.

Then Billy Jurges singled to keep the inning alive, and Secory came up to hit for Schmitz and drove one onto the left-field catwalk for a 2-0 victory.

It was one of the last times Frank Secory would be cheered in Wrigley Field.

By the way, the Cubs won the nightcap 1–0, with Hank Wyse firing the shutout.

Sundberg—Not Sandberg—the Hero

Like so many of their predecessors, the 1987 Cubs were going to end up in last place. But as July 8 dawned, the Cubs were quite respectable. They were 44–39 and just a half-game out of second place in the NL East, even with Ryne Sandberg still on the disabled list with a sprained ankle.

On this particular Wednesday afternoon, not only was Sandberg out of the lineup, but so was Andre Dawson, getting three days off to rest his troublesome knees. In the cleanup spot instead of "the Hawk" was Jerry Mumphrey, never to be accused of being a cleanup hitter.

So when the San Diego Padres rocked Cub starter Jamie Moyer for seven runs in the first three innings, some in the turnout of 31,278 must have entertained thoughts of an early departure. But why leave early when the seventh-inning stretch and local virtuoso Harry Caray awaited? Besides, the Cubs had cut the lead to 8–4 in the sixth. The wind was blowing out, the sun was shining, the Old Style was flowing. Why leave, indeed?

Those who stayed were rewarded with a shocking eighth-inning rally. Here's what transpired:

Keith Moreland led with a single and took second when Jody Davis walked. San Diego right-hander Lance McCullers replaced lefty Mark Davis and walked Manny Trillo, bringing to the plate a pinch batter

> ## At a Glance
>
> **WP:** Lancaster (2–0)
>
> **HR:** Sundberg (4)
>
> **Key stat:** Moyer allowed 10 hits, four walks and seven runs (all earned) in 3-plus innings.

for reliever Les Lancaster—reserve catcher Jim Sundberg, a man noted for his Gold Glove defense but certainly not his offense. He had gone into this series with a .226 average, three homers and six RBIs.

And, of course, Sundberg launched a blast to the back of the bleachers in left for a grand slam, and the game was tied. The rest was anti-climactic. Dave Martinez singled and was bunted to second by Sandberg's replacement, Paul Noce. Leon Durham was walked intentionally, and Bobby Dernier batted for Mumphrey and singled in the go-ahead run. The final three runs in the eight-run eighth came across on a Moreland double, a passed ball charged to Benito Santiago and a triple by Davis.

Lefty Frank DiPino came on to retire the stunned Padres in the ninth, and the Cubs were six games above .500. They went 31–46 the rest of the way.

In the Sweet Suite

Billy Williams, also known as Sweet-Swinging Billy from Whistler, Ala., enjoyed some big days in a major league career that covered 18 years. Certainly one of the biggest came at age 34, in the midst of a season that would end with him having batted .333 with 37 homers and 122 RBIs and being named Major League Player of the Year by *The Sporting News*.

He had sat out the second game of a Sunday doubleheader two days before in Cincinnati, and Monday was an off-day before the Cubs faced Houston in another doubleheader, this one at Wrigley Field. When that twinbill was finished, and 27,170 folks were marveling at what a fully rested Williams had just accomplished, he delivered this bit of understatement:

At a Glance

WP: Hands (7–6)

Sv: Aker (4)

HR: Monday 2 (9), Williams (18), Pepitone (2)

Key stat: Willliams' 8-for-8 day raised his batting average 18 points to .328.

"The rest was good for me, mentally and physically."

Apparently so. In the opener, a 6–5 Cubs defeat, Billy went 3-for-3, belted his 17th home run and drove in three runs. Then came Game 2, with Bill Hands facing the hard-throwing Houston right-hander Don Wilson. It soon became obvious that Williams was far from through for the day.

In the first inning, with two out, he lined a double to right center, then scored on Joe Pepitone's single. In the third, he got an infield hit off the glove of shortstop Roger Metzger, a brilliant defender who had grown up in the Cubs' system. Then, in the fifth, Williams homered into the bleachers in right to break a 2–2 tie. So now he was 6-for-6 on the day.

But there was more. In the five-run seventh that broke the game open, Billy lined a single to center and scored on a home run by Pepitone. Then, for good measure, he came up in the eighth and lined a one-out single to right. That made him 8-for-8 for the afternoon: five singles, a double, two homers in eight official at-bats, plus a sacrifice fly and a total of four RBIs.

Not a bad day's work. The fact that the Cubs won the game 9–5, that Rick Monday had broken out of a 1-for-33 slump with a pair of home runs and that Bill Hands (7–6) had finally won after dropping four in a row made it even better.

A Big Day for Peanuts

The Wrigley Field crowd this Friday was a loud one. Of the 36,605 people on hand, some 11,451 were ladies and girls, quite boisterous in their hatred for the first-place Brooklyn Dodgers and their love for the third-place Cubs.

The home team was responsible for most of the noise, the Cubs having shut out the Dodgers 1–0 the day before (Johnny Schmitz topping Joe Hatten) to move to 40–33 and to within seven games of the league leaders.

The pitchers this day were young and wild 21-year-old Rex Barney for Brooklyn and the veteran Hank Wyse, who had gone 22–10 for the pennant-winning Cubs of 1945. Barney still was having control problems: Through 44 $^2/_3$ innings this season, he had walked 39 batters. As one New York sportswriter, Bob Cooke, put it: "Barney pitched as if the plate were high and outside."

This outing would be no different.

The Dodgers staked Barney to a 2–0 lead in the first inning, but Stan Hack doubled, Don Johnson walked and, with one out, Phil Cavarretta also walked to fill the bases. Next up was Cubs center fielder Peanuts Lowrey, a native of Culver City, Calif., and something of a movie star: He had been in episodes of the *Our Gang* comedy series and had appeared in *Pride of the Yankees* in 1942 and eventually would have roles in *The Stratton Story* and *The Winning Team*. Now he was about to take center stage at Wrigley Field.

The right-handed hitter lined a single to center, two runs scored and the game was tied. The Cubs went on to KO Barney and cakewalked to a 13–2 romp.

And the big gun was Lowrey.

In the fifth inning, Lowrey, all of 5 feet 8 inches and 170 pounds, faced Dodgers reliever Art Herring, who stood 5-7 and weighed 168. Peanuts won this encounter of giants, driving a three-run homer into the left-field bleachers. Now the Cubs led 9–2.

At a Glance

WP: Wyse (9–7)

HR: Lowrey (3), Rickert (5)

Key stat: Of the 26 players in this game's box score, five became big-league managers—Eddie Stanky, Cookie Lavagetto, Phil Cavarretta, Stan Hack and Billy Jurges. Two others were coaches with the Cubs under, among others, Leo Durocher—Pete Reiser and, of course, Peanuts Lowrey.

In the sixth, Lowrey added a two-run single off Hal Gregg to highlight a four-run burst that closed the scoring. When it was all over, Peanuts was 3-for-5 with three runs scored and a career-high seven RBIs.

Cool Koonce Conquers Reds with One-Hitter

Fourteen months before, he was pitching for the baseball team at Campbell College in Buies Creek, N.C., the same school that had produced Jim and Gaylord Perry.

Just 12 months before that, after signing for a $30,000 bonus, he was pitching—without that much success (he finished 6–10)—for the Cubs' Class B farm team in Wenatchee, Wash.

Now here was Cal Koonce, pitching against the defending National League champion Cincinnati Reds at Wrigley Field, seeking to improve his won-lost record to 8–2—an incredible feat for a 21-year-old rookie employed by a team that was then 25 games under .500.

Make it 24 under. Reds second baseman Don Blasingame lined a single over second base with one out in the fourth. Gordy Coleman walked in the fifth. Wally Post reached in the ninth on Ron Santo's error. They were the only Reds to get on base against Koonce, who with his one-hit gem indeed moved to 8–2 on the season, thanks to Santo's sixth-inning sacrifice fly that brought in Ernie Banks with the afternoon's lone run.

In beating Reds ace Bob Purkey, whose record dropped to 14–3, Koonce needed only minimal defensive support. George Altman, in right field, made a leaping catch at the wall to retire Johnny Edwards in the third inning, and rookie second baseman Kenny Hubbs went behind second base in the fourth to turn Marty Keough's bid for a base hit into a force out.

The Cubs tried to pad Koonce's lead in the eighth when they loaded the bases with no outs. But catcher Elvin Tappe, perhaps an even weaker hitter than Koonce, struck out, as did Koonce. Rookie Lou Brock, who already had three hits on the day, grounded out.

At a Glance

WP: Koonce (8–2)

Key stat: Number of punches thrown in benches-clearing flareup between Purkey and Santo in sixth inning: 0.

In the ninth, Koonce registered his third and fourth strikeouts, getting Leo Cardenas and pinch-hitter Jerry Lynch, the noted Cub-killer, before Post reached on the Santo error. But, fittingly, Koonce ended it by retiring Blasingame on a roller to Banks at first base.

Koonce, who finished the '62 season with a 10–10 record, never won in double figures again but he won a ring—as a member of the 1969 world champion New York Mets—and later became the winningest baseball coach in the history of his college alma mater. He died of lymphoma in 1993, three weeks shy of his 53rd birthday.

Hands Hands Mets a Loss

Bill Hands was one outstanding pitcher in the Cubs' fateful 1969 season. The right-hander from Rutherford, N.J., won 20 games, worked 300 innings and recorded a 2.49 ERA. He also was something of a stopper: He ended a four-game skid in June, a five-game losing streak in July (when he won 6–2 in New York in the series finale) and an eight-game tailspin in September.

He also was the undisputed chess champ of the Cubs' clubhouse.

Perhaps his most clutch performance took place at Wrigley Field on this Monday afternoon, the opener of a three-game series with the surprising, second-place Mets, who the week before had won two of three from the Cubs at Shea Stadium and who trailed NL East-leading Chicago by five games. This obviously was to be a key series, and a standing-room-only crowd of 40,252, including 37,473 paying customers, was there to witness the proceedings.

What those fans saw was, as Cubs manager Leo Durocher put it afterward, "a World Series game." Despite the heat, the atmosphere was October-like. And when this one was over, the Cubs' lead had increased by a game.

There was no score when the Cubs came up in the sixth against young Tom Seaver, who five days earlier had shut out the North Siders on one hit, losing his bid for a perfect game when Jim Qualls singled with one out in the ninth.

Here, with one out, Don Kessinger dropped a marvelous bunt between third and home. Seaver mishandled the ball, but Kessinger likely would have beaten the play regardless. "Seaver," Kessinger said later, "is a good fielder and bounces off that mound well, but I had a feeling that was a base hit, because that's as good as I can bunt a ball."

Now Durocher flashed the hit-and-run sign, and Glenn Beckert, with Kessinger running on the pitch, grounded to second baseman Ken Boswell.

Mets	AB	R	H	RBI
Agee cf	4	0	0	0
Boswell 2b	4	0	1	0
Jones lf	4	0	1	0
Shamsky rf	4	0	0	0
Garrett 3b	3	0	1	0
Kranepool 1b	3	0	0	0
Martin c	4	0	2	0
Harrelson pr	0	0	0	0
Weis ss	3	0	1	0
Clendenon ph	1	0	0	0
Seaver p	1	0	0	0
Totals	**31**	**0**	**6**	**0**

Cubs	AB	R	H	RBI
Kessinger ss	3	1	1	0
Beckert 2b	4	0	1	0
Williams rf-lf	3	0	2	1
Santo 3b	3	0	0	0
Banks 1b	3	0	1	0
Smith lf	2	0	0	0
Hickman lf-rf	1	0	0	0
Hundley c	3	0	0	0
Qualls cf	3	0	0	0
Hands p	3	0	0	0
Regan p	0	0	0	0
Totals	**28**	**1**	**5**	**1**

NYM 0 0 0 0 0 0 0 0 0 - 0 6 0
CHI 0 0 0 0 0 1 0 0 X - 1 5 0

Mets	IP	H	R	ER	BB	SO
Seaver L (14-4)	8	5	1	1	1	4
Totals	**8**	**5**	**1**	**1**	**1**	**4**

Cubs	IP	H	R	ER	BB	SO
Hands W (11-7)	8.2	6	0	0	3	5
Regan S (9)	0.1	0	0	0	0	0
Totals	**9**	**6**	**0**	**0**	**3**	**5**

DP—New York. 2B—New York Martin. SH—New York Seaver. LOB—New York 8; Chicago 4. Attendance: 37,473.

Bill Hands recorded 20 wins and a 2.49 earned-run average in the Cubs' ill-fated 1969 season.

Kessinger moved into scoring position. Then Billy Williams lined a 1-0 delivery to left-center for a single that sent the Chicago shortstop sprinting across home plate with the Cubs' first run off Seaver in 19 innings.

Hands went out to protect his lead, but it wasn't easy. With one out, J.C. Martin, one of three former White Sox players in the Mets' lineup (Al Weis and Tommie Agee were the others), sent a long double off the right-field wall that, said right fielder Williams, "missed being a home run by six inches." Weis popped to first baseman Ernie Banks for the second out, but Seaver walked, bringing up Agee, the 1966 AL Rookie of the Year who, after two off years, had regained his stroke.

The best that Agee could manage was a fly ball to center, so the score remained 1–0.

Soon it was the ninth, Hands and the Cubs still up 1–0. Hands struck out Wayne Garrett and retired Ed Kranepool on a bouncer to Beckert, but Martin looped a base hit to left, and the Mets were still alive. The batter was Donn Clendenon, the former Pirates slugger, batting for Weis. When Hands missed with his first two pitches, Durocher arrived with his hook.

"I was surprised to see Leo come out," Hands said, "but I told him I was out of gas, finished. I'm thinking that Clendenon is a good hitter and can hit the ball out, and I'm tired. I can't think of myself in that situation. I've got to think of the ballclub."

In came Phil Regan, who went to 3-2 on Clendenon before the tall right-handed batter finally hit a soft liner that a leaping Beckert gloved for the final out.

The next two days did not go as well for the Cubs. The Mets won 5–4 and 9–5 as Agee and Weis each went 3-for-9. Weis hit two homers and drove in four runs and Agee had a double, triple and home run. It would be a long time—months, in fact—until the Cubs beat the Mets again. That was in the season finale at Wrigley Field, when the Mets finally lost a game after their amazin' 38–10 run.

At Last, Broglio Wins One

It was with much fanfare that the Cubs had announced the acquisition of former 21-game-winner Ernie Broglio from the St. Louis Cardinals almost exactly one month earlier. Broglio, who had won 18 the season before with a 2.99 ERA, was to be the starting pitcher who could put the Cubs over the top in the tight National League race.

It sounded good. The Cubs were 27–27, in sixth place but only 5.5 games out of the lead. Their pitching staff boasted starters Dick Ellsworth, Larry Jackson and Bob Buhl, the Big Three from the 1963 team that had finished in that magical, fairy-tale land north of .500—first Cubs team to do so since 1946. Now Cubs GM John Holland and head coach Bob Kennedy agreed that one more quality starter could mean a pennant flying on the North Side.

Broglio, they decided, was that man. So they had traded second-line pitchers Paul Toth and Jack Spring plus third-year right-fielder Lou Brock to St. Louis for Broglio, reliever Bobby Shantz and Doug Clemens, an outfielder to help fill the outfield vacancy.

At a Glance
WP: Broglio (4–9)
HR: Cowan (13)
Key stat: Losing pitcher was Tracy Stallard, the man who gave up Roger Maris' 61st homer in 1961.

By July 16, two things had become clear. The vacancy in the Cubs' starting rotation remained, while the vacancy in the Cubs' outfield was getting larger with each passing day.

Broglio, who had arrived from St. Louis with a 3–5 record, a 3.50 ERA and amid whispers that he might be damaged goods, had pitched in seven games (six starts) and gone 0–4 with a 6.99 ERA. Brock, meanwhile, was hitting .339 as a Cardinal with nine steals—after hitting .251 with 10 steals in two-plus months for the Cubs. Also, St. Louis, 28–31 on the day of the deal, was now 44–42 and 7.5 games out of first place. The Cubs stood at 41–43, 9.5 back.

But on this Thursday afternoon at Wrigley Field, Broglio at long last emerged with his first "W" as a Cub. He went the distance and defeated the lowly New York Mets 11-1, despite walking four batters and allowing 10 hits.

Broglio made nine more starts that year, including three consecutive triumphs over Milwaukee (5–1), Pittsburgh (4–3) and Philadelphia (3–1 on a three-hitter), before being shut down for the season with a sore right elbow.

The soreness was the result of damage to the ulnar lateral ligament. Surgery didn't help: He pitched only 113 innings the next two seasons, posting a 3–12 record, before the Cubs released him in July 1966.

And Brock? All he did was lead the Cardinals to the World Series in 1964, '67 and '68 on his way to the Hall of Fame.

Cubs Win in 21 Thanks to Flack

Max Flack was the big star of this Wednesday afternoon game at Weeghman Park. His teammate, pitcher George "Lefty" Tyler, deserved star treatment as well, for reasons that will soon become obvious, but if it hadn't been for Flack, the Cubs and Phillies might still be playing.

As it was, the first-place Cubs, with a six-game lead over second-place New York, had to play 21 innings before they finally put away Philadelphia, then in fourth place in the eight-team NL. Astonishingly, both pitchers—Tyler and the Phils' Milton Watson—worked all 21 innings.

The details:

Flack, a 5-foot-7, 148-pounder from downstate Belleville, Ill., collected five hits on the day and scored the Cubs' first run way, way back in the first inning. The Phillies tied it in the fourth on Gavvy Cravath's RBI single. It stayed 1–1 until the 21st, which was going to be the last inning, anyway: The teams had agreed on those terms earlier in the afternoon so the Phils could catch an 8 p.m. train to Pittsburgh.

The Phils put men at first and third with one out in their half of the 21st, but Rollie Zeider stopped Fred Luderus' hot smash to third and held the runner before firing to first for the second out, and Tyler grabbed Irish Meusel's comebacker and threw to first to end the threat.

In the bottom half, Turner Barber batted for Zeider and reached on a scratch infield hit. Bill Killefer was hit by a pitch, and then Bill McCabe, batting for Tyler, put down a bunt that rolled to a stop, in fair territory, halfway down the line toward third base. Now the bases were loaded with nobody out. Seconds later, Flack—who batted just .257 that season—hit the first pitch into left field for the base hit that brought the marathon to an end.

> ## At a Glance
>
> **WP:** Tyler (12–5)
>
> **Key stats:** At this point, the longest game in NL history was Brooklyn's 22-inning win at Pittsburgh on Aug. 17, 1922. The longest game in NL (and big-league) history is a 26-inning 1–1 tie between Brooklyn and Boston on May 1, 1920. Longest Cub game? May 17, 1927, a 22-inning 4–3 win at Boston.

Incidentally, the Cubs took on last-place Brooklyn the next afternoon on the North Side and lost 3–2, this time in 16 innings. Brooklyn went on to sweep the four-game series, but fret not: In a season halted on Labor Day because of the war, the Cubs wound up 84–45 and 10.5 games ahead of the runner-up Giants.

Wood Stars in Preview

It was once Joe Robbie Stadium. That was during the time Harry Caray called it Joe Rudi Stadium. Later it was named Pro Player Park, then Pro Player Stadium. Then it became, simply, Dolphin Stadium, until inevitably it had another name change, this time to Land Shark Stadium. Today the structure is called Sun Life Stadium.

Regardless of the place's name, very few among the 30,432 fans that day at the football/baseball venue just south of the Dade-Broward county line in Florida would have suggested that they were seeing a preview of the 2003 National League Championship Series.

After all, here were the Marlins at 50–46, not only 13.5 games behind Atlanta in the NL East, but even four back of Arizona and Philadelphia in the race for the wild card. The Cubs, meanwhile, stood at 47–48 and trailed Houston by 4.5 in the Central.

> ## At a Glance
>
> **WP:** Wood (10–6)
>
> **Key stat:** The Florida starting lineup included three future Cubs—Juan Pierre, Derrek Lee and Todd Hollandsworth.

Two young hard throwers, Kerry Wood for the Cubs and Brad Penny for Florida, were dominating in the south Florida heat. Penny retired the first 12 Cubs before Moises Alou opened the fifth with a double, moved to third when Marlins shortstop Alex Gonzalez bobbled Hee Seop Choi's grounder and scored on a sacrifice fly by the Cubs' Alex Gonzalez (no relation).

That was the game's lone run, as Penny went eight innings on a yield of four hits and fanned eight while walking but one. Wood, notching his fourth career shutout, gave up a first-inning double to Ivan Rodriguez and a single in the sixth to Juan Pierre. He also walked five but, like Penny, struck out eight.

Wood had to face the top of the batting order in the Marlins' ninth. Pierre lined to second and Luis Castillo grounded to short. Next was Rodriguez, who drew a walk on a 3-2 pitch. Manager Dusty Baker had the hook ready as Juan Encarnacion approached the plate, and when the count reached 3-0, it seemed almost certain he would have to use it.

But Wood came back with two strikes and then threw a fastball—his 130th pitch of the game—that Encarnacion grounded to Choi at first for the final out. The Cubs were at .500 again.

"I'm tired, beat, drained, dizzy," Wood said in the clubhouse. "I was running on fumes, but I've said it a million times before: We start the game and we want to finish it. I felt like it was my game to lose, and I'm glad they stuck with me."

One Day, 25 Innings, Two Victories

The National League pennant race moved toward late July with four teams still very much in contention. The St. Louis Cardinals couldn't quite shake the Cubs or John McGraw's Giants, and even the Cincinnati Reds were within 6.5 games of the top spot.

Some 35,000 fans showed up at Wrigley Field this Saturday for a double-header between the Giants and Cubs. And this bargain bill turned out to be exactly that. Those in attendance saw 25 innings of baseball—and a pair of Cub victories.

Game 1 was a pitchers' duel between the Cubs' Art Nehf, a former Giant, and "Fat Freddie" Fitzsimmons, optimistically listed at 185 pounds and on his way to a 20–9 season. The Giants struck first in the third inning when Jimmy Welsh singled home Shanty Hogan, who had reached on an error by shortstop Woody English. Clyde Beck's home run tied things in the sixth, and that was all the scoring until the 15th.

In the visitors' half, the Giants loaded the bases with no outs. Fred Lindstrom hit a grounder to Beck at third, and Clyde fired to catcher Mike Gonzalez for a force out at the plate. Due up next was New York's slugging first baseman, the lefthanded-hitting Bill Terry, who eventually ended the season at .326 but had opened the day at .298 and was 0-for-6 thus far. Cubs manager Joe McCarthy, playing the percentages, called for lefty Percy Jones to replace Guy Bush, who had relieved Nehf in the 14th.

McGraw, in a bit of a surprise, called Terry back and sent up Jack Cummings, a right-handed batter who was 6-for-17 (all as a pinch-hitter) for a .353 average and who had belted a grand slam eight days earlier in St. Louis. Not this time. Cummings hit a one-hopper to Beck, who threw to the plate for one out, and Gonzalez relayed to first baseman Charlie Grimm to complete the double play.

Freddie Maguire singled to begin the Cubs' 15th, took second on Kiki Cuyler's sacrifice bunt and third on Hack Wilson's long fly to right-center. Then

> **At a Glance**
>
> **Game 1**
>
> **WP:** Jones (8–3)
>
> **HR:** Beck (3)
>
> **Game 2**
>
> **WP:** Bush (10–6)
>
> **Key stat:** English was 5-for-10 on the day with four doubles.

Hall of Famer Hazen Shirley "Kiki" Cuyler had a lifetime .321 batting average and 328 stolen bases.

Riggs Stephenson, hitless in six tries so far, ripped a single between Lindstrom and shortstop Travis Jackson, and the Cubs had won 2–1.

New York led 3–2 in the seventh inning of Game 2 until English, with two out, drove a double off the wall in left, sending Beck across with the tying run. The Giants went ahead 4–3 on a pinch sacrifice fly by Les Mann, but the hosts came right back in their half. With two out and the bases empty, English drew a walk and scored when Maguire's long drive hit the wall in right-center for an RBI double.

Finally, in the last of the 10th, after the Giants had gone out quietly, the Cubs put an abrupt end to the proceedings. There were two outs and the bases were empty when Stephenson lined a single to right. And then Gabby Hartnett, who had sat out the opener and was 0-for-4 in the nightcap, launched a triple off the barrier in left-center, Stephenson scoring from first with the decisive run.

The sweep moved the Cubs into second place, four games off the Cardinals' pace, and dropped the New Yorkers to fourth, 6.5 behind. On Sept. 12, after a 6–1 decision over eventual champion St. Louis before 45,000 at Wrigley Field, the Cubs trailed by three games. They would get no closer.

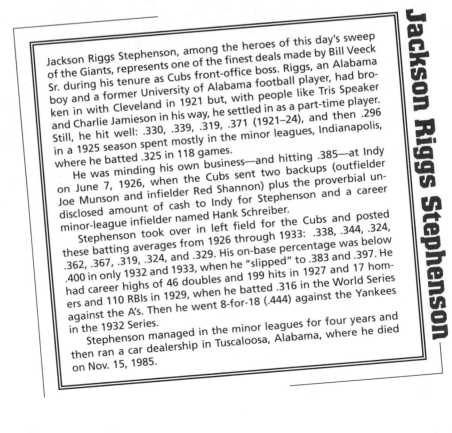

Jackson Riggs Stephenson

Jackson Riggs Stephenson, among the heroes of this day's sweep of the Giants, represents one of the finest deals made by Bill Veeck Sr. during his tenure as Cubs front-office boss. Riggs, an Alabama boy and a former University of Alabama football player, had broken in with Cleveland in 1921 but, with people like Tris Speaker and Charlie Jamieson in his way, he settled in as a part-time player. Still, he hit well: .330, .339, .319, .371 (1921–24), and then .296 in a 1925 season spent mostly in the minor leagues, Indianapolis, where he batted .325 in 118 games.

He was minding his own business—and hitting .385—at Indy on June 7, 1926, when the Cubs sent two backups (outfielder Joe Munson and infielder Red Shannon) plus the proverbial undisclosed amount of cash to Indy for Stephenson and a career minor-league infielder named Hank Schreiber.

Stephenson took over in left field for the Cubs and posted these batting averages from 1926 through 1933: .338, .344, .324, .362, .367, .319, .324, and .329. His on-base percentage was below .400 in only 1932 and 1933, when he "slipped" to .383 and .397. He had career highs of 46 doubles and 199 hits in 1927 and 17 homers and 110 RBIs in 1929, when he batted .316 in the World Series against the A's. Then he went 8-for-18 (.444) against the Yankees in the 1932 Series.

Stephenson managed in the minor leagues for four years and then ran a car dealership in Tuscaloosa, Alabama, where he died on Nov. 15, 1985.

A Long but Profitable Afternoon for Cubs, Kingman

They started the game on May 10, when darkness caused it to be suspended after nine innings. They finished it on a Monday afternoon in July, and it took nine more innings to do so. And then they played the day's regularly scheduled game.

The Cubs did not mind, however. When Game 2 was completed, the North Siders had won a pair of thrillers from the Cincinnati Reds and found themselves in third place in the NL East, just 1.5 games behind division-leading Montreal. The Reds had dropped to five games behind West-leading Houston.

The suspended game, officially listed as having lasted 5 hours 17 minutes, actually took 75 days to finish. Several players who had taken part in the May 10 action were now elsewhere. One player, Kenny Henderson, began the game in the Reds' dugout and finished it as the Cubs' right fielder.

Another note: Attendance back in May for the suspended contest had been 9,164. On July 23, there were 36,993 on hand, a figure that put the Cubs over the million mark (at 1,017,843).

The first game resumed with the top of the 10th inning. Bruce Sutter was touched for a run in the 11th, and Cincy led 8–7. The first two Cubs went down in the bottom half against Doug Bair, but then came consecutive singles by Bill Buckner, Dave Kingman and Steve Ontiveros, and the game was tied 8–8.

At a Glance

Game 1

WP: McGlothen (4–3)

HR: Foote (3), Kingman (9), Sizemore (1)

Game 2

WP: Hernandez (2–0)

HR: Kingman (30)

Key stat: Kingman was 6-for-12 with five RBIs in the two games.

Neither team threatened until the 18th, when Henderson opened with a base hit off new pitcher Manny Sarmiento. Cubs pitcher Lynn McGlothen, who had shut down the Reds since the 16th, then bunted Henderson to second. Kingman was given an intentional walk, and Ontiveros—getting his third hit and third RBI of the game—singled home Henderson for a 9–8 Cubs triumph.

Then came the regularly scheduled game, and this one, a pitchers' duel matching Tom Hume against 23-year-old Cub rookie Bill Caudill, took just 2:23 to complete. The Reds broke serve with a run in the fifth, Ray Knight's sacrifice fly scoring Dan Driessen, and that's how it stayed until the ninth. The

Reds loaded the bases with one out against lefty reliever Willie Hernandez, but Knight rapped into a 6-4-3 double play, and the Cubs were still within a run.

Larry Biittner, who'd had one of the four Cub hits off Hume to that moment, led off the home ninth with a single to right. Miguel Dilone went in to run for Biittner, and stole second, and now the batter was Kingman, in the midst of his monster 48-homer season. With first base open, Reds manager John McNamara decided against an intentional walk (which would have put the winning run on base) and instead chose to have Hume pitch to "Kong."

On the 1-2 delivery, Hume got Kingman to swing at a low, outside slider. Kingman, swinging seemingly with one hand, drilled the ball into the left-field bleachers for his 30th home run of 1979 and a 2–1 victory.

"You couldn't ask for anything more," Kingman said. "Driving in the tying and winning runs with the people pulling for me in that situation was what I tried to do. . . . It's a great feeling."

"Kingman's so strong," said McNamara. "It looked like he just reached out and flipped the ball into the stands."

Then he added about the team that had just swept his: "They have as good a chance to win the East as anybody."

The Reds went on to win the West. The Cubs were fourth in the East.

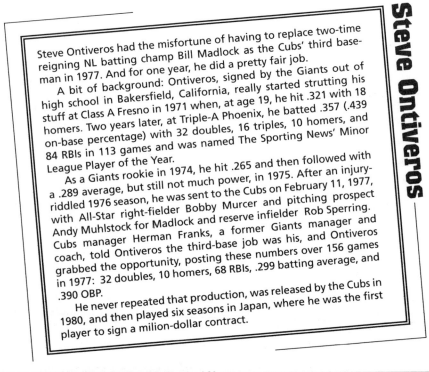

Steve Ontiveros had the misfortune of having to replace two-time reigning NL batting champ Bill Madlock as the Cubs' third baseman in 1977. And for one year, he did a pretty fair job.

A bit of background: Ontiveros, signed by the Giants out of high school in Bakersfield, California, really started strutting his stuff at Class A Fresno in 1971 when, at age 19, he hit .321 with 18 homers. Two years later, at Triple-A Phoenix, he batted .357 (.439 on-base percentage) with 32 doubles, 16 triples, 10 homers, and 84 RBIs in 113 games and was named The Sporting News' Minor League Player of the Year.

As a Giants rookie in 1974, he hit .265 and then followed with a .289 average, but still not much power, in 1975. After an injury-riddled 1976 season, he was sent to the Cubs on February 11, 1977, with All-Star right-fielder Bobby Murcer and pitching prospect Andy Muhlstock for Madlock and reserve infielder Rob Sperring. Cubs manager Herman Franks, a former Giants manager and coach, told Ontiveros the third-base job was his, and Ontiveros grabbed the opportunity, posting these numbers over 156 games in 1977: 32 doubles, 10 homers, 68 RBIs, .299 batting average, and .390 OBP.

He never repeated that production, was released by the Cubs in 1980, and then played six seasons in Japan, where he was the first player to sign a milion-dollar contract.

Steve Ontiveros

No Grace Period for Phillies

Mark Grace spent 13 seasons with the Cubs. In nine of those years, he hit better than .300 and in three of them his on-base percentage was .400-plus. Three times he drove in 90 or more runs, and four times he won Gold Gloves.

And yet in all those years the Cubs had a winning record just four times (one was 73–71 in the late-starting 1995 season) and won just one division title. They finished 20 games out of first place once, 24 out once and 30 out twice.

That he managed to remain so productive during such misery is a compliment to him.

And it's probably not surprising to learn that the biggest RBI game of Grace's career came on a rainy night in dreary Philadelphia and in the ugly facility called Veterans Stadium—against a Phillies team that, like the Cubs, would finish last in its division.

This was the night Grace drove in a career-high six runs. And the Cubs needed them all, because, after getting out to an 8–3 lead, they had to rally in the ninth inning for a 14–9 victory.

On hand to watch this matchup of losing clubs were 17,825 on an evening that included delays of 1 hour 22 minutes during the fourth inning and 29 minutes during the eighth.

Grace singled but was stranded in the first inning, then helped get the Cubs rolling with his two-out bases-loaded single in a four-run second. In the fourth, he walked ahead of Sammy Sosa's three-run homer that made it 7–3 Cubs.

A two-run homer by Ron Gant brought the Phils to within 8–5 in the sixth. Grace singled in the eighth, when the Cubs loaded the bases before Gary Matthews Jr. lined out to Doug Glanville in center to end the threat and keep the Cub lead at three.

Cubs	AB	R	H	RBI
Young 2b	4	3	2	0
Gutierrez ss	4	1	1	3
Grace 1b	5	2	4	6
Sosa rf	5	2	3	4
Buford cf	5	0	2	0
H. Rodriguez lf	4	1	1	1
Matthews ph-lf	2	0	0	0
Nieves 3b	6	0	0	0
Girardi c	4	3	1	0
Tapani p	2	1	0	0
Meyers ph	1	0	0	0
Van Poppel p	0	0	0	0
Heredia p	0	0	0	0
Greene ph	0	1	0	0
Rain p	0	0	0	0
Totals	**42**	**14**	**14**	**14**

Phillies	AB	R	H	RBI
Glanville cf	5	0	1	0
Morandini 2b	2	1	0	0
Brock p	0	0	0	0
Abreu rf	4	1	1	2
Rolen 3b	5	0	0	0
Burrell 1b	4	2	1	1
Gant lf	3	3	2	2
Prince c	3	0	1	1
Brogna ph	1	0	0	0
Bennett c	1	0	1	0
Relaford ss	4	1	1	0
Chen p	0	0	0	0
Holzemer p	1	0	0	0
Sefcik ph	1	0	0	0
Vosberg p	0	0	0	0
Hunter ph	1	1	1	3
Byrd p	0	0	0	0
Jordan 2b	0	0	0	0
Totals	**35**	**9**	**9**	**9**

```
CHI  0 4 0 3 1 0 0 0 6 - 14 14 0
PHI  0 1 2 0 0 2 0 3 1 -  9  9 1
```

Cubs	IP	H	R	ER	BB	SO
Tapani	6	5	5	5	3	5
Van Poppel	1.2	2	3	3	4	1
Heredia W (6-3)	0.1	0	0	0	0	0
Rain	1	2	1	1	0	2
Totals	**9**	**9**	**9**	**9**	**7**	**8**

Phillies	IP	H	R	ER	BB	SO
Chen	3	5	4	4	3	8
Holzemer	3	5	4	4	2	3
Vosberg	2	1	0	0	2	1
Byrd L (2-9)	0.1	2	6	5	2	0
Brock	0.2	1	0	0	0	0
Totals	**9**	**14**	**14**	**13**	**9**	**12**

E—Philadelphia Relaford. 2B—Chicago Sosa; Philadelphia Gant, Prince. HR—Chicago Grace (9), Rodriguez (18), Sosa 2 (30,31); Philadelphia Burrell (9), Hunter (6), Gant (20), Abreu (15). SH—Philadelphia Chen. HBP—Chicago Young; Philadelphia Morandini. LOB—Chicago 11; Philadelpia 8. SB—Chicago Young; Philadelphia Morandini. Attendance: 17,825.

July 26, 2000
Cubs 14, Phillies 9

In the Phils' eighth, Todd Van Poppel walked Gant and Desi Relaford and then gave up a game-tying home run to pinch-hitter Brian Hunter, who was in the final year of a less-than-spectacular career in which he would finish with a .234 batting average. So the game moved to the ninth, tied 8–8.

Paul Byrd took over the pitching duties for Philly, and, with one out, Joe Girardi reached on Relaford's 23rd error of the season. Pinch-hitter Willie Greene walked and Eric Young was hit by a pitch to fill the bases. Ricky Gutierrez walked to force in the go-ahead run, and then Grace crushed a grand slam into the seats in right, and the Cubs were up 13–8. Sosa then aded a solo shot for a 14–8 lead. Big right-hander Steve Rain allowed a home run to the Phils' Pat Burrell before finally getting the final out.

With the victory, the Cubs were 45–54, in third place, 11.5 games behind NL Central leader St. Louis. Indeed, they were a respectable 50–56 in early August. Then they went an incredible 15–41 the rest of the season, throwing in losing streaks of six, seven and eight games for good measure.

It surely was not Mark Grace's fault.

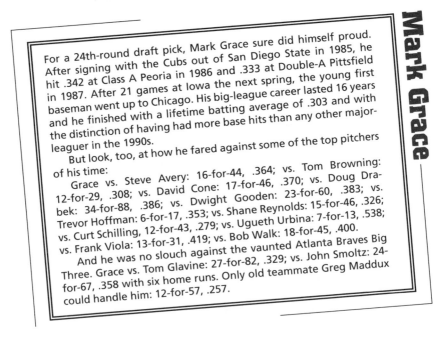

Mark Grace

For a 24th-round draft pick, Mark Grace sure did himself proud. After signing with the Cubs out of San Diego State in 1985, he hit .342 at Class A Peoria in 1986 and .333 at Double-A Pittsfield in 1987. After 21 games at Iowa the next spring, the young first baseman went up to Chicago. His big-league career lasted 16 years and he finished with a lifetime batting average of .303 and with the distinction of having had more base hits than any other major-leaguer in the 1990s.

But look, too, at how he fared against some of the top pitchers of his time:

Grace vs. Steve Avery: 16-for-44, .364; vs. Tom Browning: 12-for-29, .308; vs. David Cone: 17-for-46, .370; vs. Doug Drabek: 34-for-88, .386; vs. Dwight Gooden: 23-for-60, .383; vs. Trevor Hoffman: 6-for-17, .353; vs. Shane Reynolds: 15-for-46, .326; vs. Curt Schilling, 12-for-43, .279; vs. Ugueth Urbina: 7-for-13, .538; vs. Frank Viola: 13-for-31, .419; vs. Bob Walk: 18-for-45, .400.

And he was no slouch against the vaunted Atlanta Braves Big Three. Grace vs. Tom Glavine: 27-for-82, .329; vs. John Smoltz: 24-for-67, .358 with six home runs. Only old teammate Greg Maddux could handle him: 12-for-57, .257.

Soriano Slam Keeps Cubs on Top

The Cubs, having won four straight, had climbed back into first place in the NL Central for the first time since April 10. Yet neither that fact nor the boisterous support of the Monday night crowd of 40,794 could get the North Siders' offense going against Houston lefty Wandy Rodriguez.

A second-inning home run off Carlos Zambrano by Cub-killer Carlos Lee, the former White Sox slugger, was matched in the fourth by Derrek Lee's 20th homer of the season. And that was all the scoring there would be for about 2 ½ hours.

The Cubs had threatened in the ninth, thanks to the wildness of Jose Valverde, who walked Milton Bradley and pinch-hitters Micah Hoffpauir and Kosuke Fukudome, Hoffpauir intentionally. The bases were filled with one out for Mike Fontenot. Here, manager Lou Piniella signaled for a suicide squeeze, but Fontenot failed to make contact and Bradley was an easy out at the plate.

> ## At a Glance
>
> **WP:** Samardzija (1–1)
>
> **HR:** D. Lee (20), Soriano (18)
>
> **Key stat:** Rookie right-handers Stevens and Jeff Samardzija, between them, got 11 of the 12 Houston extra-inning outs.

The game dragged on, both teams putting together mild threats, the biggest coming in the Houston 10th when Jason Michaels tripled with two out. But Jeff Stevens struck out Ivan Rodriguez.

It was still 1–1 when the Cubs came up in the 13th against reliever Chris Sampson, one day removed from a stint on the disabled list. Sampson walked Derrek Lee, and then Aramis Ramirez lashed his third hit of the night past shortstop Miguel Tejada, sending Lee to third. Bradley was given an intentional walk to set up a force at any base. The batter was Alfonso Soriano, whose night had not gone well. He was 0-for-5, having struck out three times, bounced into a double play and grounded out—failing to run on the latter, supposedly because the ball had hit him in the foot.

So there was The Fonz, at the plate with a chance to make up for the evening's transgressions. Here came Sampson's 1-0 pitch, and Soriano chose that moment to come up with "my best swing of the second half," as he put it later. The ball disappeared into the night, a majestic grand slam, and the Cubs had won 5–1.

"I went 0-for-5," Soriano said, "but in my last at-bat I got the victory."

Cubs, and Homers, are Flying against Reds

Over the decades, the legendary Wrigley Field jetstream has driven many a pitcher to drink. The history of baseball at Clark and Addison is replete with routine fly balls that have landed in those oh-so-inviting bleachers.

Turk Lown, a Cubs reliever for several years before helping the White Sox win a pennant in 1959, was still cowering in fear decades later at mere mention of the North Side ballpark.

"At Wrigley Field, you had Ernie Banks' wind blowing out, boy oh boy," he once said. "Driving to the ballpark, as I approached it, I'd look at the flags to see which way the wind was blowing and say a 'Hail Mary' if the wind was blowing out. And most of the time it was."

And that's when you'd get these marvelous 12–10 or 9–7 or 15–12 scores and instant elevation to hero status for newcomers who might have hit a couple of lazy fly balls into the seats, helped along by the friendly breezes. It was baseball as 16-inch softball: double-figure scores, and the team batting last wins.

But those types of games could be quite exciting—and sometimes meaningful. Such was the case on this particular Thursday, when the powerful Cincinnati Reds, two-time defending world champs but floundering now at 49–48 and 11.5 back in the NL West, met the East-leading Cubs (59–39) on a humid afternoon with the wind blowing straight out to center field at 15 mph.

"We were hitting a lot of homers in batting practice," said Cubs catcher George Mitterwald later that day, "but the Reds were bombing them out on the street. When the wind is blowing out like that, all you can do is hope the pitchers keep the ball down."

The unfortunate men whose turn it was to start this game were the Reds' Dale Murray, usually a reliever, and the Cubs' Ray Burris. Murray lasted one inning, Burris two. Murray was tagged for six runs, five hits and three home runs,—Burris for seven hits, eight runs and three home runs. By the end of two innings, the Cubs led 7–6, and the 32,155 people in the stands were beginning to suspect they were witnessing something special.

A quick rundown on the first few innings:

The Reds' Pete Rose, who had predicted a 15–14 final score, opened the game with a home run. After singles by Ken Griffey and Joe Morgan and a George Foster strikeout, Johnny Bench homered, and it was already 4–0. With two out, Davey Concepcion singled and Mike Lum, a reserve first baseman-outfielder, hit a home run also. It was 6–0, and this was getting silly.

But then the Cubs came up, and it quickly became apparent that they didn't find anything silly about this game. Ivan DeJesus doubled, Larry Biittner walked and Bill Buckner launched a blast over the wall in right to cut the lead in half. Bobby Murcer followed that shot with one of his own, and it was 6–4 Reds after one.

Cincinnati, believe it or not, went out 1-2-3 in the second. The Cubs did not. First came a Mitterwald home run, then a Burris double, a pitching change, then an RBI single by Biittner and a fielder's-choice grounder from Murcer that brought in the go-ahead run.

The Reds came back with an RBI double by Cesar Geronimo, a two-run single by Concepcion and a run-scoring single by Griffey, and just like that the Reds were up 10–7. The Cubs closed it to 10–8 in their half of the third when reliever Donnie Moore tripled home Manny Trillo. A strange game had become even stranger.

Paul Reuschel escaped from a mess created by Moore in the Reds' fourth, leaving the door open for the hosts. The Cubs took advantage by scoring twice for a 10–10 tie, Steve Ontiveros and Trillo delivering two-out RBI singles.

Nothing happened in the fifth, but Griffey made sure such would not be the case in the sixth when he led off with a homer that put Cincy ahead 11-10.

Griffey was the man again in the seventh, crossing up Cubs strategy with a two-run double off lefty Willie Hernandez. Now it was 13–10, and when the Cubs went down in order in the seventh against Manny Sarmiento and Geronimo belted a leadoff home run in the eighth, the Reds led 14–10.

The Cubs, though, were not through. In the home eighth, Biittner singled and Buckner homered, and it was 14–12. After Murcer struck out, Jerry Morales lofted a Sarmiento pitch out among the bleacherites, and it was 14–13. The Cubs then loaded the bases with two out, but Jose Cardenal, in a pinch role, flied to center.

Reds	AB	R	H	RBI
Rose 3b	6	1	2	1
Griffey rf	8	2	5	4
Morgan 2b	8	1	2	0
Foster lf	6	2	3	0
Bench c	5	2	1	3
Geronimo cf	8	2	2	2
Concepcion ss	6	2	2	2
Lum 1b	5	3	2	2
Murray p	1	0	0	0
Borbon p	2	0	0	0
Armbrister ph	1	0	0	0
Sarmiento p	1	0	0	0
Hoerner p	0	0	0	0
Norman p	0	0	0	0
Summers ph	1	0	0	0
Billingham p	0	0	0	0
Totals	58	15	19	14

Cubs	AB	R	H	RBI
DeJesus ss	5	2	1	0
Cardenal ph-2b-ss-rf	2	0	0	0
Biittner lf	7	3	3	1
Buckner 1b	8	2	2	5
Murcer rf-ss-2b	8	3	3	2
Morales cf	6	1	2	1
Broberg p	0	0	0	0
R Reuschel p	1	1	1	0
Ontiveros 3b	8	0	3	2
Trillo 2b	3	1	1	1
Hernandez p	0	0	0	0
Wallis ph	1	0	0	0
Rosello ss-2b	3	0	1	1
Mitterwald c	7	2	3	2
Burris p	1	1	1	0
Moore p	1	0	1	1
P Reuschel p	1	0	0	0
Kelleher 2b	1	0	0	0
Gross ph	0	0	0	0
Sutter p	1	0	1	0
Clines cf	1	0	1	0
Totals	63	16	24	16

CIN 6 0 4 0 0 1 2 1 0 0 0 1 0 - 15 19 1
CHI 4 3 1 2 0 0 0 3 1 0 0 1 1 - 16 24 3

Reds	IP	H	R	ER	BB	SO
Murray	1	5	6	6	1	1
Borbon	5	7	4	3	2	6
Sarmiento	2	4	3	3	2	2
Hoerner	0.2	1	1	1	0	1
Norman	2.1	2	0	0	2	3
Billingham L (8-8)	1.2	5	2	2	0	0
Totals	12.2	24	16	15	7	13

Cubs	IP	H	R	ER	BB	SO
Burris	2	7	8	8	1	2
Moore	1	5	2	2	1	0
P Reuschel	3	0	0	0	1	6
Hernandez	1.2	2	1	1	2	1
Sutter	3	0	0	0	1	6
Broberg	1.1	2	1	0	3	2
R Reuschel W (15-3)	0.2	0	0	0	0	0
Totals	13	19	15	14	10	12

E—Cincinnati Lum; Chicago Cardenal, Buckner, Rosello. DP—Chicago 2. 2B—Cincinnati Griffey 2, Foster, Geronimo Morgan; Chicago Mitterwald, Clines, DeJesus, Burris. 3B—Chicago Moore. HR—Cincinnati Griffey (9), Lum (2), Bench (23), Geronimo (7), Rose (7); Chicago Bucker 2 (3,4), Mitterwald 2 (7,8), Morales (8), Murcer (15). SH—Cincinnati Rose. LOB—Cincinnati 15; Chicago 16. SB—Cincinnati Concepcion 3, Lum, Rose, Morgan. Attendance: 32,155.

July 28, 1977
Cubs 16, Reds 15 (13 innings)

In came Bruce Sutter, sidelined since July 16 because of a sore shoulder muscle. To this point, the second-year man with the amazing split-fingered fastball had worked 81 ⅓ innings and allowed only 49 hits and 13 walks while striking out 94. But he was used to seeing special players like DeJesus and Trillo at shortstop and second base, and here—due to myriad lineup changes (Cubs manager Herman Franks ended up using 21 of his 25 players)—were Dave Rosello at short and Cardenal at second.

Sure enough, Rose's leadoff groundball found Cardenal, and Jose booted it. Later, even Buckner fumbled a grounder, and the Reds had men at second and third with Foster and Bench coming up. Sutter struck out both, as the crowd roared and Jack Brickhouse reached for the throat lozenges.

Who knew? The Cubs might have a chance, after all. But hopes fell when lefty Joe Hoerner fanned Biittner and got Buckner to fly out. Then Murcer singled to right, and Sparky Anderson summoned another lefty to replace Hoerner—Freddie Norman, a Cub rookie in 1964. Norman walked Morales to move Murcer into scoring position, and Ontiveros singled to left to score Murcer, and the game was tied.

Extra innings brought the almost comical sight of Rosello and Murcer—unlike Cardenal a former infielder—switching from shortstop to second base and vice versa, depending upon from which side of the plate the Cincinnati batter swung. It also brought a successful Reds rally, after Sutter had departed, having thrown three scoreless innings and striking out six.

The Reds went up 15–14 in the 12th when Foster doubled and eventually scored on an error by Rosello, but the Cubs tied it in their half on another home run by Mitterwald. Then the Reds put runners at first and second with one out against Pete Broberg in the 13th, so in from the bullpen came the Cubs' top starting pitcher, Rick Reuschel. Reuschel got Bench to ground into a force out at second, leaving Griffey at third and Bench at first with two gone. Geronimo was next, but the best he could do was an inning-ending roller to Buckner at first.

Jack Billingham, normally a starter but a reliever on this abnormal afternoon, got Buckner on a grounder to short and Murcer on a fly ball to center. Now it was Reuschel's turn to bat, and those remaining in the stands began wondering if they should stay for the 14th inning or go home. There would be no 14th inning.

Reuschel surprised some with a base hit to right and then surprised many by racing to third on Ontiveros' third single of the day. Next was Rosello, eager to atone for his 12th-inning misplay. He did so, lashing a single between Rose at third and Concepcion at short, sending Reuschel across the plate for a 16–15 triumph, one of the most memorable in club history.

Wondered Franks aloud: "Wouldn't this have been the greatest game ever if it was the last day of the season and the Reds had to win it for the pennant? It might be as good as the Bobby Thomson thing." He was referring, of course, to Thomson's "Shot Heard 'Round the World," the ninth-inning, three-run homer that lifted the Giants over the Dodgers for the pennant in 1951, when Franks was a coach for the Giants.

Murcer, for one, said this game topped them all: "I never saw anything like this."

Added Biittner: "This was the greatest game I've ever been in, especially considering the happy ending."

Finally, Rosello was asked about his feelings after his error. "I never felt so bad. I wanted to find a hole and dive into it."

And how about after his game-winner? "I never felt so good!"

Davey Rosello

Davey Rosello, out of Mayaguez, Puerto Rico, was going to be the replacement for Don Kessinger at shortstop for the Cubs. As it turned out, he wasn't much of a replacement for Paul Popovich. Even so, he did have his moments, one of which came in the July 28, 1977 battle royal with the Reds.

The main reason he did not have more was he could not consistently hit major league pitching. And defense was not a strong point, either.

The Cubs thought Rosello might be able to hit enough after he managed a .271 average at Triple-A Wichita in 1972 and followed up with .313 in 99 games with the same team in 1973. But he never showed much with the bat at the major league level. His glove wasn't of the gold variety, which was evident from the 40 errors he committed at San Antonio in 124 games in 1971 and the 35 he tacked on in 137 games the next summer at Wichita. As for his speed, he only tried to steal four bases at Wichita in 1972, and he was thrown out each time.

In short, he was a backup who, like lots of backups before and since, had his moment of glory and his name in the headlines—if for only one glorious day.

After parts of six seasons with the Cubs, Rosello closed out his career with three seasons at Cleveland. For his career, he averaged just .236.

Let the Skipper Do It

One week before, the Cubs, in seventh place and going nowhere, had cashiered manager Frankie Frisch and replaced him with Chicago native, Lane Tech alum and longtime Cub hero, good ol' No. 44, Phil Cavarretta, then a player-coach. Since then, the Cubs had gone 1–6 under their new, 37-year-old manager. And they had gone 31 straight innings without scoring. Now, in the first game of a Sunday doubleheader at Wrigley Field, the Cubs trailed the defending NL champion Philadelphia Phillies 1–0 in the sixth. Things were about to change.

With pitcher Paul Minner and Eddie Miksis on base, Cavarretta, hitting in the No. 2 spot, tripled off Phils ace and eventual Hall of Famer Robin Roberts for a 2–1 lead. Moments later, "Cavvy" came home on Frankie Baumholtz's fly to deep right, and the Cubs were up 3–1.

The Cubs couldn't hold the lead, though, and found themselves behind 4–3 as they came to bat in the eighth against 1950 NL MVP Jim Konstanty. But Miksis singled, stole second and went to third on catcher Andy Seminick's bad throw. Cavarretta then flied deep to Richie Ashburn in center, and Miksis came home with the tying run.

Finally, in the ninth, the Cubs won 5–4 on an error by shortstop Granny Hamner.

In Game 2, the Cubs were reverting to form, trailing Jocko Thompson and the third-place Phils 4–2 in the last of the seventh. With one out, Baumholtz was hit by a pitch and Hank Sauer walked. Bubba Church, 8–0 vs. the Cubs in his career, entered and was greeted by Randy Jackson's RBI single. Roy Smalley was called out on strikes, but first baseman/TV Western star Chuck Connors rifled a double to left to score Sauer with the tying run and send Jackson to third.

At a Glance

Game 1

WP: Kelly (2–0)

Game 2

WP: Leonard (9–3)

HR: Cavarretta (3)

Key stat: Cubs pitchers held the Phillies' table-setters, Eddie Waitkus and Richie Ashburn, to a combined one hit in 17 at-bats on the day.

Here, Phils manager Eddie Sawyer called for Roberts, his Game 1 starter, and had him walk pinch-hitter Smoky Burgess with first base open. Due up was reliever Dutch Leonard, but Cavarretta surveyed his dugout and decided he himself was the best man for this job. Was he ever. Cavarretta swung at Roberts' first pitch and drove it into the right-field bleachers, the Cubs were ahead 8–4 and 25,840 people cheered their hometown hero.

Some 40 years later, Cavvy told sports columnist Ira Berkow that he hadn't been at all nervous about calling upon himself in that situation. "I always loved a challenge," he said. "And if I had struck out? Well, they'd have to say I at least had the guts to try. That was anything but defeatist, wouldn't you say?"

He was taking a little jab at his former boss, Cubs owner Phil Wrigley, who, after hearing Cavarretta's rather pessimistic but quite accurate size-up of the ballclub's possibilities in 1954, called Cavvy's attitude "defeatist" and fired him before the Cubs had even finished spring training—a first in baseball history.

"I told the truth," Cavarretta said. "I was raised that way. My dad would always say: 'Tell the people the truth. Tell them what's on your mind.' I told the truth to Mr. Wrigley and got fired."

But that was three years in the future. On this day, Wrigley and Cavarretta were all smiles after the 8–6 Cubs victory in Game 2. "Robin threw me an inside slider," Cavarretta remembered many years later, before he and Roberts passed away, "and I was ready. Roberts lives near me (in Florida), and he still kids me about that doubleheader: 'Who would be dumb enough to be manager and put himself in as a pinch-hitter?'

"I tell him, 'You were dumb enough to pitch me inside, cousin!'"

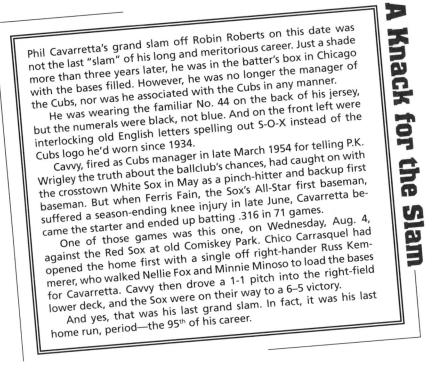

Phil Cavarretta's grand slam off Robin Roberts on this date was not the last "slam" of his long and meritorious career. Just a shade more than three years later, he was in the batter's box in Chicago with the bases filled. However, he was no longer the manager of the Cubs, nor was he associated with the Cubs in any manner.

He was wearing the familiar No. 44 on the back of his jersey, but the numerals were black, not blue. And on the front left were interlocking old English letters spelling out S-O-X instead of the Cubs logo he'd worn since 1934.

Cavvy, fired as Cubs manager in late March 1954 for telling P.K. Wrigley the truth about the ballclub's chances, had caught on with the crosstown White Sox in May as a pinch-hitter and backup first baseman. But when Ferris Fain, the Sox's All-Star first baseman, suffered a season-ending knee injury in late June, Cavarretta became the starter and ended up batting .316 in 71 games.

One of those games was this one, on Wednesday, Aug. 4, against the Red Sox at old Comiskey Park. Chico Carrasquel had opened the home first with a single off right-hander Russ Kemmerer, who walked Nellie Fox and Minnie Minoso to load the bases for Cavarretta. Cavvy then drove a 1-1 pitch into the right-field lower deck, and the Sox were on their way to a 6–5 victory.

And yes, that was his last grand slam. In fact, it was his last home run, period—the 95th of his career.

A Knack for the Slam

It's Good to Have More Than One Hobbie

Glen Frederick Hobbie will always remember Saturday, July 30, 1960, and not just because he happened to shut down the world-champions-to-be Pittsburgh Pirates that sunny afternoon at Wrigley Field.

Something began that day that evolved into a rather special tale of family and sports. But it all began with that ballgame.

The Pirates were leading the league; the Cubs, 33–60 and 23.5 games back, were trailing the league. The were, however, building for the future—or at least that was the company line. You sure couldn't tell it from the lineup manager Lou Boudreau trotted out that day. Leadoff man was Bob Will, age 29; then came Richie Ashburn, 33, followed by 29-year-old Ernie Banks and second-year man George Altman, 27. The No. 5 hitter was indeed a kid to get excited about, third baseman Ron Santo, 20, who was completing his fifth week in the big leagues.

After Santo was another veteran, ex-Pirate Frank Thomas, age 31. Then came 37-year-old second baseman Grady Hatton, who until his summons the week before had been player-manager at the Cubs' San Antonio farm club. Batting eighth was the catcher, Elvin Tappe, 33.

Apparently it mattered little to Hobbie, whose mind, as we shall see, was on other things that day. The 24-year-old right-hander from Witt, Ill., less than an hour's drive south from Springfield, gave up a run in the first inning when Roberto Clemente's two-out single to right scored Bob Skinner. Thereafter, though, he allowed just four hits as Hobbie, entering the day 9–13 with a 4.50 ERA, dueled All-Star Bob Friend (11–6, 3.03 ERA) pitch for pitch.

> ## At a Glance
>
> **WP:** Hobbie (10–13)
>
> **HR:** Altman (8)
>
> **Key stat:** Ace reliever Elroy Face (24 saves, 2.90 ERA in '60) was touched for 4 hits and 4 runs in 1 inning.

The Cubs broke through in the sixth on Santo's two-out, two-run double, and Altman's three-run homer off legendary reliever Elroy Face capped a seventh-inning rally ignited by Hobbie's double. Not much later, Hobbie retired Bill Mazeroski on a game-ending fielder's choice to wrap up a tidy 6–1 victory that ended an eight-game Cub skid.

Glen had received a bit of inspiration earlier in the afternoon. As he walked off the field after the top of the third inning, Pat Pieper made this announcement over the public-address system:

"Ten-chun! . . . Ten-chun please . . . . Glen Hobbie's wife . . . . has just given birth . . . . to the couple's first child . . . . a boy."

The 13,365 on hand applauded politely. Nearly five decades later, Hobbie remembered: "That was a special, special day. And you know what? (Cub teammate) Dick Ellsworth's wife had a baby boy that same day, and (the Dodgers') Larry Sherry had a baby daughter."

The rest of the story...

Glen's baby boy, Glen Kenneth Hobbie, grew up to become a high school baseball and basketball star in Hillsboro, Ill., a few miles up the road from Witt, and was selected by the Detroit Tigers in the 24th round of the 1978 amateur free-agent draft. Unlike his dad, a two-time 16-game winner whose career was cut short by arm troubles, the younger Hobbie couldn't blame physical problems for his giving up baseball.

"I didn't get hurt—I just wasn't very good," he said. "I pitched at Bristol, Tenn., that first summer. Went to spring training in Lakeland, Fla., the next year. I pitched three innings for the Lakeland club and four for (Detroit's Double-A) Birmingham team. And that was it."

The cut was not painful, he said. "Actually, they did me a favor. I got a real job and I raised a family."

The story doesn't end there. One of his three children, Eric, at 6-foot-6 a former All-State basketball player, averaged 23.5 points and 12.6 rebounds at Vandalia High School his senior season (2006-07) and won the Illinois High School Association's annual slam-dunk competition in March 2007 at Peoria. And fret not: Glen Hobbie's grandson played baseball, too.

"I play center field," he told a reporter that night in Peoria.

A 6-6 center fielder?

"These long legs," he said, smiling, "cover a lot of ground."

AUGUST

Second baseman Johnny Evers was part of the Cubs' most famous infield of all time,

More Hawk Talk

The listed winner of this game is a misnomer. It should read Andre Dawson 5, Phillies 3. Happened a lot in 1987.

The Hawk's long overdue election to the Hall of Fame revived the story: Dawson was a free agent in the winter of 1986, but he found himself with no offers—in a clumsy attempt to keep salaries down, baseball owners had agreed to stay away from other team's players. The practice is known as collusion, and it's a violation of labor law.

When spring training began in 1987, Dawson was without a job, even though a poll of MLB players taken by the *New York Times* just three years earlier found him to be the best all-around player in baseball.

Dawson was not alone in his belief that the rock-hard artificial surface at Montreal's Olympic Stadium contributed to the knee problems that plagued him as he entered his 30s, so he was determined not to return to the Expos. Now the Cubs … real grass, all day games, a ballpark where he had always smoked the ball … Dawson signed on the dotted line at a figure of general manager Dallas Green's choosing. Some reports said $500,000, other said $650,000. Either way, it was the sweetest deal since the Louisiana Purchase more than doubled the land mass of the United States.

A crowd of 33,002 at Wrigley Field on this Saturday was treated to a vintage Dawson performance. Batting in the first inning with the bases loaded and nobody out, he lined into a double play, and the Cubs failed to score. Dawson silently vowed to make amends.

Facing Tom Hume with Dave Martinez and Leon Durham on base in the third, Dawson cracked a three-run homer to give rookie Les Lancaster a 3–0 lead. After Chris James' two-run homer off

Phillies	AB	R	H	RBI
Samuel 2b	5	0	0	0
Thompson cf	5	0	2	0
Hayes 1b	4	1	1	0
Schmidt 3b	5	0	1	0
Wilson rf	3	1	0	0
James lf	4	1	2	2
Parrish c	3	0	1	0
Daulton pr-c	0	0	0	0
Jeltz ss	2	0	1	0
Gross ph	0	0	0	0
Aguayo ss	0	0	0	0
Hume p	2	0	0	0
Ritchie p	0	0	0	0
Roenicke ph	0	0	0	0
Jackson p	0	0	0	0
Stone ph	1	0	0	0
Calhoun p	0	0	0	0
Totals	34	3	8	2

Cubs	AB	R	H	RBI
Martinez cf	2	1	1	0
Sandberg 2b	3	0	0	0
Durham 1b	3	1	1	0
Dawson rf	4	3	3	5
Mumphrey lf	3	0	1	0
Moreland 3b	3	0	1	0
Smith p	0	0	0	0
Sundberg c	3	0	0	0
Noce ss	4	0	0	0
Lancaster p	3	0	0	0
DiPino p	0	0	0	0
Trillo 3b	1	0	0	0
Totals	29	5	7	5

											R	H	E
PHI	0	0	0	2	0	1	0	0	0	-	3	8	0
CHI	0	0	3	0	1	0	1	0	X	-	5	7	0

Phillies	IP	H	R	ER	BB	SO
Hume L (1-3)	4	5	4	4	7	0
Ritchie	2	1	0	0	1	3
Jackson	1	1	1	1	0	0
Calhoun	1	0	0	0	1	1
Totals	8	7	5	5	9	4

Cubs	IP	H	R	ER	BB	SO
Lancaster W (3-1)	6.2	5	3	3	4	4
DiPino	0.1	0	0	0	0	0
Smith S (26)	2	3	0	0	2	2
Totals	9	8	3	3	6	6

DP—Philadelphia 2; Chicago. 2B—Philadelphia Jeltz; Chicago Durham, Moreland. HR—Philadelphia James (11); Chicago Dawson 3 (29,30,31). LOB—Philadelphia 10; Chicago 9. SB—Philadelphia Thompson. Attendance: 33,002.

Hall of Famer Andre Dawson watches the first of his three home runs on Aug. 1, 1987, against the Philadelphia Phillies. Dawson's three home runs accounted for all five Cub runs in a 5–3 victory.

Lancaster made it a one-run ballgame in the fourth, Dawson led off the fifth with another homer, restoring the Cubs' two-run lead and finishing Hume's work day.

The Phils got within 4–3 in the sixth when Von Hayes walked, took second on Mike Schmidt's single, went to third on Glenn Wilson's fly ball and scored when Lancaster was called for a balk. But Dawson had one more bullet in the chamber and he fired it, taking Phils reliever Mike Jackson deep to lead off the seventh for the 5–3 final.

Dawson's line for the game: 3-for-4 with three homers and five runs batted in. For the season: a .287 average with 49 homers and 137 RBIs, both league-leading figures. Fifteen of those homers came in the month of August. Dawson also won a Gold Glove (his seventh) for his exemplary play in right field and was a runaway winner of the National League MVP award, the first player from a last-place team so honored.

Dawson's choice of the Cubs and Wrigley Field was an inspired one. Chicago acknowledged his classy presence on and off the field and embraced him with an ardor that persists to this day, even though he wears a Montreal Expos cap on his Hall of Fame plaque.

Cubs Unveil Their Killer B's against Giants

This was another one of those days at Wrigley Field when the starting pitchers begin entertaining thoughts of an early shower almost from the moment they enter the ballpark. On this Friday afternoon, the starting pitchers were pretty good ones, too.

They were Jack Sanford, 24-game-winner the year before for the NL champion San Francisco Giants and 10–11 this season with a 3.40 ERA; and Cubs lefty Dick Ellsworth, having an incredible year, having gone 15–7 with a league-best 1.86 ERA thus far.

So, naturally, Sanford lasted only four batters and Ellsworth didn't get through the third inning. What happened? In the home first, Lou Brock singled, as did Ellis Burton, and Billy Willliams cracked a home run. When Ron Santo followed that sudden outburst with another base hit, Sanford was gone, Jim Duffalo replacing him. Duffalo restored order, and in the meantime the Giants began an assault on Ellsworth.

It started in the second inning. Orlando Cepeda and Jim Davenport singled, Jose Pagan doubled for one run and Tom Haller singled for two. When even Duffalo singled for a run in the third to make it 5–3 Giants, Ellsworth was led to safety and Don Elston replaced him.

Burton doubled home Brock in the fifth, and Willie Mays homered in the visitors' seventh, so it was 6–4 San Francisco at stretch time. The Cubs cut it to 6–5 in the bottom half on Williams' RBI single off Bobby Bolin, but with teammates at the corners, first Santo and then pinch-hitter deluxe Merritt Ranew, his batting average still a lofty .405, went down swinging.

And then the action really began, although not all the 24,242 fans enjoyed the first part. That was the top of the eighth, when Lindy McDaniel, rookie Tom Baker and the just-recalled Cal Koonce were touched for five runs, the big blow a three-run homer by Cepeda off Koonce.

Down 11–5 now, the Cubs managed to come right back. Kenny Hubbs led off the eighth with a double and came home on catcher Jimmie Schaffer's single to center. Andre Rodgers drew a walk, and manager Bob Kennedy sent up Leo Burke to bat for Koonce. Burke was a stocky right-handed hitter who

At a Glance

WP: Hobbie (5-8)

HR: Williams (16), Burton (8), Burke (2)

Key stat: The teams combined for 35 hits, with Brock, Burton, Hubbs and the Giants' Pagan, Harvey Kuenn and Felipe Alou each getting three.

didn't really have a position but could swing the bat, although at that moment he was hitting just .176 in eight games since coming from St. Louis June 24 for reliever Barney Schultz.

So much for numbers. Burke connected with a Bolin pitch and the ball sailed high and deep into the bleachers in left-center, and now it was 11–9. Out went Bolin and in came lefty Billy Hoeft, who was touched for a Brock single. The switch-hitting Burton turned around to bat right-handed for the first time all day and promptly drove one into the seats in left, and the game was tied.

It was getting late, and it also was getting dark. Dark clouds rolled in during the top of the 10th, and it seemed certain the game would soon have to be called—either by darkness or by rain. So the Cubs took the decision out of the umpires' hands.

Santo lined a one-out double off Don Larsen, and Ernie Banks, who had entered as a pinch-hitter earlier, was walked intentionally. Hubbs struck out, but then Schaffer blooped a single into short right-center, bringing in Santo with the winning run. The Cubs, 12-11 winners, were 58–48, in fourth place in a 10-team league and just 5.5 games out of first.

"We're going to win it," Burton proclaimed in the clubhouse. "We're going to be in first place by September."

He was wrong, of course, but by season's end the Cubs were 82–80, an improvement of 23 wins over 1962. For those who had gone through '62 in Cub uniforms, that had to feel a bit like first place.

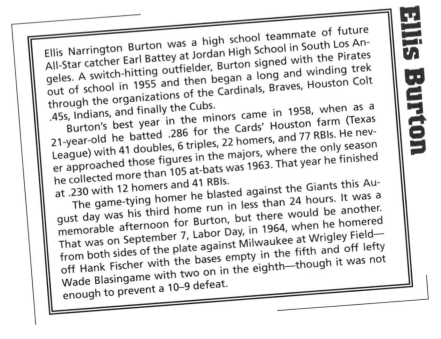

Ellis Burton

Ellis Narrington Burton was a high school teammate of future All-Star catcher Earl Battey at Jordan High School in South Los Angeles. A switch-hitting outfielder, Burton signed with the Pirates out of school in 1955 and then began a long and winding trek through the organizations of the Cardinals, Braves, Houston Colt .45s, Indians, and finally the Cubs.

Burton's best year in the minors came in 1958, when as a 21-year-old he batted .286 for the Cards' Houston farm (Texas League) with 41 doubles, 6 triples, 22 homers, and 77 RBIs. He never approached those figures in the majors, where the only season he collected more than 105 at-bats was 1963. That year he finished at .230 with 12 homers and 41 RBIs.

The game-tying homer he blasted against the Giants this August day was his third home run in less than 24 hours. It was a memorable afternoon for Burton, but there would be another. That was on September 7, Labor Day, in 1964, when he homered from both sides of the plate against Milwaukee at Wrigley Field—off Hank Fischer with the bases empty in the fifth and off lefty Wade Blasingame with two on in the eighth—though it was not enough to prevent a 10–9 defeat.

'The Immaculate Deflection'

The Cubs don't necessarily subscribe to the old sports axiom that it's better to be lucky than good, for rarely does it apply to them. Their star-crossed history is not exactly replete with examples of outrageous good fortune.

But as they pursued their first postseason berth since 1945, the Cubs had to sense things were breaking their way on this Thursday afternoon at Wrigley Field. Two run-scoring groundouts and Keith Moreland's home run staked them to a 3–2 lead over Montreal, but the Expos mounted a ninth-inning challenge to Rick Sutcliffe when Tim Wallach singled and pinch-runner Miguel Dilone scooted to third on pinch-hitter Mike Stenhouse's single with one out.

Lee Smith replaced Sutcliffe, and Pete Rose pinch-hit for Expos pitcher Bryn Smith. Rose, 43 years old and closing in on Ty Cobb's career hits record, smoked a liner back through the middle, but the ball glanced off the 6-foot-6 Smith's shoulder on his follow-through and went right to shortstop Dave Owen. Owen caught it to retire Rose, then fired to first and caught Stenhouse scrambling back for a game-ending double play.

"I guess the Cubs are destined," Bryn Smith said after taking the loss despite pitching a complete-game six-hitter.

At a Glance

WP: Sutcliffe (8–1)

S: Smith (23)

HR: Moreland (12)

Key stat: The Cubs won 8 of their first 9 games in August and stretched their lead to 4.5 games in the NL Central.

Singles by Leon Durham and Moreland preceded Ron Cey's RBI groundout in the fourth inning, and Moreland's homer tied the game at 2–2 in the sixth. In the seventh, Cey doubled, took third on pinch-hitter Jay Johnstone's grounder and scored the go-ahead run on Henry Cotto's RBI fielder's choice.

Andre Dawson reached future Cubs teammate Sutcliffe for a two-run homer in the fifth for a 2–1 Expos lead.

The victory, witnessed by 22,485 fans, was the Cubs' sixth in seven games and gave them a 1.5-game in the NL East. Following a loss to the Expos the next day, they would reel off six wins in a row.

"The Good Lord wants the Cubs to win," broadcaster Harry Caray declared after witnessing the "Immaculate Deflection." People were beginning to take him seriously.

In This Corner...

Billy Martin might not have been the best fighter in baseball, but he certainly was the busiest. A Wrigley Field crowd of 4,209 and a WGN-TV audience got a first-hand look at Martin's quick hands and truculent disposition on this Thursday when he tangled with the Cubs' Jim Brewer.

Martin, a wiry middleweight at 165 pounds, was 32 and in his first year as a National League player when his Cincinnati Reds faced the Cubs and Brewer, a rookie left-hander. Batting leadoff, Martin walked and scored on Gus Bell's single as the Reds jumped on Brewer for two first-inning runs. There were two outs and nobody on when he batted again in the second inning.

Brewer's first pitch sailed up and in on Martin, and he took exception. His bat sailed toward the mound when he lost his grip on it after swinging and missing at the next pitch. Words—nasty words—were exchanged as Martin walked out to retrieve the bat, and as Brewer eyed him warily Martin's street-fighter instincts took over—he belted Brewer with a right hand that landed just below Brewer's eye socket, shattering the orbital bone on the right side of his face.

Both benches emptied as Brewer went down, but nothing happened—Martin's surprise attack was an individual matter, not a consequence of any bad blood between the teams. He was ejected, replaced at second base by Eddie Kasko, and Brewer was taken to Illinois Masonic Hospital.

When the game resumed, Ernie Banks and Berwyn native Bob Will took it upon themselves to win it for the Cubs. In the third inning, Will doubled to left and scored the Cubs' first run on Banks' single. In the sixth, Richie Ashburn reached on a bunt single, and the Cubs had a 3–2 lead when Banks pumped his 30th home run into the left-field seats.

The Reds pulled even in the seventh on Jerry Lynch's run-scoring pinch single, but after Sammy Taylor singled and Don Zimmer doubled in the

Reds	AB	R	H	RBI
Martin 2b	1	1	0	0
Kasko ph-2b	2	0	0	0
Pinson cf	4	1	2	0
Bell rf	4	0	1	1
Post lf	4	0	0	0
Cook 3b	4	0	1	1
Coleman 1b	4	1	1	0
Bailey c	4	0	2	0
Osteen pr	0	0	0	0
Cardenas ss	2	0	0	0
Lynch ss	1	0	1	1
McMillan ss	1	0	0	0
McLish p	2	0	0	0
Henry p	0	0	0	0
Brosnan p	0	0	0	0
Totals	33	3	8	3

Cubs	AB	R	H	RBI
Will rf	4	1	3	2
Ashburn lf	3	1	1	0
Kindall 2b	1	0	1	0
Banks ss	4	1	2	3
Altman cf	4	0	1	0
Santo 3b	4	0	0	0
Thomas 1b-lf	4	0	0	0
Hatton 2b	2	0	1	0
Bouchee 1b	2	0	0	0
Taylor c	3	1	1	0
Brewer p	0	0	0	0
Schaffernoth p	2	0	0	0
Zimmer ph	1	1	1	0
Morehead p	0	0	0	0
Totals	34	5	11	5

```
CIN  2 0 0 0 0 0 1 0 0 - 3 8 0
CHI  0 0 1 0 0 2 2 0 X - 5 11 0
```

Reds	IP	H	R	ER	BB	SO
McLish L (3-7)	6.1	9	5	5	0	3
Henry	0	1	0	0	0	0
Brosnan	1.2	1	0	0	0	1
Totals	8	11	5	5	0	4

Cubs	IP	H	R	ER	BB	SO
Brewer	1.2	3	2	2	1	1
Schaffernoth W (1-2)	5.1	3	1	1	0	4
Morehead S (4)	2	2	0	0	0	0
Totals	9	8	3	3	1	5

DP—Cincinnati; Chicago. 2B—Chicago Zimmer, Will. HR—Chicago Banks (30). SH—Cincinnati McLish. LOB—Cincinnati 5; Chicago 5. Attendance: 4,209.

Cubs' seventh, Will broke the tie with a two-run single. Reliever Joe Schaffernoth earned the victory with 5 $\frac{1}{3}$ innings of one-run relief after taking over for Brewer. He beat veteran Cal McLish, whose adjustment to the National League was a little rocky; McLish, 19–8 with the Cleveland Indians in 1959, was 4–14 for the Reds in 1960 after being dealt with Martin and first baseman Gordy Coleman for second baseman Johnny Temple.

Will, used as a pinch-hitter for most of his six-season Cubs tenure, appeared in a career-high 138 games in 1960, batting .255 with six of his nine career homers and 53 RBIs. Banks, the National League's MVP in 1958-59, failed to three-peat despite batting .271 with 41 homers and 117 RBIs.

Martin's sneak attack had repercussions for Brewer. He missed the rest of the '60 season after spending several days in the hospital and never pitched effectively for the Cubs, going 4–13 with a 5.66 ERA over parts of four seasons. Brewer sued Martin for damages and was awarded $10,000 in 1969.

Traded to the Dodgers in 1963, Brewer reinvented himself as a reliever and enjoyed an outstanding career, compiling a 61–51 record with a 2.62 ERA and 125 saves in 12 years and pitching in three World Series. Brewer was just 50 when he died of injuries sustained in an auto accident in 1987.

Martin played for seven teams and managed five teams during his turbulent career. He managed the Yankees on five separate occasions and was between jobs with the team when the pickup truck he was riding in skidded on ice and crashed into a culvert on a road near Binghamton, N.Y., on Christmas Day in 1989. Martin died at the scene. He was 61.

He's Wonderful Juan Again After One-Hitter

During the first half of the previous decade, Juan Pizarro had been one of the aces of the pitching staff that made the crosstown White Sox annual pennant contenders. A left-hander from Puerto Rico who threw consistently in the mid-90s with a screwball mixed in, Pizarro won 14 games in 1961, a dozen in '62, was 16–8 in 1963 (and missed the final month with a shoulder strain) and 19–9 in '64.

Injuries wrecked his 1965 season (6–3, 3.43 ERA in 18 games), and he spent 1966 in the Sox's bullpen, still not completely healthy. Then he began a Dick Littlefield/George Brunet-style tour of the big leagues, pitching for six organizations in the next four years. He moved from Pittsburgh to Boston to Cleveland to Oakland and to California before landing with the Cubs in July 1970.

Pizarro impressed no one at Wrigley Field, working fewer than 16 innings and posting a 4.60 ERA in 12 games that season. The Cubs brought him back in '71, but the 34-year-old lost the extra lefty-reliever's spot to Earl Stephenson and was sent to Triple-A Tacoma, his big-league career seemingly over.

By late June, however, Pizarro, a starter once again, was the best pitcher in the Pacific Coast League. In one game, he struck out seven Tuscon Toros in succession. The Cubs could not ignore him any longer.

They called him up to pitch Game 2 of a July 7 twinbill in Los Angeles. He responded with 7 2/3 innings of five-hit ball and downed the Dodgers 4–3. An ineffective outing—at San Diego—followed, as did relief appearances against Philadelphia and Montreal. But Leo Durocher gave him the start against the Mets on Sunday, Aug. 1 in New York, and Pizarro went the distance, scattering six hits, and defeated Tom Seaver 3–2 before 43,733 at Shea Stadium. Ten years ago that month, he had beaten Whitey Ford and the record-setting '61 Yankees 2–1 in front of 49,059 at Yankee Stadium.

Next for Pizarro was a Thursday assignment

Padres	AB	R	H	RBI
Hernandez ss	3	0	0	0
Jestadt 2b	3	0	0	0
Murrell ph	1	0	0	0
Gaston cf	4	0	0	0
Colbert 1b	3	0	0	0
Brown rf	3	0	1	0
Spiezio 3b	3	0	0	0
Lee lf	3	0	0	0
Barton c	2	0	0	0
Kirby p	2	0	0	0
Campbell ph	1	0	0	0
Totals	28	0	1	0

Cubs	AB	R	H	RBI
Kessinger ss	4	1	1	0
Beckert 2b	4	0	1	0
Williams lf	4	1	2	2
Pepitone 1b	3	0	1	1
Hickman rf	3	0	0	0
Santo 3b	3	0	0	0
James cf	3	0	0	0
Martin c	3	1	1	0
Pizarro p	2	0	0	0
Totals	29	3	6	3

SD	0	0	0	0	0	0	0	0	0	-	0	1	3
CHI	0	0	0	0	0	0	0	3	X	-	3	6	0

Padres	IP	H	R	ER	BB	SO
Kirby L (10-9)	8	6	3	0	1	4
Totals	8	6	3	0	1	4

Cubs	IP	H	R	ER	BB	SO
Pizarro W (3-1)	9	1	0	0	2	9
Totals	9	1	0	0	2	9

E—San Diego Lee, Jestadt 2. DP—San Diego. SH—Chicago Pizarro. LOB—San Diego 3; Chicago 4. SB—Chicago Williams, Kessinger. Attendance: 25,233.

against San Diego, and 25,233 watched the old South Side All-Star come all the way back. Juan fanned nine, walked only two and threw a one-hitter to beat the Padres 3–0 for his first one-hitter since he blanked Washington 7–0 on Aug. 11, 1965.

The lone hit was a fifth-ining single, a grounder to left, by Ollie Brown.

"I knew it was a bad pitch when I let it go," Pizarro said later.

But it was about the only bad pitch he threw all day. Meanwhile, the offense was supplied by Billy Williams, whose two-run single in the eighth broke the scoreless tie, and by Joe Pepitone, who singled home Williams.

Pizarro closed with a flourish, striking out Cito Gaston to end it.

"We probably made a mistake, keeping Stephenson instead of Juan," Durocher admitted.

No one could disagree, especially when Pizarro followed up his one-hitter by downing the NL East-leading Pirates 2–1 on five hits the following Tuesday in Pittsburgh, striking out Al Oliver with the bases loaded for the final out.

Suddenly the Cubs were in second place, just six games back. They would finish third, 14 back, through no fault of Pizarro's, however. Juan won three more starts, the most memorable of which was the one on Sept. 16 in New York, when he again outdueled Seaver 1–0.

The game's lone run? An eighth-inning homer by Juan Pizarro.

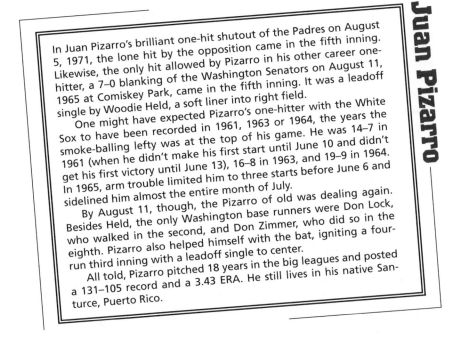

Juan Pizarro

In Juan Pizarro's brilliant one-hit shutout of the Padres on August 5, 1971, the lone hit by the opposition came in the fifth inning. Likewise, the only hit allowed by Pizarro in his other career one-hitter, a 7–0 blanking of the Washington Senators on August 11, 1965 at Comiskey Park, came in the fifth inning. It was a leadoff single by Woodie Held, a soft liner into right field.

One might have expected Pizarro's one-hitter with the White Sox to have been recorded in 1961, 1963 or 1964, the years the smoke-balling lefty was at the top of his game. He was 14–7 in 1961 (when he didn't make his first start until June 10 and didn't get his first victory until June 13), 16–8 in 1963, and 19–9 in 1964. In 1965, arm trouble limited him to three starts before June 6 and sidelined him almost the entire month of July.

By August 11, though, the Pizarro of old was dealing again. Besides Held, the only Washington base runners were Don Lock, who walked in the second, and Don Zimmer, who did so in the eighth. Pizarro also helped himself with the bat, igniting a four-run third inning with a leadoff single to center.

All told, Pizarro pitched 18 years in the big leagues and posted a 131–105 record and a 3.43 ERA. He still lives in his native Santurce, Puerto Rico.

Hello, Billy

Amid the nondescript likes of Art Schult, Jim Marshall, Sammy Taylor and Earl Averill, Billy Williams didn't really stand out in a Cubs lineup that faced the Phillies and gnarly right-hander Jim Owens in a Thursday game that drew 6,477 fans to Wrigley Field.

Williams, a 21-year-old outfielder, had hit .327 with 11 home runs and 84 RBIs at Double-A San Antonio and Triple-A Houston in the first four months of the 1959 season. Everyone who had seen him agreed he had a picture-book-pretty left-handed swing, and he came highly recommended by Buck O'Neill, who had sent Ernie Banks, Gene Baker and George Altman to Chicago. So the Cubs decided to have a look.

In the first inning, Tony Taylor was on third base and Marshall was on first when Williams came to the plate for the first time in the big leagues, wearing No. 4. He went out on a sharp grounder to first baseman Ed Bouchee, but Taylor scored on the play, so Williams had an RBI to show for his first at-bat.

The rest of the day was rather quiet: a grounder to second in the third, a fly to center in the fifth, a strikeout in the seventh. The Cubs added a second run in the sixth inning on singles by Schult, Averill and Bobby Thomson, but the Phils pulled even in the eighth when Gene Freese's bases-loaded single off reliever Don Elston scored ex-Cub Jim Bolger and future Cub Richie Ashburn.

Humberto Robinson took over the pitching for the Phils in the bottom of the eighth, and Ernie Banks greeted him with a double. Schult put a bunt down and Robinson threw it away, enabling Banks to score the go-ahead run. Schult reached second and scored on Thomson's single, so Williams debuted with a victory.

At a Glance

WP: Elston (6–4)

Key stat: Williams never struck out more than 84 times in a season. In 1972, when he won the batting title (.333) and hit 37 homers with 122 RBIs, he struck out 59 times.

He would wait three more days for his first major league hit, a third-inning single off Pittsburgh's Vern Law on Aug. 9. And, when his 18-game audition was over, the Cubs still weren't sure what they had; Williams was 5-for-33 with two RBIs. He would open the 1960 season at Triple-A Houston and earn another call-up by hitting .323 with 26 homers and 80 RBIs.

Wearing No. 41 this time, the Sweet Swinger from Whistler, Ala., looked major league-ready, batting .277 with two homers and seven RBIs in 12 games. And he was—the Cubs installed him as their left fielder for the '61 season. Wearing No. 26, Williams hit .278 with 25 homers and 86 RBIs and won the National League Rookie of the Year award, and a Hall of Fame career was launched.

Rehabilitated Tinker

"Tinker to Evers to Chance" remains the most famous double-play combination in baseball history, immortalized by a Franklin P. Adams poem celebrating their sure-handed, game-changing efficiency.

The nimble cohesiveness they demonstrated as the bulwark of the infield defense on three Cubs pennant-winning teams is what captured Adams' fancy, but it ended with each day's ballgame. Tinker and Evers went years without speaking to each other off the field, and they had a shared disdain for Chance, the player/manager, who seemed to take his "Peerless Leader" nickname seriously—he was cold, aloof and above the fray in his dealings with the other Cubs.

Infielders Joe Tinker (left) and Johnny Evers (right) pose with a Frank Chance plaque on Jan. 15, 1943. Tinker, Evers, and Chance formed the most memorable double-play combination in the history of baseball. Their consistently solid fielding and hitting led the Cubs to four National League pennants (1906–08, 1910) and two World Series wins (1907–1908). The Hall of Fame inducted all three simultaneously in 1946. In 1910, New York newspaper columnist Franklin Pierce Adams immortalized the three ballplayers in a short verse entitled, "Baseball's Sad Lexicon."

Cubs 8, Giants 6

Fredi Gonzalez, the Florida Marlins' manager early in the 2010 season, might have been channeling Chance when he upbraided and benched star shortstop Hanley Ramirez for his lack of hustle in a May game against the Arizona Diamondbacks. Chance, deciding that Tinker had given less than his best effort on two short popups that fell for base hits in a loss to the Brooklyn Superbas on Aug. 5, yanked his star shortstop from the game and suspended him for "listless, indifferent play," with the backing of team owner Charles Murphy.

"I don't care whether the winning of a pennant depends on the retention of Tinker or any other player," Chance announced. "I want to emphasize that while I am the manager, no player can loaf. Without Tinker I may lose the pennant, but I am going to have discipline on the club."

If Chance intended to light a fire under Tinker by embarrassing him, he evidently succeeded. The suspension was to cover the rest of the season at the time it was levied, but Tinker was reinstated two days later. Facing the New York Giants and Hall of Fame pitcher Christy Mathewson in his first game back, Tinker went 4-for-4 with four RBIs and a steal of home in a performance that drew raves from the *New York Times* reporter covering the game.

"There was no difficulty in deciding who won the game for the Cubs," the unsigned account read. "Even a novice could have discerned this fact. It was Tinker all the way."

The story recounts how Tinker started an inning-ending double play with the bases loaded in the first inning, preventing the Giants from scoring. He singled and scored the first run of the game on rookie Vic Saier's double in the second. An RBI single scored Heinie Zimmerman in the fourth. Tinker was described as "pestiferous" after delivering an RBI triple and unnerving Mathewson with a steal of home in the sixth. Finally, he smacked a two-run double to seal the Cubs' victory after the Giants had cut the lead to 5–4 in the eighth.

At a Glance

WP: Brown (13–9)

Key stat: Joe Tinker batted .262 with 31 homers and 783 RBIs in 15 big league seasons. He was 304–308 in four seasons as a manager. And he's in the Hall of Fame, elected in 1946.

Not that his heroics were limited to hitting.

"Tinker also played the most wonderful game at short seen at the West Side grounds in a long time," the story added.

Back in Chance's moderately good graces, Tinker batted .278 with four homers, 40 extra-base hits and 69 RBIs for the 1911 Cubs. But he couldn't pull them through; they finished second in the National League, 7.5 games behind the pennant-winning Giants.

Beanball Game vs. Mets Puts 1969 in Rearview

"Two teams that just don't like each other"—it's one of sports' most tiresome clichés, but in the case of the Cubs and the New York Mets, it's true. Has been since 1969, when the Cubs' ignominious collapse cleared a path for the Miracle Mets' run to a World Series championship.

At least it's true in the minds of Cubs fans with reasonably long memories.

The Mets were within a half-game of the first-place Cubs and poised to charge when they came to Wrigley Field for a four-game series in early August of 1984. Cubs fans could only close their eyes and hope it wasn't 1969 all over again.

It wasn't—not by a long shot. The Cubs swept the series, and the Mets left town trailing by 4.5 games. But the rivalry was more intense than ever thanks to a beanball war, a benches-clearing melee and four ejections.

Bob Dernier, Ryne Sandberg, Gary Matthews and Keith Moreland were the first four hitters in manager Jim Frey's lineup, and they were a combined 8-for-14 with six runs and five RBIs in the series finale. Moreland's 2-for-4, four-RBI day was especially satisfying, as he'd been in the middle of everything that had taken place in the previous day's doubleheader. Moreland slammed a three-run homer to back Rick Sutcliffe's 8–6 win in the first game, then reverted to his Texas football days and charged the mound to tackle Ed Lynch and ignite a brawl after the future Cubs GM drilled him with a fastball in the fourth inning of the second game, which the Cubs won 8–4.

"That's part of the competitive game of baseball," Moreland said. "[Lynch] was probably doing what he thought was best and so was I."

Perhaps, but the umpires wanted no more of it and warned both teams before a pitch had been

Mets	AB	R	H	RBI
Martin rf	4	0	2	0
Wilson ph-cf	1	0	0	0
Chapman 2b	4	1	1	0
Hernandez 1b	4	1	2	0
Foster lf	4	0	0	1
Brooks 3b	4	4	4	1
Strawberry cf-rf	1	0	0	0
Fitzgerald c	5	0	3	2
Santana ss	4	0	1	2
Staub ph	1	0	0	0
Terrell p	3	0	0	0
Gardner p	0	0	0	0
Heep ph	1	0	0	0
Gaff p	0	0	0	0
Totals	36	6	13	6

Cubs	AB	R	H	RBI
Dernier cf	2	2	1	0
Sandberg 2b	4	2	1	1
Matthews lf	4	1	3	0
Cotto lf	0	0	0	0
Moreland 1b	4	1	3	4
Davis c	4	0	0	0
Bosley rf	4	0	2	1
Cey 3b	4	0	0	0
Owen ss	4	0	0	0
Trout p	2	0	0	0
Brusstar p	0	0	0	0
Johnstone ph	1	1	1	0
Smith p	1	0	0	0
Stoddard p	0	0	0	0
Totals	34	7	11	6

NYM 0 0 0 1 0 1 3 0 1 - 6 13 0
CHI 0 0 1 0 2 0 4 0 X - 7 11 0

Mets	IP	H	R	ER	BB	SO
Terrell	6	8	5	5	2	7
Gardner L (1-1)	1	3	2	2	0	1
Gaff	1	0	0	0	0	1
Totals	8	11	7	7	2	9

Cubs	IP	H	R	ER	BB	SO
Trout	6.1	10	4	4	4	6
Brusstar	0.2	1	1	1	2	0
Smith W (7-4)	1.1	0	0	0	0	0
Stoddard S (7)	0.2	2	1	1	1	1
Totals	9	13	6	6	7	7

DP—Chicago 2. 2B—New York Santana. 3B—Chicago Johnstone. HR—New York Brooks (11). SF—New York Foster. HBP—Chicago Dernier. LOB—New York 11; Chicago 6. SB—Chicago Sandberg. Attendance: 37,292.

Cubs 7, Mets 6

thrown the next day. When Mets starter Walt Terrell hit Dernier in the batting helmet with a man on third and nobody out in the seventh inning of a 5-3 game, he and manager Dave Johnson were ejected, despite their insistence that hitting a batter at that point made no sense. With Moreland and Thad Bosley delivering RBI singles off reliever Wes Gardner, the Cubs scored four times in the inning and gave closer Lee Smith a 7–5 lead to protect.

But the umpiring crew was really jumpy. Smith's up-and-in fastball to George Foster was deemed too close for comfort in the ninth, so he and Frey were ejected. After a Hubie Brooks homer, the Mets put the tying and go-ahead runs on base, but Tim Stoddard retired pinch-hitter Rusty Staub on a grounder to end the game and let 37,292 Wrigley spectators breathe a little easier.

Finally, and ever so slightly, the memory of 1969 began to recede in the minds of Cubs fans.

Let There Be Lights II

For all the hoopla that accompanied the first night game at Wrigley Field—Cubs vs. Phillies on Monday, Aug. 8, 1988—there was reason to wonder if the baseball gods endorsed the idea. Maybe it was the "8/8/88" implication of the date.

In any case, not long after 91-year-old Cubs fan Harry Grossman and retired Hall of Fame broadcaster Jack Brickhouse flipped the switch to engage Wrigley's new lighting system, a rainstorm of Biblical severity descended on the ballpark, drenching the place.

Ryne Sandberg had hit a home run, and the Cubs led 3–1 after 3 ½ innings. The umpires did not want to deprive the SRO crowd of their place in history, so they waited for a let-up. But when rain was still falling heavily after two hours, they had no choice and called the game. Greg Maddux, Jody Davis and Les

A day after Hall of Fame broadcaster Jack Brickhouse flipped the light switch for the first night game at rainy Wrigley Field, the Cubs and Mets made it official on Aug. 9, 1988.

August 9, 1988
Cubs 6, Mets 4

Lancaster flopping around on the tarp that covered the field during the delay turned out to be the evening's entertainment highlight.

The Mets were in the house the following night for the first "official" night game. The hoopla meter was turned way down, the weather cooperated and the teams played baseball, with Sid Fernandez opposing Mike Bielecki.

Lenny Dykstra's two-run homer staked the Mets to a 2–0 lead in the fifth inning. The Cubs got on the board with Rafael Palmeiro's RBI triple in the fifth and squared it in the sixth when Shawon Dunston singled, stole second and came around on two groundouts.

They won it with a four-spot in the seventh, chasing Fernandez when Jody Davis pinch-hit for Bielecki and stroked a double to left-center to score Palmeiro, who had singled. Roger McDowell relieved, and the Cubs peppered him with consecutive two-out singles by Dunston, Sandberg, Mark Grace and Andre Dawson, building a 6–2 lead.

Howard Johnson homered in the Mets' eighth, and they got within 6–4 in the ninth when Gary Carter doubled and Dave Magadan singled him home. But Goose Gossage retired Tim Teufel, Lee Mazzilli and Dykstra to save it for Frank DiPino, who earned the win with two innings of scoreless relief.

The Cubs' agreement with the city allowed them six night games in 1984. They went 3–3 in them. It was obvious to all who were there for any of them that night baseball was here to stay on the North Side.

Mets	AB	R	H	RBI
Dykstra cf	5	1	2	2
Johnson ss	4	1	2	1
Hernandez 1b	4	0	0	0
Strawberry rf	4	0	1	0
McReynolds lf	4	0	1	0
Carter c	3	1	1	0
Magadan 3b	4	0	1	1
Backman 2b	3	1	1	0
Teufel 2b	0	0	0	0
Fernandez p	3	0	1	0
McDowell p	0	0	0	0
Leach p	0	0	0	0
Mazzilli ph	1	0	0	0
Totals	36	4	10	4

Cubs	AB	R	H	RBI
Dunston ss	5	2	2	0
Sandberg 2b	4	1	1	1
Grace 1b	3	0	2	1
Dawson rf	4	0	1	2
Law 3b	4	1	1	0
Webster cf	4	0	0	0
Palmeiro lf	4	1	3	1
Berryhill c	4	0	1	0
Bielecki p	1	0	0	0
Trillo ph	1	0	0	0
DiPino p	0	0	0	0
Davis ph	1	0	1	1
Jackson pr	0	1	0	0
Perry p	0	0	0	0
Mumphrey ph	1	0	0	0
Gossage p	0	0	0	0
Totals	36	6	12	6

NYM	0	0	0	2	0	0	1	1	-	4	10	0
CHI	0	0	0	0	1	1	4	0	X	- 6	12	0

Mets	IP	H	R	ER	BB	SO
Fernandez L (6-10)	6.2	6	4	4	1	5
McDowell	0	4	2	2	0	0
Leach	1.1	2	0	0	0	2
Totals	8	12	6	6	1	7

Cubs	IP	H	R	ER	BB	SO
Bielecki	5	7	2	2	0	4
DiPino W (2-3)	2	0	0	0	1	1
Perry	1	1	1	1	0	0
Gossage S (12)	1	2	1	1	0	0
Totals	9	10	4	4	1	5

DP—Chicago. 2B—New York Carter; Chicago Davis. 3B—Chicago Palmeiro. HR—New York Dykstra (4), Johnson (20). LOB—New York 6; Chicago 7. SB—New York Strawberry, McReynolds; Chicago Dunston. Attendance: 36,399.

Cavvy's Kindness Rewarded

The Cubs were winding up a 20-game road trip this Sunday afternoon in Pittsburgh, where a surprisingly decent crowd of 17,773 had shown up to watch their youthful, bumbling Pirates, who were on their way to a 42–112 finish.

So awful were the Pirates that Cubs manager Phil Cavarretta did something unheard of in the kick-'em-while-they're-down world of professional sports. And, perhaps because of his act of kindness, the baseball gods smiled down upon the Cubs that very same day.

The Cubs had won the first game of the afternoon's doubleheader 9–5, though Cavarretta missed most of it: Umpire Artie Gore had ejected him for arguing a play at the plate a bit too strenuously. Now, thanks to fine pitching by Paul Minner and reliever Dutch Leonard (three scoreless innings) plus RBI singles by Bill Serena and Randy Jackson during a four-run sixth, the Cubs were leading 4–3 in the ninth inning of Game 2.

That's when Pittsburgh catcher Clyde McCullough, who had been a Cub before and would be one again, had a fingernail torn off by a foul tip. He could not continue. So Pirates manager Billy Meyer had a real problem: He had already used his other two catchers, Joe Garagiola and Ed FitzGerald, as pinch-hitters. He had no one else who could catch.

It was time for Cavarretta's good deed. He told the umpires that, if it was all right with them, the Cubs would allow Meyer to re-insert either Garagiola or FitzGerald, even though, officially, they were out of the game. The umpires gave their OK, Meyer thanked Cavvy profusely and FitzGerald hurriedly put on his gear. And when the Forbes Field public-address announcer told the crowd that FitzGerald was going to be allowed to replace McCullough "through the courtesy of manager Cavarretta," Cavvy received perhaps the biggest hand he ever had received in an opponent's ballpark.

Not only that, when Leonard set down Clem Koshorek, rookie Dick Groat and Tony Bartirome in order to wrap up the victory, the Cubs—so dreadful just a year before, when they were 45-58 on this same date—were above the .500 mark at 54–53.

At a Glance

WP: Minner (11–7)

S: Leonard (9)

Key stat: The game's lone homer was the career first for Pirates rookie center fielder Lee Walls, a future Cub.

August 11, 1966
Cubs 9, Astros 8 (11 innings)

Hundley Rides the Cycle

One of the finest trades made by the Cubs was one engineered by their new manager, Leo Durocher, at the December 1965 winter meetings, when "The Lip" talked the San Francisco Giants into giving him two young players from their farm system for veteran reliever Lindy McDaniel and outfielder Don Landrum.

Astros	AB	R	H	RBI
R. Davis cf	6	0	1	0
Jackson ss	5	1	0	0
Staub rf	5	1	1	1
Nicholson ph-rf	0	0	0	0
Harrison 1b	6	1	2	1
Morgan 2b	3	2	0	0
Maye lf	5	2	5	0
Bateman c	4	0	1	1
Aspromonte 3b	5	1	2	4
Bruce p	2	0	0	0
Farrell p	2	0	1	0
Heath ph	1	0	1	0
Colbert pr	0	0	0	0
Owens p	0	0	0	0
Totals	44	8	14	8

Cubs	AB	R	H	RBI
Phillips cf	5	1	1	3
Beckert 2b	5	0	2	0
Williams rf	5	1	1	1
Santo 3b	5	1	1	0
Banks 1b	5	1	1	0
Browne lf	5	0	0	0
Hundley c	5	3	4	3
Kessinger ss	5	1	3	1
Roberts p	1	1	1	0
Keough ph	0	0	0	0
Simmons p	0	0	0	0
Koonce p	1	0	0	0
Thomas ph	1	0	1	1
Totals	43	9	15	9

HOU 0 4 1 1 1 0 0 1 0 0 0 - 8 14 0
CHI 0 0 3 3 0 0 1 1 0 0 1 - 9 15 1

Astros	IP	H	R	ER	BB	SO
Bruce	3.1	7	6	6	0	5
Farrell	6.2	5	2	2	2	1
Owens L (4-7)	0	3	1	1	0	0
Totals	10	15	9	9	2	6

Cubs	IP	H	R	ER	BB	SO
Roberts	4	5	6	6	1	4
Simmons	3.2	6	2	2	1	2
Koonce W (2-4)	3.1	3	0	0	2	1
Totals	11	14	8	8	4	7

E—Chicago Hundley. DP—Houston 2; Chicago 2. 2B—Houston Maye, Harrison; Chicago Santo, Hundley. 3B—Houston Harrison; Chicago Hundley. HR—Houston Maye (8), Staub (13), Aspromonte (5); Williams (21), Phillips (14), Hundley (16). SH—Houston Jackson. LOB—Houston 8; Chicago 6. SB—Houston Jackson; Chicago Keough, Kessinger 2.

The Cub newcomers were catcher Randy Hundley and pitcher Bill Hands. Durocher was confident Hands could become a big winner, which he did. About Hundley, then 23, he said: "I know he can catch, throw and run. I just hope he can hit."

By August, Hundley indeed had shown he was going to be just fine defensively (he was to win a Gold Glove the very next season, in fact). He had shown he could run as early as May 19, when he stole home against the Astros. And now he was starting to show he could hit, too. In the two games before this Thursday afternoon matchup at Wrigley Field, the rookie from Virginia had gone 5-for-8 with three home runs and seven RBIs.

The mashing was to continue this day, when his batterymate was future Hall of Famer Robin Roberts, the Springfield, Ill., native who was nearing his 40th birthday. Randy didn't catch him for long: Roberts lasted four innings and allowed six runs and five hits, three of them homers—a grand slam by Bob Aspromonte and solo shots by Rusty Staub and Lee Maye.

With the Cubs down 4–0 in third, Hundley led off against Bob Bruce and struck out. Things would get better. It was 6–3 Houston in the fourth when "The Rebel" tripled high off the vines in left-center, the ball eluding left fielder Maye and center fielder Ron Davis. It was a 6–5 game now, and Bruce gave way to Turk Farrell, who would work until the ninth.

In the sixth, with Houston leading 7–6, Hundley stroked a one-out double but could not advance. Billy Williams' home run, however, tied the game 7–7 in the seventh and, after John Bateman singled in a Houston run in the top of the eighth, Hundley hit his 16th homer of the year in the bottom half to make it 8–8. So Hundley had his homer, triple and double—but was missing a simple single for the cycle. And it was quite possible he might not get another at-bat.

The game, though, went into extra innings, and it was still 8–8 when Hundley came up to lead off the 11th against Jim Owens. Randy hit a grounder into the hole between short and third, but shortstop Sonny Jackson could not make a play, and Hundley was aboard with a single. He had become just the ninth catcher in big-league history to hit for the cycle. It had last been done by Bill Salkeld of Pittsburgh in 1945. (Since Hundley did it, only six more catchers have accomplished the feat.)

What made it even better was this: Don Kessinger followed with a base hit and pinch-hitter Lee Thomas delivered another hit, a single to left, to score Hundley with the winning run.

The performance improved Hundley's batting average to .263 and gave him 10 RBIs in his last three games. That Giant trade was looking like a giant mistake for San Francisco.

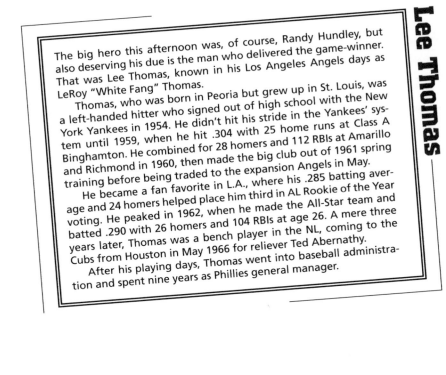

The big hero this afternoon was, of course, Randy Hundley, but also deserving his due is the man who delivered the game-winner. That was Lee Thomas, known in his Los Angeles Angels days as LeRoy "White Fang" Thomas.

Thomas, who was born in Peoria but grew up in St. Louis, was a left-handed hitter who signed out of high school with the New York Yankees in 1954. He didn't hit his stride in the Yankees' system until 1959, when he hit .304 with 25 home runs at Class A Binghamton. He combined for 28 homers and 112 RBIs at Amarillo and Richmond in 1960, then made the big club out of 1961 spring training before being traded to the expansion Angels in May.

He became a fan favorite in L.A., where his .285 batting average and 24 homers helped place him third in AL Rookie of the Year voting. He peaked in 1962, when he made the All-Star team and batted .290 with 26 homers and 104 RBIs at age 26. A mere three years later, Thomas was a bench player in the NL, coming to the Cubs from Houston in May 1966 for reliever Ted Abernathy.

After his playing days, Thomas went into baseball administration and spent nine years as Phillies general manager.

Lee Thomas

Cubs 8, Expos 7

A Pair of Bosley Blasts

Expos	AB	R	H	RBI
Raines lf	4	2	3	1
Law 2b	4	0	1	1
Dawson rf	5	0	2	0
Reardon p	0	0	0	0
Brooks ss	5	1	2	2
Francona 1b	4	1	2	0
Burke p	0	0	0	0
Webster rf	1	0	0	0
Wallach 3b	5	2	2	3
Winningham cf	4	0	1	0
Fitzgerald c	3	0	0	0
Washington ph	0	1	0	0
Nicosia c	0	0	0	0
Youmans p	2	0	0	0
Shines ph	1	0	0	0
St. Claire p	0	0	0	0
Thompson 1b	1	0	1	0
Totals	39	7	14	7

Cubs	AB	R	H	RBI
Dernier cf	5	1	1	0
Matthews lf	3	1	2	1
Gumpert p	0	0	0	0
Lopes rf	0	0	0	0
Sandberg 2b	3	1	1	2
Moreland rf-c	4	0	1	0
Cey 3b	4	0	0	0
Durham 1b	4	0	2	0
Speier ss	4	1	2	0
Bowa pr-ss	0	1	0	0
Lake c	3	1	1	0
Hebner ph	1	0	0	0
Smith p	0	0	0	0
Sorensen p	1	0	0	0
Hatcher ph	1	0	0	0
Brusstar p	0	0	0	0
Bosley ph-lf	2	2	2	5
Totals	35	8	12	8

MON 0 0 1 2 2 1 0 1 0 - 7 14 1
CHI 0 0 0 0 3 3 0 2 X - 8 12 0

Expos	IP	H	R	ER	BB	SO
Youmans	5	7	3	0	1	2
St. Claire	1	3	3	3	0	1
Burke	1	0	0	0	1	0
Reardon L (2-5)	1	2	2	2	0	2
Totals	8	12	8	5	2	5

Cubs	IP	H	R	ER	BB	SO
Sorensen	5	9	5	5	0	2
Brusstar	1	2	1	1	1	0
Gumpert W (1-0)	2	3	1	1	1	0
Smith S (24)	1	0	0	0	0	1
Totals	9	14	7	7	2	3

E—Montreal Brooks. DP—Montreal; Chicago. 2B—Montreal Dawson; Chicago Matthews, Dernier. 3B—Chicago Durham. HR—Montreal Raines (6), Wallach 2 (10,11), Brooks (10); Chicago Bosley 2 (3,4), Sandberg (16). SF—Montreal Law. LOB—Montreal 8; Chicago 5. SB—Montreal Winningham; Chicago Durham, Sandberg. Attendance: 28,195.

It certainly didn't seem like it, but it really had been more than seven years since Thad Bosley had first burst upon the Chicago baseball scene.

The highly regarded speedster had come to the White Sox from the Angels as part of the Bobby Bonds trade in December 1977. Only 21, the slender outfielder got the call to report to Chicago on the last weekend in May '78, at a time when the Sox were struggling to get untracked. Bosley provided an immediate spark with his speed and his bat, as the Sox won 11 of the first 13 games in which he played. At that point, he was hitting .309.

He never was quite able to fulfill that initial promise on the South Side, though. The "dream" outfield of Bosley, Chet Lemon and Claudell Washington—all top prospects, all in their early 20s—never did materialize, and Thad drifted to Milwaukee in 1981, to Seattle in 1982 and, the following February, to Oakland. The Cubs picked him up at the end of March '83, so he was back in Chicago, a city with which he was quite familiar. Perhaps that was one reason he ran off, in successive seasons with the Cubs, batting averages of .292, .296, .328 and .275.

By '85, this man of many talents (he was also a poet/songwriter/singer who had recorded an album of Christian music) had become something of a pinch-hitter deluxe, having entered this Monday game on the North Side with a major-league-high 12 pinch hits. The call came relatively early this day, with the Cubs—who had lost seven straight to drop to 54–54 and into fourth place in the NL East—having fallen behind Montreal 6–3 in the sixth.

After one-out singles by Chris Speier and Steve Lake off right-hander Randy St. Claire, manager Jim Frey sent Bosley in to bat for reliever Warren Brusstar. "I feel very comfortable sending Bosley up there in a pinch-hitting role," Frey said later. "I know there is an excellent chance for him to make contact."

He made contact, all right, crushing a 1-0 pitch from St. Claire into the bleachers in right to tie the game 6–6. Frey kept him in the lineup, batting in the No. 9 hole and playing left field. That turned out to be a good move when, in the seventh with the Cubs down 7–6 and a man on, Bosley drove a 1-2 pitch from Expos closer Jeff Reardon over the center-field wall. The Cubs had an 8–7 lead, which stood up, and Bosley got a standing ovation from 28,195 fans, who demanded and received a Bosley curtain call.

"I have tried to let my performances speak for themselves," he said. "I don't consider myself a part-time player, and I think the fact that I haven't has made me a better pinch-hitter."

He was the best there was during the '85 season, when he was 20-for-60 in the pinch, a .333 batting average. It had taken a while, but he had proved that he belonged.

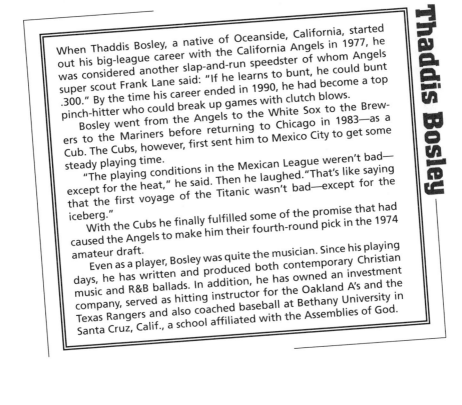

Thaddis Bosley

When Thaddis Bosley, a native of Oceanside, California, started out his big-league career with the California Angels in 1977, he was considered another slap-and-run speedster of whom Angels super scout Frank Lane said: "If he learns to bunt, he could bunt .300." By the time his career ended in 1990, he had become a top pinch-hitter who could break up games with clutch blows.

Bosley went from the Angels to the White Sox to the Brewers to the Mariners before returning to Chicago in 1983—as a Cub. The Cubs, however, first sent him to Mexico City to get some steady playing time.

"The playing conditions in the Mexican League weren't bad—except for the heat," he said. Then he laughed. "That's like saying that the first voyage of the Titanic wasn't bad—except for the iceberg."

With the Cubs he finally fulfilled some of the promise that had caused the Angels to make him their fourth-round pick in the 1974 amateur draft.

Even as a player, Bosley was quite the musician. Since his playing days, he has written and produced both contemporary Christian music and R&B ballads. In addition, he has owned an investment company, served as hitting instructor for the Oakland A's and the Texas Rangers and also coached baseball at Bethany University in Santa Cruz, Calif., a school affiliated with the Assemblies of God.

A Rout of Giant Proportions

The more one thinks about it, the more one realizes how strange it was for the Cubs to fire manager Bob Scheffing at the close of the 1959 season. The move made absolutely no sense. Not only had Scheffing taken the Cubs from 62–92 his first year (1957) to 74–80 in 1959 and made them relevant again in Chicago, his teams had played the top clubs to a stalemate. In '59, the Cubs were 12–10 against third-place San Francisco, 10–12 against second-place Milwaukee and 11–11 against NL and World Series champion Los Angeles. Indeed, the Cubs' two-game sweep of the Giants at Wrigley Field the last week of the season was the death blow for San Francisco.

But by then, the Giants were getting used to losing in Chicago. On their next-to-last visit, they had dropped three of four. The series opener, played on a breezy Thursday afternoon before 17,963 delighted fans, had set the tone. It took a then-NL-record 3 hours 50 minutes to complete, but this game was replete with excitement.

Cubs lefty starter Art Ceccarelli was shelled immediately. Jackie Brandt walked, Jim Davenport tripled and Willie Mays hit one out onto Waveland Avenue for his 19th homer of the season, and the first-place Giants led 3–0 before a single hitter had been retired. Ceccarelli settled down and got Orlando Cepeda, Willie Kirkland and Daryl Spencer on infield grounders, and then it was the Cubs' turn.

Giants starter Jack Sanford walked Tony Taylor and then gave up a homer to rookie George Altman. When the count on Jim Marshall reached 3-0, Sanford—with vocal support from Spencer, the second baseman—berated plate umpire Hal Dixon for his ball-and-strike calls. Dixon chased them both, and in came Gordon Jones, who got out of the inning but ran into trouble later.

In the second inning, after Brandt's RBI double had made it 4–2, Jones walked Tony Taylor again and, like Sanford, served up a two-run homer to Altman, and now it was 4–4. The third inning—at the end of which the Giants led 7–6—featured a three-run homer by Kirkland, the ejection of Scheffing, the departure of Ceccarelli and arrival of reliever John Buzhardt, plus a two-run home run by Cub pinch-hitter Dale Long off future White Sox All-Star reliever Eddie Fisher.

More fun was coming. After rookie Ed Donnelly allowed a Mays triple and yet escaped the top of the fourth unscathed, the Cubs jumped on Fisher and Stu Miller for four runs in their half. The big hit was a bases-loaded, two-out pinch single by Art Schult. The Cubs led 10–7.

Don Elston, the Cubs' top reliever, entered in the fifth and didn't get knocked around until the sixth, when Dusty Rhodes delivered a pinch double and scored ahead of Brandt's home run, and now it was 10–9. The Cubs, though, got those runs right back on successive RBI singles by Tony Taylor and Altman off Al Worthington, and the game headed to the seventh, the inning the Cubs put this one away.

Leading off against lefty Mike McCormick, Ernie Banks got things going with a double and then scored on Earl Averill's single. Irv Noren walked and former Giant Bobby Thomson singled to load the bases for another ex-Giant, Alvin Dark. Dark promptly belted his fourth career grand slam and his third homer in three days. A bit later in the inning, Tony Taylor also homered, and the Cubs were now up 18–9.

That was more than enough, but the Cubs still had to bat in the eighth, and Noren tripled and scored on Thomson's infield out to make it 19–9. And when Tony Taylor tripled home Dark minutes later, it was 20–9. The Cubs then rested.

Eleven pitchers had combined to give up 29 runs and 31 hits. It was not a good day for ERAs. It was, however, a good day for the Cubs. They had shown again they could play with the best, and by the end of the weekend their record had improved to 57–58.

Yet somewhere in the Cubs hierarchy, someone was deciding that Bob Scheffing would have to go.

Giants	AB	R	H	RBI
Brandt lf	3	2	2	3
McCormick p	0	0	0	0
Davenport 3b	5	1	1	1
Mays cf	3	2	2	2
Cepeda 1b-lf	5	1	2	0
Kirkland rf	5	1	1	3
Spencer 2b	1	0	0	0
O'Connell 2b	2	0	1	0
McCovey ph-1b	1	0	1	0
Bressoud ss	5	0	0	0
Schmidt c	2	1	1	0
Landrith ph-c	2	0	0	0
Sanford p	0	0	0	0
Jones p	0	0	0	0
Fisher p	1	0	0	0
Miller p	0	0	0	0
Rhodes ph	1	1	1	0
Worthington p	0	0	0	0
Byerly p	0	0	0	0
Wagner ph	1	0	0	0
Pagan 2b	1	0	0	0
Totals	**38**	**9**	**12**	**9**

Cubs	AB	R	H	RBI
Taylor 2b	4	3	3	3
Altman cf	6	3	5	5
Marshall 1b	4	1	2	0
Walls rf	1	0	0	0
Banks ss	2	2	1	0
Taylor c	4	0	0	1
Averill ph-c	2	1	1	1
Noren lf-1b	4	3	2	0
Moryn rf-lf	2	2	0	1
Thomson ph-lf	2	1	1	1
Dark 3b	4	2	1	4
Ceccarelli p	1	0	0	0
Buzhardt p	0	0	0	0
Long ph	1	1	1	2
Donnelly p	0	0	0	0
Schult ph	1	0	1	2
Elston p	3	1	1	0
Totals	**41**	**20**	**19**	**20**

SF	3	1	3	0	0	2	0	0	0	-	9	12	0
CHI	2	2	2	4	0	2	6	2	X	-	20	19	1

Giants	IP	H	R	ER	BB	SO
Sanford	0	1	2	2	2	0
Jones	1.2	3	2	2	2	0
Fisher L (2-3)	1.1	3	4	4	0	0
Miller	2	1	2	2	5	0
Worthington	0.2	3	2	2	1	1
Byerly	0.1	0	0	0	0	0
McCormick	2	8	8	8	3	1
Totals	**8**	**19**	**20**	**20**	**13**	**2**

Cubs	IP	H	R	ER	BB	SO
Ceccarelli	2	5	7	6	2	0
Buzhardt	1	1	0	0	0	0
Donnelly W (1-1)	1	1	0	0	1	1
Elston S (12)	5	5	2	2	3	2
Totals	**9**	**12**	**9**	**8**	**6**	**3**

E—Chicago Marshall. DP—Chicago. 2B—San Francisco Brandt, Rhodes; Chicago Banks, Marshall. 3B—San Francisco Davenport, Mays; Chicago Taylor, Noren. HR—San Francisco Brandt (10), Mays (19), Kirkland (20); Chicago Altman 2 (6,7), Taylor (5), Dark (4), Long (13). SH—San Francisco Jones; Chicago Altman. HBP—Chicago Moryn. LOB—San Francisco 9; Chicago 12. Attendance: 17,963.

August 15, 2006
Cubs 8, Astros 6 (18 innings)

Murton Ends Marathon with Astros

The Cubs were headed for a 66–96 finish. They were 50–68, in fifth place and 12.5 games behind the first-place St. Louis Cardinals. Houston was 57–61 and in third place, 5.5 back. Still, a sellout crowd of 41,531 was at Minute Maid Park in Houston for this Tuesday night Astros-Cubs matchup. Roger Clemens was the starting pitcher for the Astros. Mystery solved.

In any event, suffice it to say that very few of those 41,531 stuck around for the finish.

The Cubs had taken a 5–2 lead over Clemens after five innings, thanks partly to Jacque Jones' three-run homer in the fourth. But the Astros went up by one with a four-run sixth, a two-out rally highlighted by Adam Everett's two-run triple and a two-run double by Orlando Palmeiro, batting for Clemens. It remained 6–5 Houston until the ninth. Matt Murton, who had entered the game in the seventh to play left field, was leading off against Astros closer Brad Lidge. Murton, a former first-round draft pick of the Boston Red Sox, had come to the Cubs in the trade-deadline deal that brought Nomar Garciaparra to the Cubs in 2004. He'd been hailed as an excellent young hitter. In addition, Peter Gammons reported, "his makeup is off the charts." Murton never became the player many had projected—he was playing in Japan in the 2010 season—but he did have his moments. This was one of them.

> ### At a Glance
>
> **WP:** R. Hill (3–5)
>
> **HR:** Cedeno (5), Jones (20), Murton (8)
>
> **Key stats:** Cubs manager Dusty Baker used all 25 of his players; the Astros used 21. The game lasted 5 hours 36 minutes.

Murton hit one of Lidge's now-famous hanging sliders over the wall for a game-tying home run. The game was tied at 6–6.

On and on it went. Murton had four more at-bats in this one, failing in his second, third and fourth tries. The fifth one was the charm. That came in the 18th, which Aramis Ramirez began with a double off Dave Borkowski, who was in his sixth inning of relief. Jones singled to right, Ramirez stopping at third. After John Mabry popped out, Ronny Cedeno grounded to third, Ramirez holding and Jones moving to second.

Here the Astros walked Michael Barrett intentionally to load the bases for Murton, who lined a single to right for two runs and the ballgame.

Murton ended the season, his only full one in the major leagues, with a .297 average, 13 homers, 62 RBIs and a .365 on-base percentage.

Hobbie, Ernie, and Big D

Along with his Hall of Fame stuff, Don Drysdale always brought a nasty disposition to the pitcher's mound, and opposing hitters knew it.

"The key to facing Don Drysdale," Orlando Cepeda once observed, "is to hit him before he hits you."

Bob Will, a journeyman outfielder for the Cubs, tried to follow Cepeda's advice against the defending world champions on this Wednesday afternoon at Wrigley Field. Leading off in the ninth inning of a 0–0 game, Will rifled a liner back up the middle. Drysdale got a hand up and deflected the ball before it struck him in the face, then retrieved it and threw to first to retire Will for the first out of the inning.

Drysdale insisted he was fine when manager Walter Alston visited the mound, and Alston left him in the game. But he grooved his very next pitch to Ernie Banks, and the reigning two-time MVP hit it out for his 34th home run, pinning a tough loss on Drysdale, who had given the Cubs just three other hits.

Glen Hobbie was the shutout winner in a snappy 1:58 before 10,901 fans.

At a Glance

WP: Hobbie (11–16)

HR: Banks (34)

Key stat: Banks hit 7 homers off fellow Hall of Famer Drysdale in his career. His No. 1 victim? Fellow Hall of Famer Robin Roberts, 15.

Hobbie, a sturdy right-hander who always wanted the ball, was the ace of the Cubs' staff as a 24-year-old. Consequently, he often found himself matched up against the other team's No. 1 pitcher. And he rarely had a good team behind him, which explains why he was 16–20 in 1960 despite a decent 3.97 ERA and four shutouts.

Hobbie completed 16 of his 36 starts and also made 10 relief appearances in working 258 2/3 innings. This one-walk seven-hitter might have been his best performance of the season, but there was nothing easy about it—Hobbie pitched out of trouble all day as the Dodgers got seven hits and put their leadoff man aboard in five of the nine innings.

Junior Gilliam began the game with a double and took third on Wally Moon's grounder to second, but Hobbie got Tommy Davis on a popup and Norm Larker on a grounder.

Davis singled and Larker walked to open the fourth, but Hobbie escaped by getting a double-play ball from Frank Howard. In the sixth, Howard hit into another double play after Moon walked and Davis singled, and in the ninth, Larker obliged him with a double-play ball after Davis' third single.

The Cubs' didn't have too many highlights during a 60–94, seventh-place season, but Hobbie and Banks turned this game into one.

Managing a Little Magic

Phil Cavarretta had done this sort of thing before as the Cubs' player-manager, putting all the responsibility on his shoulders and taking the pressure off of his players. Now, on this Monday afternoon at Wrigley Field, with only 4,911 paying customers to witness it, Cavvy was about to do it again.

But we're getting ahead of ourselves.

The Cubs, needing a victory to climb to the .500 mark at 58–58, entered the last of the eighth inning trailing Murry Dickson and the last-place Pirates 3–0. It was time to go to work.

With one out, Frankie Baumholtz walked, scooted to third on Gene Hermanski's single to right and scored on Hank Sauer's sacrifice fly. After reliever Bob Schultz struck out the dangerous Ralph Kiner with a man aboard to end the Pirates' ninth, Bill Serena opened the Cubs' half with a walk.

Cavarretta chose Bruce Edwards to hit for Roy Smalley, and the sore-armed catcher responded by driving the ball into the right-field corner, far out of the reach of right fielder Gus Bell, who had been shading Edwards toward center. Serena came around to score, and Edwards wound up at third with a triple. Now it was 3–2.

Decision time, again, for Cavarretta.

First he sent in Hal Jeffcoat to run for Edwards. Then he decided that if there were to be a pinch-hitter for his pitcher, Schultz, it would be him. Cavarretta worked the count to 3–2, then swung and drove the ball against the back screen fence in right field for a game-winning home run—the last homer he would hit in a Cubs uniform.

Pirates	AB	R	H	RBI
Koshorek 2b	5	0	0	0
Groat ss	5	0	2	0
Davis cf	3	0	0	0
Kiner lf	4	0	0	0
Walls lf	0	0	0	0
Bell rf	4	1	1	0
Metkovich 1b	4	1	1	0
Garagiola c	3	1	0	0
FitzGerald 3b	3	0	2	1
Dickson p	4	0	1	1
Totals	**35**	**3**	**7**	**2**

Cubs	AB	R	H	RBI
Miksis 2b	3	0	0	0
Baumholtz cf	3	1	1	0
Hermanski rf	2	0	1	0
Sauer lf	4	0	0	1
Atwell c	4	0	1	0
Fondy 1b	4	0	0	0
Serena 3b	3	1	1	0
Smalley ss	3	0	1	0
Edwards ph	1	0	1	1
Jeffcoat pr	0	1	0	0
Lown p	1	0	0	0
Addis ph	1	0	0	0
Schultz p	0	0	0	0
Cavarretta ph	1	1	1	2
Totals	**30**	**4**	**7**	**4**

PIT	0 1 0 1 0 1 0 0 0 -	3	7 1
CHI	0 0 0 0 0 0 0 1 3 -	4	7 3

Pirates	IP	H	R	ER	BB	SO
Dickson L (11-17)	8	7	4	4	5	4
Totals	**8**	**7**	**4**	**4**	**5**	**4**

Cubs	IP	H	R	ER	BB	SO
Lown	7	6	3	1	4	6
Schultz W (3-1)	2	1	0	0	1	1
Totals	**9**	**7**	**3**	**1**	**5**	**7**

E—Pittsburgh Groat; Chicago Fondy, Smalley, Baumholtz. DP—Pittsburgh; Chicago. 3B—Chicago Edwards. HR—Chicago Cavarretta (1). SH—Chicago Lown. LOB—Pittsburgh 10; Chicago 8. SB—Pittsburgh Davis, Bell. Attendance: 4,911.

Outfielder Hank Sauer's MVP season in 1952 featured 37 home runs and 121 RBIs.

'A No-Hitter for Kenny Holtzman!'

It was one of the true highlights of a season in which highlights abounded ... at least for the first five months.

A crowd of 37,514 packed Wrigley Field on a Thursday afternoon, anticipating a pitcher's duel between Cubs lefty Ken Holtzman, an emerging star at 23, and Phil Niekro, the ace of the Braves' staff at 30. In the first year of division play, the Cubs were leading the NL East and the Braves were only 1.5 games behind in the NL West, so the game had possible postseason implications as well.

Niekro got off to a shaky start, touched for singles by Don Kessinger and Glenn Beckert, the first two Cubs hitters. When Ron Santo reached the bleachers with a liner driven through the teeth of an incoming breeze, the Cubs had a 3–0 lead.

Niekro settled down and allowed only two singles thereafter. Holtzman, though, was overpowering, cruising through a formidable Atlanta lineup that featured Felipe Alou, Henry Aaron, Rico Carty and Orlando Cepeda. The Braves were hitless through six innings.

That appeared to change when Aaron, leading off the seventh, snapped his wrists into a fastball and sent it soaring "toward Evanston," Holtzman recalled. "I thought it was gone for sure."

So did the crowd, based on the telltale crack of the bat. But left fielder Billy Williams never gave up on the ball. He drifted back into the "well area" where the left-field wall curved back into the outfield. The ball was hit nearly as high as it was far, and Williams was there to grab it when it hung up in the wind, then drifted back into the ballpark, as if pulled back on a string.

"Only the wind saved that ball from being a home run," Holtzman acknowledged, recalling the quizzical look Aaron gave him as he circled back to the dugout. "I thought it was going to land in those houses across the street."

Given a reprieve, Holtzman retired eight of the

Braves	AB	R	H	RBI
Alou cf	4	0	0	0
Millan 2b	4	0	0	0
H Aaron rf	4	0	0	0
Carty lf	2	0	0	0
Cepeda 1b	3	0	0	0
Boyer 2b	3	0	0	0
Didier c	2	0	0	0
Garrido ss	2	0	0	0
Niekro p	2	0	0	0
T Aaron ph	1	0	0	0
Neibauer p	0	0	0	0
Totals	**27**	**0**	**0**	**0**

Cubs	AB	R	H	RBI
Kessinger ss	4	1	2	0
Beckert 2b	4	1	1	0
Williams lf	4	0	0	0
Santo 3b	4	1	1	3
Banks 1b	3	0	0	0
Hickman rf	3	0	0	0
Heath c	2	0	0	0
Oliver c	0	0	0	0
Young cf	2	0	1	0
Holtzman p	3	0	0	0
Totals	**29**	**3**	**5**	**3**

ATL 0 0 0 0 0 0 0 0 0 - 0 0 0
CHI 3 0 0 0 0 0 0 0 X - 3 5 0

Braves	IP	H	R	ER	BB	SO
Niekro L (16-11)	7	5	3	3	2	4
Neibauer	1	0	0	0	0	0
Totals	**8**	**5**	**3**	**3**	**2**	**4**

Cubs	IP	H	R	ER	BB	SO
Holtzman W (14-7)	9	0	0	0	3	0
Totals	**9**	**0**	**0**	**0**	**3**	**0**

HR—Chicago Santo (25). LOB—Atlanta 3; Chicago 4. Attendance: 37,514.

next nine hitters, but a walk to Carty meant he had to face Aaron again, with two outs and nobody on in the ninth inning. Second baseman Beckert made a nice play on Aaron's sharply hit grounder, then appeared to stumble just a bit. "Throw it, kid," announcer Jack Brickhouse implored, and Beckert did, retiring Aaron for the final out.

"He did it! A no-hitter for Kenny Holtzman!" Brickhouse declared, and the celebration was on.

Holtzman threw 112 pitches. As dominant as he was, he did not strike out a single batter, getting 15 of his 27 outs on fly balls, most of them harmless as the Braves kept popping up his high, hard fastball.

"Sure, things have to be in your favor to pitch a no-hitter," Cubs manager Leo Durocher said. "A couple of those line drives today, on another day they might have been base hits. But a no-hitter is a no-hitter. His fastball was really humming today."

The Cubs improved to a season-best 77–45 with the win and maintained their eight-game lead over the second-place Mets. It was their last hurrah. They would lose seven of their next nine games and 25 of their remaining 40. Holtzman was not immune to the slump, dropping six of his last nine decisions.

The lead would be gone in less than a month as the Mets went 33–11 after August 19 and won the division going away. Some Cubs fans still aren't over it.

Cubs 6, Phillies 5

Koenig Makes His Mark

This thrilling victory could not have happened without the "help" of Violet Valli, a 21-year-old dancer who accidentally shot Billy Jurges as the Cubs' shortstop tried to wrest a pistol away from her in a Chicago hotel. The two had been romantically involved until Jurges broke things off, and now Violet was intent on committing suicide, something Jurges was attempting to prevent when the gun went off.

Jurges was wounded in two places—a rib and the little finger on his left hand. Fortunately, the wounds were not considered serious, but they were serious enough to keep him out of action for 2 ½ weeks. His absence prompted Cubs president Bill Veeck Sr. to purchase the contract of former New York Yankees shortstop Mark Koenig from the Mission Reds of the Pacific Coast League.

Koenig had played in three straight World Series with the Yankees, had gone 9-for-18 in the 1927 World Series and batted a career-best .319 in 1928. Having lost his starting job to Leo Durocher in 1929, Koenig spent most of 1930 and all of 1931 with Detroit. He was batting .335 in the PCL when he was summoned to Chicago in mid-August.

Now he was about to show his new teammates how they did things at Yankee Stadium.

The Cubs, in first place by 1.5 games, were on the verge of having that lead cut by a game. In a wacky contest that had seen the ejection of Cubs manager Charlie Grimm and three of his players, the North Siders were down 5–2 to the Phillies and Ray Benge in the last of the ninth. There were two outs and the bases were empty.

Then it started. Johnny Moore singled to left and Marv Gudat drew a walk. Gabby Hartnett then ripped a hot grounder off the leg of second baseman Bernie Friberg, the ball ricocheting into short center for an error as Moore crossed the plate and Gudat raced to third. Now the Phils led 5–3, with runners at the corners and Koenig coming up.

To this point, Koenig, a switch-hitter, had gone 5-for-10 in a Cubs uniform, four of the hits coming on first pitches. This time was no different. Koenig,

Phillies	AB	R	H	RBI
Davis cf	5	1	2	1
Bartell ss	4	0	2	0
Klein rf	4	1	1	0
Hurst 1b	4	1	0	0
Whitney 3b	3	1	2	2
Lee lf	4	0	1	0
Davis c	4	0	0	0
Friberg 2b	4	1	1	0
Benge p	4	0	2	0
Totals	**36**	**5**	**11**	**3**

Cubs	AB	R	H	RBI
Herman 2b	4	0	1	0
Hack 3b	4	0	0	0
Cuyler rf	4	0	0	0
Stephenson lf	4	1	1	0
Moore cf	4	2	3	1
Grimm 1b	1	0	0	0
Gudat 1b	2	1	0	0
Hartnett c	4	0	0	0
Jurges pr	0	1	0	0
Koenig ss	4	1	2	3
Bush p	1	0	0	0
Smith p	1	0	0	0
Demaree ph	1	0	0	0
May p	0	0	0	0
Totals	**34**	**6**	**7**	**4**

PHI	1 1 0 0 2 0 0 1 0	-	5	11	0
CHI	0 1 0 0 1 0 0 0 4	-	6	7	0

Phillies	IP	H	R	ER	BB	SO
Benge L (10-11)	8.2	7	6	1	1	7
Totals	**8.2**	**7**	**6**	**1**	**1**	**7**

Cubs	IP	H	R	ER	BB	SO
Bush	4.2	7	4	2	2	1
Smith	3.1	2	1	1	0	3
May W (1-1)	1	2	0	0	0	0
Totals	**9**	**11**	**5**	**3**	**2**	**4**

2B—Philadelphia Klein; Chicago Stephenson. 3B—Philadelphia Whitney. HR—Philadelphia Whitney (8); Chicago Moore (12), Koenig (1). SH—Philadelphia Bartell. LOB—Philadelphia 7; Chicago 3. SB—Philadelphia Hurst, Klein.

batting left-handed, swung at Benge's first pitch and drilled it on a line into the bleachers in right to win the game and ignite not only a celebration at home plate but a 14-game winning streak. The string of success brought the Cubs from a 1.5-game lead to one of seven by Sept. 3.

The story doesn't end here. Koenig, despite his heroics this particular day and his .353 batting average for the Cubs in 33 games down the stretch, was awarded just a half-share of the World Series swag in voting by Cubs players on Sept. 21. That fired up the Yankees, the Cubs' World Series opponents that fall, and they never missed a chance to remind one and all of the Cubs' cheapness in their treatment of Koenig.

They also happened to sweep the Cubs in four straight.

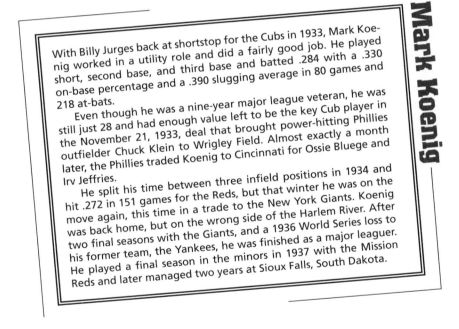

Mark Koenig

With Billy Jurges back at shortstop for the Cubs in 1933, Mark Koenig worked in a utility role and did a fairly good job. He played short, second base, and third base and batted .284 with a .330 on-base percentage and a .390 slugging average in 80 games and 218 at-bats.

Even though he was a nine-year major league veteran, he was still just 28 and had enough value left to be the key Cub player in the November 21, 1933, deal that brought power-hitting Phillies outfielder Chuck Klein to Wrigley Field. Almost exactly a month later, the Phillies traded Koenig to Cincinnati for Ossie Bluege and Irv Jeffries.

He split his time between three infield positions in 1934 and hit .272 in 151 games for the Reds, but that winter he was on the move again, this time in a trade to the New York Giants. Koenig was back home, but on the wrong side of the Harlem River. After two final seasons with the Giants, and a 1936 World Series loss to his former team, the Yankees, he was finished as a major leaguer. He played a final season in the minors in 1937 with the Mission Reds and later managed two years at Sioux Falls, South Dakota.

A Brother Act by Reuschels Lifts Cubs

The Niekro brothers combined for 539 wins, the Perry brothers 529 and the injury-plagued Martinez brothers 354. The Reuschel brothers produced 230 wins between them. But on this day, before 8,377 fans at Wrigley Field, the defending NL champion Dodgers probably would have ranked Rick and Paul Reuschel, from tiny Camp Point, Ill., among baseball's best brother acts.

Starter Rick Reuschel, 26, blanked the Dodgers on five hits over 6 ⅓ innings. When a blister on his pitching hand forced Rick to leave in the seventh, 28-year-old Paul Reuschel took over, allowing just three baserunners in completing the shutout, the first by two brothers in the majors.

Don Kessinger, the only survivor from the fabled, ill-fated '69 Cubs, had two of the team's eight hits, as did Rick Monday and Bill Madlock.

The Cubs jumped on loser Andy Messersmith for two first-inning runs, one scoring on Madlock's RBI single and the other on Jerry Morales' groundout. Manny Trillo's double and Kessinger's RBI single made it 3–0 in the second, and Monday followed with a two-run homer, his 16th, for a 5–0 lead. Jose Cardenal doubled home Kessinger and Madlock to complete the scoring in the seventh.

The Reuschels' only anxious moment occurred in the top of the seventh. Steve Garvey singled, and Rick Reuschel departed with his blistered finger after coaxing a forceout grounder from Willie Crawford. Paul Reuschel then hit Steve Yeager with a pitch, giving the Dodgers two baserunners, but he retired pinch-hitter Leron Lee on a fly ball to end the inning.

Paul Reuschel was 1–3 with a 3.50 ERA and five saves that season, and 16–16 with a 4.51 ERA and 13 saves in 198 games over five seasons with the Cubs and the Cleveland Indians.

At a Glance

WP: R. Reuschel (10–13)

HR: Monday (16)

Key stat: Former Dodgers outfielder Leron Lee is the uncle of Derrek Lee, the Cubs' first baseman from 2004 to 2010. Derrek Lee was born in 1975, a month after this game.

Rick Reuschel was an excellent athlete despite his "Big Daddy" girth, a decent hitter, an excellent bunter, a frequent pinch-runner and a two-time recipient of the Gold Glove Award for fielding excellence. He won 135 games in a Cub uniform, including a career-high 20 in 1977.

Zambrano Three-Hitter Provides Pick-Me-Up

Mark Prior and Kerry Wood were the headline acts for the Cubs' pitching staff in 2003, but all season long, 22-year-old Carlos Zambrano demonstrated the importance of a dependable No. 3 man.

This game was a case in point. The Cubs arrived in Arizona a bit down on themselves, having lost two out of three in Houston and failing to gain ground on the first-place Astros in a tight Central Division race. Awaiting them in Friday night's series opener was Curt Schilling, who had a 45–13 record over the previous two seasons. Manager Dusty Baker's crew was in need of a pick-me-up, and Zambrano gave it to them, pitching a complete-game three-hitter.

"Z was huge," Baker said. "We needed a well-pitched game, big-time."

Zambrano took a shutout into the ninth inning, but lost it when Raul Mondesi pulled a two-out double down the left-field line to score pinch-hitter Carlos Baerga, who had walked and taken second on Luis Gonzalez's single. After a cursory visit to the mound, Baker stuck with Zambrano, who retired Alex Cintron on a grounder to short to nail down his 12th win, tying Prior for the team lead.

Sammy Sosa—remember him?—did the heavy lifting at the plate, reaching Schilling for a two-run homer in the first inning and a solo shot leading off the fourth. Sosa had 30 homers and was on his way to 40, rebounding from a painfully slow start that featured a beaning, a toe injury and an embarrassing corked-bat incident that cost him a seven-game suspension.

Sosa hit only one home run in May and had a total of six when he was caught using a doctored bat in the first inning of a game against Tampa Bay on June 3. After sitting out his suspension, he got himself going with 13 homers in July and would reach 40 for the seventh time in his career.

Kenny Lofton and Aramis Ramirez continued paying dividends on the trade that brought them

Cubs	AB	R	H	RBI
Lofton cf	4	1	1	0
Womack 2b	4	0	0	0
Alou lf	4	0	1	0
Sosa rf	4	2	2	3
Simon 1b	4	0	0	0
Ramirez 3b	3	1	1	1
Martinez ss	4	0	0	0
Bako c	3	0	1	0
Zambrano p	3	0	0	0
Totals	33	4	6	4
Totals	**34**	**6**	**9**	**6**

Diamond-backs	AB	R	H	RBI
Kata 3b	4	0	0	0
Hammock rf	3	0	0	0
Baerga ph	0	1	0	0
Gonzalez lf	4	0	1	0
Mondesi cf	3	0	1	1
Cintron ss	4	0	0	0
Spivey 2b	3	0	0	0
Hillenbrand 1b	3	0	1	0
Barajas c	3	0	0	0
Schilling p	2	0	0	0
Valverde p	0	0	0	0
Counsell ph	1	0	0	0
Totals	**30**	**1**	**3**	**1**

CHI	2	0	0	1	0	0	1	0	0	-	4	6	0
ARI	0	0	0	0	0	0	0	0	1	-	1	3	0

Cubs	IP	H	R	ER	BB	SO
Zambrano W (12-9)	9	3	1	1	2	4
Totals	9	3	1	1	2	4

Diamond-backs	IP	H	R	ER	BB	SO
Schilling L (7-7)	8	6	4	4	0	14
Valverde	1	0	0	0	0	1
Totals	9	6	4	4	0	15

2B—Arizona Mondesi. HR—Chicago Ramirez (19), Sosa 2 (29,30). HBP—Chicago Ramirez. LOB—Chicago 3; Arizona 4. SB—Chicago Lofton 2. Attendance: 39,612.

from Pittsburgh on July 23. Lofton, taking over in center field after a season-ending knee injury to Corey Patterson, led off the game with a bunt single and stole second and third before scoring on Sosa's homer. Ramirez tagged Schilling for a homer leading off the seventh inning, the seventh of 15 he would hit after joining the Cubs.

Aside from the homers, the Cubs managed just three singles off Schilling, who struck out 14.

The Phoenix area is home to thousands of Chicago-area transplants. They and their pro-Cub sentiments were well represented in the crowd of 39,612 at Bank One Ballpark, a fact that wasn't lost on Arizona manager Bob Brenly. The D-backs evened the series with a 13–2 romp on Saturday, jumping out to a 10–0 lead against Cubs starter Shawn Estes after five innings.

"It was good that we could score early," Brenly said, "and take the crowd out of the game."

His own crowd.

Durocher's Doctrine

As a manager, Leo Durocher was never big on team meetings. He always said he treated his players as men and as professionals, provided they acted accordingly. But desperate times call for desperate measures. Durocher sensed the 1971 season slipping away, and as the nucleus of the still beloved '69 team grew older, the pennant dreams that had so painfully eluded the Cubs that year were fading away once again.

So after two bad losses in Houston, Durocher convened a clear-the-air meeting when the Cubs returned to Chicago. "We weren't hustling," he said in his autobiography, *Nice Guys Finish Last*. "We weren't bearing down. We were slipping back into the sloppy, uncaring ways that had beaten us for three straight years."

Durocher singled out Billy Williams and Glenn Beckert for their consistent effort and heads-up play and said the other Cubs should follow their lead. He chided Ron Santo for declining to take batting practice, though Santo said Durocher had told him he didn't have to hit every day if he preferred to save his energy—sapped by his diabetes—for the games. When Durocher referred to the upcoming "Ron Santo Day" as an honor Santo had asked for in his last contract negotiation, Santo lost it and attacked the manager. Teammates had to pull him off the 66-year-old Durocher, and not all of them could be bothered to do so.

Santo cooled down, but the meeting grew more contentious when Joe Pepitone and Milt Pappas tore into Durocher. Pepitone said he was out of line ripping Santo, and Pappas said the criticism was an example of Durocher's inability to manage veteran players. Durocher was stunned. He felt he had rescued Pepitone (Houston) and Pappas (Atlanta) from untenable situations and he expected more loyalty. He threatened to quit on the spot, but general manager John Holland talked him out of it.

The Cubs had a game to play, and they put aside their differences and whipped Cincinnati phenom Don Gullett behind Juan Pizarro's five-hit pitching. Santo went 3-for-4 with two doubles and three RBIs. Cleo James was 3-for-5 with a home

Reds	AB	R	H	RBI
Rose rf	4	0	0	0
McRae lf	4	0	0	0
Perez 1b	4	0	1	0
Bench c	3	1	1	0
Foster cf	3	1	1	0
Helms 2b	3	1	0	1
Woodward 3b	2	0	0	0
Concepcion ss	3	0	1	1
Gullett p	1	0	0	0
May ph	1	0	1	1
Cloninger p	0	0	0	0
Bradford ph	1	0	0	0
Gibbon p	0	0	0	0
Ferrara ph	1	0	0	0
Totals	**30**	**3**	**5**	**3**

Cubs	AB	R	H	RBI
James cf	5	2	3	2
Beckert 2b	4	1	3	0
Williams lf	4	1	2	0
Pepitone 1b	3	0	0	0
Santo 3b	4	1	3	3
Torres ss	2	0	0	0
Kessinger ph-ss	2	0	0	0
Cannizzaro c	3	0	0	1
Callison rf	3	1	0	0
Pizarro p	4	0	0	0
Totals	**34**	**6**	**11**	**6**

										R	H	E
CIN	0	0	0	1	0	0	0	2	-	3	5	0
CHI	2	0	1	0	0	2	1	0	X	6	11	0

Reds	IP	H	R	ER	BB	SO
Gullett L (14-5)	4	5	3	3	1	6
Cloninger	2	3	2	2	3	0
Gibbon	2	3	1	1	0	3
Totals	**8**	**11**	**6**	**6**	**4**	**9**

Cubs	IP	H	R	ER	BB	SO
Pizarro W (5-2)	9	5	3	3	6	4
Totals	**9**	**5**	**3**	**3**	**6**	**4**

DP—Chicago 2. 2B—Cincinnati Foster, Bench; Chicago Santo 2, James. HR—Chicago James (1). SH—Chicago Beckert. SF—Chicago Cannizzaro. LOB—Cincinnati 6; Chicago 10. Attendance: 31,893.

August 23, 1971
Cubs 6, Reds 3

run, Beckert was 3-for-4 and Williams was 2-for-4.

The Cubs won that battle, but they gradually lost the war, dropping their next two games, six of the next seven and 22 of their remaining 36 to finish third at 83–79, 14 games behind eventual world champion Pittsburgh. As the season deteriorated, owner Phil Wrigley took out a full-page ad in Chicago newspapers reaffirming his support for his manager and advising the "Dump Durocher" clique to give it up.

Durocher survived into the following season but stepped aside on July 23, replaced by Whitey Lockman with the Cubs muddling along at 46–44. He never did get the air cleared.

Rainey's Near-Miss Ends with One-Hitter

No Cub pitched a no-hitter between Milt Pappas' gem against the San Diego Padres in September of 1972 and Carlos Zambrano's against the Houston Astros in September of 2008.

Chuck Rainey was an unlikely candidate to interrupt that 36-year stretch, but the 29-year-old right-hander came the closest of all the pitchers the Cubs employed between Pappas and Zambrano.

Facing Cincinnati on a warm Wednesday afternoon before 17,955 fans at Wrigley Field, Rainey set down the first 18 Reds in order.

Eddie Milner walked to lead off the seventh inning and stole second, but Rainey got Duane Walker on an infield popup, Dave Concepcion on a grounder to short and Dan Driessen on a fly to left.

Johnny Bench worked him for a leadoff walk in the eighth, but Ron Oester forced Bench and Paul Householder rapped into a 6-4-3 double play, leaving Rainey with 25 batters faced through eight innings.

The crowd was on its feet exhorting Rainey as he came out for the ninth inning. He retired pinch-hitter Tom Foley on a grounder to short and pinch-hitter Alan Knicely on a sharply hit comebacker. He was one out from the record books, with Milner left to face.

Rainey started Milner with a fastball, and he slapped it into center field for a soft but clean single. Rainey was left with a one-hit shutout victory when Walker popped to short for the final out. Keith Moreland's sacrifice fly scored Leon Durham with the only run Rainey would need in the sixth inning, and Mel Hall doubled home two insurance runs in the Cubs' seventh.

If it was any consolation—and it probably wasn't—Milner made a habit of this. On four other occasions he had the only hit a pitcher allowed in a one-hitter … though he never before waited until there were two outs in the ninth inning to get it.

Reds	AB	R	H	RBI
Milner cf	3	0	1	0
Walker lf	4	0	0	0
Concepcion ss	3	0	0	0
Driessen 1b	3	0	0	0
Bench 3b	2	0	0	0
Oester 2b	3	0	0	0
Householder rf	3	0	0	0
Trevino c	2	0	0	0
Foley ph	1	0	0	0
Soto p	2	0	0	0
Knicely ph	1	0	0	0
Totals	**27**	**0**	**1**	**0**

Cubs	AB	R	H	RBI
Bosley lf	4	0	2	0
Woods pr-lf	0	1	0	0
Sandberg 2b	4	0	0	0
Hall cf	4	0	2	2
Durham 1b	2	1	1	0
Moreland rf	3	0	0	1
Cey 3b	2	0	2	0
Veryzer 3b	1	0	0	0
Lake c	4	0	1	0
Bowa ss	4	0	1	0
Rainey p	4	1	2	0
Totals	**32**	**3**	**11**	**3**

CIN	0	0	0	0	0	0	0	0	0	-	0	1 0
CHI	0	0	0	0	0	1	2	0	X	-	3	11 0

Reds	IP	H	R	ER	BB	SO
Soto L (14-10)	8	11	3	3	3	5
Totals	**8**	**11**	**3**	**3**	**3**	**5**

Cubs	IP	H	R	ER	BB	SO
Rainey W (13-10)	9	1	0	0	2	5
Totals	**9**	**1**	**0**	**0**	**2**	**5**

DP—Cincinnati 2; Chicago. 2B—Chicago Hall. 3B—Chicago Durham. SF—Chicago Moreland. LOB—Cincinnati 2; Chicago 9. SB—Cincinnati Milner. Attendance: 17,955.

August 24, 1983
Cubs 3, Reds 0

Rainey's near-gem wasn't the only bit of history to occur on this day. Chicago got its last look at Johnny Bench as a player when the Hall of Fame catcher walked in the seventh inning. Bench, who moved to third base late in his career, retired after the 1983 season.

And Charlie Fox was in his third day as the Cubs' interim manager, having taken over when Lee Elia was fired with the Cubs (54–69) in fifth place on Aug. 21. Some observers were surprised Elia lasted four months after his infamous rant against Wrigley Field boo-birds earlier that season. Jim Frey would be named manager for 1984.

It was the best day in the best year of Rainey's professional life. Obtained from the Red Sox in a trade for reliever Doug Bird in December 1982, Rainey was a rotation starter all season and went 14–13 with a 4.48 ERA. The 14 wins were nearly a third of his career total (43) over six seasons. Dealt to the Oakland A's for Davey Lopes in July of 1984, the mustachioed Rainey was gone from the big leagues by 1985.

But he'll always have this one day in the sun.

The Hits Kept on Coming

Now it can be told: The famous May 17, 1979 Cubs-Phillies game, a 23–22 Phils victory in which the teams combined for 11 home runs at windy Wrigley Field, was actually payback for this game played at the same site nearly 57 years earlier. On that occasion the Phillies lost despite scoring 23 runs. And they didn't have Mike Schmidt in their lineup.

The New York Times' game account referred to "two world records being smashed" as the teams collected 51 hits in a "weird slugging match" that drew 7,000 fans to Cubs Park. There were 11 doubles, two triples and three homers—two by Cubs outfielder Hack Miller, who had a game-high six RBIs with two three-run shots.

Cliff Heathcote went 5-for-5 and knocked in four runs and Miller and Marty Krug were 4-for-5 as the Cubs erased a 3–1 deficit by scoring 10 times in the second inning. It was 11–6 when they batted in the fourth, when their record 14-run outburst appeared to settle matters. And it might have if Cubs pitchers had been able to find the plate—they walked 11 batters, in addition to surrendering 26 hits.

As a result the Phils kept scoring—three times in the fifth inning, eight times in the eighth inning, six times in the ninth. They had the bases loaded and the potential go-ahead run at the plate when the final out was recorded. They stranded 16 baserunners. Russ Wrightstone and Curt Walker had four hits apiece for the Phils, with Wrightstone driving in a team-high four runs.

At a Glance

WP: Kaufmann (7–8)

S: Osborne (2)

HR: Miller 2 (10, 11), O'Farrell (3)

Key stat: The '22 Cubs batted .293 as a team and averaged 5 runs per game, but the dead-ball era persisted on the North Side—they hit just 42 homers.

The Phils used just two pitchers. Both Jimmy Ring and Larry Weinert got pummeled, but 12 of the 26 runs they allowed were unearned because of five Philadelphia errors (the Cubs made four). As their losing streak reached five, the Phils surrendered a double-figures run total for the third straight game. For the season they allowed 5.97 runs a game.

The Cubs just didn't play them often enough during an 80–74, fifth-place season.

Here's a Salute to Charlie Root

Charlie Root is one of the more overlooked and underappreciated players in Cubs history. Nearly 70 years after retiring, he remains the franchise leader in wins (201) and innings pitched (3,171 $\frac{1}{3}$) and is third in strikeouts.

His 200th career victory, achieved before a meager crowd of 3,204 in the second game of a doubleheader at Braves Field in Boston, was typically low on fanfare.

Root, 42, had already announced that the '41 season would be his last. He had helped the Cubs win four pennants, and the team saluted him on "Charlie Root Day" on Aug. 10. He was not the scheduled starter as the Cubs sought to salvage a split of the doubleheader in Game 2 against the Braves, but manager Charlie Grimm called on him after Ken Raffensberger retired only one of the five hitters he faced in the first inning, surrendering two runs.

Root went the distance, scattering six hits and allowing two additional runs

Playing for the Cubs from 1926 through 1941, Charlie Root (far right) set team records for games, innings pitched, and career wins.

while squaring his record at 7–7. With Bill "Swish" Nicholson hitting his 24th home run, the Cubs tied the game at 3–3 heading into the ninth inning. With the bases loaded, Grimm let Root hit for himself, and he delivered a two-run single to break the tie.

Stan Hack also drove in two runs for the Cubs, and Dom Dallessandro had two of their eight hits.

Root was 201–156 over his 16-season Cubs career. Sturdy, durable and all business at 5-foot-10 and 190 pounds, he led the National League with 26 wins and 309 innings pitched in 1927. That was his only 20-victory season, but he won 19 games in 1929 and 18 in 1926 and was a double-figures winner for eight straight seasons.

Nonetheless, Root is best known for an event that probably didn't happen: Babe Ruth's "called shot" home run in Game 3 of the 1932 World Series. There was a bad-blood backdrop to the Series even before it started: The Cubs had acquired Mark Koenig to fill in at shortstop after Billy Jurges was injured in a shooting stemming from a domestic dispute, and they voted the popular ex-Yankee only a half-share of their World Series money even though Koenig batted .353 in 33 games for them.

The haughty Yankees were all over the Cubs, ridiculing them as cheapskates, with Ruth the most vocal. The Cubs returned fire. The bench-jockeying escalated throughout the Series, and as Ruth faced Root in the fifth inning of Game 3 at Wrigley Field, he directed a dismissive wave at his hecklers in the Cubs' dugout. When he blasted Root's 2-2 pitch more than 400 feet for a home run to center field, the gesture was somehow interpreted as Ruth pointing to the spot where he intended to hit the ball, and the legend of the "called shot" home run was born.

Most eyewitnesses refuted it, none more vociferously than Root. "If Ruth had pointed to the bleachers," he said, "I would have put one in his ear."

At a Glance

WP: Root (7–7)

HR: Nicholson (24)

Key stat: "Called Shot" aside, the World Series was never Root's finest hour. He was 0–3 with a 6.75 ERA in 6 games over 4 World Series.

Given Root's reputation as a tough, hard-eyed competitor who never backed down, no one doubted him.

Then again, Root wasn't immune to the star-crossed foibles of the Cubs. He lost 3–1 to Johnny Vander Meer and the Cincinnati Reds on Aug. 10, "Charlie Root Day."

Sauer Day Ends with Three Homers

Before there was "Mr. Cub," there was "the Mayor of Wrigley Field." That would be lumbering Hank Sauer, a Cubs outfielder from 1949-55 who didn't offer much in the way of speed or agility but became a fan favorite by virtue of the long home runs he hit and his cheerful disposition.

"It doesn't sound like the right word to describe a big, strong guy like Hank, but he's just … sweet," Cubs owner Phil Wrigley once said.

Sauer hit 30 or more home runs six times in his career, and Wrigley Field patrons took to showering him with packets of chewing tobacco as a reward each time he connected. There were 19,756 of them at Wrigley for this rare Monday doubleheader against the Phillies, and Sauer kept them busy in the opener.

The Phils led 1–0 on Andy Seminick's RBI double in the second inning when Sauer stepped in to face Curt Simmons. He tied the game with a solo home run. It was a 3–1 game when he batted in the fourth, and Sauer connected again off Simmons. In the sixth, with Phil Cavarretta on base with a single, Sauer slammed a third home run off Simmons, a two-run shot that gave the Cubs a 4–3 lead.

Light-hitting Wayne Terwilliger homered in the seventh and Roy Smalley followed with a two-run double as the Cubs pinned a loss on Simmons, a 21-year-old left-hander who would win 17 games for the pennant-bound Phillies.

The Phils bounced back for a 9–5 victory in the second game, getting 3 $^2/_3$ innings of scoreless relief pitching from Jim Konstanty, the NL MVP who was 16–7 with a 2.66 ERA and 22 saves for the "Whiz Kid" Phillies.

Sauer's story of perseverance seemed to resonate with Cubs fans. He was buried in a loaded farm system after signing with the Yankees, then spent

Phillies	AB	R	H	RBI
Waitkus 1b	4	0	0	0
Ashburn cf	5	0	2	1
Sisler lf	4	0	0	0
Ennis rf	3	1	1	0
Jones 3b	3	0	0	0
Hamner ss	4	2	3	1
Seminick c	4	1	3	3
Goliat 2b	2	0	0	0
Caballero pr	0	0	0	0
Simmons p	2	1	0	0
Candini p	0	0	0	0
Whitman ph	1	0	0	0
Heintzelman p	0	0	0	0
Lopata ph	0	0	0	0
Church pr	0	0	0	0
Totals	**32**	**5**	**9**	**5**

Cubs	AB	R	H	RBI
Borkowski rf	5	1	1	0
Cavarretta 1b	4	2	2	0
Smalley ss	4	0	1	2
Sauer lf	3	3	3	4
Pafko cf	4	0	1	0
Serena 3b	1	0	0	0
Mauro ph	1	0	0	0
Ramazzotti 3b	0	0	0	0
Owen c	4	0	0	0
Terwilliger 2b	3	1	1	1
Leonard p	4	0	0	0
Vander Meer p	0	0	0	0
Totals	**33**	**7**	**9**	**7**

```
PHI   0 1 1 1 0 0 0 0 2 - 5 9 0
CHI   0 1 0 1 0 2 3 0 X - 7 9 0
```

Phillies	IP	H	R	ER	BB	SO
Simmons L (16-8)	6.1	9	7	7	2	1
Candini	0.2	0	0	0	1	0
Heintzelman	1	0	0	0	1	0
Totals	**8**	**9**	**7**	**7**	**4**	**1**

Cubs	IP	H	R	ER	BB	SO
Leonard W (4-1)	8.2	9	5	5	2	2
Vander Meer	0.1	0	0	0	2	0
Totals	**9**	**9**	**5**	**5**	**4**	**2**

DP—Chicago. 2B—Philadelphia Seminick, Hamner; Chicago Smalley, Pafko. 3B—Philadelpia Ashburn. HR—Philadelphia Seminick (20); Chicago Terwilliger (8), Sauer 3 (24,25,26). SH—Philadelphia Jones. HBP—Philadelpia Ennis. LOB—Philadelphia 6; Chicago 6.

three years in the Navy during World War II. He was 31 by the time he became a full-fledged major leaguer with the Cincinnati Reds, who never seemed to appreciate Sauer and traded him to the Cubs with center fielder Frank Baumholtz for Peanuts Lowrey and Harry Walker in 1949.

Sauer hit .274 with 32 homers and 103 RBIs for the Cubs in 1950. He won the National League MVP award after hitting 37 homers and driving in a league-high 121 runs in 1952, and he slugged a career-high 41 homers in 1954. Clearly, his 6 ½ seasons in Wrigley were the high point of a 15-season major league career in which he hit 288 homers.

"They treated me royally in Chicago," Sauer said.

Sauer was a creature of habit. He had two three-homer games in his career, the second one coming two years later, on June 11, 1952. The pitcher? Curt Simmons.

Ultimate Comeback Erases 9-0 Deficit

Don Zimmer was never known as a by-the-book manager, relying instead on hunches, gut instinct and feel. A baseball lifer, Zimmer hadn't really established himself as a dugout genius in previous managerial stops with the Padres, Rangers, and Red Sox, but so many of his unconventional moves paid off in 1989 that the Cubs developed an eerie sense of calm in the face of trouble.

So a 9–0, fifth-inning deficit to the Houston Astros wasn't all that daunting. Zim will think of something.

Houston shortstop Rafael Ramirez, the former Atlanta Brave, was the chief architect of that deficit. He had a two-run double off Mike Bielecki in the Astros' fourth, and after Bielecki departed in the fifth, Ramirez tagged rookie Dean Wilkins for a grand slam that gave Houston its 9–0 lead.

The Cubs began pecking away in the third. Shawn Dunston, whose error opened the door to two Astros runs in the third inning, singled home Mark Grace with the Cubs' first run, then scored their second on Domingo Ramos' single.

Lloyd McClendon hit a two-run homer in the Cubs' seventh, and Dwight Smith followed with an RBI single to make it a 9–5 game. In the eighth, the Cubs pulled even on RBI singles by McClendon, Ryne Sandberg, and Grace, plus Smith's sacrifice fly.

After relievers Calvin Schiraldi, Scott Sanderson, Les Lancaster, and Paul Assenmacher gave them five score-

> ### At a Glance
>
> **WP:** Assenmacher (2–3)
>
> **HR:** McClendon (11)
>
> **Key stat:** Dean Wilkins, who gave up the fifth-inning slam to Ramirez, was 1–0 with a 4.60 ERA for the Cubs in '89. A Blue Island, Ill., native, he was obtained from the Yankees in the Steve Trout trade in 1987.

less innings, the Cubs won it in the 10th against Astros closer Dave Smith. Rookie of the Year Jerome Walton walked, took second on Sandberg's sacrifice and held third when McClendon singled to left. After an intentional walk to Grace, Smith banged a single through the drawn-in infield, bringing Walton home with the winning run before 25,829 delighted spectators at Wrigley Field.

It was a rare rough outing for Bielecki, who went 18–7 with a 3.14 ERA in his first full season as a Cub. The lanky right-hander was Pittsburgh's first-round draft choice in 1979 but struggled with the Pirates, going 10–17 over parts of four seasons before his trade to the Cubs.

The Cubs had endured a six-game losing streak earlier in August, but their fourth win in five games kept their NL East lead at 2.5 games over St. Louis.

The Hack Man Cometh

The Cubs drew a crowd of 30,000 to Wrigley Field for this Sunday matinee against the rival Cardinals, but they ended the suspense early. Hack Wilson slugged a three-run homer in the first inning and George "High Pockets" Kelly connected for a two-run blast in a five-run second as the Cubs took an 8–0 lead after two innings.

And they didn't stop hitting. Wilson, on his way to one of the best seasons ever by a National Leaguer, homered again off Al Grabowski in the fourth, and catcher Zack Taylor delivered a three-run shot in the eighth.

Wilson was 3-for-3 with two homers and six RBIs for the day, on his way to season totals of 56 and 191, which still stands as the major league RBI record. The beer-barrel-shaped slugger batted .356 and drew 105 walks. With a .454 on-base percentage and a .723 slugging average, Wilson's OPS was a hefty 1.177—clearly one of the best seasons in league history. It was his fifth straight season with 100 or more RBIs and his fourth straight with at least 30 homers.

Kelly went 4-for-4 with three RBIs, Footsie Blair and Woody English had two hits apiece and Kiki Cuyler scored four runs as the Cubs collected 15 hits, nine of them for extra bases. They improved to 77–50 and stretched their lead to 5.5 games over the second-place Giants.

The Cardinals were in fourth place, 7.5 games back, but this one-sided loss was evidently a wake-up call for them. They won seven in a row and 12 of their next 13, igniting a finishing kick in which they went 22–4 in their last 26 games, overhauling the Cubs, who were a pedestrian 13–13 in their final 26.

Nobody knew it at the time, of course, but it might have been a harbinger of 1969.

Cardinals	AB	R	H	RBI
Douthit cf	4	0	1	0
Adams 2b	4	0	0	0
High 3b	4	0	1	0
Bottomley 1b	4	0	0	0
Mancuso c	4	1	1	0
Fisher lf	1	0	0	0
Puccinelli	3	2	2	2
Watkins rf	1	0	0	0
Blades	3	1	2	1
Gelbert ss	4	0	2	1
Lindsey p	1	0	0	0
Grabowski	2	0	0	0
Wilson	1	0	0	0
Totals	**36**	**4**	**9**	**4**

Cubs	AB	R	H	RBI
Blair 2b	4	2	2	2
English ss	5	2	2	0
Cuyler rf	1	4	1	0
Wilson cf	3	3	3	6
Taylor lf	2	1	0	1
Kelly 1b	4	2	4	3
Bell 3b	5	0	0	0
Taylor c	5	1	1	3
Teachout p	5	1	2	0
Totals	**34**	**16**	**15**	**15**

												R	H	E
STL	0	0	0	0	1	0	2	0	1	-		4	9	0
CHI	3	5	0	2	0	1	0	5	X	-		16	15	0

Cardinals	IP	H	R	ER	BB	SO
Lindsey L (7-5)	1	4	5	5	1	1
Grabowski	7	11	11	10	4	3
Totals	**8**	**15**	**16**	**15**	**5**	**4**

Cubs	IP	H	R	ER	BB	SO
Teachout W (8-3)	9	9	4	4	0	2
Totals	**9**	**9**	**4**	**4**	**0**	**2**

2B—St. Louis Gelbert, Mancuso, Puccinelli; Chicago Cuyler, Teachout 2, Kelly. 3B—St. Louis Douthit; Chicago English. HR—St. Louis Blades (3), Puccinelli (3); Chicago Taylor (1), Wilson 2 (45,46), Kelly. SH—Chicago Wilson 2, Taylor 2. BP—Chicago Blair, Taylor. LOB—St. Louis 5; Chicago 5. Attendance: 30,000.

The Kiki Cuyler Game

By Kiki Cuyler's Hall of Fame standards, 1932 was a down year. A .321 career hitter, Cuyler batted just .291 with 10 homers and 77 RBIs for the Cubs, missing more than 40 games because of various injuries.

But the Giants would swear he was the picture of health on this Wednesday afternoon at Wrigley Field.

Cuyler went 5-for-6 with five RBIs, one coming on a single that tied the game at 5–5 in the ninth inning. The Giants scored four times in the 10th and were one out away from winning when Mark Koenig hit a home run to keep the Cubs alive. Three straight hits produced another run, left two men on base and brought Cuyler to the plate again. His three-run walk-off home run off Sam Gibson was a grand finale to what a young Bill Veeck described as the greatest game he ever saw.

Veeck, then 18, was at the game with his father, William Veeck Sr., the Cubs' team president. A reserved, taciturn man, the elder Veeck was the polar opposite of his outgoing, rambunctious son, but Bill Veeck, in his autobiography *Veeck as in Wreck*, remembered the game prompting a rare instance of his father cutting loose a bit—one moment he was in his president's box, the next he was on the field joining the mob that greeted Cuyler as he crossed home plate.

Lon Warneke, the Cubs' 23-year-old pitching ace who was 22–6 with a 2.37 ERA in '32, was knocked out in the first inning without retiring a batter, but the Cubs won anyway. Guy Bush, a 19-game winner that season, was knocked out in the 10th without retiring a batter, but the Cubs won anyway. Bill Terry, Hughie Critz and Mel Ott were a combined 11-for-18 with six RBIs for the Giants, but the Cubs won anyway.

At a Glance

WP: Herrmann (2–0)

HR: Koenig (2), Cuyler (8)

Key stat: The Cubs' 14-game winning streak was part of a 19–2 stretch in which they extended their lead from a half-game to six games over Pittsburgh in the National League race.

Billy Herman and Charlie Grimm had three hits apiece for the Cubs and Koenig and Woody English had two each.

Cuyler's heroics completed a 22–6 month of August for the Cubs and gave them their 12th win in a streak that would reach 14 as they opened up a 7.5-game lead on the second-place Pirates. Cuyler was making up for lost time. He batted .298 with six homers and 34 RBIs in August, and .330 with two homers and 16 RBIs in September.

The Cubs were en route to the National League pennant, but the fearsome Yankees awaited them in a World Series that would end badly.

SEPTEMBER/ OCTOBER

Sammy Sosa waves to fans after he hit his 62nd home run of the season on Sept. 13, 1998.

Pappas Flirts with Perfection

This didn't figure to be much of a game. The Cubs, in second place in the NL East but 11 games behind Pittsburgh, were playing out the string. Their opponents, the San Diego Padres, were last in the West at 46–79 and 33 games out of first place. Only 11,144 bothered to pay their way to see it.

Milt Pappas, the Cubs' starter, was almost a lock to pick up his 12th win of the year. He was facing a lineup that included such "threats" as Enzo Hernandez (hitting .186 at the time), rookies Dave Roberts (.246) and Derrel Thomas (.240) plus John Jeter (.230) and Fred Kendall (.218). His only concerns might be the established Cito Gaston as well as Leron Lee (hitting .318) and Nate Colbert, the big first baseman who was to finish the season with 38 homers and 111 RBIs.

Indeed, Pappas was having little difficulty. The Padres went up and down in order, inning after inning. The Cubs, with big hits from Don Kessinger and Jim Hickman, had built an 8–0 lead. Now, as the game moved to the ninth, all eyes turned to Pappas, who had retired the first 24 batters in a row. No one had reached first base.

Leading off the inning was Jeter, who wound up in Chicago (with the White Sox) in 1973 and was the father of Shawn Jeter, who also got to the major leagues with the Sox. Jeter hit a line drive, but Billy Williams was there in left to flag it down. Kendall, whose son Jason was to become a Cubs catcher, grounded out to Kessinger. It was 26 up, 26 down.

All that stood between Pappas and the eighth perfect game of the 20th century was a pinch-hitter, Larry Stahl, a 31-year-old lefty-swinging outfielder from Belleville, Ill., who had started his career with the Kansas City A's. Pappas didn't realize it, but second-year plate ump Bruce Froemming also stood between him and the perfecto.

Pappas, in an interview with writer Bruce Amspacher of Professional Sports Authenticator, picked up the story:

Padres	AB	R	H	RBI
Hernandez ss	3	0	0	0
Jestadt ph	1	0	0	0
Roberts 3b	3	0	0	0
Lee lf	3	0	0	0
Colbert 1b	3	0	0	0
Gaston rf	3	0	0	0
Thomas 2b	3	0	0	0
Jeter cf	3	0	0	0
Kendall c	3	0	0	0
Caldwell p	2	0	0	0
Severinsen p	0	0	0	0
Stahl ph	0	0	0	0
Totals	27	0	0	0

Cubs	AB	R	H	RBI
Kessinger ss	5	1	2	3
Cardenal rf	4	1	2	1
Williams lf	4	1	2	0
Santo 3b	3	1	0	0
Hickman 1b	4	1	3	1
Fanzone 2b	3	1	0	1
Hundley c	4	1	2	0
North cf	4	1	2	1
Pappas p	4	0	0	0
Totals	35	8	13	7

SD	0 0 0	0 0 0	0 0 0	- 0 0 1
CHI	2 0 2	0 0 0	4 X -	8 13 0

Padres	IP	H	R	ER	BB	SO
Caldwell L (6-8)	7.2	13	8	6	2	4
Severinsen	0.1	0	0	0	0	0
Totals	8	13	8	6	2	4

Cubs	IP	H	R	ER	BB	SO
Pappas W (12-7)	9	0	0	0	1	6
Totals	9	0	0	0	1	6

E—San Diego Hernandez. DP—San Diego 3. 2B—Chicago Kessinger, Hickman. HBP—Chicago Santo. LOB—San Diego 1; Chicago 6. Attendance: 11,144.

"Larry Stahl was sent up to pinch-hit, and I got two strikes on him immediately. Randy Hundley called for a slider. Ball one. Slider. Ball two. Slider. Ball three. Slider. Ball four. Stahl walks and the perfect game is gone.

"Any one of the four could've been called a strike, and the last two were definitely strikes. Froemming came out to the mound after Stahl walked and I called him every name that I knew in the English language. When I ran out of names in English, I started calling him names in Greek.

"There's no way in hell that he was going to kick me out of the game. Not that game. Not if he wanted to get out of Wrigley Field alive. Everybody was too mad at him. The players, the fans—everyone. So I went back to pitching and got the final out on a (Garry Jestadt) pop-up to second base to preserve the no-hitter."

But Pappas was still hot. And he hadn't cooled off much by the next day.

"Believe it or not, Froemming comes over to me and asks me to autograph a baseball for him. So I autographed it for him and then made a suggestion as where he might want to put it. He was incredulous. 'You're not still angry at me, are you?' he asked.

"I told him, 'You have no idea what you did. You blew it! You had a chance to call one of the few perfect games in the history of baseball, and you blew it.' And he said, 'Show me an umpire who ever called a game without making a mistake.' I couldn't believe he said that."

Then Pappas ran into Stahl, who told him something else that was startling. "He said that he had wanted me to get the perfect game, so after he got two strikes on him he decided not to swing anymore."

So Milt could have grooved a batting-practice fastball and he would have had his perfect game. Of course, Bruce Froemming might have missed that call, too.

Down Six, Cubs Rally Past Cardinals

This was the series of the season. The St. Louis Cardinals came to town with a one-game lead over Houston and a 2.5-game lead on the Cubs in the NL Central race. In Monday's series opener, Mark Prior overwhelmed the Cards, and the Cubs won 7–0 before 38,410.

The next afternoon, in Game 1 of a day-night doubleheader, 31,990 saw Sammy Sosa's two-run homer in the 15th give the Cubs a 4–2 victory. And another 39,290 were at Wrigley Field that evening to watch Matt Morris outduel Kerry Wood 2–0.

Meanwhile, the Astros had split a pair with the Dodgers, so, entering action on Wednesday, Sept. 3, St. Louis led the Astros by a half-game and the Cubs by 1.5. Cubs manager Dusty Baker sent Matt Clement, though bothered by asthma attacks, to the mound to oppose the Cards' Danny Haren.

Clement got into trouble almost immediately, as Fernando Vina singled and J. D. Drew doubled and, with one out, Tino Martinez singled them both home. Then came some Cubs-Cards unpleasantness, with Clement hitting Haren with a pitch and Haren returning the favor, as Baker and his St. Louis counterpart, Tony La Russa, had a profanity-laced exchange from their respective dugouts.

La Russa earlier had accused the Cubs' Wood of being a head-hunter. "I'll tell Dusty who told me, and he can go to that guy and straighten it out if he wants to. He says Wood likes to hit people because he likes to scare them."

Said Baker, who had played for La Russa in Oakland at the end of his career and had his differences with him back then: "I've heard Tony say things before. As far as I'm concerned, tricks are for kids, and I don't take kindly to threats."

The Cards, still on top 2–0, threatened in the sixth. Orlando Palmeiro and Mike Matheny reached and, with one out, Haren's sacrifice bunt moved the runners to second and third. Here Baker called for 22-year-old lefty Felix Sanchez, making his big-league debut, to face the next two batters, both left-handed. Sanchez first walked Vina and then was rudely welcomed to the big leagues by Drew, whose grand slam made it 6–0.

But the Cubs rebounded with three runs of their own, as Sosa led with a double, and Moises Alou plated him with his third straight hit. After Haren was replaced by Jeff Fassero, Aramis Ramirez made it 6–3 with a two-run shot to left. Edgar Renteria singled in Scott Rolen in the St. Louis seventh for a 7–3 Cardinal lead, but in the bottom half, Sosa walked and scored on Alou's homer off Russ Springer, who also served up a home run ball to Alex Gonzalez, and now it was 7–6 St. Louis entering the eighth.

When the Cardinals wasted Vina's leadoff triple in the eighth, the St. Louis fans among the assembled 32,710 had to be feeling that momentum had deserted their team. Lefty Steve Kline relieved Springer and allowed a leadoff single by Tony Womack and Kenny Lofton's sacrifice bunt. Now La Russa brought in one of his top starters, 14-game-winner Woody Williams, for his first relief appearance since 1996.

Mark Grudzielanek promptly tripled to tie the game, and after Sosa popped up for the second out, LaRussa let Williams pitch to Alou instead of on-deck hitter Randall Simon with the go-ahead run at third. Alou singled to left, and the Cubs, once behind by six, were ahead by one.

Cubs closer Joe Borowski, who had entered in the eighth, then retired Palmeiro on a fly to left, struck out Renteria and fanned Jim Edmonds to wrap up one of the biggest victories of the Cubs' 2003 season.

"We've been lacking the big hits all year," Grudzielanek said. "To have a game like this is huge. To get (Alou) going and swinging the bat like he can is big for this team. This hopefully can carry us a long way, hopefully to a division title."

That's exactly what it did. The Cubs took a 7–6 decision from the Cards the next day, won 10 of their next 13 and nosed out Houston by a game for the Central title.

Cardinals	AB	R	H	RBI
Vina 2b	3	2	2	0
Drew cf	5	2	3	4
Pujols lf-1b	3	0	1	0
Martinez 1b	4	0	1	2
Williams p	0	0	0	0
Rolen 3b	5	1	1	0
Palmeiro rf	4	1	2	0
Renteria ss	5	0	1	1
Matheny c	4	1	2	0
Edmonds ph	1	0	0	0
Haren p	1	0	0	0
Fassero p	0	0	0	0
Springer p	1	0	0	0
Kline p	0	0	0	0
Taguchi lf	0	0	0	0
Totals	36	7	13	7

Cubs	AB	R	H	RBI
Lofton cf	3	0	0	0
Glanville ph	3	0	2	0
Alfonseca p	1	0	0	0
Guthrie p	0	0	0	0
Grudzielanek 2b	1	1	1	1
Ojeda ss	0	0	0	0
Sosa rf	3	2	1	0
Alou lf	5	2	5	4
Simon 1b	5	0	0	0
Ramirez 3b	4	1	1	2
Gonzalez ss	3	1	1	1
Borowski p	0	0	0	0
Miller c	4	0	1	0
Clement p	1	0	0	0
Sanchez p	0	0	0	0
Karros ph	1	0	0	0
Womack 2b-ss-2b	1	1	1	0
Totals	35	8	13	8

STL	2 0 0 0 0 4 1 0 0 -	7	13	1
CHI	0 0 0 0 0 3 3 2 X -	8	13	0

Cardinals	IP	H	R	ER	BB	SO
Haren	5	6	2	2	1	1
Fassero	0.2	2	1	1	2	1
Springer	1.1	2	3	3	1	0
Kline	0.1	1	1	1	0	0
Williams L (14-8)	0.2	2	1	1	0	0
Totals	8	13	8	8	4	2

Cubs	IP	H	R	ER	BB	SO
Clement	5.2	9	4	4	3	1
Sanchez	0.1	1	2	2	2	0
Alfonseca	1	2	1	1	0	1
Guthrie	0.2	1	0	0	1	0
Borowski W (2-2)	1.1	0	0	0	0	2
Totals	9	13	7	7	6	4

E—St. Louis Rolen. DP—St. Louis; Chicago 2. 2B—St. Louis Rolen, Drew; Chicago Martinez, Miller, Sosa. 3B—St. Louis Vina; Chicago Grudzielanek. HR—St. Louis Drew (13); Chicago Ramirez (21), Gonzalez (18), Alou (20). SH—St. Louis Haren; Chicago Lofton. HBP—St. Louis Haren; Chicago Clement. LOB—St. Louis 10; Chicago 9. Attendance: 32,710.

Sammy Passes the Hack Man with 57th Homer

The Cubs were in Pittsburgh for a Friday night series opener. They were chasing a wild-card berth, Sammy Sosa was chasing Mark McGwire, and both men were chasing Roger Maris' all-time single-season home run record of 61.

The Cubs were in a tight scramble with the Giants and Mets in the wild-card quest, and McGwire was leading Sosa 59-56 in the long-ball battle. McGwire had hit No. 57 three days earlier, thereby surpassing the old National League homer mark of 56, set by the Cubs' Hack Wilson in 1930.

At a Glance

WP: Karchner (3–0)

S: Beck (43)

HR: Sosa (57)

Key stat: Grace and Gary Gaetti each went 3-for-4 for the winners.

Now, with two out and the bases empty, Sosa was facing the Pirates' Jason Schmidt in the first inning, hoping to move past the Cub icon himself. He swung and sent No. 57 screaming toward the seats in left-center, 36,510 people cheered lustily and the Cubs led 1–0.

They went on to win 5–2 with a three-run ninth, keyed by Mark Grace's two-run, bases-loaded single that gave him a .415 batting average over his last 10 games. Matt Karchner, retiring all six Pirates he faced, got the win in relief of starter Mark Clark, and Rod Beck picked up his 43rd save.

"Nothing against the other pitchers," Beck said afterwards, "but it almost seems like Sammy is playing against Little Leaguers. He is making it look easy to hit homers, and it's not easy."

Intoned Sosa: "My team needs me right now. That's what makes this so great, being in a playoff race."

Sammy's home run was his eighth in the last 12 games; the Cubs had won five straight and eight of their last nine.

Slugger Sammy Sosa leaps in the air as he watches his 62nd home run of the season leave Wrigley Field in the ninth inning against the Milwaukee Brewers on Sept. 13, 1998.

A Work of Art by Ceccarelli

Art Ceccarelli was a stockily built left-handed pitcher who, from 1955 till the end of his big-league career in May 1960 was employed solely by losing clubs— the A's, Orioles, and Cubs. He finished with a lifetime won-lost record of 9–18 and a career ERA of 5.05.

And yet, he had his moments, in particular with the '59 Cubs. Called up from the minors at the All-Star break, Ceccarelli won his first four starts— three of them complete games—and suddenly was a 4–0 pitcher with a 2.65 ERA. Understandably, he fell off after that but still had some decent starts, like his six-inning, one-hit, zero-walk 2–0 loss Aug. 23 at Milwaukee and an eight-inning, four-hit effort at San Francisco Sept. 2, when he received a no-decision in the Cubs' 4–3 defeat.

But his most remarkable performance came four days later in the Los Angeles Coliseum, where, with 39,432 people watching in surprise, Art Ceccarelli outdueled an on-the-rise lefty named Sandy Koufax and beat the world-champs-to-be Dodgers 3–0 in 10 innings.

Not only that, the Cubs hours later made it a sweep for the day—first by a visitor that year at the Coliseum—when Walt Moryn's three-run homer off Don Drysdale in the ninth provided a 5–3 victory that left L.A. in second place, three games back of the Giants and a half-game ahead of the Braves. The Cubs were tied for fifth at 65–69, 10 games in arrears.

But the big story, as far as the Cubs were concerned, was Ceccarelli's brilliance. Remember, the Coliseum was a football stadium. The distance from home plate to the left-field foul pole was 251 feet. A 42-foot-high chain-link fence stretched toward center field; distance to the fence in left-center was about 320 feet. The Coliseum, then, was no place for a left-handed pitcher.

Still, on this day, Ceccarelli and Koufax proved a lefty could survive there, if for only one day. The

Cubs	AB	R	H	RBI
Taylor 2b	4	1	0	0
Dark 3b	3	0	0	0
Walls rf	3	1	1	0
Banks ss	4	1	1	3
Schult 1b	5	0	1	0
Marshall pr-1b	0	0	0	0
Averill lf	4	0	1	0
Eaddy pr	0	0	0	0
Moryn lf	1	0	0	0
Altman cf	0	0	0	0
Thomson cf-lf	2	0	0	0
Neeman c	4	0	1	0
Ceccarelli p	4	0	0	0
Totals	34	3	5	3

Dodgers	AB	R	H	RBI
Gilliam 3b	5	0	0	0
Neal 2b	5	0	4	0
Moon cf-rf	4	0	0	0
Hodges 1b	5	0	0	0
Furillo rf	3	0	0	0
Demeter pr-cf	1	0	0	0
Essegian lf	0	0	0	0
Zimmer pr-ss	0	0	0	0
Pignatano c	3	0	2	0
Wills ss	2	0	0	0
Repulski ph-lf	1	0	0	0
Koufax p	4	0	0	0
Totals	34	0	6	0

```
CHI  0 0 0 0 0 0 0 0 3 - 3 5 2
LAD  0 0 0 0 0 0 0 0 0 - 0 6 2
```

Cubs	IP	H	R	ER	BB	SO
Ceccarelli W (5-3)	10	6	0	0	6	8
Totals	10	6	0	0	6	8

Dodgers	IP	H	R	ER	BB	SO
Koufax L (8-5)	10	5	3	3	7	10
Totals	10	5	3	3	7	10

E—Chicago Taylor, Ceccarelli; Los Angeles Gilliam 2. DP—Chicago 2; Los Angeles 1. 2B—Chicago Schult. HR—Chicago Banks (39). SH—Chicago Dark. LOB—Chicago 9; Los Angeles 10.

only Dodger to give Ceccarelli problems was Charlie Neal, who collected four of the hosts' six hits. Weak-hitting catcher Joe Pignatano had the other two. The only innings in which the Dodgers actually threatened were the seventh and ninth, when in each case they had two on with one out. But Ceccarelli escaped, ending each inning by striking out Koufax. L.A. manager Walter Alston elected not to remove his young lefty from the game.

In the 10th, finally, the Cubs broke through. Tony Taylor drew a walk and, after Alvin Dark's sacrifice bunt, Lee Walls walked as well. That brought up reigning NL MVP Ernie Banks, hitless thus far. Ernie broke up the shutout with his 39th homer, a drive over the fence in left, and the Cubs led 3–0.

Ceccarelli returned to the mound for the Dodgers' 10th, intent on finishing what he had started. First he got Junior Gilliam on a fly to Walls in right, but Neal singled to center. Lefty-hitting Wally Moon, trying to dump another of his "Moonshots" toward the opposite field and over the short fence, could only manage a popup to shortstop Banks. Next was veteran slugger Gil Hodges. Within moments, Gil had become Ceccarelli's eighth strikeout victim.

Ceccarelli thus became only the second lefty to beat the Dodgers in the Coliseum in 1959. (The Reds' Joe Nuxhall was the other.) In addition, he was just the second lefty to shut out the Dodgers since Johnny Antonelli of the Giants did it in August 1956. This also happened to be the first extra-inning shutout of the Dodgers since the Cardinals' Joe Presko stopped them in June 1952.

"But," Ceccarelli said when it was over, "I really thought I had better stuff in the game at Milwaukee. Today, I didn't have a curveball the last two innings."

That made his accomplishment all the more remarkable.

No. 1 for Maddux

The Cubs, with a putrid 55–80 record, were on a seven-game losing streak and had dropped the first two games of the weekend series at Riverfront Stadium. Now they were up against the Reds' best pitcher, Bill Gullickson, a Chicago-area product out of Joliet Catholic High School.

Opposing him was 20-year-old Greg Maddux, the Cubs' second-round pick in the 1984 amateur draft who had gone 4–3 in Double-A ball and 10–1 at Triple-A Iowa that season before his summons to the big leagues. He had made his big-league debut five days before, giving up a game-winning homer to Houston's Billy Hatcher in the 18th inning of a suspended game.

So the Cubs went out and hammered Gullickson and the Reds 11–3 in front of 25,035, with Maddux going the distance for his first major league victory. He even chipped in with a pair of hits in becoming the youngest pitcher to win a game for the Cubs.

"I'm kind of awestruck right now," he said. "Some of the guys I saw in the clubhouse when I first walked in, I watched when I was 10 years old. I remember watching Gary Matthews play at Dodger Stadium when I was about 6. That's kind of nice."

The Cubs scored three runs in each of the first three innings to chase Gullickson from the scene. Chico Walker homered, Leon Durham singled in a run and Jody Davis contributed an RBI double in the first inning.

At a Glance

WP: Maddux (1–1)

HR: C. Walker (1), Dunston (15), Durham (16)

Key stat: Maddux, in a preview of what was to come, induced 13 groundball outs.

In the second, Ryne Sandberg delivered a two-run single and scored on a single by Keith Moreland. Gullickson was history. Shawon Dunston, Davey Martinez, and Sandberg all had run-scoring singles in the third, and it was 9–0.

Maddux's final pitching line wasn't all that impressive—11 hits and three walks allowed in nine innings with four strikeouts—but this Maddux triumph was memorable because it was the first of oh, so many, many more.

"I don't think it's fair to expect Greg to lead the league in strikeouts," said Jim Colborn, his pitching coach at Iowa, said that afternoon. "He's not a strike-out pitcher and he probably won't ever win 25 or 30 games in the big leagues. But he should have a good big-league career."

Greg Maddux won 355 games, four Cy Young awards, four earned-run average titles and 18 Gold Gloves. Yes, he had a good big-league career.

On Sept. 7, 1986, Greg Maddux became the youngest player ever to win a game for the Cubs. The 20-year-old pitched a complete game in his first major league victory.

Sutter Simply Too Much with Six Ks in a Row

Before second-year reliever Bruce Sutter, master of the split-finger fastball, began having shoulder and back miseries in mid-July 1977, the Cubs were on top of the NL East.

Expos	AB	R	H	RBI
Cash 2b	4	1	1	0
Cromartie lf	5	0	1	0
Dawson cf	4	0	1	0
Perez 1b	3	0	1	1
Valentine rf	4	0	1	0
Carter c	3	0	0	0
Parrish 3b	3	1	0	0
Frias ss	4	0	2	0
Rogers p	2	0	0	1
Alcala p	1	0	0	0
Kerrigan p	0	0	0	0
McEnaney p	0	0	0	0
Totals	33	2	7	2

Cubs	AB	R	H	RBI
DeJesus ss	5	0	1	0
Biittner lf	5	0	0	0
Buckner 1b	4	0	0	1
Murcer rf	2	1	1	0
Ontiveros 3b	4	0	0	0
Gross cf	3	1	1	0
Trillo 2b	4	0	1	1
Mitterwald c	2	0	0	0
Cardenal ph	1	0	0	0
Swisher c	1	0	0	0
Burris p	1	0	0	0
Clines ph	1	0	1	0
P Reuschel p	0	0	0	0
Morales ph	1	0	0	0
Sutter p	0	0	0	0
Rosello ph	1	1	1	0
Totals	35	3	6	2

```
MON 0 0 1 1 0 0 0 0 0 0 - 2 7 2
CHI 0 0 0 0 0 0 2 0 0 1 - 3 6 0
```

Expos	IP	H	R	ER	BB	SO
Rogers	5	2	0	0	1	2
Alcala	1.1	3	2	1	1	2
Kerrigan L (2-5)	2.2	1	1	0	1	0
McEnaney	0.2	0	0	0	0	0
Totals	9.2	6	3	1	3	4

Cubs	IP	H	R	ER	BB	SO
Burris	6	6	2	2	3	4
P Reuschel	1	0	0	0	0	1
Sutter W (6-1)	3	1	0	0	1	6
Totals	10	7	2	2	4	11

E—Montreal Carter, Parrish. DP—Montreal; Chicago. 2B—Montreal Cash. SH—Montreal Kerrigan. SF—Montreal Perez; Chicago Buckner. LOB—Montreal 7; Chicago 7. SB—Montreal Cromartie. Attendance: 2,841.

He made two appearances between July 16 and Aug. 23, the day he returned to action after three weeks on the disabled list. On July 16, the Cubs were 54–34, in first place by 3.5 games over the Phillies. On Aug. 23, they were 70–53, in third place and 8.5 games behind division-leading Philadelphia.

That's a swing of 11 games in the standings, and that's why, come September, the Cubs were playing out the schedule instead of battling it out for the East title. The key now for the North Siders was to make sure Sutter would be as unhittable in 1978 as he had been the first half of 1977.

On this day, when Sutter was called in against Montreal at Wrigley Field, he was making his sixth appearance since his DL stint. He had worked 5 $^2/_3$ innings and in that time had allowed five hits, three walks and two runs (both earned) while striking out five. Those were not Sutter numbers, but he had said it would take a little time to get back in form.

And this was the day it happened. Too bad there were only 2,841 on hand to see it.

Manager Herman Franks called for Sutter to start the eighth inning with the Cubs and Expos tied 2–2. He proceeded to strike out Warren Cromartie, Andre Dawson and Tony Perez on 16 pitches. After the Cubs failed in their half, the Expos gave it another shot against Sutter in the ninth. This time he needed only three pitches apiece to strike out Ellis Valentine, Gary Carter and Larry Parrish. The three Ks on nine pitches tied a major-league record, and

Known for his dominance with the split-fingered fastball, Bruce Sutter went on to win the National League Cy Young Award in 1979.

September 8, 1977
Cubs 3, Expos 2 (10 innings)

the six straight strikeouts by a reliever tied an NL mark. Sutter actually gave up a hit in the 10th, a leadoff single by Pepe Frias, who went to second on reliever Joe Kerrigan's sacrifice bunt. Sutter then walked Dave Cash, and up stepped the dangerous Cromartie, who grounded into a fielder's choice, leaving men at first and third with two out and Dawson in the batter's box. Cromartie stole second, but Dawson ended the threat by flying out to left.

The least the Cubs could do after a three-inning performance like Sutter's was to get him the win. That they did. Dave Rosello batted for him and reached on an infield hit, then went to third on a throwing error by Carter, who grabbed Ivan DeJesus' bunt and threw wildly in an attempt to force Rosello at second. Lefty Will McEnaney entered and got Larry Biittner to ground to Perez at first. Rosello couldn't score on that play, but he did on Bill Buckner's fly ball to left, and the Cubs—and Sutter—were 3-2 winners.

"This was the first time since I came off the DL that I had real good stuff," he said afterward. "My pitches were down, and the velocity was there. I got a save the last time I pitched (in San Diego four days before), but my control wasn't sharp. When I warmed up in the bullpen today, it was all there."

It certainly was, much to the chagrin of the Expos—especially Cromartie, Dawson, Perez, Valentine, Carter and Parrish.

Ex-White Sox Turns Cubs' Hero

When the NL East-leading Cubs traded Darrin Jackson, Calvin Schiraldi and Phil Stephenson to the Padres on Aug. 30 for backups Luis Salazar and Marvell Wynne, most Cub followers likely shrugged their shoulders.

But manager Don Zimmer liked the deal because it gave him a deeper bench. Salazar could play just about anywhere, Wynne provided more speed and neither was an automatic out. Salazar was the better known of the two in Chicago because of his two years on the South Side, having come to the White Sox in December 1984 with pitchers Tim Lollar and Bill Long and a 20-year-old minor-league shortstop named Ozzie Guillen in a deal for former Cy Young winner LaMarr Hoyt.

Salazar was then primarily a third baseman, but he also started several games in the outfield, hit decently and demonstrated surprisingly good speed. He had shown himself to be a tough cookie at the plate as early as the Sox's 1985 home opener. After a high and tight fastball from Boston's Mike Trujillo caused him to hit the dirt, Salazar got up and hit the next pitch into the upper deck in left for a two-run homer.

But his greatest day in a Chicago uniform was this Saturday contest with the hard-charging St. Louis Cardinals, who had sliced the Cubs' lead to a half-game the day before. The Cubs, who had dropped six of their last nine, had blown a 7–1 lead and lost 8–6 when closer Mitch Williams gave up a three-run homer to Pedro Guerrero and a two-run blast to Terry Pendleton, both in the eighth inning.

Now it was the eighth inning of the series' second game, the Cubs trailed 2–1 and many in the rain-soaked crowd of 37,633 likely had conceded first place to the evil Redbirds. Rookie Dwight Smith, though, opened with a line-drive base hit

Cardinals	AB	R	H	RBI
Coleman lf	5	0	1	0
Smith ss	5	0	2	0
Thompson cf	5	0	1	0
Guerrero 1b	3	1	1	0
Pendleton 3b	3	0	0	0
Brunansky rf	4	1	1	1
Dayley p	0	0	0	0
Oquendo 2b	4	0	1	1
Pena c	4	0	1	0
DeLeon p	2	0	0	0
DiPino p	0	0	0	0
Quisenberry p	0	0	0	0
Morris rf	1	0	0	0
Totals	36	2	8	2

Cubs	AB	R	H	RBI
Walton cf	5	1	2	0
Sandberg 2b	4	0	0	0
Smith lf	3	1	1	1
Grace 1b	4	0	0	0
Dawson rf	4	1	0	0
Law 3b	1	0	1	0
Smith pr	0	0	0	0
Salazar 3b	2	0	2	2
Dunston ss	4	0	1	0
Girardi c	1	0	0	0
Wynne ph	1	0	0	0
Wrona c	1	0	0	0
Sutcliffe p	2	0	0	0
Varsho ph	1	0	0	0
Lancaster p	0	0	0	0
Wilson p	0	0	0	0
Pico p	0	0	0	0
Ramos ph	0	0	0	0
Dascenzo pr	0	0	0	0
Assenmacher p	0	0	0	0
Totals	33	3	7	3

												R	H	E
STL	0	0	0	0	2	0	0	0	0	-	2	8	1
CHI	1	0	0	0	0	0	0	1	0	1	-	3	7	0

Cardinals	IP	H	R	ER	BB	SO
DeLeon	7	5	2	1	5	2
DiPino	0.1	0	0	0	0	1
Quisenberry	0.1	1	0	0	0	0
Dayley L (3-2)	1.2	1	1	1	3	0
Totals	9.1	7	3	2	8	3

Cubs	IP	H	R	ER	BB	SO
Sutcliffe	7	5	2	2	1	5
Lancaster	0.1	1	0	0	1	0
Wilson	0.1	0	0	0	0	0
Pico	1.1	0	0	0	0	1
Assenmacher W (3-3)	1	0	0	0	0	0
Totals	10	8	2	2	2	6

E—St. Louis Brunansky. 2B—St. Louis Thompson; Chicago Salazar. 3B—St. Louis Smith; Chicago Law. SH—St. Louis DeLeon; Chicago Smith. LOB—St. Louis 7; Chicago 11. SB—St. Louis Thompson, Brunansky; Chicago Walton 2. Attendance: 37,633.

September 9, 1989
Cubs 3, Cardinals 2 (10 innings)

near the line in right, and when right-fielder Tom Brunansky hesitated, Smith took off for second and made it safely. "I knew he was holding the ball on me," Smith said later. "It's wet, and he was standing a long way away. I figured he had to make a perfect throw."

He did not, so the tying run was at second base. Lefty Frank DiPino replaced Cards starter Jose DeLeon and struck out Mark Grace, and Dan Quisenberry was summoned to face Andre Dawson, who grounded to short, Smith getting to third base on the play. That brought up Salazar, a seventh-inning replacement for Vance Law at third. Salazar, 8-for-24 thus far as a Cub, took a strike but lined the next delivery into left field, and the game was tied.

Jeff Pico retired the Cardinals in order in the ninth, Smith flied out to end the Cubs' ninth with two men aboard and Paul Assenmacher set the Cards down 1–2–3 in the 10th. Grace, leading off the home half of the inning against hard-throwing lefty Ken Dayley, bounced to second before Dawson drew a walk. Salazar then lashed a 2–1 fastball down the right-field line and into the corner. Dawson, despite aching knees, raced around and scored the winning run, and, just like that, Wrigley Field had become the madhouse on Addison.

"I've got pennant fever in my blood," Salazar said after he had cooled down a tad. "This is what you want to be in—a pennant race in a tough situation."

This game was the spark the Cubs, now leading by 1.5 games, needed. It marked the start of a six-game winning streak, at the close of which the North Siders were 5.5 games ahead of the Mets and six ahead of the Cardinals. The race would soon be over.

Luis Ernesto Salazar

With his excellent work down the stretch in 1989, Luis Ernesto Salazar of Barcelona, Venezuela, won himself a job with the Cubs for the next year and beyond. He hit .325 that September, drove in a dozen runs and played a solid third base, then hit .368 (7-for-19) with a home run in the NLCS against San Francisco. Had he not performed, the then-33-year-old might well have been cut loose.

He instead received steady work the next two seasons on the North Side, adding 12, 14, and 5 home runs to his career total in 1990, 1991, and 1992, when he dropped to a .208 batting average in what would be his final year.

Salazar managed the Brewers' Beloit club in the Midwest League in 1996 and 1997 and also was manager of the Dodgers' Gulf Coast Rookie League team during 2002–05. The lifetime .261 batter has also served as a hitting instructor, most recently in the Dodgers' organization.

Phils Get Their Fill of Jurges

The 1933 season, for Cubs shortstop Billy Jurges, was a bittersweet one. He got married in June, but his team failed to repeat as NL champions, finishing in third place with a 86–68 record and six games behind the pennant-winning New York Giants.

That's not to say the season was a total bust for him. It wasn't. He fielded well and hit a decent .269. And during this Sunday twinbill with the visiting Phillies, although he only had one hit on the day, he demonstrated anew the feistiness that made him a favorite with Chicago fans and teammates and a despised enemy by opponents.

After Bud Tinning shut out the Phils 4–0 in the opener, the Cubs led 2–1 in the last of the fourth in Game 2. That's when Jurges, perhaps with malicious intent, came sliding into second base, his spikes waist high, aimed at his Phillies counterpart, Dick Bartell. Bartell avoided him, and the matter seemed to have been forgotten. But then . . . well, let's let Irving Vaughan of the *Chicago Tribune* tell the story:

"The Phils immediately began jockeying Jurges from the bench, and the Cub shortstop could not see the humor of it. He retaliated by deliberately throwing two balls into the Phils' dugout (during infield warm-ups) before the fifth inning started. One of the balls was returned with bullet-like speed and almost plunked the Cub belligerent. Then the Phils decided to get tough about it.

"They came over the top of their trench and charged toward short, where Jurges was standing. Jurges rushed forward to meet the charges. Cubs came running from every place except up out of the drain pipes. As usual, nothing happened. Umpire George Magerkurth jumped between the belligerents, shoved a few this way and a few in that direction and finally restored quiet."

And Jurges? He didn't even get ejected.

Back to the game. The Cubs broke a 2–2 tie in the sixth when Riggs Stephenson walked and September call-up Dolph Camilli, just arrived from the Pacific Coast League, cracked his first major-league hit, a home run, to give the Cubs a 4–2 lead. Thanks to the pitching of Lynn Nelson, who finished with a four-hitter, that's how the score remained.

At a Glance

WP: Nelson (5–4)

HR: Camilli (1)

Key stat: Jurges was ejected 12 times during his playing career, with a career-"best" three in 1936.

A Comeback Not To Be Forgotten

It was a Saturday afternoon that began rather bleakly. But oh, how it ended.

The Cubs, tied with the New York Mets in the wild-card race, had fallen behind the visiting Milwaukee Brewers 10–2 in the fifth inning and still trailed 12–5 in the seventh. Yet almost all of the crowd of 39,170 was still on hand, if only to see Sammy Sosa get another at-bat or two with which to tie Babe Ruth with homer No. 60 on the year and stay close to Mark McGwire, who had broken Roger Maris' mark of 61 earlier that week and was still at 62.

The fans got more than that. Much more.

To start the last of the seventh, lefty reliever Valerio de los Santos came on and immediately walked Lance Johnson, the Cubs' lefty-swinging leadoff man. After Jose Hernandez struck out, Mark Grace doubled Johnson to third, and Sosa then lost one on Waveland Avenue, a majestic, 430-foot blast that would have made The Bambino proud. The crowd roared, then roared some more when the next Cub hitter, Glenallen Hill, crushed one even farther. Now it was 12–9 Milwaukee.

After Felix Heredia retired the Brewers in the eighth, Tyler Houston batted for the afternoon's starting catcher, Scott Ser-

> ## At a Glance
>
> **WP:** Beck (2–2)
>
> **HR:** Hernandez (22), Sosa (60), Houston (8), Gaetti (17), Hill (6), Merced (1)
>
> **Key stat:** Sosa, Houston and Merced each drove in three runs; the teams combined for 34 hits.

vais, and hit a home run off right-hander Chad Fox, who had replaced de los Santos. So it was 12–10 when the Cubs came to bat in the ninth against Brewers closer Bob Wickman.

Sosa led off with a single to left, and the tying run was at the plate in the person of Hill, who singled to center. The place was going nuts. Gary Gaetti bunted the runners to second and third, and Mickey Morandini followed with a walk to bring up Houston. Brewers manager Phil Garner stayed with Wickman, who gave up a two-run single to Houston, and the game was tied.

Now, with runners at first and third and one out, Cubs manager Jim Riggleman sent up a pinch-hitter—left-handed-hitting Orlando Merced—for Manny Alexander. Merced had spent most of the season with the Twins and then one month with the Red Sox, who had released him on Sept. 1. The Cubs, remembering his successful days with the Pirates, had picked him up on Sept. 5, and thus far he had gone 1-for-4 as a Cub, strictly in pinch roles. Wickman threw, Merced swung, and the ball disappeared into the right-field bleachers for a 15–12 Cub triumph. Merced's home run had topped No. 60 by Sosa. "If you had said that one or two weeks ago," Merced noted, "I'd have said you were crazy."

Wrigley Field, at that moment, was a crazy place. The joyous fans refused to leave the ballpark. They were still celebrating. So were the Cubs.

"It's probably the sweetest win I've ever been associated with—if not the strangest," Riggleman said.

Said Sosa: "Unbelievable. I could never feel more happy than I feel today."

Finally, writers gathered around Grace, who had been on hand for the wild, August 1989 comeback from a 9–0 deficit against Houston. That one, he said, couldn't compare with this one.

"This ranks as the best I've ever been in, without a doubt," he said. "Sammy's 60th . . . Merced winning it with a homer . . . Unbelievable, unbelievable, unbelievable."

. . . *and by the way* . . . The Cubs were hardly finished. The next afternoon, before 40,846, Sosa blasted No. 61 off the Brewers' Bronswell Patrick in the fifth inning to put the Cubs up 8–3 before Milwaukee rallied for a 10–8 lead entering the home ninth. But Sosa, facing Eric Plunk, parked No. 62 onto Waveland Avenue and suddenly it was 10–9. Sosa thus was tied with McGwire in the home run race, which was now every bit as wild as the race for the wild card.

Henry Rodriguez batted for pitcher Chris Haney and doubled to center. Jason Maxwell ran for him and Gaetti, delivering his third RBI of the day, singled home Maxwell, and it was 10–10. Rod Beck set down the Brew Crew 1-2-3, and the first two Cub hitters in the 10th—Johnson and Hernandez—both were retired by Alberto Reyes. Reyes was not as successful against Grace, who launched his 16th home run of 1998 to win the game 11–10.

"Mine went a little farther than Sammy's, don't you think? He can't hang with me," laughed Grace, who with Sosa was carried off the field by teammates. For the Cubs, who went on to win a one-game playoff with the Giants for the wild card two weeks later, this was their 46th come-from-behind victory of the season and the 23rd in their final time at bat.

Debut of the Famed Combo Tinker to Evers to Chance

Frank Chance was the first of a rather well-known double-play combination to reach Chicago, doing so in 1898. The son of a banker in Fresno, Calif., he had begun his career as a catcher but by 1902 was the Cubs' first baseman.

Then came Joe Tinker, whose dad was a paper hanger in Muscotah, Kansas. Tinker got to Chicago in time for the opening of the 1902 season and soon settled in at shortstop.

Arriving too in 1902 was tiny but tough Johnny Evers, who reported to the Cubs at the start of September after spending the summer playing in Troy, N.Y., where he also worked in a collar factory. Evers, who stood 5-foot-9 and tipped the scales at about 105 pounds at that time, was essentially laughed off the team's horse-drawn bus. Undeterred, he climbed up onto the top of the vehicle, an admittedly less comfortable seating area but one that enabled him to go where the team was going. He soon became the Cubs' second baseman.

> ## At a Glance
>
> **WP:** P. Williams
>
> **Key stat:** Jimmy Slagle and Johnny Kling each collected three hits for the Cubs, referred to in some news reports as the Colts.

These three were destined to become one of the most storied double-play combinations in baseball history, immortalized in a short poem (a portion of which follows) written by a New York newspaper columnist, Franklin Pierce Adams, who too often had seen the trio turn double plays to end New York Giants threats:

"These are the saddest of possible words:

Tinker to Evers to Chance.

Trio of bear cubs, and fleeter than birds,

Tinker and Evers and Chance."

They formed the backbone of great Cubs teams that, from 1906 through 1910, went 116–36, 107–45, 99–55, 104–49 and 104–50, winning four National League pennants and two world championships. The first time they played together in the infield was on this date in 1902, when the Cubs pounded out 15 hits and romped past St. Louis 12–0 at West Side Grounds.

The box score shows that Chance, batting third, went 1-for-2 and committed an error before getting tossed out of the game. Tinker, in the No. 5 hole, was 1-for-5 and Evers, hitting seventh, went 1-for-4. Tinker and Evers were flawless defensively. They would've turned their first double play that day, too, but because of Chance's ejection, the twin killing the Cubs turned went from Tinker to Evers to backup first baseman John Menefee.

The box score also shows that only 750 people were on hand to witness this unveiling. Not to worry: Within a few short years every Cub fan would know that the trio was always ready for a good fight, even amongst themselves; that Tinker and Evers were base-stealers supreme and Chance was the clutch hitter every good club needs; and that Chance was one of baseball's great managers.

The three went into the Hall of Fame together in 1946, but they weren't as close as one might think. Tinker and Evers got into at least one dugout fight, plus another during between-inning warm-ups at second base, and went 33 years without speaking to each other. Also, Chance and Evers once exchanged punches in a dugout scrap.

Tinker, Evers, and Chance played their final game as a unit on April 12, 1912, when Chance announced he was retiring as a player. (He was fired as manager that September after compiling a 768–389 record as Cubs skipper, a percentage of .664, best in club history.) Evers was named to replace Chance in October, and two months later Tinker was traded to Cincinnati.

An era had ended.

Hendley Outduels Koufax in Rematch

Just five days before, in Los Angeles, Cubs lefty Bob Hendley had thrown a one-hitter—and lost 1–0, because his opponent that evening, the great Sandy Koufax, did him one better.

Koufax threw a no-hitter—in fact, a perfect game, retiring 27 Cubs in a row. Hendley was almost as good. The only run the Dodgers got that night was in the fifth, when former Cub Lou Johnson walked, moved to second on a sacrifice bunt, stole third and came home when catcher Chris Krug's throw sailed into left field. The only hit Hendley allowed was Johnson's pop fly double just back of first base in the seventh.

Now the venue had switched to Wrigley Field, where the turnout of 6,220 on a Tuesday afternoon didn't quite measure up to the 29,139 who saw Koufax's perfecto. The pitching did, however. Hendley, who had broken in with the Milwaukee Braves at age 22 in 1961, had been acquired from the Giants earlier in the '65 season with former batting champion Harvey Kuenn and catcher Ed Bailey for catcher Dick Bertell and outfielder Len Gabrielson. Mostly he had been ineffective, but he had turned in two successive excellent starts: the L.A. game the week before and a Sept. 2 outing against the Cardinals in which he went 7 1/3 innings and allowed just six hits and two earned runs.

On this afternoon, he was more unhittable than Koufax. He gave up a ground single to Wes Parker in the third inning, two bunt singles by Maury Wills and a pinch RBI single by Don Drysdale, who delivered for Koufax in the seventh after two-out walks to Parker and Jeff Torborg.

> ## At a Glance
> **WP:** Hendley (3–3)
>
> **HR:** Willliams (31)
>
> **Key stat:** Koufax, who began the day with 352 strikeouts and had fanned 14 Cubs in his perfect game, had only three Ks this time.

Koufax, meanwhile, had fallen behind 2–0 in the sixth when Billy Williams, with Glenn Beckert aboard, hit his 31st home run of the season. "It was a fastball, low and away," Koufax said. "It was a good pitch. Billy just went out and got it."

That was all Hendley needed. He mixed his pitches, including the slip pitch, a type of changeup taught to him by teammate Billy Hoeft. He was in command all afternoon and closed strong. Wills reached with his second bunt single to begin the Dodger eighth, but Hendley promptly picked him off. Next Junior Gilliam flied to center and Willie Davis fanned. In the ninth, Johnson struck out, Jim Lefebvre flied to right and Al Ferrara popped to kid shortstop

Don Kessinger, and the Cubs had snapped their eight-game losing streak and helped drop the Dodgers 3.5 games behind NL-leading San Francisco.

But the story was Hendley. "This is the third game in a row," he said, "that I've felt I was in the groove and that my timing and rhythm were just right."

He didn't stay in that groove. His next complete game didn't come until July 23, 1967, when he was a New York Met. On that day, he fired a four-hitter, striking out seven, for a 4-1 victory over—that's right—the Dodgers.

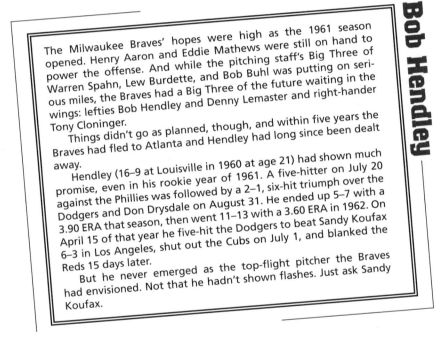

Bob Hendley

The Milwaukee Braves' hopes were high as the 1961 season opened. Henry Aaron and Eddie Mathews were still on hand to power the offense. And while the pitching staff's Big Three of Warren Spahn, Lew Burdette, and Bob Buhl was putting on serious miles, the Braves had a Big Three of the future waiting in the wings: lefties Bob Hendley and Denny Lemaster and right-hander Tony Cloninger.

Things didn't go as planned, though, and within five years the Braves had fled to Atlanta and Hendley had long since been dealt away.

Hendley (16–9 at Louisville in 1960 at age 21) had shown much promise, even in his rookie year of 1961. A five-hitter on July 20 against the Phillies was followed by a 2–1, six-hit triumph over the Dodgers and Don Drysdale on August 31. He ended up 5–7 with a 3.90 ERA that season, then went 11–13 with a 3.60 ERA in 1962. On April 15 of that year he five-hit the Dodgers to beat Sandy Koufax 6–3 in Los Angeles, shut out the Cubs on July 1, and blanked the Reds 15 days later.

But he never emerged as the top-flight pitcher the Braves had envisioned. Not that he hadn't shown flashes. Just ask Sandy Koufax.

Big Z's No-Hitter Ends Drought for Cubs Pitchers

It's not that Carlos Zambrano was an unlikely candidate to pitch the Cubs' first no-hitter since 1972. He'd been a consistently successful, occasionally dominant starting pitcher since moving into the rotation in 2003, a three-time All-Star with a career winning percentage of .617 (95–60) when he went to work at Milwaukee's Miller Park on this Sunday evening.

That's right, Milwaukee's Miller Park. The opponent was the Houston Astros, but the Houston area was under siege from Hurricane Ike, so the weekend series was moved to a neutral site.

Neutral? The crowd of 23,441 could not have been more pro-Cub if the game had been played under the Red Line tracks in Wrigleyville.

Still, a friendly atmosphere didn't ease concerns over Zambrano. He hadn't pitched in 12 days, having removed himself from a Sept. 2 start against Houston complaining of soreness in his shoulder. He hadn't won a game in three weeks, having gone 1–1 with a 7.43 ERA in August.

With the Cubs not knowing what to expect from him, perhaps it made some kind of oddball sense for the always unpredictable "Big Z" to throw a no-hitter, the Cubs' first in 36 years.

As Zambrano breezed through Darin Erstad, Michael Bourn and Miguel Tejada in the first inning, manager Lou Piniella sensed that the fire-breathing right-hander was on his game.

> ### At a Glance
> **WP:** Zambrano (14–5)
>
> **HR:** Soriano (28)
>
> **Key stat:** Soriano's 54 home runs leading off a ballgame are second only to Rickey Henderson's 81.

"From the first few pitches of the ballgame, his arm was live and the ball was coming out easy," Piniella said. "He had everything going."

The Cubs batted first as the visiting team, and Alfonso Soriano got Zambrano a 1–0 lead with a leadoff home run off Randy Wolf. Zambrano had to run the bases in the third inning, hitting a single and scoring from first on Derrek Lee's two-run double, and the Cubs eventually made it a 5–0 game in the third

---

Carlos Zambrano reacts after the final out in the ninth inning against the Houston Astros on Sept. 14, 2008, in Milwaukee. Zambrano pitched the first no-hitter for the Cubs in 36 years. The game was played at Miller Park because of the effects of Hurricane Ike in Houston.

after Aramis Ramirez singled Lee home and Geovany Soto doubled Ramirez home.

Thus the only remaining suspense about the evening was whether Zambrano would throw the team's first no-hitter since Milt Pappas came within one pitch of a perfect game against the San Diego Padres in September 1972.

He did, and he made it look relatively easy. Zambrano (14–5) walked one batter and struck out 10. Only two balls left the infield all night, and nothing spectacular was required of his fielders in a 110-pitch effort that gave the Cubs a 7.5-game lead in the NL Central and reduced to seven their magic number for clinching a second straight division title.

"We were thinking 90 pitches before the game," Piniella said, "but as it went on I said to [bench coach] Alan Trammell, 'If he has to come out of the game, you go get him. I'm not.'"

Zambrano got Humberto Quintero and pinch-hitter Jose Castillo on grounders to short to open the ninth. With the crowd on its feet, he struck out Erstad to end it, and a mob scene ensued at the pitcher's mound.

"I'm a little confused right now—I still can't believe it," Zambrano said. "It's a great feeling. This is one of the things that you most enjoy in baseball.

"I guess I'm back."

Hooray for Hooton

The schedule was winding down, the Cubs were out of it and it was time to play the kids. A kid outfielder, Bill North, just up from San Antonio, was in left field for the second game of a twi-night doubleheader at Shea Stadium, the Cubs having won the opener 6–2. And on the mound was a 21-year-old right-hander out of the University of Texas, Burt Hooton, the Cubs' No. 1 draft pick that June.

Hooton, who had been given a start on June 17 but couldn't last four innings against St. Louis, had gone down dutifully to Tacoma to gain experience and soon had become the talk of the Pacific Coast League. In just 102 innings he had struck out 135, baffling hitters with his knuckle curveball. Cub bosses now wanted to see what he could do in the big leagues.

Hooton gave them and the 21,302 paying customers an eyeful. Having been given a 2–0 lead on the strength of RBI singles by Paul Popovich in the first inning and Ron Santo in the third, Hooton fired fastballs and knuckle curves past one Mets hitter after another. With two outs in the seventh, the Texan had struck out 10—and, more impressive, had a no-hitter going.

That's when Mike Jorgensen lined a single to right and Ken Singleton followed with a game-tying home run. Said Hooton later: "The first hit was on a fastball away. And the homer was on a curve that was up a little bit."

Thoroughly entertained by his rookie pitcher, manager Leo Durocher sent Hooton back out for the eighth. Tim Foli struck out, Cleon Jones grounded out and Ted Martinez struck out, becoming victim No. 13. But the game was still tied. Hooton needed a run, and Billy Williams got it for him. Batting for North and facing Danny Frisella, Billy slugged his 26th homer of the year over the wall in right for a 3–2 lead.

Now it was up to Hooton, and he was up to it. After a one-out single by John Milner, Hooton struck out Ed Kranepool swinging and got Jorgensen looking for his first major-league victory. He had also tied the modern Cubs record for strikeouts with 15.

"I probably won't sleep tonight," he predicted.

Hooton pitched against the Mets six days later in Chicago. This time he struck out only five, but he shut them out 3–0 on two hits. Not a bad encore.

At a Glance

WP: Hooton (1–0)

HR: Williams (26)

Key stat: Hooton finished his career with 151 wins—only 34 of them with the Cubs.

Ramirez a One-Man Wrecking Crew

Aramis Ramirez has had lots of big games since coming to the Cubs from Pittsburgh in July 2003 in one of the great heists ever pulled off. He and Kenny Lofton came to Chicago for Jose Hernandez and the much-hyped but much-overrated Bobby Hill—and the Cubs even got the Pirates to send along some cash.

One of Ramirez's best performances came on this Thursday night at Great American Ballpark in Cincinnati. He socked three home runs, accounting for all the Cubs' scoring, in a 5–4 decision over the Reds that kept manager Dusty Baker's crew a half-game back of the Giants in the NL wild-card race.

He went 4-for-5 and with his last home run (No. 33) tied Ron Santo's record for most homers in a season by a Cub third baseman. (Ramirez finished the year with 36 and two years later belted 38.)

He began his show in the first inning when, after Neifi Perez reached on pitcher Josh Hancock's error, Ramirez hit a line shot over the wall in left for a 2–0 lead. He followed that up with a solo blast in the fifth, and the Cubs led 3–1. The Reds got to Kerry Wood for three runs in their half of the inning, the big blow Felipe Lopez's two-run double, and now the Cubs trailed 4–3.

That was still the score when Ramirez came up with Corey Patterson on base with two out in the seventh. Ryan Wagner replaced Hancock, but Wagner couldn't stop the Cubs' third baseman, either. Ramirez drove one over the fence in center field, and the Cubs were up 5–4.

He came up in the ninth for a chance at a fourth homer, and he hit the ball well off Joe Valentine, but right-fielder Austin Kearns was there to make the catch.

"That would've brought the house down—brought the world down," Baker said. "It was a great night for him. This is when you need somebody like that, or somebodies, to put the whole team on his back and carry them."

"If it's not me, it's going to be somebody else," Ramirez said. "We have to play every game like it's the last one."

At a Glance

WP: Wood (8–7)

S: Hawkins (22)

HR: Ramirez 3 (31, 32, 33)

Key stat: Ramirez's other hit was a double, his 31st; he raised his average to .315.

Aramis Ramirez (right) is congratulated by third base coach Wendell Kim after hitting a solo home run against the Cincinnati Reds in the fifth inning on Sept. 16, 2004, in Cincinnati. Ramirez hit three homers in the game.

Bloom Is on DeRosa

The signing of free agent Mark DeRosa in November 2006 had not caused much of a stir on the North Side when it was announced, and for good reason. Here was a career utility player who had come up first with Atlanta in 1998 and hadn't played regularly until '06, when he hit .296 for Texas with 40 doubles, 13 homers and 74 RBIs.

He was already 31 years old, had had just the one good season and didn't figure to get much better. Before the 2007 season had ended, however, the former Penn quarterback had won over Cub fans everywhere.

He played all four infield positions plus left and right field that year, had 500-plus at-bats and hit .293 with 10 homers and 72 runs batted in and was a big reason why the Cubs were one game ahead of second-place Milwaukee on this Monday night as they faced the Cincinnati Reds at Wrigley Field.

DeRosa singled to center in the second inning, followed Cliff Floyd's homer with his own in the third off Bronson Arroyo to put the Cubs ahead 3–1, singled to left in the fifth and singled to right in the seventh, but they trailed 6–4 when Ryan Theriot led off the last of the ninth against Reds closer David Weathers. Yovani Gallardo and the Brewers had shut out the Astros 6–0 in Houston, so a loss would drop the Cubs into a first-place tie.

Theriot drew a walk and stopped at second on Derrek Lee's base hit, and now the crowd of 39,075 came to life. When Aramis Ramirez's triple, a shot up the alley in right-center, sent across the tying runs, the noise was deafening. Now the Reds walked Daryle Ward intentionally, preferring to face the right-handed-hitting DeRosa. DeRosa, making it a 5-for-5 night, slashed one

> ## At a Glance
>
> **WP:** Ohman (2–4)
>
> **HR:** Floyd (9), DeRosa (10)
>
> **Key stat:** Cubs starter Rich Hill struck out seven and walked one in 4 2/3 innings but gave up seven hits and four runs.

off Weathers' glove for another hit, and pinch-runner Sam Fuld came across with the winning run.

"This was huge," DeRosa said. "There was never a doubt, though. We had the top of the lineup coming up in the ninth. We have a lot of respect for David Weathers; he's an accomplished pitcher. But we look up at that scoreboard, too, and see 6–0, Milwaukee, and you can't quit in that situation."

The Cubs went on to take the Central Division title with an 85–77 record but were swept by Arizona in the first round of the playoffs.

Reuschel Finally Wins 20th

Rick Reuschel was struggling, just like the Cubs.

His record had stood at 15–3 on July 28. The Cubs were 60-39. Now his mark was 19–8. And the Cubs were 77–71.

After losing two (Aug. 8 and 12), Reuschel had reeled off four straight wins and was 19–5 on Aug. 30. People were talking 25 victories for the big right-hander. Then he went out and lost his next three starts.

But on this Sunday afternoon at Shea Stadium, the native of Camp Point, Ill., finally bagged No. 20, becoming the first Cub to win 20 since Fergie Jenkins in 1972.

He did so by going six innings, his outing cut short by a blister on his right forefinger. He did so without having his usual good sinker, and he did so with offensive support from only second baseman Mick Kelleher, who drove in two runs. Another run scored on a ninth-inning error by New York shortstop Bud Harrelson. The other three? Reuschel himself doubled in one run in the third and tripled in two more in the fourth.

His older brother Paul followed him to the mound, but he needed help from Willie Hernandez and finally Bruce Sutter, who notched the save. "I had another chance to save his 20th," noted Sutter, recalling a blown opportunity on Sept. 3, "but I messed it up in San Diego."

Reuschel, unimpressed with his winning 20, simply said "It's nice" when asked his reaction to his feat afterward. But that was his personality. It might have meant more when his career was over, Reuschel having completed it with 214 victories—and just that one 20-win season.

Cubs	AB	R	H	RBI
DeJesus ss	5	0	0	0
Biittner lf	4	0	0	0
Buckner 1b	5	0	1	0
Murcer rf	4	0	0	0
Ontiveros 3b	4	1	1	0
Gross cf	4	1	2	0
Mitterwald c	4	2	2	0
Kelleher 2b	3	2	2	2
R Reuschel p	3	0	2	3
P Reuschel p	0	0	0	0
Hernandez p	0	0	0	0
Sutter p	0	0	0	0
Totals	36	6	10	5

Mets	AB	R	H	RBI
Randle 3b	4	0	2	0
Mazzilli cf	3	0	0	0
Boisclair rf	4	0	1	0
Henderson lf	3	0	0	0
Baldwin p	0	0	0	0
Staiger ph	1	0	0	0
Apodaca p	0	0	0	0
Myrick p	0	0	0	0
Kranepool 1b-lf	3	0	0	0
Foster ph	1	0	0	0
Stearns c	4	1	0	0
Youngblood 2b	4	1	3	0
Flynn ss	2	0	0	0
Milner ph-1b	2	1	2	1
Todd p	1	0	0	0
Siebert p	0	0	0	0
Mangual ph-lf	2	0	1	2
Harrelson ss	0	0	0	0
Vail ph	1	0	0	0
Totals	35	3	9	3

```
CHI  0 0 2 3 0 0 0 0 1 - 6 10 1
NYM  0 0 0 0 0 0 3 0 0 - 3  9 2
```

Cubs	IP	H	R	ER	BB	SO
R Reuschel W (20-8)	6	4	0	0	1	4
P Reuschel	0.1	3	3	2	0	0
Hernandez	2.1	2	0	0	0	0
Sutter S (28)	0.1	0	0	0	0	1
Totals	9	9	3	2	1	5

Mets	IP	H	R	ER	BB	SO
Todd L (3-5)	4	7	5	5	0	1
Siebert	2	2	0	0	0	1
Baldwin	2	0	0	0	0	1
Apodaca	0.2	1	1	0	1	0
Myrick	0.1	0	0	0	0	0
Totals	9	10	6	5	1	3

E—Chicago DeJesus; New York Harrelson, Henderson. DP—Chicago 2. 2B—Chicago R Reuschel, Mitterwald, Kelleher; New York Youngblood, Milner. 3B—Chicago R Reuschel. SH—Chicago Hernandez. HBP—Chicago Kelleher. LOB—Chicago 6; New York 6.

Division Champs Again!

The Cubs entered this Saturday afternoon game at Wrigley Field with a 92–60 record, nine games better than second-place Milwaukee. The magic number for clinching their second straight Central Division title was down to one. Who better to clinch against than the franchise's age-old rivals, the St. Louis Cardinals?

With 41,597 jammed into the old ballpark, the Cubs struck first with a three-run second. They filled the bases with two outs, and Alfonso Soriano lined a pitch from Joel Pineiro into left field, two runs scored and, when the ball got by left-fielder Brian Barton for an error, a third run scored.

In the fourth, Mark DeRosa doubled in Geovany Soto, and DeRosa scored on a perfectly executed suicide-squeeze bunt by pitcher Ted Lilly to make it 5–0. But the Redbirds stirred in the sixth, when Felipe Lopez's run-scoring infield single and Troy Glaus' two-out, three-run homer cut the lead to 5–4.

After that, things moved swiftly. Lilly worked a 1–2–3 seventh, and Carlos Marmol did the same in the eighth, getting Albert Pujols on an infield popup. Now it was up to Kerry Wood, the fireballer whom the Cubs had converted into a closer.

Wood walked the first man he faced, Glaus, but then got Adam Kennedy to ground into a force play. Skip Schumaker struck out, Aaron Miles lifted a soft fly ball to Jim Edmonds, and that was it. Lilly had won his 16th game, Wood had registered his 32nd save and the Cubs were division champs a second consecutive season.

> ## At a Glance
>
> **WP:** Lilly (16–9)
>
> **S:** Wood (32)
>
> **Key stat:** The turnout of 41,597 enabled the Cubs to break their all-time single-season attendance record of 3,252,462, set in 2007; the final tally for 2008 was 3,300,200.

The party in Wrigleyville began immediately: Folks stayed in the stands and applauded their heroes, who came out of the clubhouse and did a victory lap, shaking hands and interacting with the fans. The festivities lasted well into the night hours.

But manager Lou Piniella warned that this was merely the first step, that the title wouldn't mean much if the Cubs went out and were eliminated in the first round of the playoffs, which is what had happened the year before.

"It's been a really, really nice year," he said, "and I'm proud of our team. Now we can start planning for the postseason, and hopefully we can give the fans what they want. And we all know what that is."

The Los Angeles Dodgers, however, were not going to cooperate.

Fergie's 284th—and Last—Big-League Win

Seventeen years before, Ferguson Arthur Jenkins had arrived at Wrigley Field, his entire career in front of him. He'd been acquired along with center fielder Adolfo Phillips in an April 1966 deal with the Phillies, for whom he had won two games as a September call-up the season before. Victory No. 1 had come in his very first appearance, when he relieved Jim Bunning—like Jenkins a future Hall-of-Famer, but 11 years his senior—in the eighth inning against St. Louis. Jenkins threw 4 1/3 scoreless innings against St. Louis and got the "W" when the Phils scored in the 12th.

His first win as a Cub came on April 23, 1966, when before 6,974 at Wrigley Field he turned in 5 1/3 shutout relief innings and hit a homer and an RBI single to beat the Dodgers 2–0. But he was just getting started. After several successful relief outings, he was given a spot in the rotation in late August and in his next nine games, all starts, he went 4–2 with a 2.13 ERA over 72 innings, in which he allowed just 52 hits and 14 walks while striking out 52.

Fergie was on his way. He won 20 games or more each of the next six seasons, won 25 for Texas in 1974 and was 18–8 for the same club in 1978. He made three All-Star teams and won a Cy Young Award and a Comeback Player of the Year trophy. The Cubs signed him as a free agent in December 1981, five days before his 39th birthday, and he ended up winning 14 games for a 73–89 club in '82.

But by 1983, he had used up most of his bullets. Fergie did start 29 games, but thereafter was shunted to the bullpen, his record just 5–9 on a team that was 67–84. He had won only two games since June 10.

On this chilly Wednesday afternoon, in front of only 3,029 people—among them the newly

Pirates	AB	R	H	RBI
Wynne cf	5	1	1	0
Ray 2b	5	1	1	0
Parker rf	5	1	2	1
Thompson 1b	4	1	1	0
Easler lf	4	1	0	0
Pena c	4	0	2	2
Hebner 3b	5	1	3	3
Dilone pr	0	0	0	0
Berra ss	2	0	1	0
May ph	1	0	0	0
DeLeon p	2	0	0	0
Mazzilli ph	1	0	0	0
Guante p	1	0	0	0
Tekulve p	0	0	0	0
Totals	**39**	**6**	**11**	**6**

Cubs	AB	R	H	RBI
Sandberg 2b	3	3	1	0
Buckner lf-1b	5	1	1	0
Hall cf	2	1	1	1
Carter pr	0	1	0	0
Woods cf	1	0	0	0
Cey 3b	3	1	2	2
Moreland rf	2	0	0	0
Davis c	3	0	1	3
Martinez 1b	3	0	0	0
Jenkins p	0	0	0	0
Johnstone ph	0	0	0	0
Smith p	0	0	0	0
Bowa ss	4	0	2	1
Rainey p	2	0	0	0
Bosley lf	2	0	0	0
Totals	**30**	**7**	**8**	**7**

PIT	2	0	1	0	0	1	2	0	0	-	6	11 4
CHI	1	0	1	0	3	0	2	0	X	-	7	8 3

Pirates	IP	H	R	ER	BB	SO
DeLeon	5	6	5	4	4	7
Guante L (2-5)	1	1	2	2	0	1
Tekulve	2	1	0	0	1	1
Totals	**8**	**8**	**7**	**6**	**5**	**9**

Cubs	IP	H	R	ER	BB	SO
Rainey	5.1	7	4	3	2	3
Jenkins W (6-9)	1.2	2	2	0	2	2
Smith S (28)	2	2	0	0	0	2
Totals	**9**	**11**	**6**	**3**	**4**	**7**

E—Pittsburgh Berra, Wynne, Pena, Thompson; Chicago Sandberg, Rainey. DP—Pittsburgh; Chicago. 2B—Pittsburgh Berra, Wynne, Hebner, Ray; Chicago Hall, Davis, Bowa. HR—Pittsburgh Hebner (5). SH—Chicago Moreland. SF—Chicago Davis, Cey. HBP—Pittsburgh Easler; Chicago Hall. LOB—Pittsburgh 11; Chicago 8. SB—Chicago Sandberg. Attendance: 3,029.

appointed president of the Cubs, Jim Finks—Jenkins was minding his own business in the bullpen when the call came to start warming up. The Pirates' Richie Hebner had homered off Chuck Rainey to cut the Cubs' lead to 5–4. Now came a double by Dale Berra. In came Fergie, who retired the next two hitters to end the sixth inning.

In the seventh, with two out, the Pirates loaded the bases with the help of a Ryne Sandberg error. Hebner doubled in two runs, and the Pirates were up 6–5. The Cubs rallied with two runs in their half on Jody Davis' sacrifice fly and Larry Bowa's RBI single, a slow roller to short that he beat out.

Meanwhile, Jenkins had been lifted for a pinch-hitter, Jay Johnstone, so Lee Smith came on to close it out. Despite another hit by Hebner in the ninth, Smith blanked the Pirates in the final two innings and the Cubs held on to win 7–6. Winning pitcher: Ferguson Jenkins.

"It feels good to win anything," said Fergie, who didn't know at the time that this victory, No. 284, would be his last.

Of those 284 wins, 167 had come as a Cub. That's 59 percent. Oh, and by the way: He beat Jim Bunning to the Hall of Fame by five years.

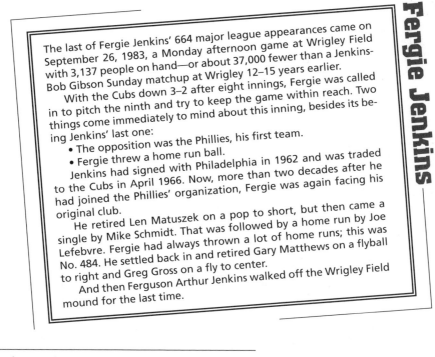

The last of Fergie Jenkins' 664 major league appearances came on September 26, 1983, a Monday afternoon game at Wrigley Field with 3,137 people on hand—or about 37,000 fewer than a Jenkins-Bob Gibson Sunday matchup at Wrigley 12–15 years earlier.

With the Cubs down 3–2 after eight innings, Fergie was called in to pitch the ninth and try to keep the game within reach. Two things come immediately to mind about this inning, besides its being Jenkins' last one:

- The opposition was the Phillies, his first team.
- Fergie threw a home run ball.

Jenkins had signed with Philadelphia in 1962 and was traded to the Cubs in April 1966. Now, more than two decades after he had joined the Phillies' organization, Fergie was again facing his original club.

He retired Len Matuszek on a pop to short, but then came a single by Mike Schmidt. That was followed by a home run by Joe Lefebvre. Fergie had always thrown a lot of home runs; this was No. 484. He settled back in and retired Gary Matthews on a flyball to right and Greg Gross on a fly to center.

And then Ferguson Arthur Jenkins walked off the Wrigley Field mound for the last time.

Fergie Jenkins

After spending 10 years with the Cubs, Hall of Famer Ferguson Jenkins had his Number 31 retired by the team.

Banks and Baker Make History

Call it a tale of two shortstops—Kansas City Monarchs shortstops, that is.

It's the story of Gene Baker, who was the first African-American to sign with the Cubs, and Ernie Banks, the second African-American to sign with the Cubs. Baker, from Davenport, Iowa, and an alum of St. Ambrose University in Davenport, had been purchased by the Cubs in the spring of 1950 from the Kansas City Monarchs of the Negro American League. He didn't get to Wrigley Field until September 1953.

Banks, six years younger, took Baker's shortstop spot with the Monarchs in 1950 but spent the next two years in the Army. The White Sox and St. Louis Browns (owned by Bill Veeck) seemingly had the inside track on Ernie, but the Cubs signed him in September of '53 and brought him almost immediately to Chicago.

Banks made his debut first, on Thursday, Sept. 17, when he started at shortstop and went 0-for-3 in a 16–4 loss to the Phillies. Baker made his first appearance three days later, as an unsuccessful pinch-hitter for Don Elston in an 11–6 loss at St. Louis.

> ## At a Glance
>
> **WP:** Minner (11–15)
>
> **HR:** Serena (10)
>
> **Key stat:** Only 3,215 people were at Crosley Field to witness history being made.

Eventually, the Cubs chose Banks to play short and Baker second base, thus making them major league baseball's first African-American double-play combination. That took place during the Sept. 22 twi-night doubleheader in Cincinnati, when the Cubs beat the Reds 4–1 in the nightcap after losing to ex-Cub Fred Baczewski 1–0 in the opener.

In Game 2, after each had gone 0-for-3 in Game 1, Banks went 1-for-4 with a fourth-inning single and Baker was also 1-for-4 with a sixth-inning double. The Cubs won behind Paul Minner's pitching and Bill Serena's three-run homer.

Next day, still in Cincinnati, Banks was 1-for-3 with a double, and Baker went 2-for-4 and was the middle man on a pair of double plays. "Bingo" and "Bango" were on their way: The two were standouts as rookies in 1954 and both were named to the National League All-Star team the following season.

But why had it taken Baker, 28 years old in 1953, so long to get to Chicago?

He had shown, in four seasons with the Cubs' top farm club, the Pacific Coast League's Los Angeles Angels, that he was ready for the big leagues. In 100 games in 1950 at L.A., he had hit .280. He followed with a .278 mark in

168 games in '51, .260 with 15 home runs and 73 RBIs in '52 and in 162 games in 1953 he had hit .284 with 20 homers and 99 RBIs.

As for his fielding, he could not possibly have been worse than the people the Cubs were trotting out to shortstop. Roy Smalley played there all 154 games in 1950 and committed 51 errors. Yes, 51. Smalley, Jack Cusick and Bob Ramazotti combined for 37 errors at short in 1951. Smalley, Tommy Brown and Eddie Miksis totaled 36 there in '52, and the same trio combined for 50 the next season, Smalley leading the way with 25 in just 77 games.

In August of '53, with the Cubs heading for seventh-place finish, two Chicago American baseball writers—Jim Enright and Wendell Smith—wondered in print without actually writing it that perhaps racism in the Cubs' front office was a reason for ignoring Baker's talent while the Cubs drifted aimlessly, some 30-plus games out of first place.

"Why are the Cubs delaying a move to bring up Gene Baker, Los Angeles shortstop?" Enright wrote. "Is it because the 28-year-old Negro isn't ready? Or are there other reasons?"

Smith, an African-American, also asked why the Cubs hadn't brought up Baker.

"The most controversial player in the Chicago Cub organization is a 28-year-old shortstop who plays 2,000 miles from here," Smith wrote. "He is Gene Baker of Los Angeles, the Cubs' No. 1 minor-league affiliate. Are the Cubs purposely overlooking this smooth-fielding shortstop for whom they paid $6,500 to the Kansas City Monarchs . . . in 1950?"

As it turned out, of course, Baker did come up, as did Banks, and the story had a happy ending. But 44 years later, when asked what he was thinking when he finally arrived at Wrigley Field that September morning in 1953, Baker told the *Chicago Tribune*'s Paul Sullivan:

"My main thought was that I should've been up years before I was."

No one could argue with that.

Sutcliffe, Cubs End 39-year Drought

It had been 39 years since the Cubs had last been in the postseason. So when Rick Sutcliffe struck out Joe Orsulak for the final out of the North Siders' 1984 division-title clincher, Cub fans around the country began a long-overdue celebration.

The *Chicago Tribune*'s Joey Reaves put it in these words:

"The suffering is over.

"Seven presidents, 60 million fans and a man on the moon later, the Chicago Cubs are finally winners.

"The team America loved to watch lose for two generations clinched the National League East championship Monday night with a 4-1 victory over the last-place Pirates in Three Rivers Stadium. . . .

"For 39 years, history and the National League swept by the Cubs, leaving a special feeling in their wake. A nation that loves a winner learned to love a loser."

For a six-year period, losing seasons ended with the Leo Durocher teams of Williams, Santo, Jenkins, Kessinger, Beckert, Banks, Hundley, Holtzman, and the rest in the late '60s and early '70s, but even that group could not win a division or league title. It took a blend of experienced stars (Sutcliffe, Gary Matthews, Ron Cey, Larry Bowa, Dennis Eckersley) and talented younger players (Ryne Sandberg, Leon Durham, Lee Smith, Steve Trout) to break down the barrier of negativity and prove that, yes, a Cubs team could be a champion.

The Cubs came into this matchup at Pittsburgh with a 92–63 record, 6.5 games ahead of New York (86–70). A Cubs win or a Mets loss would bring the NL East title to Chicago. The Cubs wasted no time, getting to lefty Larry McWilliams in the first inning on a Sandberg double followed by Matthews' RBI single. In the second, Sutcliffe (14-for-56 that year for a .250 batting average) singled in a run. In the next inning, an error by third baseman Jim Morrison on Keith Moreland's grounder scored Sandberg.

At a Glance

WP: Sutcliffe (16–1)

Key stat: The Cubs were 34–25 when the Sutcliffe deal was made. Thereafter they were 62–40 (a .608 clip).

Pittsburgh, which had won six straight, cut it to 3–1 in the fourth when Orsulak tripled and came across on Johnny Ray's infield out, but the Cubs restored their three-run margin in the fifth when a bases-loaded double-play grounder by Jody Davis got Matthews in from third.

Suddenly the ninth inning was at hand. Three outs to go. The crowd of 5,472, the majority of it made up of Cub fans, seemed to roar with every pitch. Ron Wotus flied to right, and pinch-hitter Lee Mazzilli flied to Bobby Dernier in center. Up stepped Orsulak, who owned both Pirate hits. From behind the plate, Davis yelled to Sutcliffe, "I want the ball!" Sutcliffe did as told: He struck out Orsulak, and Davis had himself a souvenir to be treasured.

"I could hear all those people cheering for us," Sutcliffe said of the noisy ninth, "and I thought we must be in Chicago."

Sutcliffe, who went on to win the NL Cy Young award, had run his personal winning streak to 14. His last loss was on June 29 in Los Angeles, where he was beaten by his original club. This night, he faced only 28 hitters, struck out nine and walked none. His NL record stood at 16–1, and with his four victories for Cleveland before the June 13 trade that had brought him to Chicago, he was a 20-game winner—an ace in every sense of the word.

The Magic Number: 19

Before this game began, the magic number for the Cubs to clinch the National League pennant was 2. And when it was over and the Cubs and Lon Warneke had beaten the Cardinals and Paul "Daffy" Dean 1–0 with a two-hitter at Sportsman's Park in St. Louis, Chicago had clinched a tie for the title and the magic number was down to 1.

So why the 19?

This also happened to be the Cubs' 19th straight victory in a streak that had begun on Sept. 4, when the Cubs were 2.5 games behind first-place St. Louis. Also, the game's lone run was supplied by Cubs rookie first baseman Phil Cavarretta, age 19 and an alum of Lane Tech, just a few blocks west of Wrigley Field on Addison Street.

Cavvy had replaced player-manager Charlie Grimm as the regular first baseman in May and batted .275 with 28 doubles, 12 triples, 8 homers and 82 RBIs.

Now, in the last week of September, the Cubs had five games remaining— all with the defending NL champions in St. Louis. Dean, younger brother of "Dizzy," opened the game firing bullets. Augie Galan and Billy Herman went down swinging in the first inning and, after a double by Fred Lindstrom, so did Gabby Hartnett, to the delight of 19,989 spectators.

In the top of the second, Dean picked up where he left off, striking out Frank Demaree. Dean's first pitch to the lefty-swinging Cavarretta was a strike, but Cavvy drove the next pitch onto the pavilion roof in right for what turned out to be the game's only run.

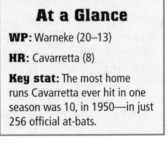

At a Glance

WP: Warneke (20–13)

HR: Cavarretta (8)

Key stat: The most home runs Cavarretta ever hit in one season was 10, in 1950—in just 256 official at-bats.

Warneke, winning his seventh straight decision, rolled after that, allowing just a single in the fourth by call-up Lynn King and a double in the eighth by Rip Collins. Collins was left stranded at third when Demaree crashed into the wall in left to haul down Leo Durocher's bid for a game-tying extra-base hit.

The Cards went meekly in the last of the ninth, not one ball leaving the infield. When Pepper Martin grounded to second baseman Billy Herman for the third out, the Cubs' World Series date with Detroit was just that much closer.

Finally, this note: Cavarretta, exactly one year earlier, had started for the first time in a big-league game and hit his first major league home run.

Cubs Clinch for 'Zim'

The 1980s was the decade the Cubs, with Harry Caray their most ardent promoter, became a consistent financial success—but hardly an artistic one. Outside of the 1984 division-title winners, the Cubs, going into the 1989 season, had compiled an overall record of 546–687 (a .443 percentage) for the decade and had finished an average of 23.5 games out of first place.

Almost universally they were picked to finish next to last in the NL East in 1989, as manager Don Zimmer and his old high school pal from Cincinnati, GM Jim Frey, hoped to bring along kid outfielders Jerome Walton and Dwight Smith and second-year catcher Damon Berryhill so that perhaps they could be pieces of the puzzle for a pennant run in 1990 and beyond.

So naturally, then, here were the Cubs on this Tuesday night in Montreal, needing a victory over the host Expos and a St. Louis loss to Pittsburgh to clinch a division championship.

What had happened? The Cubs had gotten solid years from veteran stars Ryne Sandberg, Mark Grace and Andre Dawson; the Big Three of Greg Maddux (19 wins), Mike Bielecki (18) and Rick Sutcliffe (16) had delivered the big wins (including three straight over Montreal Aug. 7-9 that put the Cubs three games ahead). New closer Mitch Williams had been wildly exciting and successful, Walton (.293), Smith (.324) and Berryhill improved day by day and people like Les Lancaster and Rick Wrona had come up from Triple-A Iowa and made key contributions.

Wrona was catching this night and, facing 16-game winner Dennis Martinez, he tripled home Luis Salazar with two outs in the second inning to open the scoring. Wrona, who hit .217 with 13 RBIs in 59 games in '89 at Iowa, now had 12 RBIs in 36 games with the Cubs. In the sixth, Sandberg (.290 that year with 30 homers) doubled and scored on Smith's looping single to right. Montreal tied it up in the bottom half against Maddux, but with two out in the eighth, Sandberg singled and came around to score when right fielder Hubie Brooks misplayed Smith's third hit of the night.

Cubs	AB	R	H	RBI
Wynne cf	4	0	0	0
Sandberg 2b	4	2	2	0
Smith lf	4	0	3	1
Dascenzo lf	0	0	0	0
Grace 1b	3	0	1	0
Dawson rf	4	0	0	0
Salazar 3b	3	0	0	0
Dunston ss	3	1	1	0
Wrona c	4	0	1	1
Girardi c	0	0	0	0
Maddux p	3	0	0	0
Williams p	0	0	0	0
Totals	33	3	8	2

Expos	AB	R	H	RBI
Raines lf	4	0	1	0
Grissom cf	4	1	1	0
Galarraga 1b	4	1	1	0
Brooks rf	4	0	1	1
Wallach 3b	4	0	0	0
Foley 2b	3	0	2	0
Nixon pr	0	0	0	0
Santovenia c	2	0	1	1
Owen ss	3	0	0	0
Johnson ph	1	0	0	0
Martinez p	2	0	0	0
Fitzgerald ph	1	0	0	0
Totals	32	2	7	2

CHI	0 1 0 0 0 1 0 1 0	-	3	8	1
MON	0 0 0 0 0 2 0 0 0	-	2	7	1

Cubs	IP	H	R	ER	BB	SO
Maddux W (19-12)	8.1	7	2	2	1	6
Williams S (36)	0.2	0	0	0	0	1
Totals	9	7	2	2	1	7

Expos	IP	H	R	ER	BB	SO
Martinez L (16-7)	9	8	3	2	2	7
Totals	9	8	3	2	2	7

E—Chicago Salazar; Montreal Brooks. DP—Montreal 2. 2B—Chicago Sandberg; Montreal Raines. 3B—Chicago Wrona. SH—Montreal Martinez, Santovenia. SF—Montreal Santovenia. LOB—Chicago 5; Montreal 7. SB—Montreal Raines, Nixon. Attendance: 11,615.

Meanwhile, the scoreboard had reported the news of Pittsburgh's victory over St. Louis. All the Cubs had to do now was hold the lead. Maddux went out to start the ninth, but with Otis Nixon on second base with one out and lefty pinch-hitter deluxe Wallace Johnson coming up, Zimmer called for Williams, the left-hander with 35 mostly exciting saves and appropriately nicknamed "Wild Thing." There was little drama this time, however: Johnson popped to Sandberg, and Williams then fanned another pinch-hitter, Mike Fitzgerald. The Cubs were unlikely NL East champions.

"I didn't think in spring training that this would happen," Sandberg said. "It was the furthest thing from my mind."

Happiest Cub of all, most likely, was Zimmer, who had played on two World Series-winning teams. "Zim," his eyes moist from tears more than champagne, yelled out, "This is the highlight of my 41 years in baseball! The greatest thing that ever happened to me in my life! These players played their hearts out all year."

Later, in the quiet of his office, he tried to explain the shocking success story that was the 1989 Cubs: "We'd bring up one guy from Iowa and he'd do a great job. We'd bring up somebody else, and he'd do great. Things started snowballing, and other teams weren't playing as well as a lot of people thought they would. And we were kind of in it. And we just kept going."

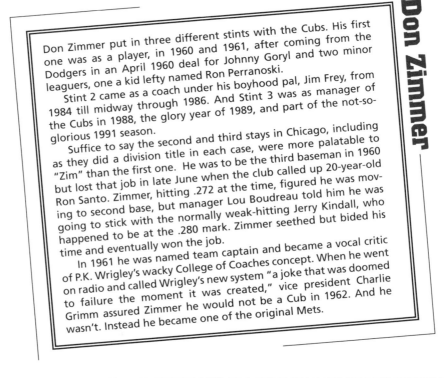

Don Zimmer

Don Zimmer put in three different stints with the Cubs. His first one was as a player, in 1960 and 1961, after coming from the Dodgers in an April 1960 deal for Johnny Goryl and two minor leaguers, one a kid lefty named Ron Perranoski.

Stint 2 came as a coach under his boyhood pal, Jim Frey, from 1984 till midway through 1986. And Stint 3 was as manager of the Cubs in 1988, the glory year of 1989, and part of the not-so-glorious 1991 season.

Suffice to say the second and third stays in Chicago, including as they did a division title in each case, were more palatable to "Zim" than the first one. He was to be the third baseman in 1960 but lost that job in late June when the club called up 20-year-old Ron Santo. Zimmer, hitting .272 at the time, figured he was moving to second base, but manager Lou Boudreau told him he was going to stick with the normally weak-hitting Jerry Kindall, who happened to be at the .280 mark. Zimmer seethed but bided his time and eventually won the job.

In 1961 he was named team captain and became a vocal critic of P.K. Wrigley's wacky College of Coaches concept. When he went on radio and called Wrigley's new system "a joke that was doomed to failure the moment it was created," vice president Charlie Grimm assured Zimmer he would not be a Cub in 1962. And he wasn't. Instead he became one of the original Mets.

21 Straight! Cubs Clinch, and Then Some

The defending world champs were in bad shape. The St. Louis Cardinals were four games back of first-place Chicago with four games to play, all against the Cubs. And all the Cubs had done was win their last 19 in a row.

The task seemed impossible, and the paid attendance for this Friday doubleheader at Sportsman's Park—an estimated 9,000—seemed to indicate that most Cardinals fans sensed the hopelessness of the situation. The Gashouse Gang of Pepper Martin, Dizzy Dean, Leo Durocher, Ducky Medwick and the rest was about to be eliminated—even with Ol' Diz himself doing the pitching in the opener.

The hosts gave some hope to the crowd by scoring two runs in the first inning off Cubs right-hander Bill Lee, although errors by third baseman Stan Hack and second baseman Billy Herman aided the rally greatly. That proved to be the champs' dying gasp, because Lee, seeking his 20th win, allowed only four hits the rest of the way and Dean simply didn't have it.

In the top of the third, the first of four hits by Freddie Lindstrom plated the tying run, and in the fourth Hack doubled and scored on a ground single up the middle by Lee to put the Cubs ahead 3–2. Lindstrom's two-out double in the seventh scored Herman, Hack lofted a home run to right in the eighth and Lindstrom's fourth hit, a single to center, drove in Augie Galan with the sixth and final Cubs run.

At a Glance

WP: Lee (20–6)

HR: Hack (4)

Key stat: Galan went 6-for-10 in the twinbill; Dean was touched for 15 hits in the opener.

And when Lee set down the Cardinals in order in the ninth, the Cubs' winning streak had hit 20 and they were returning to the World Series after a two-year absence. It certainly was difficult to believe that on July 5, the Cubs had been in fourth place, 10.5 games out of first.

For good measure, the Cubs won the second game as well, 5–3, behind the pitching of Charlie Root and Roy Henshaw and three hits each from Galan and Herman. That put the club-record winning streak at 21. The next day the streak died, but its memory lives.

Cubs Claim 2003 Division Title

When one realizes that the 2003 Cubs were just five outs from going to the World Series, it is somewhat surprising that as late as July 26 they were just 51–52 and in fact entered September with a modest 69-66 record.

But on the final Saturday, the Cubs were on top of the NL Central, leading second-place Houston by a half-game. The Cubs were to face Pittsburgh in a doubleheader at Wrigley Field while the Astros were playing the Brewers that afternoon in Houston. The Cubs' magic number was 3.

Mark Prior, who finished 18–6, allowed a Craig Wilson home run in the fourth, but the Cubs went ahead in their half, with Randall Simon's sacrifice fly bringing in the go-ahead run. In the fifth, Damian Miller homered and Sammy Sosa drove in a run with a sacrifice fly, and the Cubs led 4–1.

Rob Mackoviak singled in a run with two out in the sixth, and with two outs in the seventh, manager Dusty Baker decided it was time to go get Prior, who had thrown 133 pitches but had struck out 10 and lowered his ERA to 2.43. Kyle Farnsworth and Joe Borowski finished up the 4–2 victory, with Borowski getting Jason Kendall to pop out with the tying runs aboard for his 33rd save.

The Astros were about to lose to Milwaukee, so now all the Cubs needed was to win Game 2, and Matt Clement (14–12), given a big early cushion, did just that. Sosa hit his 40th home run in the first inning, and the Cubs broke it open in the second with five runs, thanks to RBI singles by Ramon Martinez and Paul Bako and a two-run single by Mark Grudzielanek.

> ### At a Glance
>
> **WP:** Clement (14–12)
>
> **HR:** Sosa (40), Alou (22).
>
> **Key stat:** Sosa reached 40 homers for the eighth straight season.

The crowd of 40,121 now simply had to wait for the ninth. With the Cubs up 7–2, Dave Veres came on to pitch and, with one on and one out, he threw a sinker to Jose Hernandez. The former Cub grounded into a 6–4–3 double play, and the celebration began. It included a victory lap led by Baker, a champagne shower for the fans, courtesy of Sosa, and general rejoicing.

It was an especially satisfying moment for Baker, who had left a league champion (San Francisco) and taken over a club that had finished 67–95 the year before and turned it into a winner.

"But I didn't think about 67 wins," he said. "You think about staying in the hunt and keeping the faith and trying to have your players keep a positive attitude and believe in themselves."

Homer in the Gloamin'
One for the Ages

When the month of September began, few would have predicted that the game played on this Wednesday afternoon would provide perhaps the most memorable moment in Cubs history.

Many Cub fans had given up on their team much earlier than September. On July 20, with the Cubs in fourth place, 5.5 games behind league-leading Pittsburgh, owner P.K. Wrigley fired manager Charlie Grimm and replaced him with catcher Gabby Hartnett. The change didn't help immediately: In the first 45 games with Hartnett as field boss, the Cubs went 23–22, the last two defeats coming in a Sept. 3 doubleheader at Cincinnati. But then came a stretch run reminiscent of 1935.

At a Glance

WP: Root (7–7)

HR: Hartnett (9)

Key stat: The Cubs won the season's biggest game even though their Nos. 3 and 4 hitters, Frank Demaree and Phil Cavarretta each went 0-for-5; Billy Herman and Rip Collins had three hits apiece.

Charlie Root beat the Reds 2–1 in 11 innings on Sunday, Sept. 4. And then, before 42,545 at Forbes Field, the Cubs swept a pair from the first-place Pirates. Bill Lee scattered 10 hits—three of them by future White Sox pitching coach Ray Berres—and won 3–0 in the opener. Later, Clay Bryant won his 15th game in Game 2 as the Cubs rallied for a 4–3 triumph. Even then, the Cubs were in third, five games back of the Bucs.

Next the North Siders swept three at St. Louis and went 4–3 against the Reds, Braves, Giants and Dodgers before taking four straight at Philadelphia. The Cubs returned to Wrigley Field for a three-game series with St. Louis and swept it. They had won 17 of 20 and had moved into second place with a week to go, having closed to within 1.5 games of the Pirates, who had arrived in town for a three-game series that would determine the race's outcome.

To pitch the Tuesday opener, Hartnett selected Dizzy Dean, the sore-armed former St. Louis 30-game winner who hadn't pitched in nine days and hadn't started since Aug. 13. Lacking any semblance of a fastball but brimming with guts and guile, Dean, with last-out relief support from Lee, beat the Pirates 2–1 before 42,238, and now the deficit was a half-game.

The next afternoon, a partly cloudy one, it was Bryant, on two days' rest, against 30-year-old rookie right-hander Bob Klinger (12-5, 2.99 ERA in 1938), with 34,465 people in the stands. The Pirates scored three times in the sixth to take a 3–1 lead before the Cubs rallied to tie in their half, due in no small part to misplays in the outfield by Lloyd and Paul Waner. In the eighth, the Bucs went up 5–3 on RBI singles by Heinie Manush and Lee Handley, but again the Cubs came back to tie when pinch-hitter Tony Lazzeri, the former Yankee, doubled in a run and Billy Herman singled home another. The bases soon were loaded with one out, but relief ace Mace Brown entered and got Frank Demaree to bounce into a double play.

Before the ninth inning began, the umpires, noting the growing darkness, met with the managers and told them that this would be the last inning, no matter what. If there was a tie, there would be a doubleheader instead of a single game on the morrow. Charlie Root, the sixth Cub pitcher of the day, allowed a one-out single by Paul Waner, got Johnny Rizzo to pop out and then received help from Hartnett, whose fine throw cut down Waner trying to steal second.

Now it was really getting darker. Phil Cavarretta began the Cubs' ninth and somehow saw enough of Brown's pitch to hit a fly ball to right for the first out. Carl Reynolds, whose 1938 numbers of three homers and a .302 batting average were a far cry from his 22 and .359 with the White Sox in 1930, was next and popped out. Now it was Hartnett, who took one curveball for a strike and swung at another and missed for strike two.

Then came another curveball. Hartnett didn't miss it this time.

"Hartnett didn't look good on either of the first two," Brown told sports columnist Dave Anderson years later. "I had a good curveball. I thought, I'm going to strike him out with another curveball. I wanted to throw it in the dirt, and he probably would've chased it. But I threw it high. If I had thrown him a fastball, he'd have taken it. But as soon as he hit it, I knew it was gone."

Gabby Hartnett knew it, too. "I swung with everything I had," he told Anderson, "and then I got that kind of feeling you get when the blood rushes out of your head and you get dizzy."

The ball came down in the bleachers in left-center, touching off a home-plate celebration that included players, hundreds of fans and dozens of ushers—who were supposed to keep the fans off the field but had failed.

Out in right field, Paul Waner watched in disbelief. "I just stood out there and watched Hartnett circle the bases and take the lousy pennant with him. That home run took all the fight out of us."

It also gave the Cubs a 6–5 victory and a half-game lead, which became 1.5 games when they routed the Bucs 10–1 on Thursday. Two days later, the Cubs clinched the pennant in St. Louis, and two days after that, an estimated 300,000 turned out for a parade through downtown Chicago to cheer the pennant-winners—especially Gabby Hartnett

Borowy Does It Again

The Cubs were just 6–16 against the St. Louis Cardinals in 1945. Yet, with three games left on the schedule, the Cubs were in first place, three games ahead of the second-place Redbirds, the defending world champions.

It was that kind of year.

Strange things happened during baseball's "war years" of 1943, '44 and '45. The St. Louis Browns won a pennant. Players in their 40s were playing regularly. The Reds brought up a 15-year-old pitcher, Joe Nuxhall. And the Cubs were able to get a 20-game winner from the Yankees.

And Hank Borowy, who was 10–5 when the Yankees sold him to the Cubs on July 27 for $100,000, might well have been the biggest reason Charlie Grimm's North Siders were on the verge of clinching the pennant this afternoon in Pittsburgh. He had won 10 of 12 decisions since coming from New

Members of the Cubs pose in the dugout before the 1945 World Series: (from left) Bill "Swish" Nicholson, Andy Pafko, Phil Cavarretta, Peanuts Lowrey, Don Johnson, and Stan Hack.

September 29, 1945

Cubs 4, Pirates 3

York to provide Grimm a legitimate, in-his-prime, major-league pitcher, of which there were very few during the 1945 season.

Borowy in fact had the starting assignment in Game 1 of a doubleheader, which drew a grand total of 4,016 fans. He again kept the contest close, the teams entering the ninth in a 3–3 tie. Stan Hack drew a leadoff walk, Roy Hughes (the 34-year-old second baseman) singled and Peanuts Lowrey bunted the runners along. Phil Cavarretta, later voted the league's MVP after he finished with an NL-best .355 batting average, was given an intentional walk to load the bases, and 24-year-old Andy Pafko (110 RBIs in '45) drove a sacrifice fly to right to score Hack with the go-ahead run.

Borowy couldn't finish it off: Grimm pulled him with two on and one out in the ninth and brought in lefty Bob Chipman to face lefty-swinging Jim Russell. Russell's infield out moved the runners to second and third, and now right-hander Paul Erickson was summoned to face pinch-batter Tom O'Brien. Erickson struck him out, and the pennant had returned to Chicago. It was the Cubs' fifth in 17 years, the third under Grimm.

Now it was on to Detroit for the World Series, which already had grabbed Pafko's attention.

"I'll be mighty happy," he said, "to pay that extra income tax."

Cubs	AB	R	H	RBI
Hack 3b	4	2	1	0
Hughes 2b	4	0	3	0
Lowrey lf	4	0	1	1
Cavarretta 1b	4	0	0	0
Pafko cf	5	0	2	1
Nicholson rf	5	0	2	0
Livingston c	3	0	0	0
Sauer ph	1	0	0	0
Williams c	0	0	0	0
Merullo ss	2	1	0	0
Borowy p	3	1	1	0
Chipman p	0	0	0	0
Erickson p	0	0	0	0
Totals	35	4	10	2

Pirates	AB	R	H	RBI
Gionfriddo cf	5	1	3	0
Barrett rf	2	0	1	1
Russell lf	5	0	0	0
Salkeld c	2	0	0	0
O'Brien ph	1	0	0	0
Elliott 3b	4	1	2	0
Gustine ss	3	1	1	0
Dahlgren 1b	3	0	0	0
Coscarart 2b	1	0	0	0
Colman ph	1	0	0	1
Zak ss	1	0	0	0
Ostermueller p	3	0	1	1
Strincevich p	0	0	0	0
Saltzgaver ph	1	0	0	0
Totals	32	3	8	3

CHI	1 0 0 0 1 0 1 0 1 - 4	10	0
PIT	1 0 0 0 2 0 0 0 - 3	8	0

Cubs	IP	H	R	ER	BB	SO
Borowy W (21-7)	8.1	8	3	3	7	1
Chipman	0.1	0	0	0	0	0
Erickson S (2)	0.1	0	0	0	0	1
Totals	9	8	3	3	7	2

Pirates	IP	H	R	ER	BB	SO
Ostermueller L (5-4)	8.1	10	4	3	5	3
Strincevich	0.2	0	0	0	0	0
Totals	9	10	4	3	5	3

2B—Chicago Hack; Pittsburgh Gionfriddo 2. SH—Chicago Borowy, Lowrey; Pittsburgh Gustine. LOB—Chicago 11; Pittsburgh 10.

Maddux Wins 20th in First Farewell

Greg Maddux might not have realized it, but when this Wednesday afternoon game at Wrigley Field was completed, he wouldn't be making another start as a Cub for a long, long time.

That's one reason why this game was memorable. The others:

• Maddux shut out the NL East champion Pirates 6–0 on seven hits;

• The victory marked his 20th of the season, the first time in his career he had won 20;

• The shutout lowered his earned-run average to 2.18 and all but clinched his first NL Cy Young Award.

When Maddux retired Carlos Garcia, Gary Varsho and Cecil Espy in a 1–2–3 ninth inning, he gave Cubs pitching coach Billy Connors good reason to claim some brilliance as a seer. In spring training, Connors, who earlier had taught Maddux the cut fastball, wrote down this prediction for the right-hander: 20–10 final record. Now, Maddux was going to finish 20–11.

"Billy," Maddux revealed, "taught me a cutter at the end of last season. That pitch has made a big difference this year—a big difference."

At a Glance

WP: Maddux (20–11)

Key stat: Mark Grace and sore-kneed Andre Dawson, of all people, pulled off a double steal—for both, it was steal No. 6 on the season.

There would be a big difference in the Cubs the following year. Greg Maddux would not be with the club; he would be with the Atlanta Braves, winning 20 games again and another Cy Young. Blame Maddux, blame agent Scott Boras or blame Cubs GM Larry Himes. In any case, Maddux and Boras turned down a five-year, $27.5 million offer from the Cubs, who would not go higher. Himes said they couldn't go higher because the money he had allocated for a Maddux signing had gone instead to free-agent pitchers Jose Guzman, Randy Myers and Dan Plesac.

Maddux went on to win 194 games for Atlanta from 1993 through 2003 and played a huge role in 10 division titles, three league crowns and one World Series championship. Had he remained a Cub, there might have been more of what he had just experienced in the last three years since the 1989 Cubs' division title: 77–85 in 1990, 77–83 in 1991, 78–84 in 1992, with the team finishing 18, 20 and 18 games out of first place. When Maddux left Chicago he was 26 years old. When he returned in 2004, he was almost 37.

Madlock Repeats as Batting Champ

Bill Madlock came to the Cubs from the Texas Rangers in October 1973, started hitting on Opening Day 1974—when he went 2-for-4 against the Phillies—and never did stop hitting during his too-brief stay on the North Side.

The graduate of Decatur's Eisenhower High School had served notice in 1973 of his ability with the bat when, at age 22, he hit .338 with 22 homers and 90 RBIs for the Rangers' Spokane affiliate in the Pacific Coast League. He opened more eyes by hitting .351 during a 21-game trial with Texas that September.

The Cubs, as part of a rebuilding program that had sent away old favorites like Ron Santo, Randy Hundley and Glenn Beckert, traded Fergie Jenkins to get Madlock—plus utilityman Vic Harris. Madlock had hit .313 his first year and had won the National League batting title with a .354 average in '75, the same year he had been named MVP of the All-Star Game. Now, on this final day of the 1976 season, he had a shot at another batting title, although it was a long shot. He was at .333, while Cincinnati's Ken Griffey was at .338.

From Cincinnati came word that Griffey was going to sit out the Reds' finale against Atlanta. In Chicago, Madlock prepared to face Expos lefty Woodie Fryman. Remembered Madlock: "A friend of mine had called and said, 'You've got a chance.' And I said, 'No, I don't have a chance.' And she said, 'OK, go 4-for-4.'"

And that is exactly what he did. In the first inning, he put down a perfect bunt for a single. During a five-run third, he singled off the glove of third baseman Larry Parrish, and in the fourth—this time facing reliever Chip Lang—he drove in Joe Wallis from third with a base hit over the head of Montreal second baseman Wayne Garrett. Two innings later, with Dale Murray pitching, Madlock lined hit No.

Expos	AB	R	H	RBI
Unser lf	3	0	0	1
Garrett 2b	4	0	2	0
Dawson cf	4	0	0	0
Valentine rf	4	0	2	0
Jorgensen 1b	4	0	1	0
Parrish 3b	4	0	0	0
Williams c	4	1	1	1
Frias ss	4	1	1	0
Fryman p	1	0	0	0
Lang p	0	0	0	0
Atkinson p	0	0	0	0
Cromartie ph	1	0	0	0
Murray p	0	0	0	0
Taylor p	0	0	0	0
Freed ph	1	0	1	0
Carrithers p	0	0	0	0
Totals	34	2	8	2

Cubs	AB	R	H	RBI
Monday 1b	5	0	1	0
Wallis cf	4	2	3	0
Madlock 3b	4	2	4	1
Sperring ph-3b	1	0	1	0
Morales rf	5	2	2	0
Trillo 2b	5	1	3	1
Mitterwald c	4	0	2	3
Biittner lf	4	1	1	0
Kelleher ss	3	0	1	1
R Reuschel p	3	0	1	2
Totals	38	8	19	8

MON 0 0 1 0 1 0 0 0 0 - 2 8 0
CHI 0 0 5 1 0 2 0 0 X - 8 19 1

Expos	IP	H	R	ER	BB	SO
Fryman L (13-13)	2.2	9	5	5	2	1
Lang	0.2	3	1	1	0	0
Atkinson	0.2	0	0	0	0	1
Murray	1.1	4	2	2	0	0
Taylor	1.2	1	0	0	0	1
Carrithers	1	2	0	0	0	0
Totals	8	19	8	8	2	3

Cubs	IP	H	R	ER	BB	SO
R Reuschel W (14-12)	9	8	2	1	0	6
Totals	9	8	2	1	0	6

E—Chicago R Reuschel. DP—Montreal 3; Chicago. 2B—Chicago R Reuschel. 3B—Chicago Wallis. HR—Montreal Williams. SF—Montreal Unser; Chicago Mitterwald, Kelleher. LOB—Montreal 6; Chicago 10. SB—Chicago Monday. Attendance: 9,486.

4 to right field, lifting his average to .3385, a shade higher than Griffey's .3375. Then he left the game.

That information reached Riverfront Stadium, where Reds manager Sparky Anderson got Griffey into the game in the seventh inning as a pinch-hitter for Dan Driessen. He struck out. Griffey then stayed in the game and, fortunately for him, the Reds had a seven-run eighth, enabling him to get one more shot at a base hit. He struck out again. The title was still Madlock's, .339 to .336. And the Cubs had won their finale 8–2.

"I was already at home when I heard that I'd won it," Madlock told author Carrie Muskat years later.

He would win two more batting titles, but not as a Cub. Madlock won them in 1981, when he hit .341 for Pittsburgh, and in 1983, when his average was .323 with the same club. No, the Pirates had acquired him not from the Cubs, but from the Giants. Before spring training of 1977, with Madlock's contract talks with P.K. Wrigley at a stalemate, the Cubs traded their two-time batting champ, who had just turned 26, to San Francisco for 31-year-old outfielder Bobby Murcer—whose 1976 salary ($170,000) was substantially higher than Madlock's ($80,000)—and a replacement at third base, Steve Ontiveros.

"I was 20-something years old," he told Muskat, "and I thought I'd be with Chicago forever, and . . . it didn't work out that way."

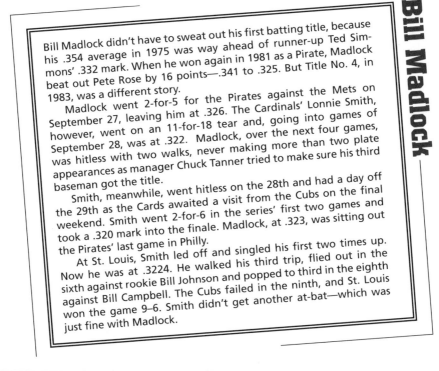

Bill Madlock

Bill Madlock didn't have to sweat out his first batting title, because his .354 average in 1975 was way ahead of runner-up Ted Simmons' .332 mark. When he won again in 1981 as a Pirate, Madlock beat out Pete Rose by 16 points—.341 to .325. But Title No. 4, in 1983, was a different story.

Madlock went 2-for-5 for the Pirates against the Mets on September 27, leaving him at .326. The Cardinals' Lonnie Smith, however, went on an 11-for-18 tear and, going into games of September 28, was at .322. Madlock, over the next four games, was hitless with two walks, never making more than two plate appearances as manager Chuck Tanner tried to make sure his third baseman got the title.

Smith, meanwhile, went hitless on the 28th and had a day off the 29th as the Cards awaited a visit from the Cubs on the final weekend. Smith went 2-for-6 in the series' first two games and took a .320 mark into the finale. Madlock, at .323, was sitting out the Pirates' last game in Philly.

At St. Louis, Smith led off and singled his first two times up. Now he was at .3224. He walked his third trip, flied out in the sixth against rookie Bill Johnson and popped to third in the eighth against Bill Campbell. The Cubs failed in the ninth, and St. Louis won the game 9–6. Smith didn't get another at-bat—which was just fine with Madlock.

Dawson's Final Game as a Cub

It had been six springs since Andre Dawson had appeared at the Cubs' Mesa, Ariz., camp, hat in hand, a free agent willing to sign a one-year contract for a base salary of $500,000.

Now, six full seasons, 174 home runs and 587 RBIs later, here he was, on the final day of the 1992 campaign, attempting to connect for the two homers that would give him a career total of 400.

Fears that he might be playing his final game in a Cubs uniform had been assuaged that week when Dawson and GM Larry Himes had met privately and given the impression that a new contract for 1993 was a foregone conclusion, despite Dawson's aching knees and advancing years.

So the more pressing matter at hand was the task of hitting those home runs, a task made more difficult than usual by the 21-mph wind blowing in from center field and by the knowledge that Montreal starter Mark Gardner had allowed only 14 homers that season in 175 innings.

After Cubs starter Frank Castillo was tagged for two runs in the first, Dawson, in his first at-bat, grounded out to end the inning. In the third, though, after two-out singles by Ryne Sandberg and Mark Grace, Dawson got hold of a Gardner delivery and, wind or no wind, this one was gone for homer No. 22 on the year and No. 399 for his career. That put "the Hawk" in a tie with Al Kaline for 25th on the all-time homer list and triggered a standing ovation that lasted close to five minutes.

In the sixth, with the Cubs still leading 3–2, Dawson, going hard for No. 400, instead singled to left, and, in his final at-bat, struck out swinging in the eighth. "The last two times up I was trying to do it for the fans," Dawson said of the crowd of 23,496 fans, who gave him another standing "O" after he went down swinging.

There were still doubts, though, as to whether or not Dawson would be back in 1993.

"I have to be optimistic," he said afterwards. "This is where I want to finish up. I think something will be worked out."

Something was worked out—with Boston. Dawson signed with the Red Sox on Dec. 9.

At a Glance

WP: F. Castillo (10–11)

S: Assenmacher (8)

HR: Dawson (22)

Key stat: Dawson, in his six seasons as a Cub, averaged 29 homers, 98 RBIs and a .285 batting average.

Thanks, Mr. Merkle

To understand the full meaning of this game, one must go back 15 days to the Sept. 23 Cubs-Giants matchup at the Polo Grounds in New York. The Cubs, two-time defending NL champs, were tied with John McGraw's New Yorkers at the top of the standings as well as in that day's ballgame.

With the score 1–1 and with two outs in the last of the ninth, the Giants had Harry "Moose" McCormick on third base and 19-year-old rookie Fred Merkle, who had just singled, on first. The next batter, Al Bridwell, New York's .285-hitting shortstop, sent a sharp single past second baseman Johnny Evers into right-center. McCormick scored from third and hundreds in the crowd of 22,000 stormed onto the field to celebrate the Giants' 2–1 victory.

But hold everything. There was Evers, standing on second base and holding the baseball aloft, trying to get the attention of umpiring crew chief Hank O'Day. The Cubs, led by Evers and manager-first baseman Frank Chance, were arguing that Merkle, instead of running to second base, had gone about halfway and then, with fans by the droves sprinting toward the center of the diamond, veered off and headed for the clubhouse, located above the center-field bleachers. Evers somehow had retrieved the ball and stepped on second base for a force out. By rule, Evers and Chance said, Merkle was out and the run thus did not score.

At a Glance

WP: Brown (29–9)

Key stat: Brown relieved in the first, finished the game and allowed just four hits.

O'Day agreed. But, noting that darkness was arriving and that the celebrating fans had left the field unplayable, he said the game could not continue and called it a tie. He then left it up to the league office to decide when the game would be played over. McGraw was livid. "If Merkle was out," he said, "O'Day should've cleared the field and gone on with the game. But Merkle wasn't out. We won, and they can't take it away from us."

He was wrong: The NL the next day upheld O'Day's ruling and decreed that, in the event the race ended in a tie, the game would be replayed Oct. 8 in New York. And that's exactly what happened, much to the chagrin of Merkle, whose baserunning gaffe forever would be known as "Merkle's boner" and who would carry the nickname "Bonehead" to his grave.

On the 8th, the Giants had the great Christy Mathewson (37–11 and a 1.43 ERA that season) ready to go against the Cubs' Jack Pfiester. This was it: the game for the pennant. The Polo Grounds was packed; the place had sold out 90 minutes before the 3 p.m. first pitch. People were watching from the bluffs overlooking the stadium and from the 155th Street elevated train station beyond the center-field fence.

Game 163: October 8, 1908
Cubs 4, Giants 2

Pfiester was not at his best. He hit Fred Tenney and walked Buck Herzog to begin the New York first, then seemed to be getting out of trouble when Roger Bresnahan struck out and Herzog was cut down on the back end of an attempted double steal. But Mike Donlin doubled home Tenney, and Chance wasn't going to take any chances. He called for Mordecai "Three Finger" Brown, who fanned Cy Seymour to end the inning.

Mathewson, who had retired the first six Cubs, was lit up in the third, which Joe Tinker (a .421 hitter against Mathewson that season) opened with a triple. Johnny Kling singled, and the game was tied. Brown bunted Kling to second, and Evers was given an intentional walk. Frank Schulte sent a double to left to score Kling, and Chance lined a double into the right-field corner, and the Cubs were up 4–1.

Mathewson shut down the North Siders after that, and the Giants scored a run in the seventh off Brown. But that was it. The Cubs, 4–2 winners, had captured their third consecutive pennant. And somewhere, Fred Merkle was hiding.

Interestingly, Merkle was sold to the Cubs several years later, in 1917, and played first base for them through 1920. His best year was 1918, when he hit .297 for a Cubs team that went to the World Series. He hit .278 in the Series and played flawless defense. That nickname just didn't quite fit anymore.

Cubs Win First Postseason Series Since 1908

Cubs fans almost outnumbered and definitely out-cheered their Atlanta counterparts on this Sunday night, even though the game was played at Atlanta's Turner Field. This was the decisive match of the best-of-five National League Division Series, the Braves and Russ Ortiz having beaten the Cubs and Matt Clement 6–4 in Game 4 in Chicago to even the series at two apiece.

Kerry Wood, 4–2 winner of the series opener Sept. 30 in Atlanta, was back on the mound for Game 5 against Braves lefty Mike Hampton before a crowd of 54,357. The Cubs struck quickly, scoring in the first inning when Kenny Lofton opened with a double and eventually came home on Moises Alou's single. They made it 2–0 in the second when Alex Gonzalez led off with a home run, and the lead became 4–0 in the sixth when Alou singled ahead of Aramis Ramirez's home run.

Atlanta scratched out a run in the bottom half, but Tom Goodwin, batting for Wood in the top of the ninth, doubled in Eric Karros to restore the four-run cushion. Joe Borowski came on to nail it down, getting Chipper Jones on a fly ball to Sammy Sosa in right and striking out Javy Lopez and Andruw Jones to end it for Wood, who had allowed just five hits and two walks while fanning seven. This marked the first time the Cubs had won a postseason series since the 1908 World Series.

Kerry Wood (left) and Mike Remlinger spray fans with champagne after the Cubs won Game 5 of the National League Division Series against the Atlanta Braves at Turner Field in Atlanta on Oct. 5, 2003.

Cubs Make Long-Awaited Return to Playoffs

The Cubs had not been in the postseason since 1945, and they were determined to make up for lost time. And did they ever. After Rick Sutcliffe retired San Diego in order in the first inning, Bobby Dernier thrilled 36,282 fans at Wrigley Field with a line drive homer into the bleachers in left off Padres ace Eric Show. Ryne Sandberg struck out, but Gary Matthews then launched the second homer of the inning, and the rout was on.

Sutcliffe ignited a three-run third with a home run onto Sheffield Avenue, and a six-run fifth—highlighted by Matthews' second homer of the afternoon, a three-run shot—lifted the Cubs into an 11–0 lead. A home run by Ron Cey and an error by San Diego shortstop Garry Templeton gave the Cubs two more runs in the sixth, and then the Cubs rested. When it was over, the Cubs had collected 16 hits, two each by Dernier, Sandberg, Matthews, Sutcliffe and Jody Davis. Sutcliffe went seven innings and allowed two hits (but five walks), and Warren Brusstar finished up. The Cubs also won Game 2 behind Steve Trout and Lee Smith, who combined to five-hit San Diego for a 4-2 victory—the last Cubs triumph in this series.

Gary Matthews only spent four seasons with the Cubs, but it was his first season (1984 and a return to the playoffs) that was most important.

'Three-Finger' Brown Guides Cubs to First World Title

The Cubs, wanting badly to wipe out the memory of their World Series loss to the rival White Sox the autumn before, led Detroit three games to none when Mordecai "Three Finger" Brown opposed George Mullin on this Saturday afternoon at Detroit's Bennett Park. The Cubs took charge early, jumping ahead with a first-inning run when Harry Steinfeldt singled home Jimmy Slagle with two outs. In the second, Johnny Evers reached on an error, took second on Joe Tinker's single and scored from third when the Tigers were unable to turn what would've been an inning-ending double play. That was all the scoring. Brown went the distance, striking out Ty Cobb to open the ninth and getting Bill Coughlin and Boss Schmidt on pop-ups. The Cubs had won their first world championship.

October 14, 1908

Cubs 2, Tigers 0
World Series Game 5

Overall, Cubs Repeat as World Champs

The Cubs, after winning the World Series' first two games, had lost Game 3 to the Tigers at West Side Park but had won the fourth one 3–0 in Detroit, thanks to Mordecai Brown's brilliant pitching. Now it was Orval Overall, who had won Game 2 of the series 6–1 in Chicago, facing Detroit's Bill Donovan. The visiting Cubs scored first on consecutive one-out first-inning singles by Johnny Evers, Frank Schulte and Frank Chance. Evers' two-out double in the fifth scored Johnny Kling for a 2–0 lead. There would be no scoring for Detroit, as Overall went the distance, firing a three-hit shutout to make the Cubs the first team to repeat as world champions.

In the 1908 World Series, Orval Overall gave the Cubs their second consecutive title by firing a complete game three-hit shutout in Game 5.

REFERENCES
BOOKS

The Amazin' Mets. New York Daily News sports staff. Champaign, Ill.: Sports Publishing, 1999.

Anderson, Dave. *Pennant Races: Baseball at its Best*. New York: Main Street, 1994.

Chicago Cubs media guides, 2008-09

Ignarski, Kasey, et al. *Cubs by the Numbers*. New York: Skyhorse, 2009.

Kahn, Roger. *The Boys of Summer*. New York: Harper & Row, 1971.

Langford, Jim. *The Game Is Never Over*. South Bend, Ind.: Icarus Press, 1980.

Muskat, Carrie. *Banks to Sandberg to Grace*. Chicago: Contemporary, 2001.

Nemec, David, et al. *20th Century Baseball Chronicle*. Montreal: Tormont, 1992.

Smith, Ron. *The Sporting News Chronicle of Baseball*. New York: BDD Books, 1993.

Snyder, John. *Cubs Journal*. Cincinnati: Clerisy Press, 2008.

Veeck, Bill, with Ed Linn. *The Hustler's Handbook*. New York: Putnam's, 1965.

NEWSPAPERS

Chicago American

Chicago Daily News

Chicago Sun-Times

Chicago Tribune

Milwaukee Journal

New York Times

WEB SITES

Baseball Almanac (baseball-almanac.com)

Baseball Biography Project (bioproj.sabr.org)

BaseballLibrary.com (baseballlibrary.com)

Baseball Reference (baseball-reference.com)

Baseball Savvy (baseballsavvy.com)

Baseball Todd's Dugout (baseballtoddsdugout.com)

Chicago Cubs: Official Web Site (Chicago.cubs.mlb.com)

Professional Sports Authenticator (psacard.com)

Retrosheet (retrosheet.org)

Smithsonian Magazine (SmithsonianMag.com)

The Baseball Page.com (baseballpage.com)

The Vault from Sports Illustrated (SI.com)